Adjust Fire

Transforming to Win in Iraq

Rita,
Best wishes
Enjoy the book

D1496827

Lt. Col. Michael A. Baumann (USA, Ret.)

Birch
Grove
Publishing

Dedication

To the soldiers of Task Force 1-21

Editor and Publisher: Paul Nockleby
Marketing Director: Chris Pederson
Cover Designer: Dawn Mathers
Web Designer: Fadi Fadhil

Library of Congress Cataloging-in-Publication Data

Baumann, Michael A.
     484 pp. XX cm.
     ISBN 978-0-9744071-6-6
     1. Iraq War, 2003-
     2. Personal narratives, American   I. Title
     DS79.76   2008   956.7044

Manufactured in the U.S.A.
1   2   3   4   5   6   7   8   9   10   11   12   13   14   15

Contents

Preface   7

Part One

Patrol Vignette   19

1   Unsuited, 1-21 Field Artillery Begins Transforming   25

2   Getting a Mission, Preparing to Deploy   49

3   Initial Training   58

4   Kuwait, the Final Preparation   75

5   Into the Cauldron   86

6   "Lay of the Land," Area of Operations Rocket   104

7   Intelligence, the Military Oxymoron   121

8   The Five LOOs, OASIS, and the Lanza Doctrine   137

Part Two

9   The Politics of Al Saidiyah   153

10   The Task Force Tactical Program   181

11   The War Becomes Personal   199

12   Patrolling & Training, Leading From the Front   228

Special Photo Section   253

13   Women in Combat for the Task Force   273

14   Character and Values in This Kind of War   293

15   Iraqi Security Forces—Keystone Cops in Action!   307

16   Civil Military Operations   325

Part Three

17   A Wind of Change   347

18   Local Political Action and Reform   372

19   Iraqi Security Forces Show Promise   389

20   Death and Respite   404

21   Wolf and Bear   421

22   First Iraqi National Elections   429

23   Taking Stock, Finding No Solace   447

24   Home Sweet Home and The Mahalla Plan for Victory   457

Endnotes   469

Glossary   472

Poem   484

Preface

"Only the dead have seen the end to war." Plato

When I returned from Iraq after a year fighting on the west side of Baghdad in a place called Al Rashid, I was tired, maybe exhausted. I felt as if a wound had been carved into my soul with a blunt dagger and it always ached.

I could close my eyes, and in my head could hear the honking horns of traffic arguing through narrow and congested streets of Al Rashid Baghdad neighborhoods. I could hear explosions, random sounds of distant gunfire, and red tracers arcing into night sky. I could recall Arab women screaming at me in sharp, rebuking, high-pitched cries of anger or pain, and could hear tiny, desperate cries of kids. I could see faces of Iraqi men quietly staring at me, their eyes empty or filled with contempt. Those were the manageable thoughts. The less manageable images and thoughts were of pools of blood; I don't know why I see pools of blood. I could conjure, without effort, the putrid smells of Iraq; the raw sewage, dried sweat, body odor, and something burning. Something was always burning in Iraq.

I would dream at night; vivid, creepy, bizarre and sinister dreams. These were dreams that were filled with carnage and personal desperation. I found myself working hard to break my habit of sleeping for only two hours. I would take strong sleeping pills to force sleep when weeks of insomnia would pass and I would feel exhausted. Sleep for the first few months back home seemed futile and interrupted. While in Iraq I never had sinister dreams and I rarely felt fearful.

The whole time I was in Iraq, I felt I was always searching for something that could not be found. It was my sworn obligation to bring change and to help Iraqis realize a better a life. Though I was keenly aware I was an outsider and that I represented an invading military Army, I always felt I needed to connect with Iraqis. I tried with great effort, but never felt I achieved the connection I sought. This caused an inner anguish because without that connection all efforts seemed exponentially more difficult.

During my entire tour I was never in any long, pitched battles. All the actions were short, violent, and over almost as quickly as they started. I had seen Iraqis shot and blown into tiny pieces. I had seen my own soldiers shot and maimed from explosions. Of the four soldiers in the battalion killed, I was with three of the four when they died. I did not make it to Sergeant First Class Michael Battles before he expired from his severe wounds, but viewed his body with Command Sergeant Major Hughes about an hour after he died at the Combat Surgical Hospital in the Green Zone.

I saw the carnage of blown-apart bodies and never felt bothered very much at the time. I didn't puke from the sight of them or from the putrid smell of death nor did I feel sickened by it. I really didn't even feel sorry for anyone who was shot or gravely wounded by an explosion. I was easily able to focus on getting wounded people medical attention and to get people to cover or remove the dead bodies as quickly as possible.

I commanded 683 American soldiers and about 300 Iraqis and I know they killed people. Sometimes I feel a sense of personal blame for that but I can't explain it. I don't dwell on it too much. I know that at least ten Iraqi men and women were killed – murdered – because they were directly associated with me. I can't push that fact away; maybe away from my mind, but not my soul.

All of these memories live in me, and despite my best efforts to suppress them I cannot. So I decided I must document what I know about this war.

I feel strongly that the war in Iraq is not well covered by the news media. Most television, radio, and print media, from my experience and analysis, have an agenda to influence the American public to withdraw from Iraq and extricate the United States from the region. There are grave consequences however this war turns out. Withdrawing from Iraq is the wrong course of action and will have lasting negative impact on the nation. My goal in writing this book is to provide Americans a coherent understanding of their Army and to better see that this war and our future challenge with countering terrorist threats against America world-wide cannot be accomplished by purely military means. Major governmental, political, military, and philosophical adjustment is necessary not only to prevail in Iraq but also to prevail in the wars to come in this lengthy confrontation between Islamic radicalism and the USA.

The U.S. Army in particular has already changed dramatically as a result of the war in Iraq. But much more must be done to shape a capable Army for the challenges that face America. The rhetorical and political battle going on in the American media obscures the most challenging issues facing America in this century. As an American citizen and retired soldier I want to influence the thinking of all Americans about this war and the future of the U.S. Army.

According to polls the majority of the American public believes that the war in Iraq is not worth the loss of American lives. They find the war disconnected from their personal lives and the majority of Americans say they are not personally threatened by the Iraqi people. All of this is well founded on the surface. But, as with all war, deeper issues are in play and much is at stake. I am gravely concerned that the war in Iraq will suffer a similar fate as the war in

Vietnam. I fear American political leaders will not be able to mount a politically acceptable campaign at home which is necessary to win decisively in Iraq. I desperately want to influence thinking to prevent that pathetic outcome.

I served in this war in Iraq as an Army battalion commander. The battalion I commanded was a Field Artillery battalion assigned to the 5th Brigade Combat Team (BCT) of the First Cavalry Division. Before deploying I had to re-train my unit to fight as an infantry/cavalry unit, a capability very different from the artillery battalion's main task and purpose in its prior configuration. We would mostly function as infantry/cavalry for our one-year tour in Iraq. We were assigned a sector in the Al Rashid district of southwestern Baghdad.

My tour was from March 2004 to March 2005. In that year I could see with great clarity the makings of the situation that exists today. What I quickly came to know is that war is highly political, personal, emotional, physical, and — by all sane accounts — horrific. Countless books, stories, documentaries, and the like have been written, published, and produced about war. This is my story and it does not profess to be impartial. At worst, this is a personal narrative with blemishes. At best, it is an insightful record of my experience commanding an Army battalion task force in Baghdad, Iraq. It is simple, direct, and factual account of a very strange war.

In this book I want to explain just how intricate, convoluted, complex, and even diabolical this task given the U. S. Army has become. This is a straightforward-insider story in which I offer a unique perspective on the political situation, my observations of the American Army, and describe what I think may lie ahead of us in the future.

This book puts an uncomfortable spotlight on me and

necessarily explains situations from my perspective. For better or worse you will see my interpretations, beliefs, and values permeating this story.

I intentionally do not tell the story of the infantry "grunt" soldier toiling daily on the mean streets of Baghdad. There are enough "Blog Books," junior military officer-authored books and enlisted soldier-authored books on that subject already on the bookshelves. Most of these are witty, satirical recollections that are highly entertaining. I doubted when writing this that I could tell the "grunt's story" better than they tell it themselves. Nor have I attempted to illuminate the inestimable contributions and leadership of the non-commissioned officers of our Army or of Task Force 1-21. That story of the truest, most-gifted, and committed soldiers of the United States Army leading the day-to-day fight in Iraq needs to be told by a more talented and skilled writer.

What you will read about is a recollection of the role of Task Force 1-21 in the war. My experiences commanding this outfit is the lens and the vehicle through which I attempt to show others what I know about this war and how it is fought.

The story was taken from notes and records I kept during the two years I served as a battalion commander. In this book I present events and dates as accurately as my personal recollection and detailed notes afford. I debated using pseudonyms for many of the people that were part of this story, but chose to keep most of the names without changing them. There are a few places, however, where names have been changed. For those places where actual names remain, I am accountable to the people for what I say.

In this book you will find my thoughts on the controversial

political issues of this war. Military men, especially active duty military leaders, lead opinion-guarded lives. Military people are not able to speak freely about their understanding of the relationship between the missions given and the political situation in which those given missions are executed. That is how the military is best able to carry out national political policy and the will of the National Command Authority. Once out of the military, however, soldiers are free to express those opinions as any citizen.

As a military veteran I think we have a duty to report to the public about our opinions and interpretations. As a former warrior who served in combat in Iraq, I believe I can provide a retired military officer's perspective on policies that put Americans into this war in the first place. The care that must always be taken when criticizing existing policy is that it needs to be balanced, fair, and offer workable alternatives. To the best of my ability, I try to adhere to these requirements.

Finally, an important note: Though this is a memoir account and invariably personal, I detest having to use the word "I" frequently. My whole professional military life was predicated on one thing: TEAM. If I have accomplished anything of value in life those successes came as accomplishments with other people. In fact, I cannot point to one thing in my life that I would consider an accomplishment of value that was attained on my own.

In writing this book I wanted to mention every single soldier, non-commissioned officer, and officer who served or supported the Task Force in the tough year the Task Force fought in Baghdad. My editor kept wrestling with me because I tried to get every single anecdote and name in here that I could. But this proved not feasible. This book represents my best effort to summarize with considerable help from others.

Acknowledgements

This project has benefited from the support of many people whose personal and professional efforts gave life to this book. I am eternally grateful for their personal dedication and invaluable work to help me produce this book.

Lisa B. Kety, an accomplished attorney and writer, trusted advisor and sister, assisted immensely with manuscript development and editing from the inception of this work.

The work also benefited vastly from the critical review of James G. McMahon. His enormous knowledge of American history, plus his tough, professional critique, wonderful ideas on story development, and recommendations improved the writing tremendously.

Filmmaker and photographer Marisol Torres also amplified this work significantly. The photo of the Iraqi woman on the cover of this book with two fingers gesturing "peace" — one of them dipped in purple ink indicating she had voted in the first Iraqi national election — came from Marisol's camera. Her feature documentary, *Interpreting Iraq*, inspired some of what I wrote in this book, as she documented the story of Task Force 1-21's preparation for the elections, and told Freddie's story as an Iraqi interpreter for Task Force 1-21. The documentary is available for purchase at www.interpretingiraq.com.

Many military colleagues assisted in the project. Lieutenant Colonel William Reinhart, who, as a major, served as the battalion S3 and Executive Officer while in Iraq, provided significant content review of the original manuscript. He personally executed extensive fact checks for this book. His contribution was essential to insuring the accuracy and fidelity of this book. Major John "Jay" Soupene, who served as the battalion S3 after Major Reinhart, also provided exceptional review and fact-checking for the book. Major Soupene was the architect of the main tactical design the battalion employed to prepare our sector for the first Iraqi National Elections in January 2005. We enjoyed fabulous success on that day of days. His review of that portion of the book insured the accuracy of this recounting. Captain Robb Dettmer's review of data and specifications on demographics, terrain, and the descriptions of the battalion's area of operations was extremely helpful to insure the correct picture of the area was provided for readers.

Major Lynn Schneider, Captains Chevelle Malone, Dorothy Butala, Denise Little, Terri Hennigan (Broussard), and Sergeant First Class Celeste Blake-Johnson were all Army leaders who directly contributed to this work. The women who served in the Brigade Combat Team and the battalion, especially the female soldiers of the 68th Chemical Company, directly shaped my thinking about women's service in the Army. Their personal actions as combat leaders and soldiers in Iraq as well as their reviews and recommendations improved the quality of this project significantly.

The contributions of Major Christian Van Keuren, Major Mathew Chambers, Captain Martin Wohlgemuth, Sergeant First Class Celeste Blake-Johnson, and Staff Sergeant Terry Saffron are acknowledged and sincerely appreciated. Their elaborations enhanced the overall story content of this book.

The book would not have been possible without the input and notes provided by Captain Eric Willis who served as my Adjutant (S-1) most of the two years I was a battalion commander. Captain Willis wrote the unit history for the battalion. Eric is without question the best writer/soldier I ever came across in the Army. The many briefings, interactions, and after-action reviews with my subordinate commanders, all of them now majors in the Army — Christian

Van Keuren, Michael DeRosier, Tom Pugsley, Roberto Mercado, Kevin Runkle, Gil Cardona, Matthew Chambers, and Kevin Kugel — were invaluable to providing the details and recalling the key events depicted in this book.

Captain Wyndel G. Darville, who served as the Staff Judge Advocate for 5th Brigade Combat Team of First Cavalry Division the year we were in Iraq, provided his review of specific parts of this book to help guide me through this challenging writing endeavor.

I especially acknowledge Specialist Anthony "Jack" Jackson, Specialist "retired" Francisco "V" Villa, and Fadi Al-Taie — my tireless combat crew who rode with me every day in Iraq and whose personal contributions to this book are beyond description.

I was the beneficiary of a great publishing team that I nicknamed, "Team Adjust Fire" consisting of Paul Nockleby, Chris Pederson, Paul Seim, and Fadi Al-Taie. The countless hours of preparation, thousands of tasks, and the creative editorial, marketing, and production meetings resulted in this book. Their commitment to the development of this publication and to the dissemination of this story were of inestimable value. I especially benefited from the professional advice, direction, and counsel of Paul Nockleby. Paul's indefatigable work ethic, willingness to listen and learn, as well as coach, teach, and mentor me through this project made all the difference.

I also wanted to acknowledge the wonderful and giving support of my in-laws, Donald and Nancy Crews. They provided me and my family with a temporary home while we had our own house built in Lakeville, Minnesota. They provided me the resources to continue writing and researching for this book so I could finish the work in a timely manner.

Without question, my family's loving support and encouragement made this process a fulfilling experience. My wife Shelly and son Alexander sacrificed tremendously to help me write this book. They gave up hundreds of hours with me while I was away at meetings, on phone conferences, in research endeavors, and ensconced in my office writing and editing this book. Their encouragement along the way kept me from giving up on this tough project.

Finally, I acknowledge my parents. My father, Allen A. Baumann, whose chief contribution was making me the soldier I became; he directed me to achieve where I wasn't sure I could reach. He imbued me with the courage to write this book. I especially acknowledge my mother, Luz Maria Serrano, whose nurture and unflagging confidence in me has always been something that only a loving mother can give to her child. Her encouragement and benevolence made this book a reality.

Enjoy the book. Always read with a critical mind. This is how the war in Iraq looked from my post . . .

Part One

1 Unsuited, 1-21 Field Artillery Begins Transforming

"God is always with the strongest battalion." Frederick the Great

The invasion of Iraq in March 2003 exemplified the superb ability of the U.S. Army and U.S. Marine Corps to maneuver aggressively and rapidly to defeat a third-rate military force and scatter the enemy to the four winds. But within a few short months after the successful offensive, what seemed to be a war with certain victory, through a series of incompetent political decisions and poor military planning, morphed into a war of insurgency. And the U.S. Army and U.S. Marine Corps were not properly organized or configured to fight that kind of war. One of the major unheralded facts about the war in Iraq is that decisive victory for the United States remains elusive largely because the U.S. Army and U.S. Marine Corps were not and are not designed and trained to fight and win a counterinsurgent war.

Anyone who is serious about understanding the war in Iraq must understand the military role and gain a sense for one of the major sources of the dysfunction that plagues the United States' ability to win decisively in Iraq. From mid-2003 until General Petraeus assumed command of the military in Iraq, the U.S. Army and U.S. Marine Corps (the land component forces of the U.S. military) were not properly focused to secure and stabilize the situation on the ground in Iraq. This was largely due to unsuitability of the forces and a severe lack of continuity for operations among forces in Iraq. The U.S. military effort pursued a course of trying to affect the security situation and the national political situation simultaneously without coherent, independent, and complementary actions among the military units across Iraq. Seeing the inherent flaw of this method, General Petraeus has focused effort on pursuing a sequential effort establishing security first in order to set the conditions necessary for political reconciliation to have a chance at the national level.

Most of the rhetoric about the war in Iraq focuses on the political issues that seem to prevent decisive victory. President George W. Bush's choice to send an additional 30,000 troops, the much heralded release of the Iraq Study Group report, and the "changing-of-the-guard" from the top of the Department of Defense to the senior generals directing the war effort that all occurred through the summer of 2007, are changes that point to the primacy of belief that political issues are the reason decisive victory is unattained.

Most Americans applaud the efforts of our military and point to the political failings as the causal factor detracting from the United States' ability to win decisively. While I assert this is true in large measure, the other quite unconsidered and rarely spoken causal factor is that the Army and Marine Corps are improperly trained for counterinsurgent warfare and wrongly configured to meet the complex challenges posed by the enemy in Iraq.

What is undeniably true about the Army and Marine Corps fighting this war in Iraq are that both services possess the mid-level leadership and ideological commitment to make needed changes within the forces; however, the time and effort considered necessary to institutionalize the changes through senior political and military leadership may prevent ultimate success in Iraq. Worse, the slow pace of change may adversely impact near-term future conflicts facing America. Additionally, the military has been poorly led at the very top echelons of command and staff to fight this kind of war and indeed the so-called "global war on terror." General Petraeus' elevation to senior commander has positively changed the leader dynamic in Iraq. Still, issues of leadership and advice abound at the next higher echelon.

I offer my experience as evidence that the Army's efforts for four years did little more than patch together its conventional forces to prosecute a counterinsurgent war without regard to a coherent doctrine or operational continuity to achieve the strategic objectives set forth by the National Command Authority. This problem coupled with an institutional lack of ability to properly prepare units and soldiers to optimally operate in Iraq, an inability at the top political and military level to clearly define the nature of the conflict at the outset, and no apparent military senior leader understanding of how to link tactics, operations, and strategy in a coherent manner with high fidelity and continuity have done more to adversely affect this nation's ability to decisively win the war in Iraq than anything else. In short, suspect generalship has significantly hindered the military effort in Iraq.

By March 2004, when the First Cavalry Division arrived in Baghdad, the insurgency in Iraq had taken root right under the noses of the Coalition military units that executed the initial attack. Several factors, I contend, contributed materially to this negative development:

1) Poor political decisions by the Coalition Provisional Authority disbanding the Iraqi Army, disenfranchising the Ba'ath officer corps, and instituting policies that disregarded cultural norms and tribal issues were seminal in creating the political conditions fostering an insurgency.

2) A delusional belief on the part of senior political leaders in the Bush Administration that Iraqis would welcome with open arms the American military allowed for a mindset that dismissed critical military planning decisions. Undeniably, there is a proven science to military operational

planning and by all rational analysis of the plan to invade Iraq it is clear that plan was grossly flawed. The plan severely limited troop strength vital to effectively consolidate the strategic objective, it failed to provide critical civil support resources, and the plan failed to connect the American political and military efforts in a synchronized, complementary manner. Even more, the plan did nothing to secure the borders and seal the problems of Iraq inside Iraq.

3) The Iraqi people were severely oppressed for 30 years under Saddam and his despotic regime. The deep-seated social complexities of this history were unaccounted for in the calculus by civil and military leaders charged with the responsibility of executing the operation that would become the war in Iraq. The military was not fashioned or ready to handle the challenges this history has presented. With the gross inability to communicate in Arabic and the insidious culture clash that is part of the reality of operating in Iraq, the U.S. military is unfortunately not suited to win decisively in Iraq. Success is only achieved through the building of relationships and the investment of time; time that the political realities of the American democracy do not allow for nurturing. Senior military leaders are inept at assimilating and retooling the force quickly enough to adapt and steal victory from the jaws of strategic political defeat because they just don't know how to fight this kind of war with the tools provided.

To fight in Iraq, I, along with many of my peers in the First Cavalry Division and throughout the rest of the Army, had to profoundly transform our units to meet the unanticipated demands of fighting a counterinsurgency war in Iraq. I was commanding a rocket artillery battalion. We were trained, outfitted, and fully resourced to move rocket artillery around on a wide open, maneuver-oriented battlefield and fire deep into enemy territory destroying key enemy targets. We would do none of that in Iraq. I was commanding a battalion in an unsuited Army heading into the cauldron of a burgeoning insurgency war. An active duty Lieutenant Colonel of Field Artillery assigned as Commander of 1-21 Field Artillery in the First Cavalry Division, I found myself leading a rocket artillery battalion headed to Baghdad, Iraq.

Figure 1.0 — The 5th Brigade Combat Team (BCT) of the First Cavalry Division was assigned this sector in the Al Rashid district of southwestern Baghdad.

Many personal emotions surged through me as I pondered the near future for the battalion. War is daunting enough to contemplate without the added burden of knowing the battalion was unsuited to fight in a counterinsurgent method given its existing configuration. Having to fundamentally change the operational structure and basic function of an entire Army battalion as part of the preparation process was intimidating. Understanding this reality is central to understanding the way America is fighting the war in Iraq.

To further explain: Most Americans are familiar with the Active Duty component units of the Army like the famed 82nd Airborne, 101st Airborne, First Infantry, First Cavalry and the like. What many Americans do not know is the Army is made up of three basic components: Active Duty, Reserve, and National Guard, and that each of these components exists and functions under laws and regulations that define their roles. Going into the war in Iraq, the Army's Active Duty component was the smallest size it's been in the modern history of the United States, sitting at just under 550,000 soldiers.

The U.S. Army in 2003 was generally organized in divisions. Army divisions traditionally have three ground maneuver Brigade Combat Teams (BCTs) organic (personnel and equipment residing in the Division) to the organization. Army divisions earmarked to deploy to Iraq in 2004 were programmed to receive National Guard BCTs to augment the known existing manpower shortages in the Active Duty component of the Army. A BCT is a combined arms organization designed to deploy and fight as a team. The term "combined arms" refers to tanks, infantry, artillery, aviation and a host of other specialties amalgamated into an organization to fight in combat. A BCT has roughly 4,000 soldiers assigned.

I served my whole career in the Active Duty component of the Army. As a Lieutenant Colonel, I was assigned to the First Cavalry Division at Fort Hood, Texas. A few weeks after notification to deploy to Iraq, the First Cavalry Division received a fourth ground maneuver BCT from the Arkansas National Guard. Despite being handed a National

Guard BCT, the Division still had to "stand up" yet another BCT to meet the critical manpower demands the Division was going to need in Baghdad. This additional BCT would make the fifth ground maneuver brigade for the Division along with the three organic BCTs and the Arkansas National Guard BCT.

Adding units to an existing Army division is not an anomaly. Piecing a BCT together using available organic assets was unique. This literally meant taking valuable resources away from existing units to make a whole new BCT. This is what all the Army divisions already in Iraq or heading to Iraq in 2004 and 2005 were forced to do. This was a reactive measure revealing, like a severe background symptom, the disease of an unsuited Army. The Active Duty component of the Army was too small in total size to meet the considerable manpower demands of the war in Iraq. Further, the Active Duty component of the Army needed Field Artillery units, Air Defense units, Chemical units and the like to transform to infantry/cavalry type units to meet the manpower demands not present within the existing conventional divisional formations. These represent units that are trained and educated to perform missions and roles distinctly different from the infantry/cavalry role required for operations in Iraq.

In addition to piecing together an extra ground maneuver BCT from organic division assets, Reservists and National Guard soldiers have been pulled into the active force in unprecedented numbers since World War II. They too figured into the Iraq "rotations" of Army divisions to meet the demands of this war. Soldiers already on Active Duty serving in deploying regular Army units in very large cohorts had their enlistments involuntarily extended or their retirements denied under a program known as stop-loss.

Some called these measures a "back-door draft." What is

meant by this term "back-door-draft" is that the Department of Defense instituted policies to meet the sudden increased manpower demands presented by fighting the war in Iraq. Using the term "back-door draft" suggested some underhanded business was being perpetrated. That was not true and nothing "back-door" occurred. No new policies were instituted but many existing policies generally not employed were suddenly invoked. Every soldier's enlistment contract and every officer's commissioning terms provides for the extension of service in situations of national emergency. Activating Reserve component and National Guard units to Active Duty is precisely defined in the law and in the contracts of soldiers under those component enlistments. The Department of Defense, through the President, merely exercised their statutory right to bring these soldiers already outfitted and through basic training to the fight — a wise action given the situation and costs of the alternative, possibly starting an actual draft.

The situation of needing National Guard and Reserve component forces to fight a war is not without precedent since World War II. President Lyndon B. Johnson faced the same dilemma in 1964. He chose to leave the National Guard and Reserve component largely untouched to fight in the Vietnam War. Leaving the National Guard and Army Reserve components largely unaffected while the Active Duty component of the Army went to fight the Vietnam War inadvertently created sanctuary for many who sought to avoid combat service in Vietnam. Additionally, Active Army units had to deploy into combat significantly under strength.

The Bush Administration policy to include the National Guard and Reserve on the scale that has been pursued was vital and necessary to meet the nation's strategic defense obligations under the existing circumstances. However, even these actions were not enough to properly provide for the manpower demands of the war in Iraq, and military leaders knew this from the outset and said as much in counsel to the Secretary of Defense and the President.

The U.S. Army and U.S. Marine Corps were too small to meet the demands placed on the force. Including the National Guard and Reserve components more equally distributed the burden of the war but did not suffice to relieve the stress on the land forces of the military. The best outcome of this policy was that Active Duty units were deployed at full strength which is vital to success against an insurgency. Unfortunately, the overall force deployed into Iraq was too small to meet the demands that would soon be levied.

The inclusion of the National Guard and Reserve Component along with the burgeoning insurgency in Iraq significantly challenged the Army to alter its operational focus as an institution. The clear situation in the early months of 2003, from those of us serving in the Active Duty Army, was that the Army was attempting a broad organizational transformation while trying to fight a war. The Army was doing large-scale, institutional, mid-stride adjustments to meet the demands of the strategic situation. This was nothing new to the Army; it's been done throughout its history. This occurs because no balance exists between senior military leaders and political leaders to continually shape military organizational design anticipating properly the strategic needs of the nation with respect to land warfare.

Senior military leaders are famously inept at anticipating and fashioning the force for the next conflict. National political leaders pay little attention until the crisis is upon the nation. National political policy, foreign policy, intelligence analysis and force design are not coordinated in our American democracy and national defense system. As a nation, we attempt to bring these components into tolerance in the midst of conflict instead of in anticipation of conflict. Reactive — rather than proactive – foreign policy, intelligence analysis, and force design are an unfortunate reality of our representative democracy and political leadership.

My command came into direct contact with the forces of change and escalating demands of a transforming Army. It fell to me and leaders of my generation to implement an Army transformation, at the same time as we were deploying into the cauldron of Iraq, and while in contact with a determined enemy. This was easily the challenge of a career.

Regardless of how anyone wants to "spin" the war in Iraq and how it has been fought to this point, the plain fact that faced the Department of Defense in June 2003 was that our conventional Army would have to bear the brunt of fighting the insurgency that evolved in Iraq because it is all the nation had at its disposal.

In 2003, the Army was not organized, trained or configured at its various echelons to fight an insurgency. But fighting an insurgency was the task. Planners at the Department of Defense quite easily assessed the manpower-intensive demands — what we in the Army call "troop-to-task" needs — could only be met by the Army (National Guard and Army Reserve components included) with Marine Corps augmentation. The nation had to put "boots on the ground" to fight the insurgency and re-build the country. All the "shock and awe" precision weapons of our Air Force could not fight an insurgency nor set the right conditions to rebuild a nation from the inside out. And the U.S. Navy had no capability to build a nation either.

General Eric Shinseki, Chief of Staff for the U.S. Army in 2002-2003 while strategic and post-Operation Iraqi Freedom I planning was going on at the Department of Defense, knew a large ground force was absolutely critical to securing and consolidating the gains of Operation Iraqi Freedom I. Any career Army or Marine Corps officer at the time understood this.

Most officers paying attention to the growing conflict in 2003 between Secretary of Defense Donald Rumsfeld and Army Chief of Staff General Eric Shinseki were bitter and somewhat cynical about the vulgar dismissal the Secretary of Defense gave to General Shinseki because "he didn't dig what he [Shinseki] had to say."[1]

General Shinseki courageously and accurately estimated and explained to the Secretary of Defense and the Congress that the numbers and plans the Secretary of Defense supported to deal with post-Operation Iraqi Freedom I were inadequate. Particularly noted was the Phase IV troop levels called for in the plan. Phase IV of an Operations Plan, in basic terms, defines the method and operations for consolidation of the objective. The Secretary of Defense appeared married to an agenda to reduce the size of the military and execute a "transformation" of the military, particularly the Army. He insisted that the Army generals were too cautious and were understating the capabilities of their formations.

Secretary Rumsfeld was a big believer in precision weapons, airpower, and lethal small ground forces poised to rapidly attack and defeat foes of the United States. This strategy had worked to great effect in Afghanistan, according to Secretary Rumsfeld.

No matter what the Secretary of Defense's motivations were, the conventional Army was the only force available to the Department of Defense with the scale necessary to fight and win in Iraq. However, the configuration and operational ability of the conventional Army to take on the very complex task of fighting an insurgency was not resident in 2002 before Operation Iraqi Freedom I. Similarly, with the Vietnam War, the Army was not properly configured nor prepared to fight an insurgency in 1964 when we committed sizeable ground forces to that war. It still is not completely resident in 2007.

The military and political leadership of America did not anticipate an insurgency in Iraq. No key civilian decision-maker or policy advisor with the Secretary of Defense's ear foresaw or believed that Iraq would morph into an insurgency. All senior military leaders, right up to the Chairman of the Joint Chiefs of Staff, knew that our Army and Marine Corps were not operationally designed to fight and win decisively against an insurgency. For political leaders, securing the peace after Operation Iraqi Freedom I did not seem to be a matter of huge concern. The Army was not designed before the war in Iraq to take on a counterinsurgent operational focus. The Army was designed to fight Desert Storm and to invade Iraq quickly defeating the Iraqi Army.

To fight an insurgency the Army needed infantry and lots of it. Not the traditional "walking the ground" light infantry but rather a more sophisticated infantry/cavalry blend of soldier and unit. This need directly characterized the essence of transformation for the Army in 2004. A more malleable and adaptive force that can function effectively in the full spectrum of conflict morphing from lethal combat force to civil affairs capable organizations within a four hour patrol defined the need for the Army fighting in Iraq.

What my battalion lacked at the time of notification to deploy and fight in Iraq was the right education, training, resources, and expertise to fight the way the situation demanded in Iraq. A synthesis of soldier-diplomat defined who and what our Army needed from its soldiers.

Leaders had to be people capable of managing military and civil affairs interchangeably and simultaneously. We were a unit, trained on the conventional, mock desert battlefields of Fort Irwin, California's National Training Center. We were not well schooled in patrolling, fire and maneuver, civil operations, psychological operations, or negotiation. All these were imperatives for success in Iraq. Recognizing these inadequacies was only part of the problem. Transforming educationally in training method, organizational structure, and equipment, needed to occur holistically and quickly.

My rocket artillery battalion in current configuration was near useless in this counterinsurgency effort. I say useless because rocket artillery provides rocket artillery and missile fires that destroy large tracts of ground or critical enemy targets deep behind enemy lines. As a rocket battalion deploying to Iraq we represented all that was wrong with our Army in the 21st century. Because the new enemy is terrorism and because insurgency is the flavor of the times, we were a force that had almost no utility in its designed configuration. We were irrelevant to the demands of this war.

Our first major task was to retool into a relevant organization with value to the First Cavalry Division. We had to transform from a rocket artillery battalion to some other, more useful unit. Determining exactly what that would be was a bit of an enigma in August 2003. Leading the battalion to become something markedly different from what we were was my number one job.

In August of 2003 my commander could not tell me what my unit needed to transform into. That is to say, he could not define precisely what 1-21 Field Artillery would do in Iraq. He could not even tell me what organizational headquarters my battalion would serve with. In turn, I could not define this for my subordinate leaders, soldiers or their families. All I could concretely state is we were going to war in Iraq.

With all this uncertainty swirling around and a pending deployment staring me in the face, I chose to define what I could and make some planning assumptions. I defined what was obscure to ease the tension of this uncertainty for subordinates and families. From my own experience and knowledge of the situation in Iraq I knew the battalion would most likely function as infantry. I also knew we would operate in a mobile or mounted configuration. I thought of us more as infantry/cavalry. We would have to develop light, fast moving units that had to operate in humvees, using reconnaissance skills to their utmost and simultaneously always being prepared for the lethal, combat engagements that would certainly come. 1-21 Field Artillery, I surmised, had to become a motorized, infantry/cavalry battalion.

It is the commander's responsibility and leadership that takes the battalion in the direction and along the path to success or failure. Dealing with the complexities of transforming a rocket battalion to what I conceived would be a motorized infantry task force was the challenge of a professional military career. A task force is a military term to define a larger unit, at or above the battalion echelon that is pieced together with smaller subordinate units placed into a combined arms organization to accomplish a particular task. I personally felt supremely capable but only because my unique career path and training experiences learning infantry maneuver as an artillery officer prepared me well. I drew my other sense of confidence and strength from a personal leader vision and intuitive knowledge that responding to change successfully was the greatest measure of effective leadership. I lived this through my entire professional career.

To transform the battalion and realize the goal of becoming an effective infantry/cavalry task force required good training, strong non-commissioned officer leadership, and a unique mental strength among the men and women in the ranks who needed to assimilate the situation successfully. Even more importantly, though, to bind the organization intellectually and from the inside out required a common vision from which all else would flow.

Having a Vision and then Following It

Develop a team of initiative-oriented leaders and a formation of prideful, self-disciplined, tough-minded soldiers that exude a strong, respectful individual and unit character which readily responds to change and routinely demonstrates mastery of combat operations in support of this division.

This was the vision statement that bound the battalion. I believed very strongly in this statement and I made sure everyone in the battalion got it and understood it as I intended. I did not hit the soldiers and leaders over the head with it. Instead, I shaped unit education processes around this vision statement. All personnel, training, logistics, operations, and leader decisions were made with this vision as the basis. The most significant aspect of this vision to me was about shaping an organization which was responsive to change.

More than anything else I thought about in the world in which I operated, responding to change, I knew, was imperative to success. I have always believed that organizations and units that are most responsive to change perform best in combat. People survive the stresses and strains best when they can adjust and respond positively to changes. As a leader, part of the "trick" is anticipating the changes and setting conditions to find success through positive anticipatory response. The natural human tendency is to resist change and avoid unfamiliarity because it's scary. However, when organizations or people are unresponsive, failure or crisis soon visits. Change happens continually and universally. If people or organizations cannot adapt or effectively anticipate change, then they truly will not survive. More importantly than responding to change is being the agent of change. This defined the kind of organization I wanted 1-21 Field Artillery to be. I wanted to develop leaders and soldiers who embodied this ideal nurturing this throughout the depth and breadth of the battalion.

I believed the best way for this unit to develop a character that was malleable and responsive to change was to encourage some specific behaviors and organizational composition of people. Diversity includes ethnic, economic, educational and gender components. It is one thing to speak about diversity within an organization, it is quite another to act on that belief when placing people into critical positions in an organization.

Diversity is strategic. Ethnic, gender, and ideological diversity are absolutely essential to achieving an organization that can respond to change. This is so because diversity brings with it different perspectives and experiences. Diversity allows for parts, when synthesized, to be brought together creating a truly unique, powerful new entity.

Another key component to my organizational vision was critical thinking and judgment. Tapping into the minds of critical thinkers — those who question what they see and hear or who look for ways to accomplish tasks better — and allowing them to voice their ideas and methods into the organizational business practices also allows an organization to continually improve and seek new paths.

Synthesizing everything that diverse and critical thinkers

bring with them exponentially strengthens organizations. I surmise too that this takes certain kinds of leaders. Leaders who exhibit confidence are mentally tough and are able to answer to and face subordinates who are critical thinkers. This is a dimension that must be developed in organizations committed to long-term success. In many military organizations this is talked about, but unfortunately, in Army combat units, it is not practiced as a norm. But in mine, critical thinking became an expected way of life.

The composition of the battalion I commanded included two rocket batteries with six M270A1 rocket launchers and 91 soldiers each to provide rocket and missile fires in support of the Division; a Headquarters and Service Battery with just over 200 soldiers who provided all the staff, maintenance, communications and logistical support to the battalion; a radar target acquisition battery with 72 soldiers that acquired counter-battery targets for the division; and a chemical company with over 200 soldiers who provided chemical reconnaissance and chemical decontamination support to the Division.

To manage the conversion of my rocket battalion into an infantry/cavalry one and to absorb the units that were earmarked to come under my command with the ultimate goal of formation of a single task force demanded flexibility. The unit had to become a motorized, infantry/cavalry battalion. The critical challenge to my vision would be to take non-infantry soldiers and make them an infantry team.

This common vision provided a compelling difference allowing the leaders in the unit to develop our soldiers along the many lines of operation that exist for any Army battalion. The senior leaders of the battalion guided the unit to achieve the unit transformation goals. More importantly, though, the leadership had to ready the outfit to fight and win on the mean streets of Baghdad. To do so meant hard work, sacrifice, and more hard work.

The focus had to be on infantry training. The problem with this crucial demand was that the battalion soldiers and all its leadership were artillerymen and chemical-trained troops. Somehow the battalion had to transform into an infantry-trained outfit with the resident leaders planning and executing the training.

With a basis of understanding through my formal military education and a mastery of fire and maneuver training, planning, and tactical execution up to the brigade level, I was well grounded in the fundamentals and prepared to guide and develop the training for the task at hand. Unfortunately, no one else on my staff or in subordinate units of the battalion had much infantry or maneuver background. This lack of expertise across the depth and breadth of the formation I was charged to command was a critical shortcoming — one that deeply concerned me. It was a situation that could prove disastrous.

All Things Infantry

I grew up as an army brat. And so, long before I "officially" became a soldier, I always saw the infantry whenever I thought of the Army. My father was commissioned a Second Lieutenant in the Army when I was two years old. So, ever since the age of two, I have always had a relationship with the Army. No other institution has had more impact on my life than the Army. I owe my very existence to the Army as the vehicle that brought my parents together from very different backgrounds. My parents met at Fort Hood, Texas in 1958, and that is where they married in 1961. My mother, Luz Maria Serrano-Fonseca, worked at Darnall Army Medical Center and my father, Allen Anthony Baumann, was an Army legal clerk. Both were enlistees in the Army.

In 1961, they married and left the Army after finishing their enlistments. My father took his Puerto Rican wife north to his home in southwest Minnesota. That's where my sister, brother, and I were born. We're from a small rural town called Olivia, Minnesota.

My father returned to the Army in 1964 as a Second Lieutenant in the Field Artillery. He earned a National Guard commission through the Minnesota Military Academy, and branch transferred to Infantry after his first tour-of-duty in Vietnam.

My mother became a schoolteacher and then public school administrator in the Saint Paul, Minnesota School District where she eventually became an Area Superintendent. Though neither had much education when they married and had three children, by the time I was graduated from college, both had acquired significant higher education.

My father earned a bachelors degree, two master's degrees and a Jurist Doctorate. My mother, by this time, had almost completed her doctorate in education administration, which she would complete shortly after I was commissioned. Along with the Army, education was always integral to my life growing up.

My parents proved to be the strongest influence on me and my siblings. Despite living through considerable life challenges as an Army family in the decades of the 1960s and 1970s, we kids did pretty well in life. My older sister became an attorney practicing in Louisiana. My younger brother, Joseph A. Baumann, has held several jobs in banking, real estate and auto sales over the years. I chose to pursue a career in the Army, a lifelong ambition.

I recall with great clarity and fondness the time my family spent at Fort Bragg, North Carolina. My father was in the 82nd Airborne Division serving in the Infantry. That's when, at age 10, my personal ideal of the Army really began to take shape. My image of the Army was of airborne infantry.

Many years later, in 1987, I was at Fort Campbell, Kentucky in the 101st Airborne Division (Air Assault) in 2nd Battalion, 320th Field Artillery. I was a Lieutenant when I was offered an opportunity to go to the U.S. Army Ranger School. At this school, for two months I learned how to be an infantryman and combat leader under the most demanding conditions the Army could throw at me. Ever since I had started college, I wanted to attend this school that I saw as the epitome of training for a lieutenant. I wanted to prove to the world and to myself that I was tough enough to make it through that rigorous training.

Little did I know then that this training would serve me so profoundly more than 15 years later, literally defining my leadership of a battalion in combat in Iraq. Back then, and throughout most of my career, I knew Ranger training would personally serve me allowing me to truly know the limits of my endurance. I knew too this training would provide me with a general ability to perform well as a leader. But Ranger School actually proved to be so much more valuable. I would always tell my lieutenants, "Everything I ever needed to know about how to lead a unit in combat I learned in Ranger School." Ranger School is focused not at battalion level but at the squad, section, and platoon level. But the principles, techniques, systems, and fundamentals for leading any organization are all part of the Ranger program.

When I was getting ready to go to Ft. Benning, Georgia, for Ranger School, I read some literature about what I could expect. The literature touted a program that "was a course designed to meet or exceed combat conditions" for sustained periods of time. Today the course scope is described as:

> *The Ranger course is 61 days in length with an average of 19.6 hours of training each day, seven days a week. The emphasis during the course is on practical, realistic, and strenuous field training, where the Ranger student is taught Ranger related skills based on current tactical doctrine. It is designed to develop combat arms functional skills relevant to fighting the close combat, direct fire battle. The student is exposed to conditions and situations, which closely approximate and often exceed those he would encounter in combat. Fatigue, hunger, the necessity for quick, sound decisions and the requirement for demonstrating calm, forceful leadership under conditions of mental and emotional stress are all experienced in the Ranger course.*[2]

I was sold and knew it was my rite of passage on my way to becoming the leader I wanted to be. Patrolling was the essential skill necessary to fight along the mean streets of Baghdad. This is where I focused the battalion training and leader development. Instilling a warrior ethos and a cavalry mindset into my soldiers and modeling all we did from the doctrinal designs of Ranger patrolling became my basis for training and transforming the battalion. Ranger training gave me the mastery I needed to truly achieve this within my organization. Of course, that was not all I needed. Thankfully, I had other infantry training to draw upon in realizing our training goals.

During my tour at the 101st Airborne Division, (Air Assault) in 1989, I sought an opportunity to attend another Army branch Officer Advance Course. For my generation, typically, once an officer completed the first three-year assignment in the Army, standard personnel practice was to send officers to their branch's Advance Course. After that course, the officer was then sent to their next assignment at another Army post serving in another unit. Although my branch was Field Artillery, I petitioned for an assignment to the Infantry Officer Advance Course.

I did this for two fundamental reasons. First, as a Field Artillery officer, one critical position I knew I might serve in was Fire Support Officer for an infantry or armor battalion. A battalion Fire Support Officer works for an infantry or armor battalion commander and is responsible for coordination of indirect fires. Cannon, rocket, missile, mortar, aircraft or naval gunfire are all indirect fires assets that require detailed coordination to integrate into a battle. This is the primary skill set of a Fire Support Officer. I believed an understanding of infantry methods, planning processes, and tactics would permit me to be more effective in that job. In my mind, there is nothing better than an intimate understanding of the branch that I would likely support.

Secondly, I believed this would broaden my knowledge as an officer. The more I understood the intricacies of maneuver warfare, tactics, and processes the more I could add that to my knowledge and experience with planning and directing indirect fires. Theoretically, this would materially expand my utility to the Army. For me, it was not enough to just master my branch of expertise; I wanted to understand the whole picture — combining fires and maneuver — because optimally that is what combat officers must do.

By developing this foundation, there was little I could not do in the world of my chosen profession. I never consciously conceived that one day I would be asked to transform a rocket artillery battalion into a motorized infantry battalion task force. Fortunately, by making some good decisions early in my career, I had the education to do what was needed at a time when the Army was undergoing an ill-prepared transformation.

In the Infantry Officer Advance Course, I went through the professional development education progression of all infantry officers. We mastered company through brigade level operations. I also learned from within the branch the infantry developmental thinking and planning processes. This was highly instructive, grounding me in the fundamentals of infantry operations. As a Fire Support Officer, understanding tactics and operations for maneuver enabled me to refine my ability to apply my primary professional forté. This experience and education allowed me to develop confidence in my ability to apply that understanding and to instruct others on the application of maneuver tactics.

Later in my career, as a senior Captain, I served as the Military Science III Course Director at Texas A&M, where I had the opportunity to teach cadets seeking to become lieutenants in the Army what I had learned about leadership and small unit infantry tactics.

My task as the Military Science III Course Director was to train junior year college students (cadets) in leadership, command, and mastery of small unit infantry tactics from squad to company level operations. During the academic year we would have classes and field time to develop the cadets' skills and to assess their performance. I had to master and then teach all the intricacies of squad and platoon infantry tactics to cadets who, for the most part, knew nothing about this. This experience forced me to master training and teaching technique.

Teaching cadets small unit infantry tactics was a pure joy and this further prepared me well for what was to come in my professional life: leading and transforming 1-21 Field Artillery.

As the Army was forced to fight in Iraq and utilize so many

non-infantry units as infantry, the rocket battalion I commanded had to make the adjustments to become an infan-
try/cavalry unit. Additionally, 1-21 Field Artillery needed
a mission in which to focus upon all the while, we had to
prepare to deploy, fight an elusive enemy in a very challenging kind of warfare, and try to find a way to win in the
cauldron of Baghdad, Iraq.

2 Getting a Mission, Preparing to Deploy

"The truth of the matter is that you always know the right thing to do. The hard part is doing it." Norman Schwarzkopf

I knew from the earliest days of my command tenure that the battalion could transform if called upon to do so. I also knew I had exceptional non-commissioned officers who would direct the effort successfully. I could see the conviction in their eyes. Once notified of deployment, despite the unclear situation, I kept the leadership of the battalion informed. Even if my seniors could not provide clear guidance, I would not allow that ambiguity to trickle below me. The leaders of 1-21 Field Artillery always had a direction and a path to walk. I made certain of that.

After deployment notification, over the course of the next few weeks, several scenarios for employment of the battalion were considered. Rumors were weaving their way through the barracks, the headquarters, and among the family members of the soldiers. Everyone was trying to "nail down" the truth of what the rocket battalion would do in Iraq.

One rumored concept had us replacing another rocket battalion from First Armor Division already in Iraq. That battalion, 1st Battalion 94th Field Artillery Regiment, was providing security for Baghdad International Airport. They operated as infantry, not artillery. This represented the likeliest model for 1-21 Field Artillery.

The Baghdad International Airport "Guard Force" rumor lasted about a month. It then shifted to having us serve as the security element and guard force for the First Cavalry Division headquarters at a place called Camp Victory. That lasted a few days when a new concept surfaced. 1-21 Field

Artillery would become part of a new maneuver brigade, the 5th Brigade Combat Team (BCT). This rumor had 1-21 Field Artillery as the forward operating base security force for the brigade and I would be "mayor" of the forward operating base, Camp Falcon.

That unfounded information lasted for about another week when it became apparent we would definitely be part of a newly forming ground maneuver BCT known as the 5th BCT. Rather than serving strictly as Camp Falcon security, we would instead provide route security for two major supply routes (highways) in the 5th BCT sector. We would also be responsible to secure a "small" sector of the Al Rashid district of Baghdad.

In the end, this concept plan became the basis for our preparations and where I directed the unit's focus. I was never privy to the discussions the Commanding General was having with his BCT commanders (known as "The Barons" in First Cavalry Division) in the early weeks after the Division was notified of its deployment. But I surmised that when the Commanding General seriously considered a fifth ground maneuver BCT with the Division Artillery Commander, Colonel Stephen R. Lanza as the most likely to command that formation, Colonel Lanza argued to get 1-21 Field Artillery in the BCT. This was a natural fit because we were a subordinate unit of the Division Artillery already. By having us in the new 5th BCT, this would give Colonel Lanza a larger force to form a viable maneuver command. Having us guard the Division headquarters, or allowing us to be sent out to Baghdad International Airport under some other organizational structure, would have reduced his potential BCT size. That would have considerably challenged his ability to deal with the situation in Al Rashid because he would have to execute that with just two maneuver battalions. It was in his best interest to see that we were assigned under this newly forming BCT.

Ultimately, the Commanding General chose to assign 1-21 Field Artillery to the 5th BCT.

From a strict doctrinal assessment of the initial mission, given the allotted troops assigned within each of the battalions that made up 5th BCT, we were each over-tasked, under-resourced, and under-strength for the mission and battle-space assigned. This was normal for almost all units sent to Iraq in Operation Iraqi Freedom II. The task and mission were enormous and we were in a "come-as-you-are" configuration. Assessing, adapting, and adjusting were vital traits needed to succeed.

The area the battalion would have to cover extended over forty square kilometers of mostly urban terrain. Demographically, our sector was densely populated in the northern area, included Camp Falcon in the central portion, and was very rural in the southern part. A major Baghdad highway ran in front of Camp Falcon and through the heart of the BCT sector. This was Highway 8. We all came to know Highway 8 as Route Irish. Highway 8 was easily the most traveled road in Baghdad if not Iraq. Route Irish was a graphical name (label) given by the First Armor Division staff planners, which the First Cavalry Division retained. Most Americans know this as "Airport Road" — the name the television media dubbed it. We would have to secure this route in the north of the Task Force assigned sector to the BCT boundary in the south.

What the Army was asking me to do was take radar, rocket and cannon artillery troops, chemical soldiers, cooks, mechanics, administrators, men and women from a variety of ethnic backgrounds, training regimens, education levels and varying ranks and make them an infantry team in combat. I had about three months to prepare.

Disconcerting was that my Modified Table of Organization

and Equipment would not be adjusted at all except the eventual provision of a small number of the M1114 armored humvees. The organizational structure and personnel numbers would not be adjusted one iota. I would fight as infantry with degraded assets, incongruent resources, and lacking capabilities basic to infantry units across the Army. It was up to me to figure out how to get it done and have the unit ready.

Becoming Part of 5th Brigade Combat Team

Another important dynamic for my battalion to manage was becoming part of the as-yet non-existent 5th Brigade Combat Team. This was an ad hoc organization, born of necessity, which did not exist as an element of the First Cavalry Division until it was directed to "stand up" for this deployment.

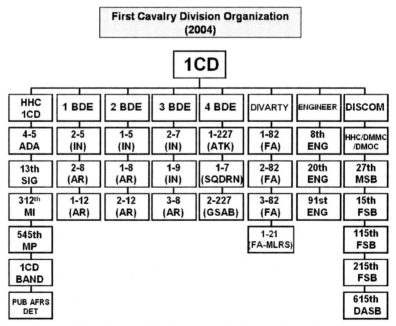

First Cavalry Division Organization (2004)							
1CD							
HHC 1CD	1 BDE	2 BDE	3 BDE	4 BDE	DIVARTY	ENGINEER	DISCOM
4-5 ADA	2-5 (IN)	1-5 (IN)	2-7 (IN)	1-227 (ATK)	1-82 (FA)	8th ENG	HHC/DMMC /DMOC
13th SIG	2-8 (AR)	1-8 (AR)	1-9 (IN)	1-7 (SQDRN)	2-82 (FA)	20th ENG	27th MSB
312th MI	1-12 (AR)	2-12 (AR)	3-8 (AR)	2-227 (GSAB)	3-82 (FA)	91st ENG	15th FSB
545th MP					1-21 (FA-MLRS)		115th FSB
1CD BAND							215th FSB
PUB AFRS DET							615th DASB

Figure 2.2 — First Cavalry Division organizational chart, September 2003, before the Division was re-organized to fight in Iraq.

Becoming part of 5th BCT was a unique and supremely challenging experience. To explain, heavy Army divisions like First Cavalry Division were organized into three-ground maneuver BCTs. The Division also had an Aviation Brigade, a Division Support Command, an Engineer Brigade, and the Division Artillery headquarters. The Division Artillery headquarters managed three cannon artillery battalions and one rocket artillery battalion.

This chart depicts how the Division Artillery was organized:

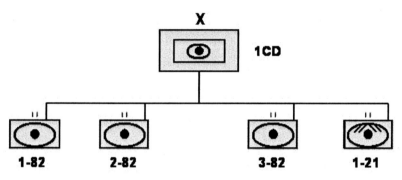

Figure 2.3 — Division Artillery organization chart, June 2003.

The Division Artillery was the headquarters element that oversaw and trained the fire support system of the Division.

The Division Artillery Commander was responsible for managing the training and fire support coordination of all indirect fires for the Division Commander. The Division Artillery was a brigade-size headquarters with a colonel commanding to exercise a functional role to coordinate fires for the division.

On a high-intensity, large-scale, set-piece, free-flowing,

modern, maneuver battlefield no Army was better organized or practiced at synchronizing fires with maneuver
to seize tactical and operational level objectives than the
U.S. Army. Iraq was not a high intensity conflict battlefield
after the initial operation to overthrow Saddam in Operation Iraqi Freedom I. The subsequent fight is an insurgency
pure and simple.

To deal with the manpower-intensive demands of the Division counterinsurgent mission the Division's senior leaders concluded, like the senior leaders of the Army, that the
Field Artillery formations in the Division were potential
sources of needed ground, maneuver troops.

The Division Commander and his staff, early in the planning process, identified the need to have a fifth ground
maneuver BCT as part of the Division (a National Guard
BCT was already earmarked with the deployment order
to go to First Cavalry Division). Senior Division leaders
and planners considered this additional ground maneuver
BCT absolutely necessary for the Division to accomplish its
mission in Baghdad, Iraq.

Major General Peter Chiarelli had to figure out quickly
who would command this new organization. Major General Chiarelli was about 6', slim with a long face, a full head
of dark, graying hair and an infectious, affable personality. Five minutes in his presence you could tell he loved
soldiering. Major General Chiarelli had served a long and
distinguished career as an Armor officer. He was steady,
courteous, confident, and approachable despite his lofty
rank and unique position commanding a premier division
in the Army.

As Major General Chiarelli pondered the selection of a BCT
commander he had at least two obvious choices. He could
select the Engineer Brigade Commander or his Division

Artillery Commander. The Commanding General selected the Division Artillery Commander, Colonel Stephen Lanza.

Colonel Lanza was the natural and right choice to take command of this newly formed organization. A strong-willed, tough-nosed Roman Catholic Italian from the Bronx in New York who graduated from West Point in 1981, Lanza was a decent choice for the task. He stood up a new ground maneuver brigade in the Division and led the counterinsurgency in the Al Rashid district of Baghdad.

Lanza's quick, intense exploitation of the Division campaign plan proved to be effective. Given the circumstances of establishing the formation, building the team, and directing the complexities of the area he was charged to secure and stabilize, Colonel Lanza performed well.

1-21 Field Artillery became part of the 5th BCT on September 12, 2003 and remained so until May 26, 2005. Two weeks after I assumed command of 1-21 Field Artillery, on June 27, 2003, until the First Cavalry Division Artillery was officially inactivated on June 30, 2005, I served as a subordinate battalion commander to Colonel Lanza. Literally, I stood with him his entire command tenure start to finish. As, together, we transitioned to a new command structure, the professional, personal and command relationship I already had with Colonel Lanza would remain in place though much around both of us would change dramatically.

Battalion-sized units added to comprise the 5th BCT were 1-7 Cavalry, 1-8 Cavalry, and 515th Forward Support Battalion. These sister battalions were commanded by officers, peers I barely knew and who barely knew me. None knew Colonel Lanza as their commander although the 1-8 Cavalry Commander, Lieutenant Colonel John "Jay" Allen, had served with him in a previous assignment at Fort Riley, Kansas.

The commander for 1-7 Cavalry, Lieutenant Colonel William "Bill" Salter, and the commander of 1-8 Cavalry, Lieutenant Colonel Allen, were armor officers by training. Bill Salter and Jay Allen had served as Observer Controllers at the National Training Center when they were captains. Lieutenant Colonel James "Jim" Hevel, Commander of 515th Forward Support Battalion, was an aviation officer and master logistician.

Each would have their own issues with Colonel Lanza's methods of command, as they were unaccustomed to the painstaking detail for which artillerymen are famous for when commanding organizations. I, on the other hand, was all too familiar with the "pain" of serving commanders in my branch of the Army. Over time this provided no particular advantage but watching the others struggle a bit did offer some comical moments.

It was this collection of senior leaders, which I stood among, and this newly-formed BCT a few months ahead of deployment, that had to grow into a fully-functional, lethal, and capable team to fight in Iraq. This was a superb personal and professional experience. It fell right in line with what was happening on a larger scale in the Army. It was exciting.

Standing Up the New 5th Brigade Combat Team

The First Cavalry Division effort to "stand up" the 5th BCT was rather unique. The First Armor Division had been confronted with a similar problem while in Iraq prior to the deployment of the First Cavalry Division and had chosen to use the Division Artillery headquarters and its attendant staff capability, forming a "pseudo BCT" at the tail end of their deployment. Theirs was an impromptu method to resource a fourth organic maneuver BCT. But the Division Artillery Commander of First Armor Division never enjoyed the true trappings, designs, and full resources of a maneuver BCT. First Cavalry Division had some time to prepare and resource a BCT, albeit little, and pursued a more deliberate course to "stand-up" this BCT.

Given the time and lessons learned from First Armor Division's experience, Major General Chiarelli directed his staff to take all prudent measures to resource 5th BCT as much like the other maneuver BCTs as possible. He had intended to give 5th BCT a large sector of ground in Baghdad. He wanted their personnel and equipment organization to be as close to fully resourced, organic BCTs in the Division as reasonable measures would allow.

Soldiers and equipment had to be pulled from existing units. Other units from section size through brigade size had to give up personnel and equipment to resource this BCT. The Division Artillery Headquarters Battery had to be re-staffed to reflect a maneuver BCT. Many additional soldiers and equipment had to be culled away from other units to become part of the 5th BCT. New relationships, operating procedures, and team dynamics had to be determined.

The battalion subordinate units had to figure out how to work together and compete for limited resources within the BCT. The actual activation date for the 5th BCT was September 12, 2003. The BCT was in combat on March 25, 2004. There was precious little time to build a team and then take it to the ultimate test.

3 Initial Training

"The best form of taking care of troops is first-class training, for this saves unnecessary casualties." Erwin Rommel

The transformation effort for 1-21 Field Artillery had multiple components. Organization was one part, integrating external units into a newly-forming organization was another part, and training was yet another. These were not independent; they were interrelated entities that had to be closely managed and synthesized. Meshing these so they worked in complementary fashion was the primary leadership goal and constantly posed a significant challenge. Of all the parts, training was the most important to ultimate success.

From the beginning of our training efforts and integration activities assimilating into the 5th BCT, the battalion had a uniquely dissimilar training requirement than that of the other two maneuver battalions of the 5th BCT. 1-7 Cavalry and 1-8 Cavalry were already maneuver units by design. Maneuver units train all facets of their unit to maneuver tasks. They are skilled in direct engagement and maneuver against a hostile enemy, unlike fire support units that train to put indirect fires on the battlefield in support of maneuver actions. 1-21 Field Artillery had to learn how to become a maneuver unit without the attendant developmental individual and collective task training that traditional Army maneuver unit's nurture. We also had unique additional tasks which were to shoot missiles, fire cannons, cue radar throughout Baghdad, and respond to a chemical emergency anywhere. Firing missiles and responding to a chemical emergency were mission requirements that transcended the BCT and potentially even transcended the Division. That meant if the Division were tapped by Multi-National Forces, Iraq, the highest Coalition Forces Command in Iraq, to fire missiles or deal with a chemical hazard emergency, 1-21 Field Artillery would represent the Division.

This situation necessitated by the nature of the conflict occurred in many other units across the Army and Marine Corps. Fielding units to conduct missions in which they are not trained, organized, and outfitted with the necessary equipment to conduct is dangerous business. This method was commonplace for the Army fighting in Iraq.

Exacerbating this situation was the constant morale issues attendant with stop-loss policies. Task Force 1-21 had about 25 percent of the soldiers serving under the Army stop-loss policy. Some complained vociferously, but most soldiers did not complain openly. In any case, the policy had an impact on morale, and I had to pay close attention to its overall effect on the organization.

My view and approach to help overcome the significant disparity was to imbue a strong spirit of the cavalry in soldiers and leaders and instill the belief that this battalion could adapt, respond, improve, and succeed through all these demands. The myriad of things we were asked to do necessarily demanded agility, poise, and intellect. We had to be able to work through these demands and not come apart from the burden. There was also the overriding demand to execute all the training safely. With this much diversity, disparity, and challenging realistic training scenarios in play, a major accident or loss of life would be catastrophic. No unit could pull this off without leader involvement at all echelons, strong discipline, and good communication throughout the unit.

In the initial assessment phase back at Fort Hood, Texas, and the early part of the actual combat tour in Iraq, Division staff and the BCT staff shaped the training. The battalion staff had voluminous and tedious reporting requirements to insure training was accomplished to standard. The leadership and battalion staff were mostly engaged in planning, coordinating, preparing, executing, and assessing. Where assessments found shortcomings, we went back and repeated the task so I was sure the soldiers and junior leaders were confident in the task.

The S3 I was blessed to have and the leaders in the battalion were magnificent. Major Rob Menti was my S3, Operations Officer, and he was "on fire." Easily, he ranks as the most intense mind I have ever served with in the Army. About 5′ 8″, physically strong like an ox, Major Menti had piercing eyes and an electric mind. When I observed Major Menti, what I saw was a guy who could think critically and who could think faster than almost everyone around him in a seemingly effortless manner. I knew immediately that I wanted to exploit that ability for the unit.

Major Menti was an officer who could look at a problem and analyze it so far down that he could conceive of multiple branches and sequels to a plan in seconds. He saw what most others could not see. I was very enamored with this talent. I was beside myself that I had this veritable genius mind working for me in the critical job of the battalion. I knew God truly was taking care of me.

Major Menti helped me direct my focus on two groups: the non-commissioned officers and the lieutenants of the battalion. If the training I wanted to implement was going to meet my overarching goal of fielding a unit that was capable of routinely executing the primary and contingency missions near flawlessly, these were the leaders who would achieve success.

The battalion's training plan was nested in the BCT's training plan, and organized into a five-phased program. Phase I focused on leader training down to the platoon leader and platoon sergeant level. Phase II concentrated on individual training. Country orientation, anti-terrorism, force protection, rules of engagement, handling of unexploded ordinance, and dealing with Improvised Explosive Devices (IEDs) were required subjects of training. The BCT added nuclear-biological-chemical procedures, individual first aid, land navigation in urban terrain, and personal weapons qualification to the training requirements.

Phase III changed the effort, focusing on collective training for platoon, squad, and team units. The battalion conducted live-fire exercises, honed troop-leading skills, practiced convoy procedures in live-fire scenarios, conducted tactical mounted road marches, and worked on medical evacuation procedures. This was done to insure all soldiers and tactical elements could effectively handle casualties from combat or accidents. We also began to work on the basic platoon and company level offensive and defensive tasks to execute those operations properly. Conditions to transition to Phase IV were thus set where battalions would work on stability operations from platoon to battalion level.

The final phase, Phase V, all the efforts in a Division-driven mission readiness exercise brought the BCT together for the first time. In this mission readiness exercise, the BCT attempted to operate as a team in an Iraq-like simulation exercise at Fort Hood. This represented capstone training and included all the units of the BCT (1-7 Cavalry, 1-8 Cavalry, 1-21 Field Artillery, and 515th Forward Support Battalion). This training allowed the brigade staff to hone their command and control skills. This also allowed the BCT to get familiar with integration and operations utilizing psychological units, Civil Affairs units, and more robust military intelligence detachments.

Major Menti worked aggressively, with unmitigated energy, all the details of training management and planning.

When I arrived in the battalion back in June 2003, the unit, I assessed, was deficient in its ability to execute training management. No unit was in more need of a process. The unit was incapable of anticipating on the scale necessary to expect to succeed consistently in their multiple, diverse, and disparate endeavors. The leaders of the battalion were expert at reacting to problems presented both internally and externally. I could not stop the external reaction immediately, but I could stop the internally-generated problems quickly. Over time, I would work on the externally-generated crisis-creation machine. The solution to the battalion's training management problems reside in Army doctrine; unfortunately, it was a doctrine that few followed.

In the early years of my Army career, training management was something I had heard about. As a battery commander, I executed training management processes but it was unrefined and only at my level. It was a buzz phrase as far as I was concerned. I learned definitively what it was when I became the S3 of a rocket battalion (1-77 FA) at Fort Sill, Oklahoma, in 1999. There, I met Lieutenant Colonel Mark Tillman, the quintessential staff perfectionist and best mentor I ever had in the Army. This man was phenomenal at staff work in the Army. Lieutenant Colonel Tillman made me a field grade officer and a true professional at my chosen profession. As a leader, he was demanding, mentally tough, and tended to the minutest detail. I had to learn how to keep up with him and then go the next step and anticipate his thoughts, questions, and expectations. Once I achieved that level I was set, maybe for life.

Lieutenant Colonel Tillman taught me training management. Early in my tenure as his S3, Operations Officer, dissatisfied with the unstructured and incompetent training management system in place, Lieutenant Colonel Tillman told me to figure out a method to run the battalion training meeting process following our doctrine. When I was tasked to develop this program I went straight to the Army doctrinal book and read it again. Nothing immediately jumped out at me as a pragmatic means to develop a systemic program for the Battalion.

I decided I needed a better brain on the problem. I had a brilliant S2 officer, Captain Steve Carroll. This guy was dazzling, eager, and magnificently talented at abstract thinking. So I delegated to him the task I was given and asked him to give me a concept the next morning. What I got was incredible. He was able to break down the details from the doctrine into a practical slide-formatted presentation that covered all the basics presented in the training doctrinal manual. I worked-in some refinement and we went final with a product to present to Lieutenant Colonel Tillman. He instantly loved it.

Over the 18 months I was the S3 for 1-77 under Lieutenant Colonel Tillman the product was refined until it had an edge and functionality that was effective and easily understood and followed. The training management process he invoked streamlined battalion operations so profoundly; all were capable of quick understanding, allowing everyone to be in step immediately. This worked so universally that it became standard practice in 1-21 Field Artillery when I assumed command.

To me, processes and systems are vital to organizations. They must be functional and effective for the people who must operate within their framework. A system can theoretically function very well but never serve the people or work for those who must operate within the system. In those cases, the process or system is a burden. Systems and processes also must conform to the norms and cultures of those who operate it. Unless a system respects the people rejecting that which is too mechanical and impersonal and incorporating that which is malleable, then it's just an encumbering weight, which will ultimately, fail demoralizing its people and dragging down the organization. People can't become slaves to a process or system. Systems have to be vibrant, interactive, and adaptable; they must honor intellectual and creative abilities of those they are intended to govern. Achieving this kind of system and process management methodology allows an organization to flourish.

Most of my career, in whatever job I had where people worked under me by hierarchical military structured dictates, I always pressed them to work with me but not necessarily for me. I've tried to create environments that elicited the ideas of all to solve problems or shape processes.

As part of the initial training program, we had to reconfigure personnel to train in units designed like infantry organizations. These units needed to be adaptive and to share ideas, training techniques, and lessons learned. Our unit preparation to deploy and fight in Iraq was not an Army-level-directed transformation conducted in a well thought out, overarching, and resourced sense. The reorganization we had to execute was localized and consisted of an adjustment of existing personnel coupled with a modification of training to build the necessary skills to fight as infantry/cavalry in Iraq. We determined that we would take the rocket artillery firing platoons, the cannon firing platoons earmarked to come to 1-21 Field Artillery, and the chemical company platoons and re-make them into what we called "SOSO Platoons." SOSO was an acronym for, Security Operations/Stability Operations.

We named these "SOSO Platoons" because the operational tasks of these platoons were not just designed around conduct of combat; combat was their primary functional role. However, these units had to be organized to conduct reconnaissance, support local psychological operations, collect information in support of information dissemination campaigns, distribute food, clothing, support medical teams bringing aid to Iraqis in need, and support civil affairs projects. These myriad of tasks could impact the platoons every day. When reorganized, we had a total of fifteen SOSO platoons that needed to be distributed in the sector and along the two highways the battalion was tasked to secure.

For each of the SOSO platoons we developed a program of instruction. That program included all the individual readiness training requirements from Division and the directed training tasks from the BCT commander. Then each had to accomplish the various individual and collective tasks that I directed each unit to master. We would have each platoon train using urban terrain in a variety of scenarios and certify them as they successfully negotiated the various gates of training.

We started first by reorganizing and identifying an officer (Lieutenant) and a non-commissioned officer (Sergeant First Class) as Platoon Leader and Platoon Sergeant for each of the SOSO platoons in the battalion. We then assigned soldiers to each platoon. After that was established, we provided the training event gates. Then, at battalion level, the staff tracked all the training accomplished through the battery and company commanders. We also overlaid the plethora of pre-deployment administrative tasks that had to be done.

To further focus the BCT planning and training beyond the obvious, the Division had worked out a pre-deployment site survey program for each of the BCTs of the division. This pre-deployment site survey would allow selected leaders and staff officers of the BCTs to get on the ground we would be operating within in Baghdad and examine the situation. The idea was for key leaders to assess, first hand, what was going on. This would then allow us to refine plans and make training adjustments before getting to Iraq.

Pre-Deployment Site Survey — Into Iraq

On January 23, 2004, the wheels of an Air Force C-130 squealed on the runway to Baghdad International Airport with the senior leaders of the 5th BCT aboard (Colonel Lanza, Lieutenant Colonel Salter, Lieutenant Colonel Allen, Lieutenant Colonel Hevel, and me) and two staff officers (Major Chris Bonheim and Captain Lou Alvarez, the BCT S3 and S2 respectively). We were going to Camp Falcon to assess the situation on the ground in order to learn what we could, see the available facilities and refine the plans that we had been feverishly developing at Fort Hood, Texas.

Before we departed on this pre-deployment site survey, the BCT Commander articulated his intent for the reconnaissance mission. He wanted each of us subordinate battalion commanders to observe what the battalions in the BCT that we were replacing were doing. With that, we would begin to make a detailed assessment of how our organization would overlay the existing program.

My task was to make an assessment of how 1-94 Field Artillery of First Armor Division operated. This was the battalion we would relieve in place. First Armor Division, which 1-94 Field Artillery was assigned to, moved this unit from Baghdad International Airport to Camp Falcon and assigned them a sector in the Al Rashid district of Baghdad. Our initial plan was to have my battalion task force directly overlay 1-94 Field Artillery's existing setup and operation. A direct overlay is the execution of a unit-for-unit swap whereby my subordinate units inherited exactly the sector boundaries of another subordinate unit of 1-94 Field Artillery. We would later refine our operation.

This, in my mind, was the right thing to do for several reasons. The units in place knew the subtleties of the area. To minimize transition disruption, this technique would allow for less consternation. This method also simplified our tasks. Complexity sets conditions for bad things to happen. My ability to focus and appreciate the status quo I was soon to inherit was also aided by falling in on existing methods. And as young leaders prepared to hand-over their areas and explain their sectors, this way of doing business kept them on familiar ground.

While on this pre-deployment site survey, I went on patrols and walked through existing facilities. I was able to take digital photos and send those back to the battalion Executive Officer, who distributed them to the battalion staff and allowed us to make assessments at Fort Hood simultaneous with my reconnaissance. This also allowed us to make decisions about equipment needs or items we would need to purchase so we could have them in country. Sending pictures of the terrain, landscape, roads, and infrastructure provided leaders and soldiers the opportunity to develop a good sense of where we were going. I also observed, in great detail, the tactics, techniques, and procedures used by 1-94 Field Artillery. I spoke directly with soldiers and the junior and senior leaders of the battalion. They gave me first-hand accounts and provided me with a sense of what we were headed into. I got to see precisely how the battalion sector was managed. I met the key Iraqi people the unit interacted with in the neighborhoods of the sector they secured. I gained a true feeling for what was important and what was not.

Several things came out of this trip. First, it was painfully obvious that armored vehicles would be essential and we could not have enough of them. The biggest threats to soldiers were IEDs. The enemy hid these along roads in garbage, behind guard rails, and buried in sand, wherever vehicle patrols might traverse. Often these devices were artillery rounds strung together with detonation cord leading to a remote spot for manual detonation. Some were rigged with washer machine timers. Others were set for electronic detonation using the coded signal from a cell phone.

These explosive devices had devastating effect on standard configured humvees. The enemy also engaged patrols using small-arms fire and rocket propelled grenades in small numbers but always from a built-up area with at least 100 meters or more of distance from their attack location and the patrol. Their small-arms engagements were generally tied to an IED event. As a rocket artillery battalion, we had armored launchers, lightly-armored command and control tracked vehicles known as M577s. That was the sum total of our organic armor. 68th Chemical Company had lightly-armored Fox Chemical Reconnaissance Vehicles (a wheeled armored vehicle) and M113 smoke dispensing tracks. C/2-82 (a unit earmarked to become part of our task force) had Combat Ammunition Track Vehicles and M109A6, Self-Propelled Paladin Howitzers, all of which were armored.

We would make use of these systems but they had significant limitations in urban terrain. Driving around the neighborhoods in tracked armored vehicles was problematic. These vehicles were difficult to maneuver and they could cause significant damage to the infrastructure in the townships of Baghdad. That kind of damage was counter to our mission. The Fox vehicles proved to be very good. But unlike my sister battalions who sported tanks and infantry fighting vehicles, armor that was designed for maneuver tasks, we had little capability to match theirs. Humvees were our best option and armored M1114 humvees would be the best asset for the Task Force.

Second, I determined from this pre-deployment site survey that mounted patrolling is what the battalion did day in and day out. 1-94 Field Artillery called it "presence" patrols or convoys. But these patrols were in fact recon patrols or combat patrols by Army doctrine. The notion of "presence patrols" was a carryover term from units who served in Bosnia.

Third, I realized from this trip that using our personal weapons, firing Anti-Tank weapons, employing automatic weapons fire from machineguns and an ability to fire and maneuver these weapons were essential skills we had to continue to hone. Artillerymen have limited training in these skills. They are trained to employ rocket and cannon fires to great effect, but fighting with a personal weapon and maneuvering in teams to engage and defeat a hidden and protected enemy was outside the professionally refined scope of their training to this point.

I also came to understand that my lieutenants had to master patrol leading skills and that this had to be emphasized immediately. Patrol leaders would also have to be skilled, effective, comfortable negotiators. To successfully accomplish our goals, the soldiers had to become true infantrymen and the chain of command had to press continual training and refinement of those skills throughout the deployment. Lacking the ability to use personal weapons and fight as an infantryman, clearly meant people were going to be killed.

This pre-deployment site survey impressed upon me the need for knowledge of basic first aid for saving lives in close combat. This required more focus and emphasis and had to be continually trained before and during our time in Iraq. I also know that my medics would have to harden and be able to function under fire, so as to apply their craft and getting other soldiers involved in setting conditions to support them. We were woefully undermanned in medics based on what I saw 1-94 Field Artillery had assigned and I was very concerned about how we would be resourced. I would have to ask for more medics and train those already assigned more extensively.

Besides the training and facilities assessments I was able to make, I was also able to appraise the area of operations. The battle space I would be covering and the assets (personnel and equipment) I would be provided were incongruous. The training we had accomplished was focused on platoon mounted and dismounted operations. Our primary mount was the humvee. The humvee was the most practical vehicle to operate in the urban terrain. The Fox vehicles looked as if they would work well but howitzers, ammunition carriers, and launchers would not suffice. Patrolling was our main tactical function but that could not be reasonably accomplished with the majority of vehicles we had. From the pre-deployment site survey, I knew I would have to seek every opportunity to upgrade. Innovation, creativity, and initiative would be in order to fight and win.

Upon my return from the pre-deployment site survey I wanted to adjust some of the training. But there were very few practical exercises I could put into action because equipment loading had already begun and by early February when we returned, limited time was available. I was able to gather leaders and we chalk-talked about some of the adjustments I knew were imperative. I found some consolation in the realization that much of what the Division directed and the BCT had us focused on for preparation was actually very good. The basis for building solid, functional tactics, techniques, and procedures was resident in the battalion from the training regimen the Division and BCT put us through already. For that I was grateful.

My immediate focus for leader training and development

was acutely directed toward the lieutenants in the battalion. I surmised these leaders were the critical connection for me to make. Battery Commanders were important but this was a lieutenant fight. By that I mean these young leaders would be at the decisive points of most engagements encountered in the sector throughout the battalion. How they led and performed would, literally, define the unit day to day.

Lieutenants: Leaders at the Point of Action

Lieutenants are a group of officers that have, over the course American military history, taken a lot of verbal abuse through jokes, admonishments and senior enlisted soldiers observing their performance, often with negative review. But this one group has done more to shape the image of an officer in the American consciousness than any other.

All officers pass through the crucible known as Second Lieutenant, and are subjected to common, derogatory slang names shave-tail, El Tee, butter bar, second luey, and rookie to name just a few. Those officers who speak honestly about this internship they served in the Army will tell you that this was the time they truly learned the most. When serving as a Second Lieutenant, an officer becomes grounded in the fundamentals of Army life and leadership. This learning experience shapes every officer and significantly contributed to the goals ultimately achieved by each.

I have always wanted to work with these young officers to help them learn and succeed. This desire came from two sources. First, I've always felt I had to teach others what I learned. Growing up, my dad put me in charge of my younger brother. I had the responsibility and expectation to care for him, "Michael, you are your brother's keeper," my father often reminded me. That shaped me into realizing I had an obligation to others beyond myself at a very young age. I probably took it all too seriously and I was not a good "keeper" of my brother.

The other source of this desire came from an officer, Major Lynn H. Hartsell, who is now a Major General. When I was a new Second Lieutenant, Major Hartsell took the time to acknowledge me and teach me some things. Doing this came naturally for him. He cared. He affirmed who I was and what I could do, and for the rest of my career I have aspired to his example. I'm sure many more officers and non-commissioned officers share similar experiences with this man. After I moved on to higher ranks, I believed it was important to stay close to lieutenants — to teach, coach, and mentor them. I consciously wanted to do my part to keep the best in the Army. That would constantly prove to be a huge challenge.

After the pre-deployment site survey, it was patently obvious that these young officers would be the decision-makers at the point of action. I would, indirectly, affect the actions of the units they led by what I taught them. Platoon leaders were my business.

My vision for training these young officers was also affected by recent professional experiences. When I assumed command of the battalion in June 2003, I had just returned from a tour of duty in Saudi Arabia. While in Saudi Arabia I had been assigned to the Joint Task Force-Southwest Asia. I was aware the First Cavalry Division would deploy to Iraq. I had access to information that showed them deploying. Shortly after I returned to Ft. Hood, in April, Operation Iraqi Freedom I had just kicked off and the programmed deployment of First Cavalry Division was canceled. Despite the cancellation, I firmly believed the Division and the battalion I was to command would deploy at some point in the next two years. I made a commitment in my mind to make sure my lieutenants would be as ready as I could make them. This is what I told them as I came into command:

Lieutenants, the ARMY wants you for your brain!

• *The greatest asset you bring to your unit, to your soldiers, to your purpose as a leader — is your* **intellect.**

• **Your ability to think and apply your ideas** *to constructive purpose is the single most profound "thing" you contribute.*

• *Think on your feet, no two situations will be the same, you must be a good problem-solver; for that you must think! Develop that quality and you will lead well.*

• *"In the absence of orders —* **you** *take charge."*

• *"Think before you act—engage brain before mouth."*

• *"Not all decisions have to be taken right NOW—tie your decisions to a reason and purpose for making it."*

• *You will make mistakes—take personal responsibility for them, take immediate action to correct them—then* **move on.** *I will underwrite honest mistakes—I will not endorse stupidity.*

• *"Protect your subordinates" from the wrath of those higher to the reasonable extent possible.*

• *"You are responsible for everything your unit does or fails to do." Know your unit. I believe strongly in this credo. If you are truly the leader, you're a believer too.*

Though many of the lieutenants found some of this difficult

to fully comprehend, they would find that I followed this very closely. The Army wants its officers to have a college degree because they must demonstrate the ability to think critically and to problem-solve. That in a nutshell is what a lieutenant must do: problem-solve. Those who do that best perform best. It's really that simple.

I involved the command team in the education and training of lieutenants from the start and I took the lead. Interacting and training them was one of my ways to go the two levels down to communicate. Army leader doctrine teaches that leaders should focus two levels below their own to communicate and effect action. I would do physical training with them once a week and have a lieutenant professional development session with them monthly if not more frequently. In these sessions I would cover a particular subject. I continued this in Iraq to great benefit. When the platoons trained, I was there to see how the lieutenant performed. I would listen to or participate in the after-action reviews, making my personal assessment of how each lieutenant performed. I also continued to do this in Iraq as a means to further coach, teach, and mentor. I wanted my lieutenants to be comfortable around me and to not fear me so much that I was unapproachable. I wanted them to see me as a coach more than anything else.

The lieutenants caught on quickly to the coaching and training I gave them. While I could not spend every minute of every day with them, I gave them all the time I could find. They, in turn, worked hard and improved quickly, knowing the imminent deployment would be a test like no other. By the end of February, most of the lieutenants were performing at high levels. Soon we would get on aircraft and head to Kuwait. My unspoken commitment was to bring every one of them back alive.

4 Kuwait, the Final Preparation

"Leadership is a potent combination of strategy and character. But if you must be without one, be without the strategy." Norman Schwarzkopf

On March 15, 2004, most of 1-21 Field Artillery boarded contracted commercial aircraft at Gray Army Airfield in Fort Hood and flew to Kuwait. The whole day seemed like a surreal nightmare. Women, children, parents, and girl-friends jammed the gymnasium where soldiers marshaled for deployment and gave the most heart-wrenching and tearful good-byes I've ever witnessed. I think that day was without question the longest of my life.

After the good-byes at the first marshalling location on Fort Hood, we boarded buses and were moved to Abrams Gymnasium in the heart of First Cavalry Division country. Here, soldiers were now separated from their families and gathered together in our battalions to execute final prep-aration tasks before flying away. At Abrams Gymnasium we received a few briefings, were fed very well and inter-minably awaited our call forward to board the airplane. The whole time very loud, blaring, irritating music was played over the loudspeakers in the gym. Of all the pains of this day, the irritation from the loud, obnoxious music bothered me most because I knew this was some contrived means to control us further. A psychological operations of-ficer told me they programmed this into the deployment process because it keeps soldiers from thinking too much about their situation. It didn't work on me. I was already a bit depressed and pissed off on top of that. Eventually, we were called forward to the buses for the ride to the tarmac to board the planes. Nothing happened quickly.

We boarded the plane and I found a spot at the front of

the aircraft. I sat scrunched in my seat feeling more like a sardine in a can than a battalion commander leading his troops into the fray in Iraq. It took the flight crew about 45 minutes to get all the soldiers loaded and settled. Eventually the engines fired and the plane taxied to the runway. Evening twilight was setting in and a wash of loneliness and emptiness filled my heart. Shortly, the plane streaked down the runway pressing me back tightly in my seat. As the plane took flight, my mind was locked on my wife and son. I had deployed many times in my Army career. I had experienced this phenomenon repeatedly, but I had never gotten used to it. I often, and very self-critically, admonish myself because I detest so strongly the feeling of loss I experience when I walk away from my family to do what the Army requires. It's not how a real warrior and soldier should feel. I am also haunted by my boyhood memories. As a kid, my father left to go to Vietnam, twice. Every time I think back on that time I remember it like he left yesterday. I've been on both ends of that experience and neither set well with me. It is the hardest thing I've had to do in my life.

As the plane climbed ever so deliberately into the bright orange sky I had a fleeting thought that this might be my last trip away. I contemplated my son who was eight years old and our only child. I was leaving for the Middle East for the second time in less than a year. Last time I was gone six months. This time I would be away much longer. He was upset earlier that morning when he and his mother dropped me off at my headquarters. I did not want them to come to the first drop point where families could say goodbye. We said our goodbyes in the parking lot of the battalion headquarters. Now, with my eyes closed I could see his face in my mind's eye and I was awash with guilt and melancholy feelings of loss.

I also worried about the plight of my wife. I left her to deal with all the other wives and families of the soldiers in the battalion and she had to literally lead them. She did not "sign up" to be a "pseudo battalion commander" in my absence. Army families have tremendous needs. Young wives often face an overwhelming situation: separated from their husband, caring for toddler children, living in unfamiliar surroundings, far from their extended families.

I was also struggling with the sudden emotional detachment from leaving my wife. The countdown to our separation was familiar but more poignant than it had been before. The days leading to this "D-day" were dreadful. And now I was living the dread. We understood the life I had chosen, and she was a supportive partner and best friend in this journey to realize my dream. Seemingly from nowhere sitting in that plane, I had recalled, with great clarity, our first date. We went to a Perkins restaurant in Bloomington, Minnesota. I had to be the worst date a girl could have. I talked incessantly about my dreams to become an Army general and lead the Army to a promised land that only I could see. In hindsight I was unbelievably naïve, but she indulged me and then went on the journey with me. And now we were at this point. I missed her already and the plane was barely off the ground.

An hour or so into the flight I was able to suppress my glum thoughts and started to transition my mind to thinking forward to the next thing for the battalion. I rationalized that this was an act of choice and others depended on me. The soldiers would take their cues from me. Gloom was something I had better shake off, quickly. I drowned my mind in the business at hand and focused on work like I never had before in my life. I wanted to lead well, be a man, serve the soldiers in my battalion, and prove to be a good combat leader. This became my exclusive concern.

After a long, tiring, and uneventful flight, we arrived in

Kuwait where we were hit with more Army briefings and herded around like cattle from point to point. Then, many hours later, we were loaded on Kuwaiti buses and rode from the Ali Al Saleem Air Force Base to Camp Udari, Kuwait. Most of us were just numb through the whole travel experience. We had to say goodbye to our families and loved ones, leaving one world and very soon thereafter entering another. These two worlds could not be more profoundly different.

The ride on the bus from the air base to Camp Udari was an odyssey along the desolate roads cutting through the desert sea of sand and endless flat emptiness. We all ducked in and out of various states of sleep throughout the interminable ride to seemingly nowhere. It was absolutely boring, arduous, and distressing but we all knew that there was still much to be done before we headed north to Iraq. Life would now sink into a Spartan, communal living situation and would not return to normal for a long time.

For most soldiers in the three batteries that remained under my direct control, deployment to the Middle East was an entirely new experience. We immediately busied ourselves with organizing, setting up operations, and shaping the area we would live in and establish our equipment. The S3, Major Menti, had busied himself with organizing the many training classes and tactical instruction the soldiers would have to accomplish in the coming weeks before we deployed to Iraq.

When we arrived in Kuwait, Major Menti was the executor of much of what the unit had to do. Due to a training requirement at Fort Hood to field the Army's newest Multiple Launch Rocket System, the M270A1, the largest portion of 1-21 Field Artillery deployed to Iraq via Kuwait with the 3rd BCT of the First Cavalry Division. The 3rd BCT would eventually deliver us to 5th BCT in Al Rashid, Baghdad, a week behind our parent organization and the main body of 5th BCT.

At Camp Udari, we were extremely limited in communications and transportation. The 3rd BCT headquarters was halfway on the other side of the camp, a 15-minute walk. We had no phones and the little nit-picking, detail problems that can plague any operation were compounded by not having a standard relationship with a higher headquarters. Something as simple as radio communications was made tediously complex. For example, to use Army radios you have to have an electronic fill. This fill is an electronic coded signal put into the radio's electronic coding. These fills changed on a scheduled basis. Units have to be accounted for by the issuing headquarters to get the electronic fill. The 3rd BCT Headquarters' communication section received these fills and then passed them to the battalions under their control. The battalions passed the fills down to their companies or batteries and so on down until all radios had the fill. Without the fill, the radios could not communicate. Since we were not accounted for in the distribution plan, we were constantly playing catch-up trying to address a simple matter like that. This condition persisted throughout the time we were in Kuwait. We worked through each of these nuisance problems and tried to anticipate as many as we could. In the end, despite the irritations, we accomplished the many tasks necessary to prepare for the trip north.

All of this work and effort reminded me of what I had learned the first week I was in a regular Army unit. Resourcefulness is next to godliness for a leader. This literally became a principle of my leadership philosophy. If, as a leader you depend on an external agency or entity and that is your only means to success, you will certainly fail. In the Army, resources are scarcer at each progressively lower echelon. Most echelons suffer the hubris of their own importance. They tend to husband resources for administrative convenience at the expense of the lower echelons.

I also know that the Army, generally, is well-resourced. The problem for the Army is one of distribution and allocation. Because decisions for distribution and allocation can be "lost in translation" and those making decisions are less aware than they ought to be about the plight of the "grunt," the distribution often runs afoul. Distribution is also adversely affected by decision-makers who focus on administrative convenience at the expense of a greater need below their level. Knowing these things about the way the Army functions institutionally was helpful in developing training and resource planning. There were many training activities the soldiers still needed to accomplish in Kuwait and I wanted my team as well-resourced as I could make it.

During final pre-Iraq preparations in Kuwait, soldiers fired at ranges, conducted more iterations of close-quarters marksmanship, convoy live-fire operations, first aid, combat-lifesaver training. We practiced mounted and dismounted movement, individual fire and maneuver as well as squad and platoon fire and maneuver. The whole process of the multitude of training tasks was geared toward readying the soldiers physically and mentally for fighting in Iraq.

Between all the training events, soldiers had to get equipment arriving on ships from the port and prepare it for convoy north to Baghdad. This had to be phased and we spent an inordinate amount of time looking for our vehicles as they arrived through various methods from the port to Camp Udari.

The process the Army executed to go into a combat theater of operations was elaborate and detailed. It was a process focused on receiving personnel, equipment, and then preparing for operations incrementally as the capability increases with the right mix of personnel and equipment. In the Army this is known as Reception, Staging, Onward Movement and Integration (RSOI).

First Cavalry Division organized the BCTs deploying into theater as Force Packages. This is an administrative method for staff managers to incrementally manage organizational movement of personnel and equipment. Each Force Package was numbered. Basically, a Force Package consisted of a BCT set (all equipment and personnel) plus a few extra units that did not fall under any particular BCT Headquarters. In total, a First Cavalry Division Force Package was nearly 5,000 soldiers, their personal equipment, and all the equipment this size force needed to conduct combat operations. Force Package management was necessary so the Division could be efficiently assimilated into theater and subsequently set to conduct combat operations in Iraq. Space and resources were limited in Kuwait. The whole Division could not fit into the available facilities in Kuwait, the staging location for all U.S. Forces sent to Iraq. 1-21 Field Artillery was broken into two of these Divisional deployment Force Packages with some units in Force Package 3 and others in Force Package 5. This occurred because our predeployment training requirements were non-standard. We were ordered to field the Army's new M270A1 Multiple Launched Rocket System during pre-deployment training for Iraq. This was done to insure the Multi-National Forces, Iraq commander had a deep strike, theater missile capability in Iraq. I had two other subordinate units of my battalion in Force Package 3 and three subordinate units in Force Package 5. This meant that the staff had to develop an elaborate plan to manage the movement and the Relief-In-Place (RIP) process with First Armor Division already in Iraq. The staff objective was to insure the timing of the departure of 1-94 Field Artillery would not be "de-synched" from the 5th BCT requirements to pick up the fight in Al Rashid. The majority of 5th BCT was programmed in Force Package 3. They were set on a Relief-In-Place timeline based on this Force Package Reception, Staging, Onward movement and Integration program. This process had to be a near-seamless execution process, as lives could be lost if gaps occurred in the execution of the transition.

The plan we devised for the Task Force was to fly the necessary leaders with my Executive Officer, Major Robert "Bob" Marshall, forward to Baghdad International Airport where we would catch up with 5th BCT, which was departing two weeks ahead of the rest of the battalion. Once there, Major Marshall would establish our Tactical Operations Center with the Battalion Operations Sergeant and a few support soldiers.

Major Marshall was well qualified and capable of handling the toughest assignments I doled out. Because he had been the Battalion S3 before becoming Executive Officer, I knew he could easily handle operations and simultaneously manage logistical establishment of the battalion. Major Marshall was ideally suited to operate independently and required minimal guidance. He always knew what needed to be done and he got it done.

Bob Marshall was about 6′ 2″ in height and a handsome man. He had an easy smile and a soothing southern drawl when he spoke. Born and raised in Mississippi, he attended Southern Mississippi University, which automatically meant he liked Brett Favre, quarterback for the Green Bay Packers. Because I was from Minnesota and a huge Viking fan, this caused some wonderfully comical jousts between us. Bob Marshall was a personable guy with a very balanced, calm, and assured demeanor.

I would characterize Major Marshall as the antithesis of me

in terms of personality. He was "low-key" and I was aggressive, always pressing. I came to learn he was the perfect executive officer for me.

Major Marshall oversaw our initial assimilation efforts in Baghdad. The leaders began the Relief-In-Place (RIP) process by conducting what we referred to as "right-seat-rides." This was a training and familiarization process where battery commanders from my unit rode on patrols and shadowed with battery commanders from the replaced unit and learned the sector. They met key Iraqi people in the sector and personally observed the tactics, techniques, and procedures the replaced unit used to operate in the sector. 5th BCT planners worked the lead elements from Task Force 1-21 into their air-flow plans. Air-flow was the administrative procedure of designating personnel to fly into Iraq on available Air Force aircraft. Each BCT had a specified allocation of aircraft to get their assigned personnel into Baghdad.

Leaders and staff worked long hours from the day we arrived. My days were 18-20 hours with little sleep. We all had to struggle with the time change and jet lag that set in on the trip. Dealing with jet lag, long hours, and initial separation anxiety are normal to any training deployment soldiers go through. Adding the dimension of impending combat to the equation compounds everything. The combined effect, if not properly mitigated and managed, can cause a serious breakdown.

Mental stress is always a factor in military operations. Most leaders acknowledge it exists but simply ignore it, reasoning that the tasks must get done and the price paid is negligible for most soldiers. Leaders at all levels have to watch their soldiers, and each other, to get through the trials of these situations. My S3, Major Menti, overstressed in Kuwait. I did not anticipate that how our soldiers might respond to the stress of this particular deployment. Of a battalion that exceeded 600 soldiers, however, he was the only one who quit due to stress. I felt I should have seen it coming. It cost the battalion the S3 leadership and experience he possessed at a critical point in the early going. Major Menti literally quit on the battalion, refusing to continue as the Battalion S3 while we were in Kuwait, an action clearly brought on by stress. Days before the battalion was to road march north into Iraq, Major Menti insisted on relief from his duties and clearly suffered a mental stress breakdown. I have often considered the circumstances of his actions and have never fully resolved why all other soldiers, non-commissioned officers, and officers of the Task Force persevered and he did not. The situation was unsettling for me as the Task Force Commander, but despite his action, I remained optimistic and decided quickly I would press on and figure out a solution best for the unit.

Because I had already sent Major Marshall forward to Baghdad, with the sudden loss of Major Menti, I now had to assume the roles and functions of the executive officer, S3, and battalion commander with the part of the battalion I was with in Kuwait. Thankfully, we hit the road in a few days.

The key leader supporting me while preparing the battalion for action was the Command Sergeant Major. Command Sergeant Major Kelvin Hughes was a rock. He was a first class warrior, impeccably sharp in dress, attitude, discipline, and mental toughness; soldiers followed this man instinctively.

Command Sergeant Major Hughes was reserved by nature. He was not one to grand-stand or yell maliciously at soldiers. His method was "Follow me. Do as I do." Everyone did, best they could. Command Sergeant Major Hughes was methodical, deliberate, and highly professional.

He communicated such high expectations of performance that, when not met, he attacked leaders and soldiers to achieve the prescribed standards. He made it his business to know everything that was going on in the battalion and was aware of the happenings of the lowest and newest soldier right up to me. He was absolutely composed.

Command Sergeant Major Hughes' leadership as well as his direct assistance to me was invaluable especially the last few days we readied to move north into Iraq. Together, we checked and re-checked all the vehicles and supplies. We participated in training events alongside the soldiers to insure the training met or exceeded standards. We went separate directions all day and into the night to cover more ground. We met mid-day and late in the evening to compare notes and discuss adjustments. Then we went out to supervise and assess the adjustments. This was something we continued to do the whole year we were in Iraq. The night before we moved north, we both agreed the battalion was ready. I trusted that my seventeen years of experience along with the Command Sergeant Majors' twenty-three years of experience spelled success for the battalion.

5 Into the Cauldron

"Well, I can't say just where we are, but we're not in Kansas anymore." Anonymous, U.S. News Reporter

The trek north into Iraq from Kuwait began for 1-21 Field Artillery on March 25, 2004. The route that we followed was named Route Tampa by the Army. Route Tampa was a four-lane highway that cut a swath through the desert in Kuwait and then traveled through southern Iraq and into Baghdad. The route in March 2004 was more like an old country road than a highway. The road was literally under construction while we marched over it heading north.

Traveling in three serials, the Battery Executive Officers and First Sergeants led their respective battery formations north on this tactical convoy. The Command Sergeant Major and I were with this contingent.

Almost none of the vehicles we had in these convoys had armor. They were what we called "soft-skinned" vehicles. The Army developed and used the humvee primarily as a command and control vehicle platform, not as the main fighting vehicle for urban combat. The Army had no vehicle specifically designed for urban, counterinsurgent combat. When Iraq transitioned to a counterinsurgency fight for the Army and Marine Corps, the fact that troops from both services did not have enough humvees became evident to all. Worse, it became painfully obvious that the existing configuration of the humvee was unarmored and inadequate for the need. The conventional forces of the Army and Marine Corps were not outfitted for the scenario each was sent to fight.

Curiously, one of my soldiers asked why humvees weren't armored regardless of whether we were fighting in urban terrain in Iraq. Fighting in a conventional situation, in his mind, did not diminish the need for protection and armor on these vehicles. I didn't have a good answer. I posited that perhaps the weight of an armored humvee in other than urban terrain might be prohibitive. I tried this answer on him. He just shook his head and knocked his knuckles on his helmet and said, "Ain't buyin' it sir, KEVLAR, man! They could make them with kevlar plates."

Of course, I knew he was right.

Needless to say, many of us were nervous having to travel more than 300 kilometers through Iraq with no armor protection. But there was absolutely nothing we could do about that. We had no recourse. The Army just did not have the armor. The mission to go north to Iraq was still there. We simply had to make do. There was no sense whining about the situation. As a battalion commander I fully understood too that armor alone does not guarantee survival in combat. It is but one element. We were not well equipped. But this was war and we did our best.

As we rolled out, we traveled north on a paved road and then, about 100 kilometers into the march, the road deteriorated gradually with a heavy construction effort until it was nothing more than a wide, unimproved dirt road. We drove for hours at a time. The trek took over two long, arduous days, bumping our backs, hips, and legs until our bodies were little more than vibrated mush.

We wore about 60 extra pounds of weight. Secured to the front of an armor outer tactical vest were all our accoutrements. On the front of the vest was fastened our ammunition in four double magazine pouches, first aid bandages, water, and a small equipment storage pouch. Small Arms, Protective, Individual (SAPI) plates of armor protection were slipped into the front and back of the vest giving soldiers true ballistic protection from up to 7.62mm bullets. Although this is what added all the bulk and weight to the vest, no one minded.

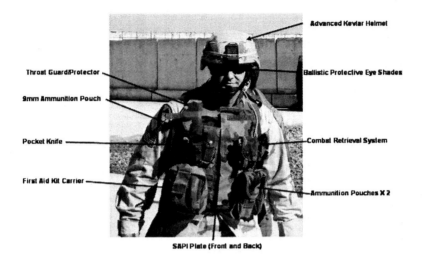

Figure 5.1 Body Armor

The weather was tolerable. These temperatures were not new to the soldiers who had trained in the heat of Fort Hood, Texas and at Fort Irwin, California at the National Training Center. None of us were fazed by the weather, but the long drive did wear on us. And we were still dealing with jet lag, fear, and the unknown.

With convoys, movement is slow and generally tedious because the convoy only moves as fast as its slowest vehicle. We averaged about 40 to 45 MPH most of the way. Along the route, the Army had placed logistical way stations. At those stations, we slept on cots next to our vehicles, which were set in staging lines by serial. We ate hot meals in the dining facilities and were able to get 6 to 8 hours rest. Most everyone took full advantage of the opportunity to sleep and eat. We were all exhausted from the drive and high level of concentration we were exerting while driving.

Vigilance takes energy, and fears can drain a person of energy. Add to that the unmerciful bumpy road, heavy gear, and the great unknown; it was a grueling trip north.

Early on the morning of March 28, 2004, we entered the southern outskirts of Baghdad. Picked up by a 1-94 Field Artillery patrol escort, we were led the last few kilometers through southern Al Rashid and into the forward operating base at Camp Falcon.

During my earlier pre-deployment site survey foray into Al Rashid, Baghdad, I was struck by the squalor living conditions around Camp Falcon. There was a constant, nasty, smell of body odor mixed with a sickly aroma of fuel, feces, and burning trash. The area was replete with piles upon piles of solid trash waste strewn along the streets and alleyways throughout the district. Broken-down cars, mud huts, and makeshift roadside lean-tos that served as store fronts lined the route near the forward operating base. The place reminded me of a gigantic junkyard. This was not a decent place to live. Despite these conditions, arriving was a relief. To my soldiers, I could tell, they felt as if we had landed on Mars. We were all mesmerized but thankful to have finally arrived safely.

Through the march north we did not lose a single vehicle. We experienced no enemy contact, and all but one soldier from the three serials made it to Camp Falcon, our home for the next year. We had a soldier injured when we stopped to help another unit with a disabled vehicle. One of my soldiers jumped off the back of the disabled truck after putting out a fire with an extinguisher. He injured his ankle when he landed on the uneven, gravel road surface, turning his ankle badly enough to break it. The unit medic patched him up to get him to the next forward way-station. From there he was evacuated to a hospital. He would join us weeks later in Baghdad.

Major Marshall met us on the road to the new battalion motor pool inside Camp Falcon and welcomed us to our new home. In the intervening two months since I had been to Camp Falcon before on the pre-deployment site survey, the base had changed with plenty of new construction going on all around. There were many local national Iraqi workers around and I took notice. The local workers did not seem to be well controlled. What came to my mind that morning was my recollection of stories my father told me about the Vietnamese when he was over there. He told me how the Viet Cong infiltrated the working groups that would come onto the base camps and would be among the American Army units doing manual labor jobs but really scouting out the place for future attacks. The Viet Cong were much craftier and better fighters than the Iraqis but the insurgent concept was no different. Though at the time I didn't know it, that was my sixth sense talking to me and I would learn to listen to that voice in the future.

I didn't say anything to Major Marshall. I just made a mental note to talk to Colonel Lanza about it later. Major Marshall started to point out the facilities to me and offered to get with me and the rest of the staff to start laying out the current situation. He also told me there had been mortars that impacted Camp Falcon the night before and we could expect more tonight. "Welcome to Camp Falcon, sir," Major Marshall said with a big grin, and then he went off to do what executive officers do.

At that point in my life, I had served seventeen years in the Army. I had never been shot at with real bullets. I had never been in a mortar attack or artillery barrage. I hoped that I would at least get a day or two to orient before I had to deal with being on the wrong end of the firing range. I wasn't scared; I was too ignorant to be scared. I was concerned and my senses seemed to perk up when he suggested we'd get attacked again tonight.

About 11 p.m. that night, the Task Force experienced its first mortar barrage. There was a distinctly different sound to mortar rounds impacting than when firing. This night, just four rounds impacted about 700 meters west of the building I was quartered in. We all talked about it the next morning. No one was wounded or killed.

Because Major Marshall had already been in Iraq at Camp Falcon for two weeks, what he typically did those early days is what I should have been doing. He executed daily coordination with the 5th BCT staff and oversaw battalion operations, insuring the units were resourced and ready to fight. Patrols were going out daily and Major Marshall was making sure they were up to standard to effectively execute their tasks. He had also set up our quartering situation for the battalion, occupied the maintenance facility, worked out the budget management system, stood up the headquarters building, established communications, and prepared a detailed operations brief to assimilate me and the rest of the battalion staff.

In those first days, too, I would have to meld the battalion into a bona fide Task Force. The day we arrived at Camp Falcon we were officially reorganized into Task Force 1-21. We absorbed C/2-82, a cannon field artillery battery, and re-established command and control responsibility for 68th Chemical Company.

The Task Force now consisted of: HHS/1-21, A/1-21, B/1-21, C/2-82 and 68th Chemical Company. The radar battery C/1-21 was organized under the Division Fire Support Element and technically was not part of the Task Force on paper. However, there was no battalion-level commander overseeing the support and command of the battery that remained with my command. Therefore, while the Task Force technically did not have direct command and control authority on paper, we retained that command relationship throughout our tour in Iraq. We provided logistical, administrative, and morale support for the C/1-21 throughout the deployment.

Task Force 1-21, Assimilating the Fight

Task Force 1-21 went through a deliberate and comprehensive process to assume control of its assigned sector in the Al Rashid district of Baghdad. 1-94 Field Artillery Regiment of First Armor Division had four batteries and the division chemical company as part of their task force.

To assimilate the fight in Al Rashid, Colonel Lanza implemented a direct overlay program he had begun preparing with us on the pre-deployment site survey. This was precisely the right choice for directing our initial assumption of security and stability operations. Direct overlay meant the subordinate units of the BCT (Task Force 1-21, 1-7 Cavalry, 1-8 Cavalry and 515th Forward Support Battalion) literally assumed the already-assigned sectors of the subordinate units of the current BCT. Iraq, and particularly the Al Rashid district of Baghdad, had some intricate subtleties that demanded understanding. By committing to a direct overlay approach, 5th BCT was postured with the best chance to garner the most comprehensive understanding of the sector as was possible.

It is said that transitions are points of greatest vulnerability for organizations. This is never truer than in military operations. Because military decision-making must be based on good information and solid understanding, which are incomplete in transitions, danger lurks. Leaders should seek to minimize consternation exacerbated by unfamiliarity in times of transition. Colonel Lanza did a magnificent job employing this direct overlay approach.

To attempt to occupy differently and cover terrain, neighborhoods, and areas in a disparate and disjointed manner would have significantly detracted from the salient method of fighting in Baghdad. Fighting in Baghdad is predicated on forming and nurturing strong relationships. Upsetting or destabilizing existing associations with little chance of growing them into stronger, more sophisticated, and binding relationships was a losing proposition.

At the battalion task force level, the process of assuming control of the sector was managed in two parts. First, there was the tactical hand-off whereby we would have to learn tactics, techniques, and procedures in a ride-along, coach-teach-mentor process. Task Force 1-21 leaders at the platoon, company and battalion level would ride in the "right-seat" and observe the soldiers of 1-94 Field Artillery as they executed their tasks in sector. This covered a variety of things: communications, weapons preparation, vehicle preparation, meetings, routes, danger zones, local national interaction techniques, talking points, fire and maneuver, IED searching and neutralization techniques, and ambush reaction to name a few. Second, the staff and unit commanders would have to start shaping assessments. We had to collectively begin to design an overarching strategy to pick up at the point where 1-94 Field Artillery was and move to the next level of securing and stabilizing the sector in a progressive manner.

Regression was something I desperately wanted to avoid. I surmised that if we had to regress that would be a damning indictment on our chances to operate and win here. We weren't in this situation in Iraq to lose or start over to begin anew. If the Army operationally chose to make this effort in Iraq a relay race, then much like a true relay race, each leg had to be progressively faster. Although the leg Task Force 1-21 was challenged to run would have to start a little slow, as we received the baton we would accelerate and then with great momentum run a stronger leg than 1-94 Field Artillery. To do otherwise spelled failure. Everywhere in Iraq where a regressive condition was allowed to occur, failure ensued.

As a military leader directing combat troops in Iraq, I felt, despite all efforts to win the tactical fight, the strategic program was working against us. That the tactical, operational, and strategic activities of this war would be disjointed did not bode well for our modest efforts. Although most of my peers intellectually and pragmatically disconnected the tactical from the operational from the strategic, I did not. Having studied in great detail the American effort in Vietnam, I saw that many of the same strategic and political mistakes of Vietnam are being repeated with the counterinsurgent fight in Iraq. The distant specter of failing to ultimately win decisive victory in Iraq loomed large. I quickly sized up the situation from the ground in Baghdad. Several factors prevail and work against our Army soldiers and marines with this fight in Iraq.

The reasons for my cynical view were easily described. First, the senior leaders of the Services and the political leaders of our nation have bought into this notion that wars can be won with either individual or unit rotations. We were living this reality and I could easily discern the adverse affect this was having for soldiers and Iraqis alike. Army units operate differently. Procedures change. Iraqis easily become confused.

The rotation of units, I consider, is a major contributing factor and reason why this country hasn't decisively won any of its armed conflicts since World War II. In World War II this practice was not part of the program. Units rotated in and out of combat but not out of the war. Rotations meter commitment and commitment can never be metered in war. In Korea, we failed to win a decisive victory even though the military did not rotate forces. In that case, the President unilaterally decided the nation would pursue a limited objective. Fifty-plus years later we stand guard in a demilitarized zone to keep the peace.

A second major contributing factor is that Presidents — not the constitutionally-mandated authority, the U.S. Congress — have committed this nation to war. Using resolutions, Presidents believe crisis is bearing down on the nation and pursue a "mandate" for committing the military to action. Political conditions raise fervor and with that the President secures his authority to commit the military to action through the device of a Congressional Resolution. But this is not the constitutionally-authorized procedure. By going to war this way, the nation dismisses the crucial public commitment and diminishes the national sacrifice necessary to fight and win decisively. Politicians are provided a non-binding means to commit this nation to war. This leads to open dissent, obfuscation, and outright lying that tears at the fabric of America and divides our national commitment when the going gets tough. The spirit and intent of the framers of the Constitution have been completely thwarted with our new-fangled method of declaring war on other nations.

A third major contributor to my sensing the outcome in Iraq will not be decisive, as was the case in Vietnam, is that military leaders directing the operations in Iraq at the tactical level are unable to connect tactics to operational and strategic-level objectives. Making this connection between tactics and operational and strategic-level objectives is vital to defeating an insurgency and it is not something Army or Marine Corps leaders are taught and able to practice. Winning tactical battles that do not accomplish the operational and strategic objectives mean nothing. Generals Casey and Abizaid pointed out to Congress on several occasions that our Army and Marines have never lost a battle with the enemy in Iraq. These were the same descriptions and words General Westmoreland uttered about the military's performance in Vietnam. It is patently ridiculous to even point this out because it disconnects the tactical from the operational and strategic objectives. A collection of tactical victories disconnected from operational objective and strategic objective are near worthless. This merely proves American soldiers and marines are better trained and skilled at executing close combat and nothing more.

Finally, America, since the Korean War, has nationally tried to run wars as a business. We will continue to fail to be decisive and fail to achieve the objective as long as American citizens believe that wars can be successfully fought in the same way that a business is run (i.e., the Robert McNamara and Donald Rumsfeld model). The Rumsfeld model, in other words, is a war fought for a limited objective, declared by Chief Executives and their administration officers, saddled with incongruent metrics to measure success or failure, and with operational and tactical decisions made by civilian amateurs who risk nothing more than reputation. Further, the McNamara-Rumsfeld model chooses to fight wars on a unit rotational basis like a corporate business practice, placing incongruent metrics on performance, and trying to make war nationally painless. This model has proven unsuccessful. Perhaps after World War II it seemed like a good way to conduct our national defense. When Harry Truman fired General MacArthur and made the resounding statement that war for a limited objective was the future for America, we started down the road to losing. This wasn't Truman's conscious failing. He just did not understand the nature of war and made an internal argument personal, which then became public at the same time, charting a losing course for others to follow for the next 55 years. I suggest we have now collected enough anecdotal evidence to decisively state the limited-war experiment has failed and ought to be terminated. Since the end of World War II, the U.S. has chosen this obtuse path. It has clearly failed.

In this American democracy, as defined through the Constitution, the will of the people is expressed through a representative Congress. With respect to war, the role of the Congress is incredibly significant. American history and experience tells us that American democracy depends on national commitment to win wars. Without national commitment, there is little chance of a decisive victory. That a war is fought so as not to impinge on the daily lives of the citizens of this nation, but rather is suppressed as an ancillary activity, dissipates our national will. Making war just one of many priorities weakens our chances for decisive victory. We, as a public citizenry, are reduced to a position where we count the dead on the evening national news and feel sorry for the families who lose loved ones. This creates a public that pities its military but certainly does not want to serve in their ranks. The military of this mighty nation does not want to be pitied. Service members swear an oath to the Constitution, not to the President. But, alas, the proof of validity in this aspect of the Constitution is borne in the results: lots of dead soldiers without a decisive victory, engaged in wars for limited objectives, for what? Continuing on this path is a loser.

As much as I wanted to ignore all this, I knew then, as I sense now, these strategic political factors worked against my humble tactical efforts with Task Force 1-21. I was also certain the Iraqis I would face could care less about all this. They would fight me every day with whatever they had. I wasn't leading for a constituency in my home district as a Congressional Representative. I was leading soldiers in the Army at war. My task was to find a way to win in my corner of Baghdad. This truth was not lost on me one iota. Furthermore, my analysis and sensing about this war and my unit's role in it could not be worn on my sleeve. I was not against the war. I was in it to win it, even if the politicians who led me and I was sworn to follow and the generals who led me were not.

Task Force 1-21 Gets its Slice of Baghdad

First Cavalry Division had the mission to secure and stabilize Baghdad. The commander who owns a given piece of terrain establishes the goals and provides the guidance to subordinate commanders to shape their operations. The First Cavalry Division was given a piece of ground: Baghdad. The Division Commander, through his staff, divided up Baghdad and gave specified missions to the four, ground maneuver BCTs. The BCT commanders further divided the ground and tasks and gave the terrain in sectors to battalion task force commanders. The battalion task force commanders further divided the ground to company commanders. Orders, directives, and the intent for operations in these areas were nested from the Division Commander down to patrol leader level through an extensive training and command information dissemination process. Some units managed this nesting and dissemination process better than others. The Task Force 1-21 command group devised a very elaborate and multi-faceted command information and education program to keep patrol leaders and soldiers well informed and educated on the policies and expectations of higher level commanders. The intricacies, ambiguity, and nuances of fighting an insurgency demanded this. The Task Force command group emphasized this to insure that the delicate business of fighting an insurgency was acted upon effectively and appropriately by soldiers who daily executed the will of their commanders. I viewed this as seminal to fighting the Task Force.

Fighting in Iraq demanded that soldiers understand, in detail, their task and purpose on all operations. Education, communication, and constant updates through subordinate leaders had to be continuous, precise, and rehearsed. Soldiers could not be discounted as means to ends and left to their own devices, not because they were incompetent but because the "devil was in the details" fighting an enemy like this. Leadership that did not work the details down to the lowest levels failed when operating in Iraq.

In conventional fighting the rigor on education and detailed intelligence dissemination to the very lowest levels is not as acute. The Army I served in was a product of the National Training Center methodology which was purely conventional. Training at the Army's National Training Centers did not emphasize the level of precision, education, and down-to-soldier-level dissemination that was essential to successful operations in Iraq. The Task Force and the leaders experienced a major paradigm shift in thinking and operating to meet the demands of this environment.

Commanding the Task Force, I had to assess this aspect of the fight. The leaders below me had to also understand the dynamic. Together we had to develop procedures to enhance the education, improve precise intelligence dissemination, and sensitize soldiers to a complex contemporary operating environment. Information and knowledge were as important as the weapons the soldiers carried to survive on this battlefield. These assessments had to be blended into the common tactical assessments of the Task Force sector.

In the first few days, the Task Force staff put together a detailed analysis and recommendation for me on how to overlay Task Force 1-21 subordinate units with 1-94 Field Artillery. This overlay supported the BCT Commander's intent and insured we properly covered and best accounted for the similarities of how 1-94 Field Artillery executed operations in sector. Our goal was to set conditions to have a near seamless transition. Depicted below was the initial tactical set we used to operate in our sector:

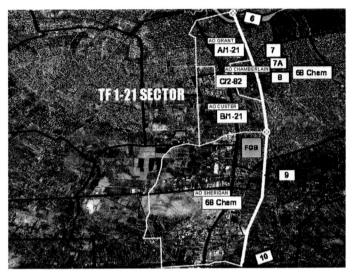

Figure 5.2 — This slide, taken from a command information briefing, depicts the Task Force's initial set in sector, April 2004.

After the staff carved up the ground based on the land distribution 1-94 Field Artillery used, I directed that each area of operation be named after Civil War Generals who served on the winning side. We chose Custer, Sheridan, Grant, and Chamberlain.

We called the total expanse of the Task Force sector area of operations "Rocket." As we assumed tactical responsibility for area of operations "Rocket", we had to make a thorough assessment of our situation and of the operations area at the battalion task force level. A key actor in this effort normally would be the S3.

The job of the S3 is a very tough one in the Army. There is no respite for an officer in this position. Even in a garrison Army, this officer is nearly overwhelmed daily. In garrison, the S3 is the planner, director, and quality assurance leader for operations and training. In war, this officer is the key director of operations. He also has to oversee all the training that must continue for a unit in war. Quite literally, he is ensconced in some aspect of operations or training twenty-four hours a day, seven days a week. He sleeps when he can, but 18-20 hour days are the norm. The S3 does have a staff to support him but he is the critical decision-maker. The S3 must be able to operate in current events and simultaneously preparing future events. Many officers have been defeated by this position and its considerable demands. Because Major Menti quit the Task Force in Kuwait, these first weeks in Iraq the Task Force had to struggle without an operations director. Other officers had to step up and fill the void, but the situation was tough at best. In the third week of fighting, Colonel Lanza finally sent me a qualified major to assume duties of the S3. I was beside myself with frustration and anger about the BCT commander waiting this long to provide my unit with an essential and fully qualified officer to serve as the S3.

The New S3 Directing Operations

Colonel Lanza sent Major William "Bill" Reinhart to Task Force 1-21 to replace Major Menti. His arrival was the beginning of a profoundly positive change in the climate of the staff and the Task Force. Major Reinhart was 6' 3," incredibly smart, and a West Point-educated officer. He was an engineer by academic training and possessed a first-rate analytical mind. Major Reinhart had a great sense of humor and a calm demeanor. He was the perfect fit for the job.

Major Reinhart previously served on the BCT staff as the BCT Fire Support Officer working in the capacity of the Information Operations officer for Colonel Lanza. Prior to coming to the Task Force, Major Reinhart was the Brigade

Fire Support Officer for 4th Brigade (the First Cavalry Division Aviation Brigade). He was assigned to 1-21 Field Artillery before we were reconfigured and deployed to Iraq. He was the third major in the battalion. As Commander of 1-21 Field Artillery, I was responsible to provide the Fire Support Element for 1-7 Cavalry, 2-227 Attack Aviation Battalion, and 4th Aviation Brigade. When we reconfigured and became part of 5th BCT, the 4th Brigade Fire Support Element became the 5th BCT Fire Support Element. I moved the Fire Support Element from 2-227, Attack Aviation Battalion, and elevated them to serve as the 4th Brigade Fire Support Element. The Attack Aviation battalion went without a Fire Support Element. Because Colonel Lanza took the major from 4th Brigade Fire Support Element, I had a captain fill that role with 4th Brigade Fire Support Element until a major became available.

In Iraq, the BCT Fire Support Elements became the basis for a lethal and non-lethal targeting cell, managed some fires — albeit very little — within the BCTs, and mostly focused their assets and capabilities as planners and co-ordinators of Information Operations for the BCT. Major Reinhart, in that BCT Fire Support Officer position, was a chief contributor and architect of the BCT campaign plan. I figured I had won the lottery getting him as my new S3.

Major Reinhart understood in depth the overarching program that the BCT sought. He and I were instantly in agreement on how to operate in sector. His most compelling attribute was his ability to think critically.

Major Reinhart's first major task upon arrival to the Task Force was to immediately take charge of operations. This included current operations and future operations. He had to get processes, procedures, and reporting set into a routine, sharp, responsive, and anticipatory program given our new circumstances and the BCT staff reporting requirements.

Major Marshall had already established the foundation, Major Reinhart had to refine, and then improve, the program.

The S3 section had been modified since arriving in Iraq because so many non-standard activities confronted the operations section of the Task Force. We had to form Advisory Support Teams to train the Iraqi Army soldiers which were known at the time as the Iraqi Civil Defense Corps. We also had to manage, administratively, the Facility Protection Services/Interpreter operations teams. We had to integrate intelligence analysis, civil operations, and psychological operations into the daily functions and decision cycles of the Task Force. This entire monolithic activity Major Reinhart had to figure out and then build into a cohesive, integrated, functional, and effective team. I didn't give him much time to get it done. In a few short weeks Major Reinhart had the S3 section, the Tactical Operations Center, and our daily combat operations regimen in top form.

6 "Lay of the Land," Area of Operations Rocket

"On dispersive ground, therefore, fight not. On facile ground, halt not. On contentious ground, attack not. On open ground, do not try to block the enemy's way. On the ground of intersecting highways, join hands with your allies. On serious ground, gather in plunder. In difficult ground, keep steadily on the march. On hemmed-in ground, resort to stratagem. On desperate ground, fight." Sun Tzu

One of the largest neighborhoods in Al Rashid, Al Saidiyah, had a population of over 250,000 people by best estimates. This was a somewhat affluent neighborhood having upper-middle-class residential areas, a large industrial park, and a few large, prosperous market places.

The religious make up of Al Saidiyah was 45 percent Shia and 50 percent Sunni with about 5 percent of others being Christian and Kurdish. Christians hid among the Muslims. Despite a large but minority-Shia population, sixteen mosques functioned openly in the neighborhood and fourteen of these were Sunni. The Shia forcefully took over one of the Sunni mosques just before U.S. forces arrived in Baghdad back in March 2003. So, the struggle for domination continued while we were there. The Shia desire to assert power in Al Saidiyah was a clear element of strife. I viewed this obtuse relationship as a subtle point for my use in future negotiation. I could exploit this desire for power to keep the general peace within Al Saidiyah.

Many retired, high-ranking Iraqi military officers also resided in Al Saidiyah. This gave the former Ba'ath party a strong representation in this area. It saddled me with another constituency I would have to balance in the process of trying to bring security and stability to the area.

Saddam Hussein had chosen this area to provide for the loyal retired officers of his armed forces. Once these former officers were disenfranchised by the aftermath policies of the Bush Administration through the Coalition Provisional Authority, this group of men proved to be difficult to control. Most of them ran scared of Americans.

Through the center of Al Saidiyah was a "market" road. Along this road were restaurants, apartments, stores, and small new family-owned shops selling everything from plumbing supplies and household appliances to sheep for slaughter. Also prevalent along this strip were the black marketers dealing mostly in gasoline (benzene, as Iraqis called it) and, I suspected, weapons. The weapons sales were never openly visible. I was convinced the deals were done in the market place but the weapons pick-ups and deliveries were done in the residential areas, at the mosques, in the dead of night.

Highway 8 was along the eastern edge of the Task Force sector. Highway 8 is the main, six-lane highway that runs through Baghdad and bends westerly to Baghdad International Airport. This road was known as Route Irish or "Airport Road." Route Irish was famous for unpredictable, devastating, vehicle-borne, suicide attacks against Coalition convoys and civilian contractors. The majority of attacks along this highway were in the northern portion closest to the Baghdad International Airport.

The mission to protect this road was a huge challenge because we had little proper equipment to execute to the expected standard. Worse, the Task Force was at a low level of training in conducting route security. The skills needed to do this task for an extended period of time and in combat were not typically part of the Military Occupational Specialty for rocket artillery and chemical soldiers. We had to learn fast.

What I came to discover was that we needed, from the outset, the M1114 Armored humvee or tanks (Abrams main battle tank) and infantry fighting vehicles (Bradleys) that have Forward Looking Infra Red (FLIR) sights, great mobility, and excellent armor protection for the crew as well as an intimidating presence to dominate the road.

One of the interesting efforts I engaged in early on in our tour in Iraq was an initiative to secure Bradley Infantry Fighting Vehicles. The staff analysis assessed, to balance the situation more in the Task Force's favor and successfully accomplish the given mission, was that we needed this kind of armor capability. I requested these assets from the BCT commander. We needed the four Bradleys that the Fire Support Teams of 1-7 Cavalry controlled but which belonged to my battalion. Equipment was assigned to 1-21 Field Artillery and then attached to 1-7 Cavalry. My battalion provided the fire support personnel and equipment to 1-7 Cavalry.

The 1-7 Cavalry Commander and his staff refused to release the vehicles to Task Force 1-21. I failed to convince the BCT commander or his staff that my need was more compelling. 1-7 Cavalry argued they had a need to use these in their portion of the Iraqi Civil Defense Corps support mission. I felt they could have "made do" without the Bradleys as they were merely using them to shuttle Advisory Support Team troops to and from the Iraqi Civil Defense Corps compound "outpost" several kilometers from Camp Falcon. Advisory Support Teams were teams of soldiers put together by each battalion task force to train a company or battalion of Iraqi Civil Defense Corps soldiers. Because the Army had no formal advisory assistance command structure in 2004, we were required to provide this capability with organic assets. I knew precisely what and how the Bradleys were being used because all the soldiers from 1-7 Cavalry conducting the Advisory Support Team mission were fire support soldiers assigned to 1-21 Field Artillery and I discussed this with them at length before making the request. Easily, other vehicles could have been used. The Route Irish security mission was more dangerous and more important to the overall BCT force protection mission. But I lost the argument and the fight to secure these assets. The battalion would have to do its best with its limited assets.

Because our fight was on an asymmetric battlefield, the argument over the Bradleys became a classic example of dealing with standard conventional problems that demanded non-standard solutions. I was constantly dealing with a BCT staff that could not think unconventionally very well or very quickly. They were mostly constrained from fears that Colonel Lanza would be displeased. It was often suffocating and quite debilitating given the fluid nature of the operating environment.

In my mind, the fire support teams and equipment should have been given back to me. This would have offset the gross disparity in mission-specific resources. Unfortunately, my inability to manage the political fight within my brigade had a stiff tertiary effect on my mission for the BCT.

I would soon come to discover that my battalion was viewed as the BCT enabler to the other two maneuver battalions of the BCT. The BCT staff would not even acknowledge that Task Force 1-21 was doctrinally a task force unit. Instead we were depicted and treated as 1-21 Field Artillery. This relationship and mindset placed the Task Force in a very difficult position at the resource bargaining table. Additionally, it just solidified the fact that convention ruled the day in the BCT and in our operating environment. Though given a completely maneuver mission, the BCT staff made decisions as if the battalion were not acting in that capacity. Rarely did the BCT staff task 1-7 Cavalry or 1-8 Cavalry to support 1-21 Field Artillery. 1-21 Field Artillery was frequently tasked for personnel and materiel to support the other two maneuver task forces.

I tried to fight this perception and treatment at first. Within a few weeks, however, it became futile and I decided to take on this role for the team and did all I could to ensure we met the needs and expectations for the BCT. As a fire support trained officer I understood this relationship very well. I didn't think that relationship was proper in these circumstances but I failed at every effort to change it.

This situation highlights the extreme futility of the war for the American military and illuminates the adverse affect conventional thinking has on the general effort fighting in Iraq. I knew as commander of a Task Force not maneuver-based in design, training, and configuration, I would have to find a way to start winning a few of these kinds of political battles within the BCT or this could become a very trying and long combat tour.

Another very clear depiction of this organizational political battle and the primacy of conventional thinking over unconventional occurred with the security of Highway 8. The northern portion of Highway 8 was patrolled by First Cavalry Division's 4th Battalion, 5th Air Defense Artillery Regiment (4-5, Air Defense Artillery). The northern portion of Route Irish was that portion of the road running from the northeast corner of Task Force 1-21's sector in Al Saidiyah to the entrance at Baghdad International Airport where Entry Control Point 1 stood.

The First Cavalry Division staff struggled with various scenarios and concepts to secure Route Irish and I know one of 5th BCT's assigned battalions, 1-7 Cavalry, was considered for reassignment to this mission. That choice would have clearly been the right one. Though second-guessing or "Monday morning quarterbacking" is considered bad form, the plain fact was that the unit the Division assigned to secure the road was not suited for the mission. That was not its fault; organizational design and Army training did not support this unit functioning optimally in that manner.

Similarly to Task Force 1-21, 4-5, Air Defense Battalion had to master infantry skills and tactics in order to perform their assigned mission. 4-5, Air Defense Artillery Battalion was not the right organization to execute such a vital task for the Division. Route security and dominating a major highway required more training, more armor assets, and frankly a larger formation than was 4-5, Air Defense Artillery.

Easily, the division cavalry squadron should have had this mission. Route Irish had strategic significance in this war. The enemy seemed to be aware of this and exploited the fact the unit on the highway was incapable of securing the road. Ill-equipped and not trained for this kind of mission, the air defenders did a noble job but they learned most lessons the hard way. They paid in blood for their inexperience and the mismatch.

The solution to securing Route Irish lay with Lieutenant Colonel Bill Salter and 1-7 Cavalry. This unit was ideally suited in every way to secure that route and had the means to do so. Major General Chiarelli should have reassigned 4-5, Air Defense Battalion to the 5th BCT and that unit could have assumed the sector 1-7 Cavalry had. This would have permitted 1-7 Cavalry a role and mission that it was ideally suited to accomplish and one that the unit was trained to do by doctrine. 1-7 Cavalry had the training, leadership, equipment, and bravado to successfully control that key route. It would have eased the burden and pressure placed on Lieutenant General Sanchez, and later General Casey, the Multinational Forces, Iraq Commander, as Route Irish was strategically sensitive to the Multinational Forces Iraq Command, the Division, and to the BCT.

Highlighting this problem, the reporter Thomas Friedman of *The New York Times* wrote an article about the inability of the Coalition to secure and stabilize Baghdad. To illustrate his case, Friedman pointed out the fact that the road to Baghdad International Airport was unsecured and incredibly treacherous. Friedman's analysis and point was that if such a vital road leading to Baghdad International Airport – the symbolic link that symbolized the recovery of Iraq — was not securable, then the effort by the Army was a failure and a losing proposition. 1-7 Cavalry could have rectified that situation.

Along the western shoulder of Route Irish, in the central zone of Area of Operations Rocket , was a bombed-out and decrepit industrial park zone. Old warehouses, a hydraulic and pneumatic machine factory, and a large, five-story, engineering-school building poked above the park. This industrial park was near a major cloverleaf intersection that managed traffic at the confluence of Highway 8 and Highway 5 in Baghdad. Many attacks against U.S. Army patrols originating from Camp Falcon occurred from insurgents who infiltrated this urban maze of abandoned and bombed-out buildings. Mostly at night, the enemy launched ambush attacks with small arms and rocket propelled grenades.

North of the industrial park area were the residential and commercial sections of Al Saidiyah. These areas were laid out into mahallas (neighborhoods). There was no zoning plan for the township such as we are accustomed to in American cities. Residential areas, shops, and public utility facilities are intermixed without much rhyme or reason.

This map shows how Al Saidiyah was laid out in mahallas:

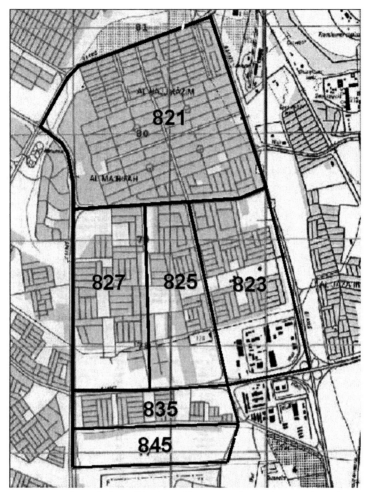

Figure 6.1 — Labeled in black with sector boundaries also drawn in black denote the mahallas (neighborhoods) of Al Saidiyah.

The terrain south of Al Saidiyah and surrounding Camp Falcon was very wide open and flat. Soldiers could observe for about five kilometers from the ground on a clear day. Many unimproved, dirt roads zigzagged across the landscape known as 40N (area 40 north) and 40S (area 40 south). At night, this terrain provided excellent ground to launch hit-and-run mortar attacks with 82mm and 60mm mortars.

The enemy took full advantage of this in April and on into May of 2004.

Camp Falcon was hit by mortar attacks, one and sometimes two attacks a night, for the first weeks until we began a vigorous counter-mortar patrolling effort. This was unnerving to many soldiers as the insurgents were not skilled in their attacks, the mortar and rocket rounds would randomly impact inside the walls of the camp. There was no "safe" place on the camp, and this weighed on the minds of our soldiers over time. Stopping the mortar attacks was critical to our long-term survival.

The enemy tactic was a very simple program whereby a mortar tube was stored in the trunk of a car usually a small, four-door Opal station wagon or the bed of a small pick-up truck. Typically, two men drove to a spot, jumped from the vehicle, set the mortar down on the ground, and aimed it by visually pointing it in the direction of Camp Falcon. They then quickly dropped two or three mortar rounds, threw the tube back in the car or truck, and drove off as though they were simply on their way home. The total time to drop these rounds wouldn't exceed 90 seconds. By the time the last round was impacting Camp Falcon, the insurgents had driven away to collect the $500 they were paid for conducting the attack.

Taking action to counter this tactic was supremely difficult. Without pre-positioned observation posts to catch them in the act, chances of catching the perpetrators were slim. Once in awhile, these insurgents made a mistake or had an equipment malfunction and they would end up killing themselves.

Many times the insurgents used a convenient source of cover along the outer wall surrounding a palm grove near Camp Falcon. Just south of the industrial park, along the edge of Route Irish and about two kilometers north of Camp Falcon, was a palm grove in a walled compound. A wealthy Iraqi family owned the palm grove and in 2003 the owner was building a mansion on the twenty-acre property. Apparently, the owner and his family left in haste when the Americans invaded. Wisely, this owner hired a religious sect of Muslims, much like the Hari-Krishna people most Americans are familiar with, to be caretakers of his property. In exchange, the owner allowed them to squat in the unfinished buildings on the compound. Multiple times insurgents backed-up against the wall of the compound and lobbed a few mortars at Camp Falcon. In response we searched every inch of that compound and dug it up. We used ground surveillance radar to see if weapons or ammunition caches were stored underground in the compound. We never found anything. Once we realized the enemy was using the sanctuary of the outer compound wall we over-watched the wall with counter-mortar patrols, denying the enemy the palm grove as a means to launch attacks.

Squatters also had begun to move into the area surrounding Camp Falcon. They erected mud-huts, forming impromptu residential enclaves, which dotted the landscape of 40-North. Neither U.S. forces nor Iraqi government officials could control or manage this. There was no local government. It was literally a free-for-all. As much as we wanted to, we were impotent to stop it. We had to patrol these areas to make sure the enemy did not exploit the situation.

On the south side of Camp Falcon, running for about ten kilometers further south in the Task Force sector, was an area we called 64W (Area 64-West). This was mostly rural terrain and largely ignored under Saddam Hussein's regime. Two villages existed here. The people farmed the land around the town for subsistence. A large irrigation canal with banked dikes cut through the center of Area 64-West and terminated 12 kilometers north in area 40-North just beyond the north side of Camp Falcon.

The villagers and farmers were extremely friendly and caused no problems for us the entire year. Our initial assessment of Area 64-West was that helping them to improve their quality of life and bringing some amenities to these people would go a long way to winning their cooperation.

Tactically, this rural terrain could provide excellent ground to launch rocket attacks north into the center of Baghdad and into what we called the Green Zone. We were very wary of this possibility and determined immediately that we would not allow Area 64-West to be used for that activity. Like 40-North and 40-South, this area was sparsely populated, flat, and wide open. Few vehicle navigable roads existed down here.

Initially, the other part of our sector responsibility was route security on the two major highways of Al Rashid. Highway 5, graphically named Route Senators, was a road that ran from the western side of Al Saidiyah straight across to the eastern side of Al Rashid.

Highway 5 was lined closely by store fronts and residential buildings. The houses sat no more than 100 meters from the highway on either side for most of the length of the road. From the cover of these buildings, the enemy frequently planted IEDs and attacked patrols transiting this route. The enemy had excellent vantage points on the rooftops and alleyways between buildings facing the highway.

1-94 Field Artillery warned us Route Senators was treacherous ground. The officers repeatedly advised us not to be on that route at night. The tactics, techniques, and procedures of 1-94 Field Artillery were to run their last patrol in the late afternoon so it would come back to Camp Falcon before dark. This was clearly to avoid enemy contact at night.

As I examined this situation several things were obvious.

First, 1-94 Field Artillery was reneging on their task and purpose by abdicating the road at night. Second, any units traveling that road at night were free game as the protection force was not present. They placed no ambushes out, patrolled no mahallas, and essentially hunkered down on Camp Falcon at night. I doubt the First Armor Division staff and leaders knew this resignation occurred willfully. If they did know and sanctioned this action, then the leadership was not meeting the obligation of their mission. I did not like or agree with this action.

Another obvious fact I discerned quickly was that the enemy did not have to go searching for American forces. We delivered ourselves to the enemy by driving humvees, tanks, and infantry fighting vehicles on the main roads. Somehow, physically occupying the road translated to securing it. I did not ever agree with that view, despite the fact many of my superiors did. It defies logic. If being on the road in plain sight of the enemy constituted security then the Army (my superiors) owed me the equipment necessary to do that job that way. This meant outfitting us with tanks and infantry fighting vehicles, not humvees. I had howitzers, Fox chemical-detection vehicles, M113 series chemical smoke tracks, and rocket launchers. But none of these vehicles were designed to do a route security or an offensive patrolling mission.

In a short time, we developed tactics where we dismounted in ambush positions. We drove mounted patrols in humvees on the side roads to "secure" the main roads. We sought to be where the enemy would attack from instead where he would attack toward.

I know that more combat casualties occur among dismounted forces than mounted forces. However, in Baghdad, the reverse was occurring. The way this enemy fights, with his penchant for using IEDs, was focused on mounted troops.

Iraqi insurgents are not good at wounding or killing dismounted troops in a head-to-head fire-fight. We can outgun and more accurately shoot our weapons in a more disciplined manner dismounted.

Unfortunately, everyone did not adopt this method. So, as other patrols drove the main roads and were attacked, our limited forces could not counter every attack. We could not be everywhere all the time. This put me headfirst into arguments with Colonel Lanza about why I was in dismounted ambushes and not driving on the roads protecting, which I found was supremely frustrating the entire year we fought in Baghdad.

As I examined the terrain and assessed this concrete jungle against the personnel I had available, I realized we were severely disadvantaged. The enemy could blend into the terrain, wear civilian clothes, and drive civilian vehicles easily hiding among the people and among families in their houses. The insurgents could hit and run, melting away in seconds into just another Iraqi walking on the street.

I knew then that our success required us to get the people living in the mahallas to rat-out the insurgents. We needed to encourage the people and not tolerate insurgents using their homes and streets to launch attacks. And that would be extremely difficult for two reasons. First, the insurgents were willing to threaten death and kill those who would not submit. Secondly, most Iraqis saw us as occupiers and, therefore, it was their Muslim duty to support the insurgents proactively or apathetically. Regardless which they chose, both behaviors achieved the same end: the insurgents could attack easily.

One of the spots in Area of Operations Rocket that insurgents operated around and at which sought to frequently attack us was the cloverleaf confluence of Highway 5 and

Highway 8. The cloverleaf was considered key terrain in Al Rashid. The graphical term the First Armor Division gave this cloverleaf was Check Point 8. Although later in our tour, First Cavalry Division staff would change this to Check Point 546, we in Task Force 1-21 always referred to it as Check Point 8.

Check Point 8, Key Terrain

Check Point 8 was contentious ground because American forces were always using it. Thousands of Baghdad citizens used it daily as well. This was a major commerce route within Baghdad. If the insurgents could ever blow up the overpass, severe traffic problems in this part of Baghdad would result. Colonel Lanza was determined that this would never happen. Task Force 1-21 was given the responsibility to secure this interchange of roads.

Figure 6.2 — Overhead view of Check Point 8 at the confluence of Route Irish, Route Force, and Route Senators.

In order to secure this route we would have to run many patrols in and around this checkpoint. Because so many other units used this area without coordination but merely passed through, our ability to positively control the vicinity was very challenging. The fact that other units from the Division and the Coalition at large drove on these routes and passed through this area not fully appreciating the threat also added to our frustration. Some units shot at the local nationals or threatened them by pointing their weapons in an attempt to scare the Iraqis. And Iraqis didn't distinguish units. An American soldier is an American soldier to an Iraqi. Since 5th BCT was responsible for the terrain, we were often blamed for the insensitive actions of other units over which we had no control.

Another aspect of securing Check Point 8 was incredibly challenging. Controlling the high volume of traffic that traveled this area was nearly impossible. Drive-by shootings were frequent. Often too, random attacks occurred with thrown hand grenades or an occasional rocket propelled grenade fired from a passing car at humvees in observation/over watch positions.

Once given responsibility for Check Point 8, I knew the vulnerabilities needed addressing. Simply occupying the position without some fortification and construction improvements would not guarantee the Task Force success. We would not meet the BCT Commander's intent to secure this key terrain unless we did more.

In the early weeks and months of our specified task to defend the key terrain we struggled with coordinating enough patrols and placing enough soldiers on the terrain to guarantee its security. We were not resourced with appropriate armor, enough personnel, or the requisite operations scheme in tempo and other assigned mission requirements to get this right and meet the BCT commander's expectations. His staff, in turn, did not resource our Task Force to meet the BCT commander's expectations. Additionally, we were not well trained as rocket artillerymen and chemical soldiers to execute this to the desired standard. We learned on the job and through minor successes and failures. Not until early November did we have the sense and understanding to better execute the requirement.

Immediately after a major IED incident, the BCT Engineer Officer and I went to Check Point 8 and walked the entire ground to develop a comprehensive construction/fortification security plan. My failure was not having the foresight and sense to strong-point Check Point 8 from the very beginning of our assignment. Though our mission analysis clearly indicated we did not have the proper resources and our operations tempo with competing tasks assigned by the BCT negated strong-pointing this location from the outset, I still felt it a personal leadership shortcoming that I did not press this issue with Colonel Lanza forcefully from the onset of the mission assignment. Nonetheless, by October we understood we had to integrate soldiers with construction improvements that would fortify Check Point 8 and develop it into a strong-point and at the same time depict an aesthetically pleasing highway system.

Several construction improvements were indicated. With staff input, I decided the best way to get the most from our effort was to develop this process into a civil project. That way we would employ Iraqis in the area and garner for the Coalition a fortified defensive network to hold that key terrain.

Three areas of the highway network needed immediate attention. First, the center area under the overpasses was highly vulnerable to IED placement. Second, fencing around the cloverleaf risers needed to be extended to prevent insurgents from tossing hand grenades to the area below where soldiers and guards patrolled on foot. Third, the backsides of the overpass extensions were obscured from direct observation. This meant dismounted infiltration was easily accommodated. Some blocking obstacle needed to be emplaced to stop that from occurring.

The initial obstacles that needed to be transformed to shape the defense of Check Point 8 and to establish the strongpoint were mostly wire, lighting, and fencing. Illuminating the entire cloverleaf at night was essential to deterring attacks. The combination of physically occupying the terrain with Iraqi security forces and American forces in mutual support; providing roving patrols with additional stand-off, employing over-watch positions consisting of heavy machineguns and anti-tank rockets (American version of the rocket propelled grenade); and controlling traffic flow all served to radically improve our ability to secure that ground.

The Task Force was able to control this ground but we never did dominate it. Task Force 1-21 could not completely deny the enemy opportunities to attack into the area. Armor vehicles were needed. More soldiers dedicated 24/7, and more permanent barriers were needed. But the Task Force was able to set the conditions for improvement. Over time, the civil project to make the defense more viable was implemented.

While Check Point 8 devoured our resources, we still had other parts of the sector to manage. Understanding the demographics and terrain were key aspects to securing and stabilizing the Task Force sector. More important to achieving success though was using intelligence resources and analysis to shape the bigger fight in our favor.

7 Intelligence, the Military Oxymoron

*"If I always appear prepared, it is because before entering an
undertaking, I have meditated long and have foreseen what
might occur. It is not genius where reveals to me suddenly
and secretly what I should do in circumstances unexpected by
others; it is thought and preparation."* Napoleon Bonaparte

Fighting in Iraq demanded superb intelligence gathering
and analysis in a manner not heretofore exercised to the
depth and level of sophistication now necessary by conventional forces. Conventional Army and Marine units, sent in
come-as-you-are configurations to prosecute an insurgency war were not resourced to meet the demands of the situation. Task Force 1-21 was no exception. Despite our woe-
ful resources, we had to adapt and overcome to succeed.

The Task Force Intelligence section was directed by Captain Robb Dettmer, a first-rate, affable young officer who
hailed from Forest Lake, Minnesota. Captain Dettmer was
a West Point graduate, about 6' 2", fair-skinned with red
hair and, soldiers joked, resembled Dale Earnhardt Jr.

Captain Dettmer was a quiet person. That demeanor belied his acute, sharp, mind. He was self-assured, always
kind-hearted, and enthusiastic about his business which
was military intelligence. Iraq is a military intelligence officer's Disney World. The challenges to collect, develop, and
shape intelligence information to drive operations is the
focal point of operations for many company teams and battalion task forces fighting in Iraq.

Robb was sent to Task Force 1-21 from 312th Military Intelligence Battalion, another unit assigned to the First Cavalry Division a few months before we deployed. He was a
Military Intelligence officer with the staff title designator

of S2 which caused us to dub him, "Deuce." He was tremendously skilled in the art and science of assessment, collation, interpretation, and recommendation. He had a superb analytical mind and he used it to great effect.

Captain Dettmer ran a very good section and made sure all his team was well integrated into the tactical and Civil Affairs operations. Serving in the S2 section were First Lieutenant Michael Brewster (a.k.a. "Baby-Deuce"), Sergeant First Class Daniel "Dan" Moody, and Sergeant Derrick Warner. Captain Dettmer frequently had his team out on patrols supporting the batteries' patrols with on-site intelligence analysis and interrogation. We never did anything in the way of plans and decisions without the intelligence section of the Task Force weighing in with their thoughts, analysis, and assessment. All decisions I made about tactical employment of assigned forces, civil operations, and political maneuvering were predicated on intelligence assessments from my S2 or the BCT Military Intelligence team without exception.

The 5th BCT had a robust and focused intelligence system and program. Colonel Lanza was well aware that intelligence was the major player in the counterinsurgency. His articulated tenets for intelligence operations within the BCT were simple and clear.

- *Intelligence **drives** all operations ("act on" or "collect")*

- *All operations generate new intelligence – must fight for new intelligence on every mission ("every Soldier a scout")*

- *Effective intelligence analysis and fusion has high return on investment – resource the Fusion Cell generously (The Fusion Cell was a intelligence staff section that collated disparate intelligence information and fused it to shape a cohesive story or what was happening in sector.)*

•*HUMINT (human intelligence information) is king in Iraq – cultivate relationships*

• *Achieving populace neutrality is the first step in deriving plentiful and effective HUMINT (human intelligence)*

• *Intelligence, information operations, and lethal fires must be seamless the ultimate objective of intelligence collection is force protection*[4]

With these tenets to guide the BCT intelligence operations, Task Force 1-21 was focused on honing our ability to support and operate along these guidelines. And Captain Dettmer and his staff followed this methodology in their efforts as well effectively supporting the BCT intelligence apparatus. Intelligence information must constantly be assessed, analyzed, synthesized, and disseminated to have utility to operators who must make decisions and act on information.

At the Task Force level, the biggest challenge for military intelligence operations was developing human intelligence sources, an absolute must in fighting an insurgency. Much of the intelligence information we received came from higher echelons. We often had to piece together disparate sources from outside the Task Force and do our own synthesis of the information, and extrapolate as accurate a picture as we could. This was normal intelligence practice. But, assets at battalion and company level needed to improve to insure more precision so vital to tactical effectiveness in counterinsurgency.

The Task Force soon learned that intelligence management is highly challenging in a war against an insurgency. Because insurgents are adept at using the populace to blend-in and, thus, they are able to create camouflage right in front of your face, intelligence resources at the company level were vital. It is with solid intelligence resources and capability that commanders can focus effort and achieve greater precision to best negate the sensitive issues associated with collateral damage.

In a conventional force, the most capable assets we had were our weapons. These weapons could quickly generate superior firepower. That is what conventional forces are designed to do. But this approach does little good in a counterinsurgency war. Precision engagement — striking at the enemy after precisely identifying and isolating him without causing collateral damage in the process — is essential; but to achieve this, conventional units must be better resourced. Effective and re-tooled assets must be available at the lowest operating level so long as Americans choose to use conventional forces to prosecute these types of fights. This has been the decided choice of our National Command Authority in two out of two modern insurgent fights (Vietnam and Iraq).

Conventional Army forces have significant limitations in this arena. As a classic conventional unit, we could not develop spies and task them. None of the BCT task force S2 sections had personnel trained and certified (i.e., the Army requirement to allow development and tasking of spies, to handle human sources for intelligence gathering). But that capability did reside at the BCT level.

Informants are absolutely essential to the successful prosecution of a counterinsurgency war. Sun Tzu counseled that a spy provided "foreknowledge" and this foreknowledge gave generals the ability to develop plans to defeat their foe. Sun Tzu said,

> *Knowledge of the enemy's dispositions can only be obtained from other men. Hence the use of spies, of whom there are five classes: Local, inward, converted, doomed and surviving spies.*

When these five kinds of spy are all at work, none can discover all of the ramifications of your secret spy system. This is called 'divine manipulations of the threads.' It is the sovereign's most precious faculty. Local spying: invaders employing the services of the inhabitants of a district.[5]

The "other men" from whom the enemy's dispositions can be obtained are, in today's vernacular, called human intelligence sources. Spies are one source of human intelligence. Although the Task Force could not task and develop spies, we had informants and we debriefed them when they wanted to bring us information.

We had many sources providing us human intelligence within our sector. There were limitations to the value of this method of collecting human intelligence. With Iraqis providing human intelligence there were several storylines the information provided would take.

There was the "News Story Report." This was the term I gave the reports we most often received, which were nothing more than a local Iraqi telling us what we already knew or that could be heard on Al Arabia news. These reports were not of much value.

Then there was the "Made-up Story." Some Iraqis, thinking they might get some money, would come to us and tell us things that were just clearly fabrications or exaggerations. Some of the stories were comical.

Another was the "Vendetta Story." This was a story that a local national would bring to us claiming a neighbor or someone they wanted to get revenge on was an insurgent or criminal. Literally, they would fabricate a sinister story and attempt to get us to act on the information to kill or detain their enemy.

Finally, there was the "Disinformation Story." Iraqi insurgents worked elaborate, plausible tales in an attempt to direct the Task Force or BCT away from planned actions.

Having the ability to discern those reports was a learning process. We were not great at it in the first month, but by the second month we had heard so many stories, we could easily discern what was credible from these that were concocted as a sort of comedy hour for the Iraqi informant.

The Task Force intelligence section developed a very good process for interrogating informants and quickly getting to the gist of their stories. As well, we had great interpreters who could tell us very quickly if an informant was legitimate or just motivated by some other personal gain.

The S2 section had developed a limited number of interpreters who mastered the interrogation procedures. These were the only interpreters who participated in the interrogation process and they truly developed a team effort with the critical task. Some interpreters were better than others. But it was vitally important to develop interpreter interrogations team tactics and skill to conduct fruitful interrogations.

Never did we use coercion or physically handle an Iraqi detainee. Much hyperbole and wild false stories are told about U.S. military interrogations being abusive. We were not well skilled in the art of interrogation nor did we have the developed training to execute this task in any sophisticated manner. The volume and soldiers available that I entrusted with the task were too limited.

Additionally, as commander, I was very sensitive to the adverse affects of allowing any interrogation situation to get out-of-hand. It was standard procedure for the Task Force field grade officers or the Command Sergeant Major to monitor interrogations.

The Task Force intelligence section was most valuable at synthesis, analysis, and collation of information. They had to weave accurate predictive analyses from the disparate information we received to aid commanders in making good decisions. The Task Force intelligence section quickly revealed that the major threat areas in our sector were the two highways and two mahallas within Al Saidiyah where insurgent cells appeared to have some sanctuary and influence. Obviously, we would have to target these areas to get precise intelligence to conduct raids and dismantle these groups.

IED emplacement between the northern most Check Point along Route Irish in our sector and Check Point 8 throughout April, May, and into June was commonplace. There was way too much road and concealment available to the insurgents than we could cover with our troop-to-task allocation. We were also subject to multiple attacks from rocket propelled grenade gunners hidden in the buildings and along the rooftops from the east side of Route Irish. This was terrain we did not have tactical control over, it belonged to 1-8 Cavalry, our sister task force in the BCT.

To counter this, we had to share information with 1-8 Cavalry and work precision targeting. Firing artillery in response to a threat such as this –an available tactic in a conventional scenario— was not an option in this counter-insurgent fight. The rules of engagement that governed the use of lethal force simply did not permit employment of such a tactic. We literally had to see an enemy position and maneuver to destroy the insurgents occupying the position. That was a nearly impossible task. And with just 100 meters of standoff distance placed between us and the enemy, insurgents could blend into the populace very quickly after firing. This was a maddening way to fight.

Counter Intelligence Efforts—Keeping the Insurgents at Bay

Another major threat that Task Force 1-21 had responsibility to deter was enemy surveillance of Camp Falcon and the immediate surrounding area. The enemy typically observed, followed, and then assassinated camp local national workers. In the summer months, the enemy focused a campaign to kill local nationals who were working for the BCT on Camp Falcon. And they were having some degree of success.

As Task Force Commander charged with responsibility to mitigate enemy surveillance of the camp, one of my most exasperating experiences in the first months in Iraq was tied to this responsibility. Most American camps employed locals to work in the laundry facilities, Post Exchanges, barbershops, and a multiplicity of other logistics needs a BCT had in that environment. Employing local nationals served a couple purposes. First, the BCT employed well over 100 people. This nurtured good relations with the local area. Second, this relationship allowed an outlet to pump money into the local economy.

Unfortunately, the insurgents determined these workers were valuable targets. In a concerted effort, insurgents attempted to assassinate as many of these Iraqi workers as they could. In the Task Force we lost over twenty Iraqi workers, interpreters, and Iraqi Army soldiers combined due to assassinations. We were about average for units in the First Cavalry Division. The murders were often very gruesome and highly effective at instilling fear in Iraqis.

One evening in late June, I had just returned from a patrol in Al Saidiyah and went into the Tactical Operations Center to get an update on the situation in the rest of our sector. About a minute into the briefing from Major Reinhart, I was interrupted with a phone call from Colonel Lanza. He was irate. "I just had nine Camp Falcon workers killed outside the FOB (Forward Operating Base) and it's your fault! Where are your patrols?" he yelled accusatorily at me into the phone.

I replied, "What are you talking about? We don't have any reports of that happening. I just got back with a patrol in Al Saidiyah." I began to wonder if something happened that I was not told about yet.

Reading from our Patrol Status Board and eyeing the S3 for positive acknowledgement, I reported, "I have a patrol on Irish, one in 64 West and another on Route Rock. I think the MPs [Military Police] have a patrol on Route Rock right now." Route Rock was a key route, a dirt and gravel road, less than 1000 meters outside Camp Falcon running east to west on the north side of the forward operating base. The road intersected on its east termination point onto Route Irish.

He got more hostile, "You don't have a patrol on Route Rock because that's where these workers got killed!" he blared back at me.

I decided I wasn't going to convince him I was right and he was getting bad reports from somewhere unknown to me but I suspected his staff was serving him their normal helping of "bad poop." I knew had that really happened I would have been called on the radio while out on patrol. My staff knew information of this nature was a command critical information report [CCIR] to me and they had never failed to pass that type of information to me. I just replied to him, "Sir, I will find out exactly what's going on and come see you."

His retort, "Yeah, you come see me!" and he abruptly hung up.

I turned to the group in our operations center and explained, as calmly as I could what I just got told. Everyone looked at me like I was insane.

I directed the S3 to call the BCT operations center and find out what was going on. I had the Task Force Operations Sergeant, Master Sergeant Joe Silvas, call the patrol leader of the Task Force patrol on Route Irish as well as the one on Route Rock to find out if either of them was dealing with such an incident. I knew that if nine people had just been shot to death at the intersection of Route Rock and Route Irish, we would have a significant traffic jam on the roads and both patrol leaders would be reporting that information.

The report back from the BCT operations center was that an incident occurred but the location was unclear and the killed local nationals were three personnel not nine. No one was sure the local nationals were from Camp Falcon either. The two patrol leaders in the vicinity reported that the situation was normal, i.e., no such incident had occurred at that intersection or anywhere else on Route Irish or Route Rock.

After about thirty more minutes and considerable investigation, we determined that three local nationals had been killed in another battalion's sector, miles away from Camp Falcon although we believed they worked at Camp Falcon. The best we could piece together was that the local nationals were followed from Camp Falcon and gunned down in another region of Baghdad.

Armed with these facts, I went to Colonel Lanza. By then he had received the updated reports from his staff with accurate information, and he had calmed down. For me, the incident was so exasperating I became disillusioned about the lack of trust and confidence communicated to me from my superior officer and the staff at the echelon above my level. But nevertheless I stayed focused on meeting Colonel Lanza's intent, as always. My peers had to manage this "fog of war" too and they managed it their own way. My method was to handle the caustic treatment and supercilious behavior from the echelon above me as the price of doing business and I committed to dealing with issues as they arose on a case-by-case basis. This, though, was easily one of the most exhausting aspects of serving the year in Iraq in the 5th BCT. Managing the local counter-reconnaissance effort was always challenging and fraught with danger from the enemy as well as from the BCT command. Despite the micromanaging from the BCT staff, the Task Force remained keenly focused on meeting Colonel Lanza's goal of stopping the enemy surveillance and the killing of local nationals working on Camp Falcon.

As mentioned previously, to meet Colonel Lanza's intent and to properly counter the enemy's reconnaissance effort along Route Rock we employed a robust and effective counter-reconnaissance effort. Mounted and dismounted patrolling, directing psychological operations team engagement of the local population, and executing combined patrols with Iraqi security forces became part of the regimen.

The other major threat to Camp Falcon was indirect fire attack. In the summer months of 2004, Camp Falcon was hit almost daily with mortars or rockets. The BCT staff assigned Task Force 1-21 to provide counter-mortar patrols. The intelligence section did a very detailed pattern analysis of the threat. This was done in an effort to determine the windows of time and general locations that presented the greatest threat. Knowing this, we could focus patrols against those times and locations. This worked well and we significantly reduced the attacks originating from within our assigned sector very quickly. Unfortunately, the other task forces did not do this as effectively and attacks originating from other parts of Al Rashid continued.

The counter-surveillance and counter-mortar effort became much like engaging in police work. Patrols were directed to check out cars that were stopped along the road, usually broken down or needing water. We would help motorists with flat tires or other minor mechanical problems to get them on their way. We would randomly stop cars and search them. We enforced a rule that no one stops along the road in front of Camp Falcon. We had to watch the area around Camp Falcon closely. Because on the east side of Camp Falcon ran Route Irish (Highway 8) there was usually a large volume of traffic that passed day and night. We developed tactics, techniques, and procedures to effectively patrol the area around Camp Falcon.

Patrols observed key terrain from hidden positions and were linked to a central command and control communications structure. We adjusted Camp Falcon's guard tower manning so that those guard towers overlooking Route Irish were manned by soldiers from Task Force 1-21. This was important to the counter-reconnaissance effort. Once we made this modification, I had the Task Force Operations Officer develop a robust training plan to teach soldiers how to detect enemy activity from those towers. This gave us the opportunity to exercise an effective system of coordinated command and control. The tactic we refined was to have the tower guards talk directly to moving ground patrols outside Camp Falcon. The tower guards, as observers, vectored mounted patrols and Iraqi Army scouts to points on the ground permitting us to challenge suspicious situations. Synthesis and practiced integration improved our counter-reconnaissance actions and optimized the situation in our favor.

One of our biggest challenges with our effort to deny traffic stopping on the road in front of Camp Falcon was managing local nationals' use of a gas station which was located along the front side of Camp Falcon immediately off Route Irish. The gas station was easily accessible to southbound traffic. I requested to Colonel Lanza that this gas station be closed down. The gas station provided the enemy an excellent location to observe the area around Camp Falcon, and it was nearly impossible to control.

I felt the gas station was a lucrative target for the enemy for a couple reasons. First, its proximity to Camp Falcon — should the insurgency blow it up — could have a profound impact on the local nationals' view of the ability of American forces and Iraqi security forces to protect the common Iraqi citizen. Second, a catastrophic attack here was consistent with the insurgent message and effort to destabilize the Iraqi Interim Government.

Colonel Lanza did not allow the gas station to close because he felt it was too valuable a support facility to the local area. To him, this consideration outweighed the potential threat it presented to Camp Falcon. I disagreed arguing there were many more gas stations along Route Irish that mitigated the economic affect of closing this particular one. But, I lost the argument and thus Task Force 1-21 spent much time and effort protecting the gas station against a potential attack.

To deal with the gas station we put patrols in and around the station 24/7. With dismounted patrols, the Task Force moved in and among the Iraqi people at the gas station area and further south in the Al Rashid market area. By placing ourselves in amongst the local nationals, we provided a visual and aggressive deterrent to enemy surveillance efforts. These patrols, well-armed and moving, were intended to keep any enemy off balance and to have the psychological effect of placing us among the locals where we were neither fearful of them nor a source of fear to them. The patrol leader knew the patrol's mission was to serve and protect much as a cop on the beat. But the patrol members had to be prepared to fight and be wary of set-ups or stand-off attacks. This was a tough mission for any young lieutenant or sergeant.

Another tactic, technique, and procedure we employed and often executed was what we referred to as a hasty traffic control point. We could place these along Route Rock or various places on Route Irish and disrupt vehicular traffic movement. Effectively done, a hasty traffic control point could disrupt enemy movement or trafficking of weapons along Route Irish. Because there were so many side roads and Iraqis took cars everywhere, it literally took a whole battalion task force to completely cut off all routes from this major urban highway. We always tried to be smart and cut off most of the routes leading away from these hasty traffic control points.

Often, we would employ Iraqi security forces to operate in autonomous supporting patrols to combine with our formations. Obviously, they brought a certain added capability to the patrols. Language and cultural barriers that otherwise stood in the way of interactions were eliminated. Some key drawbacks operating with the Iraqi security forces were that they could be heavy-handed with the local nationals. For example, if they came across an Iraqi civilian who refused to listen to their instructions, Iraqi security forces personnel would fire their weapon into the air or at the feet of the Iraqi civilian. Sometimes the Iraqi security forces guard or soldier would point their weapon directly at the face or chest of an uncooperative Iraqi civilian. In the worse cases, the guard or soldier would hit or even begin to beat a dissenting Iraqi civilian. This was learned behavior from more than thirty years of Saddam's rule.

Sometimes Iraqi security forces were hazardous to themselves. They had a penchant for shooting warning shots into the air or operating with the safety off their weapon and their fingers on the trigger. This practice sometimes resulted in the negligent discharge of their weapon. Several times when we were with an Iraqi security forces unit, bullets would zing past me or other soldiers in our patrol due to an Iraqi soldier's negligent discharge of his weapon. This was scary and added an unnecessary dimension of danger to our patrols.

Another monitoring technique we employed was one devised by Captain Dettmer. He developed a system within our Task Force where patrols would take digital photos and record pre-fabricated data collection sheets. This information was used to build a database of vehicles that we had stopped and challenged. This practice allowed us to find patterns of repetitive vehicles or people in the area. Once patterns were determined, we could target and focus our efforts in that direction.

The other key action the Task Force operations center systematically executed was to query our sister task forces and the BCT headquarters to gather alternate source information on activity along Route Irish in the vicinity of Camp Falcon.

From our experience in Iraq, we concluded that the Task Force could have benefited from some changes the Army might consider in the future. The following are policies I believe need to be considered by the Army in its continued campaign in Iraq:

• Effective human intelligence collection depends on precise geo-location and the required target description. Conventional units need more assets to accomplish this. Every patrol of every unit, regardless of Table of Organization and Equipment prescribed by the Army and branch, must be allocated more tools like digital cameras, GPS telemetry, Lo Jack, cell phones, and infra-red strobes to better exercise intelligence gathering operations.

• Place a Tactical HUMINT [human intelligence] Team in every platoon in a maneuver BCT.

• Significantly increase foreign language training. Every soldier should have to learn and certify in a foreign language. At a minimum, get foreign language training into the Army at large.

• Tactical questioning is a soldier skill that has utility in any theater whether fighting an insurgency or a high intensity conflict. Get this into basic training systems.

To further refine our efforts, we operated from a framework that was derived from the Division campaign plan. This framework was a construct of what was termed the Five Lines of Operation (Five LOOs) from which all military operations in the division flow.

8 The Five LOOs, OASIS, and the Lanza Doctrine

"You [military professionals] must know something about strategy and tactics and logistics, but also economics and politics and diplomacy and history. You must know everything you can know about military power, and you must also understand the limits of military power. You must understand that few of the important problems of our time have, in the final analysis, been finally solved by military power alone." John F. Kennedy

As we arrived in Al Rashid, we were not exactly sure how to conduct business most effectively. We had ideas and theories, but as most military leaders learn early, the most carefully-drawn plan rarely survives the first shots of battle. We knew that our method had to be smart, non-standard, and that we were committed to the Full Spectrum Operations model as a foundation in our fight. Full spectrum refers to the various places along a continuum where operations must be conducted to affect the battle space. Commanders who accomplish specified missions by combining and sequencing offensive, defensive stability, and support operations to a defined purpose conduct this type of fighting. [6]

What was new and materially different about how we fought the insurgency in Vietnam compared with the way we are fighting the insurgency in Iraq is our method and commitment to operating on multiple levels. In Iraq we embrace "Full Spectrum Operations" as a doctrinal method to fighting. In the Vietnam era, this doctrine did not exist. I suspect some younger officers and Special Forces leaders were operating in this methodology but it was not until years later that a doctrine was codified.

To operate on multiple levels effectively, leaders and soldiers had to intellectually understand what Full Spectrum

Operations entails. Then they had to implement in a committed fashion the tactics, techniques, and procedures that support that method. Soldiers and leaders in the 5th BCT were, for the most part, able to do that.

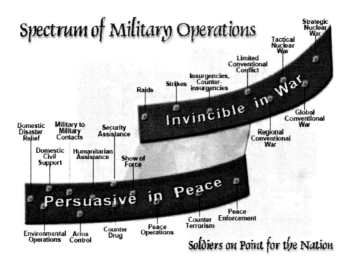

Figure 8.0 Spectrum of Military Operations

The First Cavalry Division and all of its subordinate units operated from a single unifying operations concept known as the Five Lines of Operation (LOO). The Five LOOs were:

• Combat Operations

• Train and Employ Iraqi Security Forces

• Essential Services

• Promote Governance

• Economic Pluralism[7]

The list did not represent a top-down priority list. Rather, the master of the Five LOO construct would work these five areas simultaneously striving to have each line of operation complement the others as flawlessly as possible. The Division termed the Five LOO campaign plan "Oasis."

Colonel Lanza seized upon the Division campaign plan immediately when we arrived in Al Rashid and then took the ideas, concepts, and policy codified in the plan to the level of implementation. What was an esoteric and tentative conceptualization Colonel Lanza shaped, molded, defined, and refined. He designed staff systems and processes to support the implementation of "Oasis" in the BCT. He developed sound tactics, techniques, and procedures supporting the lines of operation. Expertly Colonel Lanza linked metrics to the Five LOOs to attempt to objectively assess effectiveness. He issued insightful guidance to subordinates and literally breathed life into "Oasis."

Charting the Five LOOs — Programming Task Force 1-21

From the 5th BCT Five LOOs the Task Force then programmed them for application within Area of Operations Rocket.

Early on, the Division seemed to struggle with what direction it wanted to go. The Division leadership and staff seemed hesitant about how to truly put "meat on the bones" of the campaign plan. I believed the campaign plan was considered very arcane and senior leaders in the Division lacked any clear understanding at the tactical level of how to implement the plan with vigor and confidence any place within the Division zone.

My personal assessment from observations and through attendance at numerous briefings in April 2004 was that the four ground maneuver BCT commanders were mostly reactive in their actions and decision-making. This was normal as the Division assimilated the fight in Baghdad. All leaders, from the Division Commander down the chain of command to patrol leaders, had to learn through experience. To effectively implement a strategy or campaign plan for fighting and winning in any particular BCT sector required experience. Only then could leaders work with the realistic expectation of seizing the initiative, an essential ingredient to fighting and winning. "Oasis" provided leaders at all echelons a basis and guide to follow.

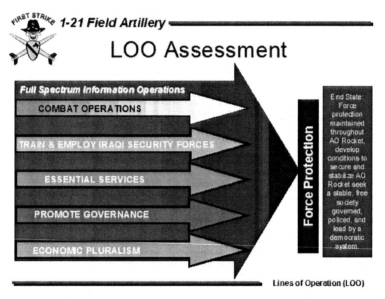

Figure 8.1 — The Five LOOs were enrobed/enhanced/empowered by Full Spectrum Information Operations Army doctrine.

Each BCT had to internalize "Oasis" and then shape the nuances of the Division campaign plan to fit the realities of their particular sectors because each was remarkably different. Just as Brooklyn is different from Manhattan, so too is Sadr City different from Al Rashid. Within days of arrival in Baghdad, Colonel Lanza was attuned to this. He very deftly pursued actions to shape "Oasis" for Al Rashid. I believe Division senior leaders saw his exuberance and effort, and then followed his lead to find the way ahead. The Divisional leadership seemed to pounce on what Colonel Lanza was doing to learn more and then further define "Oasis" in real terms for the overarching Division campaign effort. Colonel Lanza shined the beacon light to illuminate the path.

Colonel Lanza was undaunted by the magnitude and complexities facing the BCT when we arrived. He knew intuitively what needed attention. With his mastery of Army systems, his personal confidence and willful manner, Colonel Lanza determinedly marched off into the ambiguity of "Oasis" and the shadowy intricacies of Al Rashid, defining "Oasis" for 5th BCT. By doing so he also fashioned the way for the Division. Though he will never be officially credited for such clairvoyance his leadership role was clearly obvious to me, a subordinate commander observing the action.

Colonel Lanza's ability to so readily define "Oasis" also served another very important leadership function. By deliberately and clearly articulating how "Oasis" worked for the 5th BCT, Colonel Lanza directly helped his battalion task force commanders who had very limited combat leadership experience at this early juncture.

Combat leadership experience mattered in Iraq. Among the BCT Command Group, there was precious little. Lieutenant Colonel Bill Salter, Commander of 1-7 Cavalry was the only senior officer among us battalion commanders who had any ground combat experience. His experience came from Desert Storm when he was a captain. Colonel Lanza had no previous combat experience though he served a tour of duty in Bosnia years earlier. This was a ground maneuver fight — an insurgency — and at the BCT level. I had no combat experience. Worse, I was a Field Artillery-trained officer. I was not an experienced or trained maneuver commander from the Infantry or Armor branch. I had not personally maneuvered more than a company of infantry in my professional experience and nothing in ground combat. Fortunately, in this insurgent fight, experience maneuvering a battalion-sized force wouldn't matter much. Except on few occasions, a patrol was the largest maneuver formation I would have to manage and I was eminently qualified for and felt extremely competent doing that.

The lack of combat experience among the BCT senior leaders meant that a well-defined, tightly-controlled program could have positive effects. Having a clearly-defined and well-articulated framework from which to work was extremely helpful. As a BCT leader, group, and staff, we were quickly able to talk in a common language with understanding. Having this capability was essential to our success. Finally, this allowed us the opportunity to seize the initiative quickly. We could easily pick up on what was left for us to build upon in our sector of Baghdad.

What Colonel Lanza seized upon and pushed for the BCT was, in essence, a counterinsurgent fighting doctrine. This permeated the entire BCT and shaped our fight. It was exactly what we needed.

The "Lanza" Doctrine

Shaping a campaign plan was a process that occurred over time and, as we fought the enemy, the details and adjustments fit into the overarching "Oasis" campaign plan. Campaigns are operational level warfare and not necessarily tactical. But I think that because operational areas in Iraq differ vastly from rural regions to urban enclaves, units at BCT level actually operate in a campaign methodology. The people and their culture make it necessary to do so.

In my mind, campaigns and campaign planning are not limited by echelon but rather by unit scope and influence. Our modern Army gives large tasks and large areas of responsibility to battalion-sized task forces. This is the norm in Iraq, not the exception. Additionally, different parts of Baghdad necessarily require different approaches to fighting. The methods used to command, influence, and fight in sector as demographics, geography, and a host of other variables influence areas differently are unique in time and space. Commanders must know the subtleties: what might work in Sadr City will absolutely not work just a few city blocks away in Al Rashid. To be successful, a Divisional campaign plan designed to fight an insurgency in this contemporary environment must account for this nuance. Even more complex is that even within a district of Baghdad the sectors can be vastly different. Again, demographics, economics, wealth, and education of the residents all play a role in how a military organization approaches the "fight" in this urban, insurgent war.

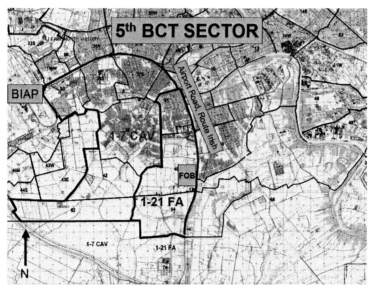

Figure 8.2 — The sector covered over 250 square kilometers.

In Al Rashid there are many mahallas. As the BCT carved up and defined the battle space, we followed the established sector lines set by First Armor Division. Colonel Lanza's direct overlay method of assimilation of the existing sector fit well and would, from that point, allow us to adjust as necessary based on what he learned or discovered over time and through engagement. This is how the BCT area was laid out and the units assigned to cover the battle space.

Any approach to counter-insurgency must have a long-term vision and a framework in which to operate. There was no such thing as a formal Army-sanctioned "Lanza Doctrine." This is a designation I alone made. I used this designation as a framework to promote common understanding and to help see the way ahead, and shaping how I would fight the Task Force. My appreciation of Colonel Lanza's game plan can be boiled into this "doctrine."

• Fight full spectrum every day.

• Work across the Five LOOs.

• Educate, down to soldier level, how to treat Iraqis and that what we are trying to do as a BCT is to influence positive change in our sector.

• Discipline in all we do from uniform, to behavior, to combat, is critical.

• Force protection is always our number one consideration.

• Leverage "powerbrokers" to advantage the BCT.

•D3A [Decide, Detect, Deliver and Assess] is our targeting process and we execute lethal and non-lethal targeting. Master the processes.

• Intelligence gathering and integration to operations lethal and non-lethal must be constantly developed and refined.

• The Five LOOs must complement your efforts, always.

• Leaders must act in direct engagement with operations and local nationals.

• Use the conventional forces allocated to the BCT from the Division and modify them organizationally and materially in whatever manner determined worked, fighting unconventionally if we expected to win.

The Division Campaign Plan concluded that the enemy center of gravity was "the popular support of the Iraqi populace." In order to successfully win the popular support of the Iraqi populace any conventional approach to fighting necessarily had to be scrapped. And by conventional approach I refer to the set-piece, fire and maneuver, kill the enemy in continual, open combat methodology. This method would never work in this kind of war. We had to be prepared to fight toe-to-toe when necessary and in fact, the BCTs of the Division had to execute these fights and fight close quarters, urban combat in places like Fallujah and Sadr City as well as other lesser-known enclaves of Baghdad. This was, however, not the norm. No senior leader in First Cavalry Division went to Iraq with the notion that we would fight entirely conventionally.

Flexibility mandated by the "Lanza Doctrine" was achieved and manifested by moving units, individuals, and/or equipment as directed for a given situation. I viewed this flexibility as an integral means to be successful in fighting the insurgency. My unit was asked multiple times to provide troops to other task forces in the BCT. I gave them up willingly and without fuss when the analysis supported the demand. This was not reciprocated well by my peers from 1-7 Cavalry and 1-8 Cavalry. In fact, there was a clear intransigence on their part to give anything to the greater good of the BCT. That this was tolerated and persisted throughout the operation in Al Rashid was the source of great personal and professional disappointment for me. My peers in the other maneuver task forces had more territory to cover and, thus, concluded they could not "surrender" a single asset. It was an unhealthy attitude. Worse, it demonstrated a lack of care for the greater need and broader situation, which I found troubling behavior from fellow professionals. That the BCT Commander tolerated this was further disheartening to me.

Parochial leadership in today's Army and in this kind of fight guarantees failure. Broad, deep thinking and decision-making, which affect long-term goals, have more utility in counterinsurgency. Leader training at the National Training Center, Joint Readiness Training Center, and Combined Maneuver Training Center up to this point taught short-term decision-making for conventional fights. In that model, company team and battalion task force commanders learn quickly that every asset relinquished proportionately reduces combat power in the simple math of the force-ratio battle calculus. BCT force-on-force at the Maneuver Training Centers was completely conventional. My peers and I grew up on that model of training and leadership decision-making. In my judgment, my peers failed to make the proper adjustment to a new way of perceiving and executing decision-making in the counterinsurgency fight in Iraq. This way of thinking was ingrained in them from their experiences as Observer Controllers at the National Training Center. They too frequently problem-solved tactics on that model which was completely obsolete for this fight. I think this more than anything else led to a mindset that actually adversely impacted the BCT while we were operating in Iraq.

Colonel Lanza reoriented himself fairly quickly and preached that leaders had to think first and act flexibly to accomplish the objectives we sought. We had to be able to "walk softly and carry a big stick", and then very judiciously apply the tools we had at our disposal.

For my leaders and me, we were intellectually in synch with Colonel Lanza from the outset. The Herculean effort we had gone through to just transform, train, and get to Iraq, coupled with my organizational vision, fit like a glove to counterinsurgency. My subordinate leaders were already attuned and in the mindset to operate in a constantly-morphing and evolving manner. We would have to refine our education and adopt new tactics nested in the ideas and doctrine espoused and encouraged by Colonel Lanza. I was committed in every way to meeting the tenets of his "doctrine" because I firmly believed in the better part of his ideology.

The ideology the BCT embraced and the execution of the "Lanza Doctrine" were sometimes pre-empted by our struggles to deal with the Iraqi people. We were in Iraq by orders of our government to help the people realize a better way of life. It is supremely difficult to explain that how we were operating in the battalion task forces needed to be tethered to a strategic political task and purpose every day.

As a Task Force Commander it was vitally important to know and communicate to soldiers why we were fighting. Always, we had to know what our task and purpose was. The task and purpose for the Army in Operation Iraqi Freedom I was to attack to destroy the regime of Saddam Hussein. The invasion was predicated on finding weapons of mass destruction, primarily in the form of chemical weapons. None were found. By Operation Iraqi Freedom II, we were still in Iraq, and now we did not have the mission to topple the government or even find weapons of mass destruction. So, what were we ordered to do? We were ordered to secure and stabilize the area in order to allow a democratic process to take root in Iraq.

This mandate demanded a significant paradigm shift in thinking and functioning day-to-day for Iraqis. Their lives to this point were not democratic and free. The masses of Iraqi citizens did not think democratically. As a people, they did not have a viable understanding of a democratic lifestyle. Expecting the American Army to somehow inject that into the social fabric of Iraq without resources to do so was supremely challenging. Worse, the politics of the Iraqis were incredibly convoluted and difficult to understand and dissect.

Delving into the politics was critical to mission accomplishment. From having no resources or earnest senior leadership commitment to confronting the political nuances of the Task Force sector (meaning a major focus on local government), I knew I had to unweave the tangled web of Al Saidiyah politics. This, more than anything, would define and characterize success or failure for our tour of duty.

The Task Force Program

Having a grasp of the politics, the terrain, and a well-developed understanding of the intelligence gathering requirements the Task Force would have to develop, I had to refine our plan of action to fit the reality of our situation. After the Relief in Place/Transfer of Authority (RIP/TOA), the staff and I were through with our initial assessments. Time was of the essence to provide the subordinate leaders and soldiers of the Task Force with an overarching method to realize our unit goals. Following the lead of Colonel Lanza, I moved quickly to disseminate my plan and vision.

This was doctrinally how I articulated my intent:

Purpose: *Provide a secure and stable environment in the greater Al Saidiyah district (41S, 40 and 64W) of Al Rashid to enable the re-establishment of critical infrastructure, the development of economic progress, and the transition to a legitimate national government.*

Key Tasks:
–Protect the force and maintain a secure environment.
–Maintain an offensive attitude and conduct combat operations when required.
–Secure ROUTE IRISH (Highway 8) from Check Points 6–10.
–Conduct aggressive intelligence-based patrolling; emphasize dismounted operations.
–Control land, people, and resources in sector to achieve positional advantage.
–Support training of Iraqi police and security forces.
–Establish, guide, and advise the Al Saidiyah Neighborhood Advisory Council.
–Sustain/improve essential services of power, waste management, health care, roads, water and education.
–Conduct decisive Information Operations promoting Iraqi success, supporting a legitimate government, and establishing economic and religious freedom.
–Enforce cultural awareness and treat all Iraqi citizens with dignity and respect.
–Maintain the force, focus on upholding discipline and standards.

Endstate: *Districts 41S, 40, and 64W are secure and stable. Security requirements and key civic functions are transferred to civil authorities; the Neighborhood Advisory Council and elected officials are empowered.*

Risk: *Majority of forces will be focused in the populated areas of the northern portion of the Area of Operations.*

Providing this intent was one step in a process to articulate and put into practical operation a Task Force program to stabilize and secure our assigned sector. Everything we did was connected and made complementary. If it was not, we did not execute. Working with my concept plan over time, I looked for when and where to apply adjustments. Many variables potentially influenced the situation. One of the major variables I would have to master was the politics of Al Saidiyah. The politics of the Iraqis in Al Saidiyah were complex, fraught with danger, and a critical element I had to understand to have any hope of winning.

Part Two

9 The Politics of Al Saidiyah

"The political object is the goal, war is the means of reaching it, and the means can never be considered in isolation from their purposes." Karl von Clausewitz

The subtleties and politics of leading a counterinsurgency fight in Iraq was what made this war and leadership in this war so dramatically different from anything I had done or trained to do as an Army leader to that point. The fight to win the popular support of the Iraqi people was the critical fight. To win that fight was mostly a political and intellectual exercise.

Fighting was worse in the parts of Baghdad where the ability of the American commanders to out-think, to intellectually overwhelm their adversary, and to control the political nuances to their favor were poorest. For those leaders who preferred to bash their way through their sector, the fight was there to have but winning the popular support of the Iraqi people could never occur.

I quickly became enamored with the politics and mental sparring I would engage in throughout the sector Task Force 1-21 was assigned. Using primarily civil affairs, psychological activities, and the precisely measured use of force to secure and stabilize my sector was the formula for success. Of the many entities influencing the sector day to day, two had more prominence than all others: the Neighborhood Advisory Council and the imams of Al Saidiyah. The former I could see plainly and quickly, the latter was discovery learning plain and simple.

My guiding principle for dealing in the murky politics of Al Saidiyah and in working with Iraqis was provided by Lawrence of Arabia, who had great success with Arabs decades before I arrived in Iraq. Lawrence of Arabia (a.k.a. T.E. Lawrence, the British legend) had much to say about Western leadership of Arab people. He fought in this region, had a very enlightened view of Arab culture, and achieved some degree of success. Lawrence advised:

Do not try to do too much with your hands. Better the Arabs do it tolerably that you do it perfectly. It is their war, and you are here to help them, not win it for them. Actually, also, under the very odd conditions of Arabia. Your practical work will not be as good as, perhaps, you think it is. It may take them longer and it may not be as good as you think, but if it is theirs, it will be better.[8]

I made my whole staff master the message here so when they spoke to me about what we were going to do, they had to speak with this understanding. When we implemented method, process, and procedure, our actions were consistent with this message from history. I gave great personal attention to master the philosophy described by Lawrence. And I worked doggedly to ensure that my personal efforts, negotiations, and behaviors remained consistent with it.

The other writing I grounded myself with as I approached all my experience in Iraq was the thinking behind the poem "If" that Rudyard Kipling gave the world. I discovered this poem when I was about twelve years old in junior high school and it set my world on fire. I've carried it on me ever since. More than anything else, I committed myself and based my leader style on the ideas the poem expressed. This denotes what I believe a leader must be:

IF

If you can keep your head when all about you
Are losing theirs and blaming it on you;
If you can trust yourself when all men doubt you,
But make allowance for their doubting too;

If you can wait and not be tired by waiting,
Or, being lied about, don't deal in lies,
Or, being hated, don't give way to hating,
And yet don't look too good, nor talk too wise;

If you can dream — and not make dreams your master;
If you can think — and not make thoughts your aim;
If you can meet with triumph and disaster
And treat those two imposters just the same;
If you can bear to hear the truth you've spoken
Twisted by knaves to make a trap for fools,
Or watch the things you gave your life to broken,
And stoop and build 'em up with worn-out tools;

If you can make one heap of all your winnings
And risk it on one turn of pitch-and-toss,
And lose, and start again at your beginnings
And never breathe a word about your loss;
If you can force your heart and nerve and sinew
To serve your turn long after they are gone,
And so hold on when there is nothing in you
Except the Will which says to them: "Hold on";

If you can talk with crowds and keep your virtue,
Or walk with kings — nor lose the common touch;
If neither foes nor loving friends can hurt you;
If all men count with you, but none too much;
If you can fill the unforgiving minute
With sixty seconds' worth of distance run
Yours is the Earth and everything that's in it,
And — which is more — you'll be a Man, my son! [9]

I was reminded of the ideas and concepts embodied in this poem repeatedly as I dealt with the politics of Al Saidiyah. Never was anything as it seemed on initial review. Always, when things were said, what I had to do was pay attention more to that which was not spoken, for therein resided all the truth of what was really happening in Al Saidiyah.

When the Task Force first assumed control of Al Saidiyah, I had to deal with a local pseudo-governing body known as the Neighborhood Advisory Council. To chart a course for the Task Force to attempt to better secure the area, I had to assess this organization and begin to work with the council within my first two weeks in Iraq.

The Neighborhood Advisory Council

Line of Operation 4 was "Promote Governance." Curiously, as I began to assess this aspect of the sector, it quickly became obvious to me no governance of any kind existed in Al Saidiyah. That was not just a passing problem. No local governance was the most significant problem of this whole effort in Iraq. No one was in charge and every Iraqi was looking for someone to truly be in charge. That the Coalition authority (military or civilian) could not be the legitimate power and leadership in Iraq, was as obvious as the sun rising.

In the first days and weeks of the Task Force conducting operations in Al Saidiyah, overtures and gestures from Neighborhood Advisory Council members and local imposter-sheiks were made to press me, as American military, to be in charge. Literally, they wanted me to be the governance entity for Al Saidiyah. The Iraqis would say, "You tell us what to do." Or they would say something more sinister suggesting, "Colonel 'Booman' (as they called me), you kill those people and the problem will go away."

But I knew this would be a huge political mistake on my part. I could not assume any role to demonstrate I was the political leader of the area. Because such a pronounced void existed, regardless of my personal desire or will, the actual situation could get so distorted and uncontrollable that I could find myself as the de facto "Mayor of Al Saidiyah." And I truly did not want that. As I deliberated about the situation I was reminded of one of my favorite stories growing up, the wonderful tale by Rudyard Kipling entitled, "The Man Who Would Be King." As you may recall, the story opens with author Rudyard Kipling working in his study. His solitude is broken by the arrival of a tattered, half-mad derelict, who is soon revealed to be his old acquaintance Peachy Carnahan. As Kipling listens in rapt fascination, Peachy relates the incredible adventures of himself and his partner-in-chicanery, Daniel Dravot. Serving in the British Army in India, Carnahan and Dravot have masterminded all sorts of underhanded money-making schemes, the most elaborate of which takes them to a remote city in the hills of eastern Afghanistan. There, through methods both foul and fair, Daniel passes himself off as the incarnation of Alexander the Great, the better to lay his hands on the vast riches all around him. Unfortunately, Daniel begins to believe his own lies, and the results are disastrous for both himself and Peachy. Inadvertently exposing Daniel's scheme is his native would-be wife. When his betrothed bites his face on the morning of their arranged wedding and draws blood, Daniel is exposed as a fraud and eventually is killed by a mob incensed by his deception.[10]

Mindful of Daniel's ill-fated outcome, I could not presume to be that which I was not. No amount of ego should get in the way of good judgment. I could not fake being the political leader in Al Saidiyah. The people had to decide who would lead them. Most importantly, the leader had to have the legitimate endorsement of the people of Al Saidiyah. Anything else was folly and failure would ensue.

The Neighborhood Advisory Council was an organization originally formed by the Coalition Provisional Authority headed by Mr. L. Paul Bremmer III. The Coalition

Provisional Authority became defunct, replaced by the Interim Iraqi Government on June 28, 2004. The Interim Iraqi
Government ruled until the first elected Iraqi Assembly
convened to define a constitutional national government.
These neighborhood advisory councils existed in all the
major enclaves if Baghdad. Neighborhood advisory councils were the lowest level of any kind of Iraqi committee.
Ostensibly put in place with the charter, and defined by the
Coalition Provisional Authority, to "provide for an initial
democratic, representative system of government in Baghdad. These councils were to serve a key role in developing
the experience and institutions upon which a democratic
Iraqi government could be based."[11] This was a distant concept for a people in a nation that had neither democratic
processes nor a working knowledge of democracy at any
level of government.

The Baghdad City Advisory Council was the highest council in the advisory council hierarchical structure. Below
the Baghdad City Advisory Council were the district advisory councils and below these were the neighborhood
advisory councils. The Baghdad City Advisory Council issued a handbook that was published by the Coalition Provisional Authority. This handbook provided detailed rules
and guidance for operation and conduct of meetings for
all the advisory councils down to Neighborhood Advisory
Council level.

After spending time with Iraqis, and then reading this
handbook, it was evident that the handbook was completely Western in design and rules. Therefore it had almost no chance of working. The Iraqis do not do business
like Americans or any other Westerners.

The neighborhood advisory councils represented a governance entity to the military leaders above me, to the Coalition Provision Authority administrators, and then later to

the political leaders at the American embassy. It was not clear to me, or any of my superiors for that matter, what other entity we could turn to for local governance. Nothing else existed. This was hugely troubling because in reality the mandate given these councils provided no means to govern anything. The neighborhood advisory councils had no budget, no election process, and no authority of any kind. Their provision was to provide "advice" to the American military. I saw this as a significant problem but was powerless to change that. Some accused me of overstating the problem and being too politically minded. I saw no way to legitimately meet the demands and efficacy of the fourth Line of Operation tenant "Promote Governance" with no governing entity to support, promote, or advise.

To frame this issue another way, by what means did the leaders and directors of the Coalition Provisional Authority expect that local governance worked in the many neighborhoods of Baghdad? What governing entity was tending to the business of the Iraqi people for their daily communal needs? The answer: there was none. I believe this is the diabolical, fundamental failure of the whole effort in Iraq. Anyone who can resolve this will make a gigantic leap forward in realizing the strategic goal of democracy in Iraq.

The notion that the American Army would get the electrical power operating, trash collected, roads repaired, traffic lights functioning and do all the thousand other things a local City Council does was preposterous. Worse, it was dangerous because this meant the American Army was the new government. But the American Army could not fill the void. At every turn we were told to facilitate these functions but do so in the background. "Put an Iraqi face on the actions," we were ordered. But there was no legitimate "Iraqi face" to place upon any of the reforms. That is to say, there was no local governing agency to place out front to take the lead and legitimately accept credit at the local level. Constantly, we struggled with making the Al Saidiyah Neighborhood Advisory Council look and act like a city council; yet they possessed no substantial power to affect anything. Almost everything the Council did was based on our direction.

Given this basic understanding, the Al Saidiyah Neighborhood Advisory Council was the entity in place when the First Cavalry Division arrived in March 2004. For Task Force 1-21, we inherited what the commander of 1-94 Field Artillery had established. His method of dealing with the Al Saidiyah Neighborhood Advisory Council was by way of a battery commander (Army captain) liaison. In the beginning I chose to follow this course, as I knew no better. The battalion staff and battalion commander of 1-94 Field Artillery were pretty much hands-off with this whole aspect of the fight in their sector. I would quickly discover that this was not a viable approach. While a liaison was an option, most battery commanders lacked the experience and professional maturity to deal with the myriad of complexities and politics required to direct and mentor this council. I was not certain that as a Lieutenant Colonel with seventeen years of service I had the right dose of either quality to do this, either.

A few weeks into my sector assessment and fighting in Baghdad, I figured out just how important the Neighborhood Advisory Council was to the stability and security of Al Saidiyah. The Al Saidiyah enclave of Baghdad was described by some as the Beverly Hills of Baghdad. Within the neighborhoods, or mahallas, lived many high-ranking former military officers, higher officials of the Ba'ath Party, and many of Saddam's strongest and most loyal mid-and-upper-level Sunni governmental officials. Those still residing in the mahallas of Al Saidiyah were either overlooked in Saddam's purges or missed in the American invasion that swept through Baghdad in Operation Iraqi Freedom I when Saddam was toppled. By no means had all the bad guys been removed, and they knew well how to hide.

Al Saidiyah was home to some strongly-entrenched Sunni Muslims. Because many were wealthy under Saddam, and educated and competent at government administration, these were not your average Iraqi citizens who had some issues with Americans on a rudimentary level. These were sophisticated people, essentially disenfranchised now, capable of planning or directing insurgent activity on a broad scale. Once I learned this and began to meet those who sat on the council it struck me as very odd that the Neighborhood Advisory Council members were not representative of the demographics of Al Saidiyah. This foreshadowed trouble that lay ahead.

The formation of this so-called advisory council, improperly constituted and not representative, was advising exactly what and to whom? This question came to mind almost immediately. The constitution of the Neighborhood Advisory Council defied basic common sense when taking the simple measure of its stated purpose. This necessarily led to many more questions.

How did these people get selected? Who were they? Why did they want to be on the council? What could I leverage from these people? What did they want out of the deal? No one seemed to be able to definitively answer these fundamental questions.

I quickly realized the mess we had on our hands. Exacerbating the problem was that Colonel Lanza was headlong into shaping conditions in the BCT area and wanted to know how we were connecting with "powerbrokers" in our respective sectors intent on developing projects and programs to improve the situation in the mahallas.

The whole notion of "powerbrokers" was frustrating to me as well. If I knew nothing before my experience in Iraq, I did know one fundamental truth about the exercise of power in war and in criminal activity, and that is, those who truly "pull the strings," do it from behind the curtain because exposure means vulnerability. Power lies in clandestine operations. I saw this dynamic clearly in operation in Al Saidiyah and I found it laughable that I was being told to "talk to the community powerbrokers" to stabilize my sector. As one interpreter warned, "If an Iraqi comes to you and introduces himself as a sheik, he is not a sheik he is a fake-sheik."

In 2004 real sheiks did not want to be openly identified to the Americans. They could be found but it required work. Colonel Lanza pressed very hard for us to work with these neighborhood advisory councils to start building momentum to secure and stabilize the area. This was part of our mission.

What I saw in the Neighborhood Advisory Council was the potential of establishing local governance. The council represented a possibility to implement a system of developing a democratic local government for the people in the township of Al Saidiyah. What all the neighborhoods of Baghdad lacked was a City Council entity to do the business of a city government. Trash pick-up, road repair, school maintenance, sports and recreation management, policing, sewer repair, traffic control, all the myriad of tasks that require city management and oversight do not exist in Baghdad through a local governance entity or any other entity. It was my vision to create this capability through the Al Saidiyah Neighborhood Advisory Council. I knew that the charter for the Neighborhood Advisory Council clearly was not to be a city council as we understand them in America. But this is what needed to be implemented to immediately impact the civil affairs of the many enclaves and districts of

Baghdad immediately following Operation Iraqi Freedom
I. Implementing this approach would have allowed huge
strides toward averting the existing insurgency in Iraq.

Immediately following Operation Iraqi Freedom I strategically, the decision was made by the Bush Administration
leadership to pursue the formation of a national government and at some point get to the business of local governance. In my estimation from personal experience that was
exactly backwards from what the Iraqi people needed. The
Iraqis had no capability resident at the local level to manage communal affairs and this was desperately needed.

By what cognitive, deliberate process did the senior leaders
in the Bush Administration conclude a top-down implementation of democracy in Iraq will work? Here, on the
streets dealing daily with Iraqis, it was intuitively obvious
to me what had to be done. The directors of the American effort in Iraq erroneously concluded that placement of
a national-level democracy took precedence over the development of a local democratic process. But this defies all
we know throughout world history about the formation of
democracies. The very example of the U.S. evolution to a
democracy holds the keys to success in Iraq. Democracies
that have succeeded and thrived have always started at
the local level and grew into national, democratic systems.
This works because democracy has a foundation and efficacy when the citizens understand how it operates practically and not just esoterically. And Iraqis could handle local democratic governance. I saw this with my own eyes.

If local governance prevailed and accomplished the necessary improvements in the neighborhoods of Baghdad, the
greatest argument of the insurgency is thwarted. The insurgency fights with the intent to demonstrate the existing
government cannot help the average Iraqi realize a better
quality of life. Effective local governance, democratically

functioning politically, destroys an insurgency. Every day I served in Iraq, I burned passionately for the desire to implement local governance across all of Baghdad. I was certain this was the road to victory.

But I was limited to proving this in my little corner of Baghdad against the grain of the disparate American military program and unclear political designs. My goal was to transform a major Sunni area of Baghdad, bringing it democracy and local-governance thinking that could grow into something meaningful. This I hoped would be Task Force 1-21's successful contribution to the bigger fight in Iraq. I pursued this goal with all I could muster, staking out the Neighborhood Advisory Council as the centerpiece for the Task Force to win against the insurgency in our assigned sector.

To press my efforts and learn all I could to figure out how to legitimately achieve my vision for an Al Saidiyah City Council with means and real political power, I had to master and truly understand the Iraqi culture. I had to respect their ways and traditions. In my mind, two critical things allow people to learn another's culture. The most profound is to learn the language and speak it conversantly. Unfortunately, I was not getting there from here. The next best thing I believe is to form deep and truly friendly relationships. This, I felt I could do and intended to pursue.

In May 2004, Colonel Lanza introduced me to Dr. Ali-Olbeidi. He was a smooth talking, American-educated (Ph.D. from Oklahoma State University) Iraqi who had returned from twenty years of self-imposed exile in the United States to help his country after Saddam's overthrow. He spoke idealistically about Iraq's future and confided he had ambitions to make Iraq the "Middle Eastern America." He was a staunch Democrat in America — claiming to have worked for Rep. Richard "Dick" Gephardt of Missouri — and had visions of attaining some political stature in the new Iraq.

Dr. Ali had two sons, Said and Saif, who also returned to Iraq from their comfortable lives in the United States. The sons were Dr. Ali's business partners and trusted body-guards. Both were in their early twenties, spoke colloquial English, and were fluent in Arabic. They were an odd but interesting trio. We joked in the Task Force that we had the next Saddam Hussein and his two sons Uday and Qusay in the personage of these three.

Dr. Ali and his sons in truth were pretty good guys. Certainly they had a personal agenda and it was not too hard to discern. But they also served a highly-functional purpose to me. They understood Americans and Iraqis and helped me see things I would have taken much longer to learn on my own. The Ali's were mostly honest with me. I never caught them lying or stealing but they didn't always deliver on their promised efforts either.

Dr. Ali's primary motivation was to earn money and seek political opportunity. As a contractor, he sought to win our favor and, thus, our money. He spoke eloquently about the many things the people in Iraq needed and he provided me with great insights about how Iraqis think and what their lives had been like under Saddam's rule. In the time of our association, the Ali's executed a few good projects. I kept Dr. Ali close to help me understand the environment and Iraqis. Curiously, Colonel Lanza who introduced us and instructed me to work with Dr. Ali., pressed me to cut ties with him a month later, advising that Dr. Ali was a scoundrel. Apparently, his two sons went to a scrap metal junkyard in the southern half of Task Force 1-21's sector and attempted to broker deals selling the metal in the junkyard and personally profiting from these sales. Colonel Lanza thought that was dishonest and subversive, which was true enough on the surface. However, this was very normal and typical behavior for Iraqis. Though objectionable by American standards, it was expected in Iraqi culture. He was right that Dr. Ali and his sons behaved as scoundrels in this instance, by our standards. But they were the "scoundrels" I knew and Dr. Ali's functional purpose allowed me to appreciate the Iraqis and understand the culture. Exploiting that was of inestimable value to me. No one on the BCT staff ever proved the accusations of corruption.

My entire tour I withstood ridicule and some odd accusations of special favors and collusion with this man and his sons from the BCT staff. I chose to ignore the pettiness and press my relationship with Dr. Ali as I was very certain I could handle him and make the most utilizing the cultural bridge he provided. Having an American-educated man with broad American culture experience as well as experience with his own people was an asset to nurture, use to my advantage, and develop inroads to understanding the Iraqis. In short, Dr. Ali facilitated my ability to communicate with Iraqis. There were risks but the risks were minimal and completely manageable. Most on the BCT staff never really understood this beyond a rudimentary level. They never understood that a huge part of this fight was about relationships and the key to success was in developing those relationships to our advantage. They understood this academically but not pragmatically. I surmised staff officers could afford to be cavalier, they weren't responsible for much. Colonel Lanza absolutely understood this dynamic but he communicated that he did not always trust I could manage it. I understood this intimately and considered building relationships as a process integral to the overall scheme of maneuver in this war.

One of the things Dr. Ali repeatedly told me was that I had the wrong people on the Neighborhood Advisory Council. I frustrated him because as we sought to execute civil affairs projects, I would insist the Neighborhood Advisory Council be involved. I knew that if I circumvented the Neighborhood Advisory Council in the projects determination process, I would never have their confidence and, in the end, the Neighborhood Advisory Council would serve absolutely no purpose from which to build upon.

This requirement and insistence on my part ultimately drove Dr. Ali away. He could not reason with the people on the Neighborhood Advisory Council and so he decided to cut his losses and disassociate with the Neighborhood Advisory Council of Al Saidiyah and me. In October 2004, he left Iraq again and headed to the United States. I did not hear from him again until after I returned from the war.

He was absolutely right. I did not have the right people on the Neighborhood Advisory Council. Nor did I have the right endorsement and association consistent with the culture and customs of the Iraqis. If ever the Neighborhood Advisory Council would become effective, self-sufficient, and politically viable, business methods on the Neighborhood Advisory Council would have to change. My goal was to form a council to benefit the people of Al Saidiyah; the representation and political process by which the Neighborhood Advisory Council operated had to change to meet the people's needs. The Neighborhood Advisory Council also had to function democratically consistent with the strategic goals of the United States government.

What was missing, in the grand scheme of the political situation in Al Saidiyah, was legitimacy to the democratic and local governance process. Colonel Lanza's insistence that we adhere to LOO 4 "Promote Governance," through the neighborhood advisory councils neither helped the situation nor made it the right choice. The simple fact of fighting in Iraq for our time was that for civil affairs efforts to take root and have a chance to work in a substantial and long-term sense required local governance. That simply did not exist in the form of the Neighborhood Advisory Council. Given that void, there was no legitimate chance for success. This point I tried to make clear to all who would listen. But no one on the BCT staff would listen. All were married to the administration of the "Oasis" Campaign Plan and providing briefings that sounded slick but had no substance or true chance of long-term success. I sensed that Colonel Lanza understood this too but he had no answer for the void and so sought to do the best that he thought could be done.

Unfortunately, the policies and procedures espoused by the Division and all higher echelons up to Multi-National Forces, Iraq, would not nurture this or acknowledge this shortcoming. I could see the desperate need plain as day. I knew if I could get a strong, capable, and representative town council operating, I could so directly and profoundly disrupt the insurgent effort that we would win hands down in Al Saidiyah.

When the police protect and serve, the lights come on, the trash gets picked up, the toilets flush, the water flows cleanly, and the streets are repaired, Iraqis in mass numbers would then see the fruits of democracy. Local governance had the best chance to develop this capability throughout Baghdad. And these things disperse the power of the insurgency.

Despite my knowledge of the weaknesses of the Al Saidiyah Neighborhood Advisory Council, I pressed forward with a plan and hope. The two fundamental things I needed to make the Neighborhood Advisory Council viable were a budget and a local election to seat the right members, i.e., those who would promote the infrastructure of the mahallas in which the council was seated. The Task Force needed to find a way to create money for a budget the Neighborhood

Advisory Council could use on the community. The Task Force also needed to conduct a local election. Having a local election to select viable, representative council members would have set off a fire for democracy the likes of which the people of Iraq would not be able to resist. The Task Force leadership surmised that if within 90 days of achieving those two things, the council began to meet the needs of the people in the township, the fight would, as a practical matter, be won.

One of the principal dynamics the political process lacked in my corner of Baghdad was legitimacy and endorsement. Because the Sunni ran Iraq before the invasion and after the invasion it was wholly unclear who was in charge, any political activity necessarily lacked the popular backing of the people who lived in the townships of Baghdad. This I discovered through personal observation in our attempts to work to build projects in the town as well as through our daily interactions with people who lived in Al Saidiyah. Iraqis wanted to tell me their problems and discuss the politics of their lives. They were generally eager to explain to me how American policy was flawed emphasizing the belief that it propped the Jews and oppressed the Arabs. There was no subtlety in the Arab expression of hatred for Jews. I often was privy to articulation of the opinion that America was fixated on preserving Israel and helping the Jews at the expense of the Arabs, including the Iraqis. This predilection coupled with the perception of an occupation force made distrust more acerbic. For the Iraqis, distrust was palpable, always.

I focused on figuring a way to develop legitimacy and thus popular support among the people in Al Saidiyah. If I could find the key to democracy, preserve local custom, insure the culture norms of the people remained in tact, and implemented T. E. Lawrence's advice of placing the means in the hands of the Iraqis, while the Task Force simultaneously progressed in community improvements, then the war in my piece of Baghdad could be won. But this would be no small trick.

I decided that in the coming weeks I would have to find a way to gain effective political influence in Al Saidiyah. By doing so, I could positively affect the Neighborhood Advisory Council and influence the course of events in Al Saidiyah. If I worked this correctly, we would also stabilize and secure the area, which was my ultimate objective. Over time, we might actually realize substantial progress in the development of the township's future, setting conditions that would allow the Iraqis to seize positive control over and start defining for themselves what tomorrow would look like. In these early weeks, I would have to be content just to start. The first step was figuring out where true political power resided. From there I would then work that entity hard and deliberately to accomplish my purpose.

Unbeknownst to me at this time in late spring 2004, the imams of Al Saidiyah were the political entity I needed to effectively influence the political situation in Al Saidiyah. When I stumbled into this discovery, I had my epiphany and made all efforts to exploit the imams to commit to the democratic future of Al Saidiyah.

Imams

My discovery-learning odyssey began with our tactical efforts in Al Saidiyah. We were having problems in mahalla 823 located in the central, eastern portion of Al Saidiyah. The Battery Commander in Task Force 1-21 who had tactical responsibility for mahalla 823 was Captain Matthew Chambers. Captain Chambers was Commander of C/2-82. An extraordinary young man, he was my most introspective and articulate battery commander. About 5'11", blond hair, blue eyes, and a strong, handsome guy and a graduate of the Army ROTC program at Saint Bonaventure University in New York, this officer was absolutely superb in so many ways. Except for his penchant to be late or sleep-in on occasion, he was otherwise physically fit, tough minded, always exercised good judgment, and unflappable in the most stressful, adverse circumstances. Captain Chambers easily grasped the nuances of the diplomatic efforts I pursued. I often consulted with him on ideas and initiatives about ongoing and planned future engagements because he was excellent at critical thinking and defining problems in unique ways. He helped me see what I might not have otherwise seen on my own. I respected his leadership style and leveraged every bit of his considerable abilities to benefit the Task Force.

His description of the tactical situation was this:

The tactical situation in April 2004 in mahalla 823, along Route Irish near its intersection with Route Senators, and in the central-eastern portion of Al Saidiyah, in general, there were no less than 30 enemy combat actions that occurred in the area over the past month. Approximately 19 of those combat incidents involved IED's. That was a sustained rate of one per day. The Shakir Al Abood mosque was located at the epicenter of that violence. Therefore, we assessed the possibility that the mosque and its imam were instigating those events and directing other enemy operations in the area. To complicate matters was the volatile and bloody situation precipitated by Moqtada Al Sadr and Mahdi's Army. Subsequently, there was no way to know precisely what faction was responsible for the attacks in mahalla 823. I surmised that either Sunni Ba'athists with assistance from Sheik Ali Al-Jabouri Hussein, Mahdi's Army, or both were responsible. As we conducted reconnaissance and surveillance, gathered information, and executed mosque message collection on and near the Shakir Al Abood mosque, we discovered overwhelming evidence that Sheik Ali at least condoned insurgent

*activity. (Mosque collection was an information-detection pro-
cess whereby we posted patrols to record or listen to a mosque
speech over the public address system with translators to assess
what was being broadcast.) Sheik Ali permitted anti-Coalition
propaganda to be posted on the walls of his mosque. His sermon
on April 23, 2004 was politically charged, linking American
and Israeli policy. In his mosque message Sheik Ali referred to
Americans as "Jews," and suggested that the recent killing of a
Haamas leader in Lebanon was the result of a joint U.S. − Israeli operation. He called for Sunnis and Shias to unite and resist those who would destroy Islam. These were the events that
pressed the Task Force Commander, Lieutenant Colonel Baumann to meet with Sheik Ali. Much was at stake.*

My objective in our first meeting was to let the imam know
who I was, what my intentions for Al Saidiyah were, and request that he give me a chance to demonstrate my honorable
and noble intentions. A major understanding from which I
operated in my dealings with the Iraqis in the Task Force
sector was to acknowledge and respect the fact that this
was their country. I had to demonstrate this not rhetorically
but in deeds, decisions, behaviors, and leadership. Though
I was sent here to secure and stabilize Al Saidiyah, my tenure was for a year. This is where the people of Al Saidiyah
lived and would spend their lives. I was a part of a new process. Potentially, we could help realize a new way of life. I
was not the change but an instrument of the change. In the
long run, success depended on their choices and convincing
them there was a better way. I wanted the imam of Shakr
Al Abood to know we were here to help. We didn't want to
fight and spill blood, his people or my soldiers'.

In this initial meeting, I would not ask anything of him nor
did I give him anything. This was a get-acquainted meeting, an opportunity for me to size him up in order to begin
a negotiation and a dialogue with him, if that was possible. I was prepared to take whatever time was necessary.

I would not be impatient. Patience and persistence were more powerful weapons than heavy guns and ammunition. My nation may have chosen a strategic course that subverted patience but I did not have to give in to that choice. This was the first meeting of what I fully believed and hoped would be many more.

Americans cannot go into a mosque. No imam would invite an American soldier into his mosque. This would be viewed by many Iraqis as traitorous. American military cannot go into a mosque of their own accord. An elaborate process of requests and purpose statements must be navigated for an American soldier to enter a mosque.

Captain Chambers arranged a meeting between the Imam of Shakir Al Abood, Sheik Ali Al-Jabouri Hussein, and me. Captain Chambers described his efforts:

The elaborate political choreography that accompanied our meeting with Sheik Ali was also made more challenging by the intricate process my unit had to navigate just to arrange a meeting with Sheik Ali Al-Jabouri. Preliminary face-to-face negotiations between subordinate intermediaries is always required. Kind of like "have your people get with my people and we'll do lunch" thing that I feel was designed to accentuate the imam's social and political status in the community, a very Arabic cultural proclivity. I believe 1-94 Field Artillery struggled in their attempts to engage imams (they were 1 for 14 in their attempts to engage the imam at the Moath Abu Jabal mosque) because they failed to respect this process. They simply rolled up to the gate unannounced and demanded to see the imam. That must have been viewed as insulting and rude. I went through this rigorous process and patiently worked with Sheik Ali's emissaries to secure a meeting for Lieutenant Colonel Baumann.

We met in the afternoon at the Shakir Al Abood mosque. The arrangements of our meeting were that the sheik would come to the main entrance gate of the walled compound around the mosque. We were out on the sidewalk that paralleled the street running in an east-west direction in front of the mosque. We would be observable, in plain sight, in close proximity to the local Iraqis. I believe he wanted it that way to make it clear to the many people who would observe that he was not cooperating. With my arrival and his obvious refusal to permit me any access other than on the street, in open, plain view, he created the appearance that he was not cooperating but rather that I was approaching him and imposing on his time. He did not want to be seen offering hospitality. I was fine with that arrangement. For security, this was a little risky. But I proceeded anyway. I decided I would stay very close to the imam. If someone wanted to take a shot, it would be certain the imam was going down too.

My tactic in this first meeting with the imam was a little unconventional. When I walked to him from my humvee I brought my chaplain, Captain John Boyer, with me.

Captain Chambers introduced my chaplain to Sheik Ali. They had a warm greeting and the sheik recognized my chaplain as a spiritual man. After their introduction, my chaplain introduced me to the sheik. What I wanted to present to Sheik Ali was that I was not here to push anything on him. I wanted him to see us as human, religious, and peaceful people, I hoped to dispel any preconceived notions he held of the members of my unit and me. I decided I would not extend my hand unless he extended his, which he did immediately. Then he and my chaplain began to engage in conversation.

Sheik Ali commenced with a theological discussion and I knew to be patient and listen. I hoped he would feel comfortable. Chaplain Boyer knew not to proselytize. I asked Chaplain Boyer to help me by keeping theological discussions focused on Christian and Muslim commonalties, which Chaplain Boyer did superbly.

When Sheik Ali finally engaged me I was kind, displayed deference, and was supremely respectful. He appreciated that because that was not his previous experiences with any other American soldier or officer.

Sheik Ali remained cordial throughout our discussion. I was somewhat successful in convincing him we were committed to helping the situation. I felt as though he understood my message that we were not dictating to him or any others in Al Saidiyah how they would live. I made sure too that I conveyed to him the harsh reality that if he wanted a fight, he would get one and he would not walk away the victor. I did not shove this in his face. I merely told him that I had the weapons, the means, the will, and the character to be aggressive. He had a say on what direction or path we would take. I recommended he choose carefully.

This kind of open, outdoor meeting is how I would meet several other imams in the battalion sector over the next few weeks. Clearly, I needed a better way but because the imams were mostly un-interested in dealing with me in face-to-face negotiation, I struggled for better means by which to engage them. As I dealt with these spiritual leaders, I began to conclude that imams were the political entity that were capable of bringing about the local governance that I clearly understood Al Saidiyah needed.

As I dealt with the imams — both Shia and Sunni — discussions about the future invariably became filled with the historical friction that has existed between the Sunni and Shia Muslims. A real rivalry and bitter hatred truly exists between the two sects. Not quite the Arab versus Jew level of dissonance but enough animosity that they advocate killing one another. It was disturbing.

Sunni versus Shia

A critical dynamic ever-present in the ongoing relationships between my Task Force and Iraqis was the Shia and
Sunni conflict. Unquestionably, my observation and experience assures me that a sectarian fight is ongoing in Iraq
between these two religious sects. Some in the Bush Administration and senior military leaders want to characterize the conflict as simply sectarian and purely religious.
I viewed it as economic and rooted in a competition for
political power and that suggested a civil war. The power
void created when Saddam was toppled gave life to this
bitterness. It is manifesting itself daily in violence throughout Iraq. There is very little Americans can do to relieve
this problem unless a democratic local governance regime
can be instituted. Without this, one sect will necessarily
have to defeat the other. I think that unless local democratic governance is established, trouble will continue long
after the Americans leave Iraq from Sunni Muslims fighting against Shia Muslims.

Shia people are the majority in Iraq. Iran, which borders
Iraq in the east, is a Shia Islamic State, Some call it a theocracy. Many Americans are familiar with U.S.-Iranian relations and history at least since 1979. Saddam is a Sunni and
used the difference in the Islamic faith tradition between
Sunni and Shia as a wedge to control the majority and keep
people further in distrust of one another.

Because in Arab culture it is virtuous to take care of your
family, tribesmen, and fellow Muslim believers through favoritism, Saddam insured the Sunni were the privileged.
Thousands of Sunnis became members of the Ba'ath Party. This was the only avenue to achieve position and some
small modicum of power. Sunnis filled the upper ranks of
the military, government ministries, higher-education positions, and legal and medical occupations, literally owning

the country. This was relevant in my world because in many negotiations on security, the resolution of these issues invariably came to discussion on the Badr Corps.

The Badr Corps was started by Ayatollah Al Hakim. This organization or unit (Badr) began its existence with a brigade then called the Badr Brigade. This brigade in a short time developed into a division and then grew into a corps-size unit. It consisted of thousands of fighters derived from Iraqi refugees who fled to Iran. It also included Iraqi migrants, military officers, and soldiers from the Iraqi armed forces who defected to Iran during the Iran-Iraq War in the 1980s. A new wave of fighters arrived in Iran after the popular uprising of March 1991, which was crushed by Saddam's regime.[12]

Sunni clerics argued the Shia were all Badr Corps sympathizers or outright supporters. There was great mutual distrust. The Shia, according to Sunni imams, helped the unwanted Iranian infiltration into Baghdad through Al Saidiyah. In meetings with Sunni leaders in Al Saidiyah, often these local leaders accused Shias in the area of supporting this Badr Corps organization as a means to get Americans to intercede on the Sunnis behalf in disputes. They reasoned that the Americans did not want the foreign intervention from Iran and so cried foul against the Shia to get an American response to protect the Sunni.

The Sunni-dominated make-up of my sector meant that we had to be among Ba'athists. Fourteen of the sixteen openly-functioning mosques in Al Saidiyah were Sunni. This presented unique challenges and opportunities.

When I walked the streets to talk to the people, I wasn't speaking to the underclass but to the disenfranchised. I found this to be remarkable. In the other two assigned sectors of Al Rashid the neighborhoods were run down and impoverished. The other sectors were also much larger in total area. My peers had a much lower ratio of soldiers to Iraqi citizens in their neighborhoods. Thus what the BCT Commander espoused for the majority of his sector was not applicable for my portion of Al Rashid. The challenges presented with this situation and the organizational politics that interceded as a result were difficult to manage. Because of the uniqueness of Al Saidiyah, the complexity and subtlety of negotiation did not limit itself to my dealings with the Iraqis. It continued in a whole different vein within my BCT. My struggles within the BCT due to the particular challenges we faced were complex, delicate to maneuver, tedious, and exhausting.

The American government cannot endorse the Shia outright without triggering a multitude of problems. Iran is indirectly given influence through any significant American endorsement of Shia in Iraq. And Iran has a clear agenda to intervene in Iraq so as to expand their brand of Shia Islamic government and their influence in the region. One fact that some American diplomats and almost all politicians miss is that Iraqis consider Iranian people Persians and not Arabs. Their kinship is less powerful than some surmise. Additionally, what kind of democracy do you achieve if the Shia overwhelmingly and subversively dominates the Sunni and Kurds of Iraq?

Sunnis, I was convinced, were the insurgents and the financiers of the insurgency in Iraq. Sunnis import the "outsiders" and recruit the destitute Shia to attack American soldiers and marines. They are primarily the ones that fight us in the streets. From planting the IEDs to firing rocket propelled grenades at a patrol to taking pot shots with AK-47s, the Sunni insurgents are directing the program.

In my earliest weeks in Al Saidiyah, I assessed the enemy's success was tied to the political dominance achieved since the invasion concluded. Not to be discounted though was the obvious weak mindset of the people as a whole. Saddam ruled the masses in a manner that rendered them weak. For example, consider the mukabarat spying system, a network where ordinary citizens—neighbors— informed on their friends and acquaintances. Saddam had an elaborate rewards system in place that made this extremely effective. To move up in this organization agents informed on and tortured people. The heinous ways in which torture was inflicted was also a measure of effectiveness for rewards. Informing on or turning in a friend as a subversive was considered good, but informing on or turning in a brother was considered even better. Electrical torture was good; disembowelment was better. If people cannot think critically, they are easily intimidated. Between the religious fervor, the passionate/emotional disposition and the natural and cultural tendencies of Iraqis, the formula is disastrous for reform initiatives and plays well into the hands of terrorist insurgents.

Finally, the willingness by Iraqis to randomly kill people without moral constraint seals the fate of many. It is easily understood why and how Iraqis have been so readily overwhelmed. But this is the climate in which the Task Force was required to operate. Time and effort could overcome some of the obstacles but the effort would not be measured in short amounts of time.

Five years may get us down the road to reform. In ten years quantifiable change may be seen but not all of our long-term goals may be met even in twenty years. Progress is up to the Iraqis, who take responsibility for nothing and I mean nothing.

The majority of the population in Al Saidiyah was Sunni, the majority of mosques were Sunni, and, thus the majority of imams I sat with were Sunni. Concluding that the Sunni were the basis for the insurgency, it logically followed that some of the spiritual, and perhaps political, leaders of the insurgency resided in the Task Force region.

Throughout the process of developing and continuing my relationship with imams, we eventually formed an informal Imam Council. With this council, I had to work through the politics of this Sunni-Shia conflict ever-mindful of the objectives of the BCT. Keeping the Shia and Sunni at the table, talking and facing each other, was absolutely critical to keeping the peace. Though there was plenty of under-the-table fighting and killing, it remained contained and limited. The sectarian fighting had not erupted into an open civil war, which would have had worse consequences for all involved.

Given the logistics of this area and its people, I understood the need to fight the enemy in a manner completely different from what most might think. Civil affairs and psychological operations had to dominate the Task Force methodology if we expect to win against this insurgency.

10 The Task Force Tactical Program

"Work relentlessly, accomplish much, remain in the background, and be more than you seem." Alfred von Schlieffen

Civil Affairs operations permeated all that we did in the Task Force sector. When the Task Force arrived, I already had a strong sense that we would have to execute our mission in our sector of Baghdad primarily through robust civil operations. My personal study of the war in Vietnam and descriptions of that war from my father convinced me of this. My personal observations during the pre-deployment site-survey trip I had made in January also buttressed my understanding this was the right course to pursue. I understood that intellectually. Civil Affairs operations, in my assessment, would be focused on LOO 3 & 5, Restoration of Essential Services and Economic Pluralism.

To rebuild a nation it takes more shovels and mechanical tools than guns and ammunition. Within the first week of arrival, I took on the clear command decision that civil operations would be the basis of all we did in Task Force 1-21. Combat operations would have to be subordinate and complement civil operations in Task Force 1-21. In my judgment this was the general approach the Division adopted in the early going of its efforts in Baghdad.

This operating concept did not mean combat operations and force protection would be subordinated per se, it meant that operational focus was predicated on civil and psychological operations.

To address the day-to-day tactical aspects of our operations I turned to Roger's Rules for Rangers as my guide to establish and disseminate the Task Force dictums for tactical operations. In a document we called "Standing Orders," I enumerated the absolutes for tactical operations that were to be universally applied across the Task Force.

The Task Force Standing Orders were outlined as follows:

1. *Remember your orders and follow the ROE.*
2. *Have your weapons clean, carry your basic load of ammo, and be ready to move on a minute's warning.*
3. *When you're on the move try to maintain proper intervals and secure formations. Try to see the enemy first.*
4. *Tell the truth about what you see; conduct a debrief after each venture outside the FOB. You can tell the stories you like when you tell other folks about your time in Iraq, but don't ever lie to an officer.*
5. *Don't ever take a chance you don't have to.*
6. *If we take prisoners, execute the five S's and insure confiscated equipment is accounted for and turned in to an S2.*
7. *Don't ever march home the same way. Take a different route so you won't be ambushed.*
8. *No matter how you move, each patrol must have scouts out front 50 meters so the main element can't be surprised.*
9. *Every patrol must designate enroute rally points.*
10. *Don't cross roads/highways at obvious points when provided a choice.*
11. *When in enemy contact, establish superior firepower and get help.*
12. *Don't expose yourself needlessly to the enemy. Kneel down, lie down, hide behind some available cover even if it's your vehicle.*

With these standards we would apply our craft.

The focus for the Task Force was civil affairs operations. The adjunct Civil Affairs Team for the Task Force was ably led by Major Robert "Rob" Dixon. Major Dixon was the assigned Civil Affairs Team Chief supporting 1-94 Field Artillery. He was handed off to Task Force 1-21. Major Dixon was a Reservist called back to active duty to ply his craft in Iraq. He was supremely capable and well trained at his job. A short, balding and stocky guy, Major Dixon was very kind, committed, and a sharp, critical thinker. Having already been in Iraq and Al Rashid for many months, he knew the area extremely well and had at least ten projects in various states of execution when we arrived on the scene.

As I assessed the terrain, people, and the overall situation in our sector, Major Dixon made a profound and immediate impact on me. Through him and his wise counsel, I began to see the situation and develop the tactical operation with greater precision. We spent time discussing theoretically what was going on in our part of Baghdad. Major Dixon imparted sagacious advice on how to deal with Iraqis in the area.

He had developed an elaborate contracting process and had formed many relationships with Iraqi men who were seeking to earn contracts in Baghdad. Major Dixon showed me several key factors that made a difference to my assessment and shaping of security and stabilization in sector.

First, Iraqis who sought contracts were generally shady characters who said whatever needed to be said to win the contract. Their scopes of work were often overstated and not well designed. There were no regulations or laws governing the process, only the rules the Civil Affairs teams imposed. I would have to learn these rules and the accompanying politics that invariably occurred in the negotiation process of letting a Civil Affairs Project contract.

Second, projects had to be constantly quality-assessed. This could only be done by going onsite and observing performance first-hand. Because I am not trained as an engineer I was limited, to some degree, in the detailed assessment I could provide. But I was easily able to look at work and discern if it was generally meeting the scope and design expected.

Third, contractors were at great risk as targets to the insurgents. A project to repair a sewer could be waylaid if insurgents killed the workers, or gunned down the contractor at home or on his way to work. The insurgents often went after these contractors in a manner similar to Mafia gangland murders. Major Dixon pointed out that we did not have the personnel to protect these contractors. But we had to be careful how we managed their individual situations to keep them from getting killed.

From an organizational operations and procedural perspective, Major Dixon's team was not well integrated into the daily business of 1-94 Field Artillery. They were treated as ancillary and allowed to operate somewhat independently. This is typical management method for conventional Army units. For me this would not work. If Civil Affairs was central to my operation, then that business had to be well-integrated into the Task Force. I had Major Dixon move his operation into my S5, Civil Affairs office in my headquarters facility. Major Dixon began working closely with my S5, Captain Michael "Mike" Levy, and started attending all my operations and targeting meetings infusing his knowledge, expertise, advice, and operations planning skill into the Task Force daily business. This proved to be invaluable right from the start. Major Dixon was amenable to this kind of integration and treatment because it elevated his position and influence within the Task Force.

The partnering of Major Dixon with my S5 was administratively necessary to leverage all I could from the Civil Affairs Team. Captain Levy was assigned as the Task Force S5 (Civil Affairs Staff Officer). About 5'9", blond-haired, a West Pointer who hailed from Louisiana, Captain Levy had a razor-sharp mind, a great sense of humor, and refined deep-thinking skills; he was an outstanding officer.

Captain Levy was one of my best staff officers because

he challenged me to think beyond my normal tendency. Captain Levy was a quick study. Within a few weeks of learning the area and interacting with the various characters seeking contracts or other inroads to the Task Force, he quickly became the true director of all civil operations for the Task Force. I also saddled him with the responsibility of serving as the Task Force Information Operations Officer and the Targeting Officer title and duties. His skill and adaptability allowed me to synthesize key functions of the Task Force under his direction.

Captain Levy swiftly became one of my closest advisors and the undisputed resident expert on civil and psychological operations and governance management for the Task Force. He also excelled in managing the murky politics of our sector. He was supremely adept at taking my ideas and thoughts and building them into coherent plans of action. More importantly, Captain Levy was fearless about presenting his own sometimes contradictory ideas and making me listen to them.

Another excellent quality of Captain Levy was his personal commitment to developing the civil affairs operation by literally going out on many of the patrols he ordered for information gathering or coordination so he had a first-hand accounting and the ability to influence situations, as he knew I wanted them to be. Captain Levy was often forced to work in ambiguous territory and functioned as I would expect a field grade (major-colonel) officer with a great deal more experience would have.

Captain Levy was in this position because a need occurred within the Task Force. Again, the conventional force structure of an unsuited Army organization attempting to adjust to fighting an insurgency was in play here. Captain Levy was originally assigned as the battalion Fire Direction Officer. This position is critical to a Field Artillery battalion because this officer literally manages the tactical fire direction of a whole battalion's worth of artillery. Obviously, because we were not operating as a rocket artillery battalion his position had to morph into something functional. The former S3, Major Menti, had the idea, before we deployed, to make the Fire Direction Officer the S5 and I felt Captain Levy could handle the job.

Captain Levy not only performed the civil affairs directorship of the Task Force, he also managed all the information operations programs and non-lethal targeting processes. These functions were closely linked to my concept of focusing the Task Force on civil affairs rather than simple combat action. Employing this procedure and organizational design was consistent with my desire to marry the civil affairs functions with the information operations and psychological operations. I did not want to separate or compartmentalize these functions. Synthesizing these functions allowed planners to focus efforts in an ideally complementary manner instead of working on them disparately and disjointed which I surmised would cause dysfunction.

The other battalions in the BCT had Fire Support Elements and their commanders chose to use the Fire Support Elements as information operations managers. It was common practice in the other two maneuver task forces to assign an officer to a commodity area and manage operations that way. This was common conventional unit management practice: compartmentalize and specialize synthesizing at a higher level. In a counterinsurgent operating environment this is dysfunctional management practice.

Easily one of the major strengths of our Army — really in all the Services — is the ingrained spirit, ability, and education among our leaders to adapt and think through problems and fashion creative and innovative means to accomplish missions. Having leaders who can assess, determine methods, decide on a course of action and do so freely within the framework of solid doctrine, and accomplish missions is very powerful. In Iraq, this was absolutely essential to success. Dealing with ambiguity and not allowing it to paralyze action matters when fighting an insurgency.

The other external team attached to 1-94 Field Artillery that we inherited was the Psychological Operations Team. This team was superbly led by Staff Sergeant Timothy P. Rogers. Sergeant Rogers was a Reservist from Arkansas.

Tall and thin, Sergeant Rogers often sported a light or thin mustache. He was older than most Sergeants of his grade, very mature, and well-studied in psychological operations. An easygoing guy and consummate professional, Sergeant Rogers quickly became entrenched in the battalion. My staff instantly liked him and he too was a very sharp critical thinker. Because of his rank I think he was a little reticent to express his opinions to me during our first few weeks of transition. After I sensed this, we had a private meeting where I made it clear to him that he had to have the courage and comfort to advise me without letting rank or protocol get in the way of effective business. As far as I was concerned, he was an officer on my staff and he had to learn "yes men" got nowhere with me. He got the point and adjusted quickly.

The Psychological Operations Team also had to become directly integrated into the S5 (Civil Affairs) and S3 (Operations) of my Task Force. Like Civil Affairs, the Psychological Operations Team also brought an element of expertise, knowledge and influence on the battlefield that I found most compelling to fighting and winning. Swaying minds was more important to me than fighting Iraqis with guns. None was better than Sergeant Rogers.

Articulating the Task Force Program

The synthesizing of civil, psychological, political, and combat operations was the tactical challenge I faced as the Task Force commander. Having a keen understanding of the politics of Al Saidiyah and having made a commitment to civil affairs and psychological operations methods to lead the efforts of Task Force 1-21, it became imperative to establish a comprehensive program for all soldiers and leaders of the Task Force to follow and implement.

I had to amalgamate all of my assessments and develop a program that traced a line of continuity from the strategic, through the operational, down to the tactical level of operations for my battalion task force. All commanders at my level and above had to conduct this analysis and develop their commensurate tactical programs each ostensibly nested in the next higher echelon's program.

The goal was to seamlessly link the three levels so that the accomplishment of tactical goals served the accomplishment of operational goals that in turn served the accomplishment and ultimate achievement of the strategic goals. This was then and is now an abject failure across the Army in the process of prosecuting the Iraq counterinsurgency effort. Few senior officers do this or even understand that they must do this in order to have a chance at success.

In American military history this connecting of strategic, operational, and tactical operations was the same critical problem that Ulysses S. Grant faced when he assumed supreme command of the Union Army. Grant succeeded as the Union Commander because he effectively combined the distributed tactical efforts with the major field Armies' accomplishment of clear operational goals which allowed for the Union Army to ultimately meet the strategic objectives given by President Lincoln.

In Vietnam the military failed at this process. The military is again failing at this in Iraq. I was keenly aware of this shortcoming but felt obligated nonetheless to try my best to establish this linkage in the Task Force program. I did so despite knowing, because others did not do this, my program would not go unimpeded.

Articulating my program, I used the metaphor of a building. Providing guidance in this manner more directly explained my vision and intent through a mental image all could rally around and support.

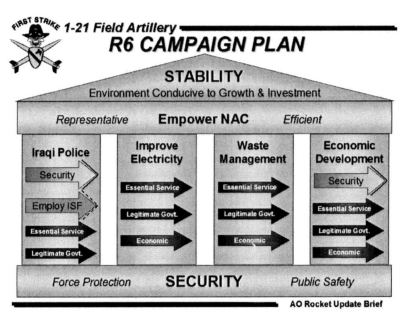

Figure 10.1 — Task Force briefing chart that depicted the strategy we would pursue to achieve my goal to neutralize or defeat the insurgency in Al Saidiyah (NAC= Neighborhood Advisory Council).

The chart shows how I envisioned the Task Force working to counter the insurgency in Al Saidiyah. I used the metaphor of a building to illustrate the strategy because so much of what we attempted to do in Iraq was accomplished by building things, not destroying them; something antithetical to the public image and media portrayal of the American military in Iraq. The metaphor of a building represented the translation of the strategic goals of the nation and operational goals of Multi-National Forces, Iraq into a tactical level plan nested in the Division and BCT plan at my battalion task force level.

This was how Task Force 1-21 internalized the Division Five LOO, Oasis Campaign. The foundation of the building from which all other pieces were fastened was security.

Security had two distinct dimensions: force protection and public safety for Iraqis. Force protection was directed at protecting soldiers in the Task Force. We sought a level of safety that would allow for the relative harmless movement of Task Force soldiers in and around Al Saidiyah. We sent multiple, mutually-supporting patrols every day into the enclave. Those patrols worked to assist in enforcement of public safety, conduct civil affairs operations, provide security for psychological operations initiatives, check on criminal activity in Al Saidiyah, and collect information on insurgent activity throughout the area.

Public safety had numerous parts. No Iraqi police station operated in Al Saidiyah, but the Neighborhood Advisory Council did convince the Iraqi police from the Al Bayaa police station just next door to patrol in Al Saidiyah. These patrols had to work to "protect and serve" the Iraqis in the mahallas that made up Al Saidiyah.

Iraqi police do not work like city police in the U.S. They are a nationalized force. This adversely impacts the effective operations of the Iraqi police to provide competent security in the neighborhoods of Baghdad. I say this because local focus and priorities are subordinated to other perceived needs. Opportunities for corruption are great. Who determines where the police patrol, how resources are allocated, and what level of effort are focused is indeterminate in the existing system.

Despite that particular shortcoming, I wanted to get a police station in Al Saidiyah and team the Iraqi police working from this station with the Neighborhood Advisory Council that I wanted to fashion more as a "Town Council" in an attempt to focus efforts on local policing of Al Saidiyah. If we could get Iraqi police into Al Saidiyah, I would work with the Neighborhood Advisory Council and the Senior Iraqi police officer at the station and teach them how to "protect and serve" with local focused policing.

My plan was to politically connect the Neighborhood Advisory Council Chairman, the strongest Sunni (Sheik Ali Al-Jabouri) and Shia (Sheik Nael) imams in Al Saidiyah, and the senior Iraqi police officer assigned to Al Saidiyah so they would have to work together for the benefit of all the residents of Al Saidiyah. The people I worked with in Al Saidiyah were capable of doing this only if the politics and supporting democratic processes were in place. They also needed to be taught and mentored how to operate democratically, representing constituencies and compromising where the common good could be realized.

Our long-term goal was to reduce the visibility of the Task Force in Al Saidiyah and increase the signature and legitimacy of Iraqi security forces. We also worked to establish Iraqi Army patrols and the Facilities Protection Service force associated with Task Force 1-21 into the commercial districts of Al Saidiyah to accomplish what police forces should, but did not, effectively do in Al Saidiyah. This security foundation would have to achieve a level of effectiveness strong enough to allow the columns to be erected.

Continuing with the building metaphor, I saw four columns erected on the security foundation. The first column was the "Iraqi police." As noted, I believe that the Iraqi police was the Iraqi security force element most likely to achieve the long-term solution to local security that I sought in Al Saidiyah. In an effort to achieve this goal, an Iraqi police station — major civil project — was constructed across from the Neighborhood Advisory Council building to get this effort going and realize this part of the renewal for Al Saidiyah.

The second column of my metaphorical building was "Economic Development." All efforts had to be made to insure the underdeveloped, burgeoning, entrepreneurial storefront districts were viable and functional. Banking barely functioned at the local level in Baghdad's many districts. Almost all capital exchanges were cash transactions. The township had two significant commercial areas, and the focus for security had to be in those zones. We were severely limited in our ability to effect the economic development and entrepreneurial interests for Iraqis in our sector. Battalion task force level leaders in the 5th BCT had no money directly available to spawn this activity.

Additionally, we had no authority and no educational process to help the people learn about investment, free market enterprise, entrepreneurship, or democracy. As military, we were purposefully restrained from pursuing this kind of educational activity. No other entity existed to provide this; Iraqis simply went without it. What we could do was give Iraqis ideas, employ groups of people on civil projects, work to provide a safe environment, and mentor activity that was occurring through other means. But this was trifling little in the overall situation in Baghdad. I knew unless we could do more, real growth would not take root. We stayed focused on what we could do and continually searched for opportunities to do more.

The metaphoric building's third column was "Waste

Management." Strewn across all of Al Saidiyah was trash, environmental hazards in the form of overflowing sewage, oil and gasoline spillage, dead animals (dogs mostly), broken-down vehicles, and abandoned factory facilities with no regard for chemical waste. Squatters inhabited these abandoned facilities and lived among the squalor at extreme risk to their health. Cleaning this up would take much more resources than those made available to the Task Force. However, to the extent we could, I pursued a vigorous effort to clean the streets and as much of the mess as possible. This also offered opportunities to employ manual laborers to collect the garbage and transport it to a central collection point to further dispose of the trash. No formal garbage collection existed in Al Rashid or Al Saidiyah. Attempts were made but corruption and poor administration prevented them from being successful. Trash pick-up and street cleaning were ongoing employment opportunities for Iraqis. Until a formal waste collection system was established, this problem persisted. In the meantime, we sought to clean up the town. This would also help demonstrate a sincere effort to re-build. Cleaning up the mess, I surmised, was critical to future success.

"Improve Electricity" was the fourth column on the security foundation of the building metaphor Task Force 1-21 rallied around. Almost all the residents in Al Saidiyah had power from a spaghetti-web of crisscrossing electrical wires strung all over the residential areas of Al Saidiyah. These lines pulled in electrical power from generators set along many streets in the mahallas of Al Saidiyah, which was how the Iraqis in our sector received electricity most of the time. It was not a reliable system. The power generation facility in Al Dora, a township to the east of Al Saidiyah, was operating at 50 percent capacity. Power was distributed to homes and businesses in Al Saidiyah in four hours on/four hours off random operation. When the power from the city facility was off, the residents relied on the generators. These generators were in varying states of repair. Most were in disrepair. Fuel was not always readily available and this adversely affected the electrical situation for residents. The overall effect was that most residents had intermittent electricity and that spelled problems for us.

Exacerbating the electrical power problem was the Iraqi perception associated with electrical power. Saddam's regime used distribution of electricity as a means to control people. Corruption also affected electrical power distribution. Iraqis believed the Americans were acting in the same manner that Saddam did: controlling the distribution as a means to punish them. When I denied their assertions, they just laughed at me and said, "You Americans can put a man on the moon but cannot get the power plant running? You do not fool us."

We made dedicated efforts to get the power plant operating at full capacity. But the infrastructure and sub-station distribution system was so poorly maintained over the years by Saddam's government that all phases in the generation and distribution of electricity had to be repaired if we hoped to produce constant supply of electricity to the homes and businesses of Baghdad. I knew that fixing the electricity system would easily be the single most profound action the Americans could take to defeat the arguments of the insurgency at this juncture in the war effort.

I wanted to implement a reliable generator back-up system in the mahallas of Al Saidiyah to work as an interim solution. We went as far as getting a contractor proposal to emplace and provide maintenance for generators in the mahallas. The proposed cost exceeded $3 million for all of Al Saidiyah.

After the BCT staff finished laughing, they rejected my proposal. Instead, it was decided that our unit mechanics would go with patrols to attempt to locate the owners of the existing generators and try to fix them. It quickly became apparent that this tedious "solution" was not tenable, and many owners hid from us believing they were going to be detained because we thought they were doing something illegal.

The four columns of the building metaphorically supported the major beam of "Empower the Neighborhood Advisory Council," which represented the only modicum of local governance that we could embrace. The two components of this empowerment were representation and efficiency. Establishing a democratic, representative Neighborhood Advisory Council could do the most to psychologically, intellectually, and pragmatically disrupt the insurgency. An efficiently functioning Neighborhood Advisory Council with administrative and political muscle was a powerful counter to the insurgency. This Neighborhood Advisory Council, efficiently operating, was the key to near-term and long-term stability.

The roof of the Task Force's metaphorical building was "Stability." If all the other parts of this structure were sound and properly fitted, the roof would hold strong to cover the building of Al Saidiyah. None of the parts were exclusive and we did not pursue any independent of the other.

This building was metaphoric structure symbolizing the Task Force implementation of the Five LOO Campaign plan, suited for the realities of the situation as presented by the inhabitants of Al Saidiyah and the capabilities of the Task Force in real, not merely symbolic or esoteric, terms.

Another very sinister reality we had to contend with while trying to implement our tactical program was the Sunni versus Shia conflict. All we tried to do tactically to neutralize the insurgency in Al Saidiyah was tangled up in the larger conflict between the Shia and Sunni. This internal national struggle was potentially subversive to all other efforts the Task Force pursued in Al Saidiyah.

The Shia detested the Sunni. Since the U.S. invasion and the ousting of Saddam, the Shia have risen from the ashes of despair and begun to exercise some real political power. The insurgents are focused on defeating the Shia. Upon examination, I surmised that Sunni objectives were not to win over the Shia; they are more sinister. The Sunni seek to destabilize anything the Shia attempt. As Shia politicians seek to consolidate power and authority over Iraq, the Sunni will aggressively subvert all efforts. Sunni firmly believe they can dominate the Shia. The wild-card for the Sunni is the U.S. presence. By continuing their menacing goals and killing as many Americans as they can, the Sunni insurgency lives. Their aim is to survive long enough to push the Americans out of Iraq because they are arrogantly certain that they can wrest power back from the Shia. And they may not be wrong. The Sunni insurgency intentionally targets the American electorate and mass media to achieve their ends to extricate the U.S. from Iraq. They are succeeding.

George Washington used a very similar strategy to defeat the British in the American Revolution. As an Army of lesser capability, the Americans avoided direct action with the British until the conditions were favorable. Simply keeping the Continental Army in the field and legitimate meant the American Revolution lived. This strategy worked for Washington and could work for the Sunnis.

But if the American military and political effort focused on avoiding a civil war among Iraqis and steered the situation to force the Sunni to bargain or parish the fight in Iraq could be over. The Shia would dominate the political landscape and end this insurgency.

The approach to defeat the insurgent effort in Al Saidiyah hinged on three essential actions:

• Local political reformation (developing and exploiting relationships, Neighborhood Advisory Council reform, good community projects and improved local governance)

• Iraqi security forces activity (Facilities Protection Services, Iraqi Army, Iraqi police, autonomous patrols, and good command and control)

• Pressuring the insurgents everywhere in sector (cordon and search, precision attacks to capture insurgents, and interdicting operations)

I know Colonel Lanza supported these three parts to my local strategy because they were directly related to his intent and program for the greater Al Rashid sector of the BCT. The only major issue he had with my program was the local government reformation objectives. I had a very detailed, deliberate, and far-sighted plan that I hoped the Task Force would perform for my sector.

I do believe that neither the intelligence planners nor the commander of the BCT felt the Shia-Sunni politics were as important a factor as I had concluded. I saw no aggressive effort to radically alter the dynamics of political action in the District Advisory Council. I know Colonel Lanza experienced all the frustrations I was having at the Neighborhood Advisory Council level with the District Advisory Council. I participated and sat in on many discussions about reforming the District Advisory Council. Alas, much was discussed but I saw no definitive action to overhaul that entity.

I could not influence or change the reality above my level, so I focused on my local area. I hoped to influence the greater area of Al Rashid through demonstration of success rather than discussions.

In April 2004 the insurgency and the First Cavalry Division along with the overall American effort in Iraq were in transition. This time also marked the maturation of the infant insurgency. The insurgents hit us hard in our sector of Baghdad. We would get a bloody nose and the war would become personal for all the soldiers of Task Force 1-21.

11 The War Becomes Personal

*"In modern war . . . you will die like a dog for
no good reason." Ernest Hemingway*

All the efforts we made to take in the nuances of our assigned sector did not allow the war to creep in too closely
to the personal psyche of the soldiers that made up Task
Force 1-21. This was all still a grand adventure. Personally,
I was continuing to adjust to the sights and sounds of the
battlefield. Occasionally, the war was close; we heard gunfire or mortars and rockets impacted inside the walls of
Camp Falcon. I had seen some Iraqis killed and listened
to some stories from my peers about combat engagements
they had been in already. I hadn't been in any firefights
personally and none of my soldiers or Iraqi workers had
been wounded or killed in these first weeks. The war had
not become personal just yet.

By mid-April, the Muslim holy time of Ar'baen was approaching and the Iraqi insurgency was getting very bold
in their efforts to throw off the yoke of occupation and
simultaneously fight the Shia for control of Iraq's future.
Patrols from the Task Force were operating in the sector
around the clock. Once Ar'baen started, there were concerns from Division about our ability to protect Shia pilgrims from insurgent attacks as they moved south along
the major highways across Baghdad.

During Ar'baen, the Shia move south in large groups to
visit the holy Mosque shrine in Karbala. The movement is
by foot and in a modern caravan of trucks, cars, and any
other motorized conveyance the pilgrims could find.

The 68th Chemical Company had responsibility for patrolling Highway 5, known as Route Senators. This was a major

travel route through Baghdad for Shia pilgrims marching to Karbala. From almost the first day we assumed control of Route Senators the company was taking fire from enemy ambushes and being hit with IEDs. Fortunately, the enemy was not capable, and though engaged, our patrols were not sustaining any wounded or killed soldiers. That changed quickly. The second week of April, the first four wounded soldiers of Task Force 1-21 were from the 68th Chemical Company; two were females.

Private First Class Kristopher Ross was the first Task Force soldier who was wounded. A rocket propelled grenade hit the side of an armored humvee in which Private Ross was riding. It was one of the few armored humvees the Task Force had. The armored humvee (M1114) was a refitted, well-armored, combat-capable humvee. By April 2004 these armored humvees were just beginning to arrive in large quantities to support all American forces fighting in Iraq.

The blast burned the rubber door seal, and flame shot through the opening, burning the right rear of Private Ross's neck and his ear. Fortunately, the rocket-propelled grenade did not penetrate the vehicle; if it had, most likely his wounds would have been fatal.

Sergeant First Class Celestine Blake-Johnson, a female non-commissioned officer in 68th Chemical Company, was the assistant patrol leader on the mission. It was her humvee Private Ross was riding in that was hit by the rocket propelled grenade. The driver of the humvee was Specialist Latonya D. Flagg. Sergeant Blake-Johnson describes her role and the incident like this:

We encountered our first enemy fire from a rocket propelled grenade which hit the side of my vehicle while on patrol along Route Senators. Upon impact, the humvee immediately became engulfed in fire. Specialist Flagg, my driver, and I kept an eye on the road despite the flames. We went racing down the road at a high rate of speed looking for a place to stop. Specialist Flagg drove like a champ. It was like we were "Cagney and Lacey" from the television show.

Once stopped, I jumped from the humvee yelling for the patrol to establish a hasty security perimeter. I knew Private Ross was wounded. I needed to assess the situation. Private Ross was badly burned and in a lot of pain. I wanted to cry. I couldn't though. As I looked at him he reminded me of my son who was just a year younger than Private Ross. We evacuated Private Ross from my humvee and put him in another vehicle from another Task Force patrol that linked up to support us. They were sent by the Tactical Operations Center when they knew we were under fire. Private Ross was writhing in pain, I wanted to scream and felt like I might break down. I felt as if one of my kids were wounded. Private Ross had so much blood on his face and the right side of his body was a sight I could barely stand to see. The patrol medic began to work on him. Private Ross kept asking for me to get him home. I looked directly in his eyes to comfort him and promised him I would get him home. I felt helpless standing next to him and trying to keep an eye out for the rest of the patrol. Squad leaders were directing their soldiers and kept the area secure. When Private Ross was stabilized he was evacuated by the other patrol. My driver told me the humvee was able to drive. I ordered the patrol to follow me, and we headed back to Camp Falcon. Another patrol was sent to Route Senators.

Private First Class Cassandra Fisher and Specialist Ellen Terry were nearly killed by an IED a few days later.

Ahmed, the interpreter who supported the patrol was killed, decapitated by a shrapnel fragment from the blast of the IED. He was the first person assigned to the Task Force killed in action. He was also the first combat casualty associated with our unit I ever saw up close and personal. I was not on that patrol, but as it returned to Camp Falcon,

I went to the Troop Medical Clinic where the patrol brought the wounded. We heard the reports over the radio in the Tactical Operations Center, and I knew I had two soldiers wounded and an Iraqi interpreter killed.

Nothing before in life prepared me for what I saw when I got to the dismount point in a gravel parking lot behind the Troop Medical Clinic. I saw the cab of the truck as I approached from the front. I noticed the remaining glass was coated in a dark red and white speckled residue: blood and brain matter. It smelled like nothing I can describe.

Specialist Marvin Deboest, an unassuming, big, soldier with a very reserved, easygoing personality, jumped in the truck cab right after the attack. He drove the truck, with Ahmed blown apart lying next to him, four kilometers back to Camp Falcon. Private Fisher and Specialist Terry who were riding in the cab of the truck with Ahmed were wounded. The Patrol Leader medically evacuated them from the location of the explosion on Route Senators. The circumstances of the situation when the IED went off prompted Specialist Deboest to hop into the cab of the vehicle and take over driving to get the vehicle and body back to Camp Falcon.

When I arrived, Specialist Deboest had just moved from the driver seat and had come around to open the passenger door where I was standing. After he opened the door, I saw, slumped over from the center of the cab, this grotesque figure. Ahmed did not exist anymore. This was some sort of ghoulish zombie body of what was once one of our Task Force's interpreters. In the very few weeks we had been in Iraq, I had barely met him. And now here he was lying in a pool of his own blood, missing most of his head, with brain material, skull fragments, and torn flesh exposed. Here was a macabre, limp body just lying on the seat. No one wanted to touch the body. Specialist Deboest helped a medic pull the body from the cab. I could not believe what I just saw; it was surreal. In my lifetime I'd seen animals killed. In Iraq, already I had seen half a dozen dead bodies, maybe more. But I never knew the dead people. And unfortunately, I would see death up close and personal again soon.

We all felt an eerie loss by the death of Ahmed. The loss of Ahmed was both an event and a statement about the war. Iraqis were going to die in greater numbers. Their deaths would be cruel. Some would die like Ahmed's death doing their duties and coming up unlucky. Others would die gangland style from drive-by shootings, in up-close assassinations, or killed in their cars driving.

I presided over a small memorial service in honor of Ahmed. All the interpreters that worked in the Task Force were present at the service held in front of our Task Force headquarters building. I was concerned many interpreters might quit. Other units had already begun to lose their interpreters from perceived maltreatment and exposure to combat; many Iraqi interpreters had little constitution for this kind of risk. I wanted to draw attention to Ahmed's significance to the Task Force and reinforce my message to the interpreters that what they were doing was meaningful and noble. They responded by staying with us, committed to the cause of building a new, democratic Iraq.

For me, this event solidified my commitment to our interpreters. I had determined their support and utility to the Task Force was vital to success with our program. They had to be protected, treated well, and encouraged to perform to their best level to meet our needs.

Days later, the combat death of Private First Class Adolfo Carballo in an enemy ambush significantly impacted every soldier in the Task Force. Ahmed's death did have an impact but it was not quite as profound as it could have been because he was an Iraqi. We had not bonded with our interpreters yet — that came later; for now, he was once removed from each of us. When Private Carballo was killed, each one of us understood now just how vulnerable we were. That reality was substantial.

Adolfo Carballo, Task Force 1-21's First KIA

On the night of April 9, 2004, the beginning of our third week in Iraq, a patrol set out from Camp Falcon to conduct a security mission in Al Saidiyah. The patrol of three humvees drove in a tactical convoy north along Route Irish to the mahallas in Al Saidiyah. As they passed the cloverleaf road network of Check Point 8, which join highway 5 and highway 8, several rocket propelled grenades were fired at the patrol from buildings on the east side of the highway. Private Carballo was a gunner for one of the humvees in convoy on that patrol.

The humvee he manned had no armor except the makeshift plates we put on the body of the truck. The machinegun station was a hole in the fiberglass roof of the vehicle. Gunners protruded from the hole where their weapon was mounted. There was an armor skirt in front of the machinegun mount but that was all the Army supply system provided for armor protection for the gunners.

Because we had not received any add-on-armor through the Army supply system yet, we had welders cut locally purchased metal and place plates in specific locations on the fiberglass body of humvees to get some semblance of protection for crews in the humvees.

Practically, the only real protection the gunners had was the swift movement of the vehicle. By driving fast, the vehicle was a more difficult target for a rocket propelled grenade gunner to hit. 1-94 Field Artillery had taught us that speed was an essential element to protecting against these ambushes. Oddly, many people (civilian safety officers) and some senior leaders in the Division told us that speeding did not equate to force protection. They discredited this as a viable method of security. Their reasoning was that accidents could occur due to excessive speed. Thus, they concluded, the increased risk assumed by speeding nullified any protection offered by this practice. This was all true, speed kills just as deadly as an enemy's rocket propelled grenade or rifle fire.

However, speeding did provide a small measure of protection in certain circumstances. A fast moving target is tougher to hit: that is physical fact. Certainly, with no armor protection, easy identification by the enemy, and highly-vulnerable positions on the roads in the urban terrain of Baghdad, driving slowly was tantamount to providing a very easy target for an enemy gunner. Early, when we did not have adequate armor, I endorsed speed in movement as a patrolling tactic to increase security. Soldiers in my formation had to wear seatbelts and leaders had to control the speed as a tactical means to an end. Drivers did not have liberty to speed arbitrarily. Patrol leaders directed speeds for movement and were accountable when they chose to speed to achieve security. When maneuvering, the vehicle commander modulated speed. The use of seat belts was the essential factor in my mind. I reasoned that Ranger patrolling doctrine, in fact, endorsed speed as a means of achieving security for a formation. In Baghdad, minimizing your target profile by multiple means, one of which was rapid movement, worked. And so we did speed in the early weeks until our armor protection was upgraded.

The enemy truly got a "lucky shot" when they hit Private Carballo. Firing from just over 100 meters away, a rocket propelled grenade hit Private Carballo square in the back.

Amazingly, the grenade did not detonate. The kinetic force of the round hitting him square in the back caused so much internal damage he died because his insides were so badly scrambled. His backside ballistic protective plate literally stopped the grenade. The grenade did not penetrate the plate. The warhead was flattened and part of it was stuck to the back of his outer tactical vest when I retrieved it from the humvee. Private Carballo collapsed from the force of the impact falling inside the vehicle.

The patrol was less than five kilometers from Camp Falcon where there was a critical-care medical facility. The medic in the patrol attempted to stabilize Carballo as the patrol raced back to Camp Falcon. The Patrol Leader was determined to get him to the next higher level of emergency care as he was trained to do. I had just returned to my headquarters from a meeting at the BCT headquarters when I was informed of the incident and went straight to the medical facility. When I got there I went straight into the emergency treatment room. There, three soldiers were struggling with Carballo's limp body pulling him from the humvee parked in the back. I ran to the truck to help. I held his waist and carried him to a gurney in the emergency room.

An Army medical doctor, Captain Lopez, MD, took control of the situation immediately. I recall that Private Carballo was experiencing seizures and foaming at his mouth. Blood was draining from his ears, and his eyes were closed. He was not breathing. I had never personally seen a person die so violently before, and I felt responsible. I tried to shake it off and I knew I could not allow my emotions to get away from me. I was mindful that others were taking their cues from me. I could do nothing for him, and I had to consider the others. The doctors began CPR and I removed my soldiers from the emergency treatment room so the doctor and medics attending could work. We all left and went in the front foyer of the medical clinic.

This was when I figured out that soldiering, commanding, and leading in combat was about one thing: mental toughness. Remaining capable despite knowing that I had ordered that patrol and that my soldiers can and will be killed required that I control my emotions well enough to think. This emotional control transferred too in situations when we were under fire. Leaders can only be inward for a split second to orient. From there, leaders must direct and focus assets to defeat the threat — calmly and coolly — until the action is complete. And that ability can only reside in leaders who are mentally tough, period.

I recall praying for Carballo and selfishly, praying a little for me asking God to allow me the inner strength to maintain my composure and absorb this with dignity and compassion at the same time. Some soldiers let their emotions go and cried. Others just stared off into space. I knew now that I was definitely at war. I was enraged, saddened, and frustrated all at once.

Private Adolfo Carballo left a very young wife and large extended family behind. After his wife was officially notified by the U.S. Army I got to a phone and called her to offer my condolence and pay my respect to her husband. This, needless to say, was an emotionally difficult call to make. It was not the last call of this nature I would make.

Some good, if that's possible, did come from the loss of Private Carballo. The BCT staff, struggling with dividing up a very limited supply of M1114 armored humvees, decided to give us more than originally allotted. Also, Lieutenant Colonel "Jay" Allen, Commander of 1-8 Cavalry, found me and advised of an enterprising soldier in his command who drew up some plans for an armored cupola design for gunners on humvees. 1-8 Cavalry had begun installing these on their humvees. Lieutenant Colonel Allen offered the designs to me, allowing us to better protect our gunners.

Once we received the plans and assessed the merit of the design and function, I got with Major Marshall and ordered all our humvees outfitted with this design immediately. We would work around the clock. My two welders looked at the design and concluded that although it was a decent design, the metal was not thick enough to afford optimum protection.

Private First Class Shalk from HHS/1-21 came up with an improvement to the design. He created a spacer and a second layer of metal that, when overlaid with a ¼ inch gap, stopped anything from penetrating. Because of the added weight, this armor protection would need some wheels at the base and hand holds on the inside of the plates so the gunner could turn the whole assembly easily. When completed, the design provided ideal protection.

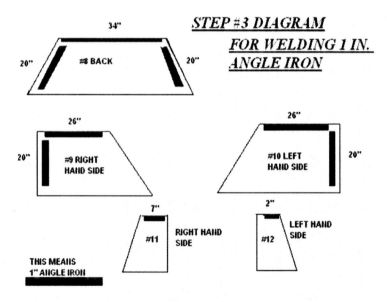

Figure 11.1 — PFC Shalk's diagram for building the turret shields.

Within three weeks, all the humvees in Task Force 1-21 were outfitted. Meanwhile Colonel Lanza made certain all the humvees of the BCT were also configured with this added protection. Later, the Army would provide a manufactured design. But the one Private Schalk modified was superior to the one the Army provided later. Protecting gunners was vital because they were exceptionally vulnerable. The enemy targeted these soldiers for obvious reasons. All patrols Americans run are movements to contact. That is, a patrol can be attacked anywhere, at any time. All have to be ready for that likelihood. No one could predict when or where they would be attacked.

We did not drive around Baghdad shooting at everything that moved. Quite to the contrary, the enemy always got the first shot. Moving as we did in convoy patrols, American military was easily identifiable day or night. The rules of engagement we operated under gave the enemy the advantage. There was little we could do except be ready to respond. It was our challenge to wrest the initiative from our enemy after absorbing the first shot.

Rules of Engagement — Advantage: Bad Guys

One of the major frustrations I came to grips with immediately following the death of Private Carballo was the clear tactical disadvantage the Rules of Engagement placed us under. The Combined Forces Land Component Rules of Engagement decidedly gave the advantage to the enemy.

Combined Forces Land Component (CFLCC) *RULES OF ENGAGEMENT SUMMARY*

NOTHING IN THESE RULES LIMITS YOUR INHERENT AUTHORITY AND OBLIGATION TO TAKE ALL NECESSARY AND APPROPRIATE ACTION TO DEFEND YOURSELF, YOUR UNIT, AND OTHER US FORCES.

*HOSTILE ACTORS: You may engage persons who commit hostile acts or show hostile intent with the **minimum force** necessary to counter the hostile act or demonstrated hostile intent and to protect US Forces.*

HOSTILE ATTACK: An attack or other use of force against US Forces or a use of force that directly precludes/impedes the mission/duties of US Forces.

*HOSTILE INTENT: The threat of **imminent** use of force against US Forces or the threat of force to preclude/impede the mission/duties of US Forces.*

You may use force, up to and including deadly force, against hostile actors:
• In self-defense
• In defense of your unit, other US Forces, and civilian personnel.
• To prevent the theft, damage, or destruction of firearms, ammunition, explosives, or property designated by the Commander as vital to national security. (Protect other property with less than deadly force.)

ESCALATION OF FORCE
When possible, use the following degrees of force against hostile actors:
SHOUT: warning to HALT or "KIFF" (pronounced "COUGH").
SHOVE: physically restrain, block access, or detain.
SHOW: your weapon and demonstrate intent to use it.
SHOOT: to remove the threat of death/serious bodily injury or to protect designated property.

FIRING YOUR WEAPON
You may open fire if you, friendly forces, or persons and property under your protection are threatened with deadly force. This means:
a. You may open fire against an individual who fires or aims his weapon at you, friendly forces, or persons under your protection.

b. You may open fire against an individual who plants, throws, or prepares to throw an explosive or incendiary device at friendly forces, or persons or property under your protection.
c. You may open fire against an individual who deliberately drives a vehicle at you, friendly forces, persons with designated special status or property designated special status.
d. You may also fire against an individual who attempts to take possession of friendly weapons, ammunition, or protected property, and there is no other way of avoiding it.

IF YOU MUST FIRE:
- *Fire warning shots if the situation permits*
- *If warning shots do not defuse the situation, fire aimed shots.*
- *Fire no more rounds than necessary.*
- *Fire with due regard for the safety of innocent bystanders.*
- *Take reasonable efforts not to destroy property.*
- *Stop firing as soon as the situation permits.*

You may use minimum force, including lethal, against an individual who unlawfully commits, or is about to commit, an act which endangers life, or is likely to cause serious bodily harm, in circumstances where there is no other way to prevent the act.

ROE DEFINITIONS
PROTECTED PERSONS: Coalition personnel. DOD civilians (MPRI) or local civilian contractors working for or with NGO's [Non-Governmental Organizations]. Government officials designated by the commander.
PROTECTED PROPERTY: Anything that would hinder Coalition forces mission or stability if destroyed.
HOSTILE INTENT: Clearly demonstrates that a hostile act is imminent (pointing a weapon or emplacing explosives, or preparing an attack).
HOSTILE ACT: Any act to kill, destroy or otherwise do harm to a protected person or property.[13]

That we surrendered tactical advantage to the enemy with

our Rules of Engagement was a necessary evil to fighting a counterinsurgent war. This very much complicates war and impacts soldiers and marines in very sinister ways. To deal with this critical aspect of the war in Iraq, all soldiers had to master this summary and know how to apply it in a variety of combat situations. But this was just a summary. The actual Rules of Engagement were lengthier and laced with "legal strychnine" for leaders to interpret and attempt to apply, quite impractical for day-to-day operations.

Rules of engagement are not new to the military. The Army has fought many wars with rules in place. Rules for Land Warfare separate the U.S. Army from many other Armies in the world. Rules are righteous and necessary, even in war. Rules of engagement should always seek to be permissive and practical. Rules must be comprehensive disallowing room for further restriction from subordinate commanders below the issuing command authority. For the Army in Iraq, the rules of engagement are frequently further restricted in application by subordinate commanders to the issuing authority. This action, above all others, should be made illegal and commanders found to be further restricting and impinging the rules of engagement established by the highest military command authority should be relieved of duty. This kind of action subverts the higher authority intent and smacks of career protectionism and is, in my opinion, toying with the lives of soldiers immorally.

Under the Combined Forces Land Component Command Rules of Engagement, which Task Force 1-21 operated under in 2004-2005, soldiers could always protect themselves. But for soldiers, the key in any fight at the tactical level is initiative. Simply "getting the drop" on your adversary was vital to winning a firefight. In infantry combat, seeing the enemy, identifying him, and then engaging him with a combination of well-aimed shots and overwhelming suppressive fire coupled with quick, controlled maneuver is what fighting is all about. Close combat is cruel and ugly. It is quite violent and fast paced. In urban terrain fighting an insurgency, identifying or seeing the enemy is supremely difficult. Add to that the dimension of terrorist tactics and it is a hell of a mess. Soldiers must be trained and capable as never before in our Army's history. Leaders are responsible for the actions of their soldiers. Rules of engagement define the terms for lethal engagement supporting the strategic goals of America.

The rules of engagement we were operating under prohibited us from firing on suspicious behavior alone. Soldiers had to clearly identify someone as hostile enemy. Even a weapon in view may not be enough evidence to allow soldiers to engage or use lethal force. Soldiers had to use a graduated, escalating response to engage the enemy. Shout, Shove, Show, and then Shoot was our organizational mantra to effectively employ the rules of engagement day-to-day on patrols.

The more menacing aspect to engagements that usurped the intended application of the rules of engagement existed in the 5th BCT most of the one year tour we were in Iraq. In the 5th BCT, if soldiers fired at an Iraqi they believed was an enemy combatant or considered Iraqis who were acting provocatively where soldiers believed their lives were threatened and a BCT soldier injured someone, a 15-6 investigation was required. A 15-6 investigation is a thoroughly-documented, command-supported investigation of an incident. By rule, a field grade officer (major-colonel rank) is assigned as an investigating officer. After a few occurrences of engagements that resulted in "innocent" local nationals having been wounded or killed, Colonel Lanza instituted a blanket 15-6 investigation policy for all incidents. That a 15-6 investigation became standard fare in the 5th BCT our last six months in Iraq became a source of some consternation for me as a subordinate battalion task force commander. The stated purpose for conducting a 15-6 investigation for any and all incidents where combat action took place was to ensure the soldiers involved were protected from prosecution. In my mind, this presupposed that soldiers who had engaged suspected or known insurgent enemy within the limits of the Combined Forces Land Component Command's issued Rules of Engagement were automatically threatened with legal prosecution. What kind of command and operating environment is that?

Regardless of all the rationalizations proffered by my superiors, this threat of looking over our collective shoulders, suspecting wrongful application of the Combined Forces Land Component Command's Rules of Engagement was the unstated result of the 15-6 investigation policy. And I believe it was absolutely the wrong way to conduct business. This kind of command activity within the Army needs addressing from the highest levels as future conflicts will find the military in the similar counterinsurgent wars.

This unwritten policy was frequently discussed by the battalion task force commanders and BCT staff officers. Unspoken to the 5th BCT commander, Colonel Lanza, it was considered by us to be a loser. We had other administrative mechanisms in place to assess the combat actions without resorting to 15-6 investigations as the standard. The unintended second-order effect of these investigations was to seed a command climate of distrust and lack of confidence in leadership below the BCT level.

An After Action Review was standard operating procedure in Task Force 1-21 for units returning from patrols. In fact, all units in the 5th BCT produced written After Action Reviews for patrols regardless of whether combat action occurred. This, however, was not considered sufficient by the BCT Commander. When Iraqis or American soldiers were injured in combat, the 15-6 investigation served to document the facts of what had occurred. Should legal action be pursued, the investigation would have the facts, and senior leaders would have reviewed the findings. My gut told me we really just had senior leaders who were "covering their ass" in the event something serious or untoward occurred.

The way I pieced this policy together was like this: We were an Army at war with a crafty enemy who freely and frequently used terrorist tactics. Tactics designed to create ambiguity included suicide attacks by the enemy. Moreover, this enemy hid among the civilian people and attacked from their houses and buildings where we could not easily see or identify them even after they fired at us. If we fired at them within the strictures of the Combined Forces Land Component Command Rules of Engagement, we still had to justify, in a detailed 15-6 investigation, why we did this. Together, it seemed like an unintelligent way to fight. We were sent to Iraq with weapons, we were trained to use them. But using them meant an incredible amount of scrutiny. Scrutiny that implied a soldier or the unit did something heinously wrong. I truly believe there were circumstances and incidents that warranted this level of scrutiny. But in those cases, I felt commanders should assess individual situations and incidents. If inappropriateness was suspected, based on a review of the facts in these incidents, then a 15-6 investigation could be ordered. The blanket application just smacked of self-protectionism that was not too hard to decode.

As if the rules of engagement were not sensitive and challenging enough, dealing with the Iraqi people every day further complicated the situation for soldiers and leaders alike. Cultural, religious, and fundamental values about life and human existence were dissimilar between soldiers and Iraqis. Staff officers in the Combined Forces Land

Component Command and lawyers who did not run the mean streets of Baghdad designed the rules of engagement. The rules of engagement were absolutely necessary to preserve the integrity of American combat action in a counterinsurgent fight that required soldiers to convince the average Iraqi that we were there to help them rebuild. Killing non-combatant Iraqis, abusing them or acting unmercifully does not achieve that end. A set of engagement rules help soldiers and leaders define the appropriate boundaries. Because the rules of engagement were focused on limiting the use of lethal force, soldiers were disadvantaged in most situations. I constantly reminded my lieutenants and senior non-commissioned officers that the enemy, in almost every situation, got the first shot. Their job was to manage and direct the response.

One of the major areas the rules of engagement fell short was in circumstances where traffic control points or hasty cordon positions were established. Early in our deployment to Iraq the Task Force found that this kind of tactical operation was particularly dangerous and challenging. For example, I recall the incident where an Italian Intelligence Agent, Nicolo Calipari, was killed at Entry Control Point 1 at Baghdad International Airport in the spring of 2005. This was solid evidence that applying the rules of engagement in traffic control point circumstances was very treacherous. The circumstances of the incident were classic to life as an American Army soldier or marine in Baghdad:

Giuliana Sgrena was captured by an insurgent terrorist group outside the University of Baghdad on 4 February 2004. Sgrena was a journalistic reporter for a publication in Italy. The captors took her in an attempt to extort the Italian government to remove their troops from Iraq.

Italy sent Nicolo Calipari, an Italian intelligence agent, to negotiate with the terrorist group to secure the release of Sgrena.

He was successful (no disclosure of the deal made has ever been proffered). Coordinating with unnamed officers of the Italian and U.S. Army at Camp Victory, a car carrying Sgrena and three other agents approached Entry Control Point 1 at Baghdad International Airport. According to Sgrena, approximately 700 meters from the Entry Control Point soldiers assigned to 1-69 Infantry, New York National Guard, without warning fired on the approaching car killing Calipari, wounding Sgrena and another agent in the vehicle. [14]

The U.S. government investigation found that the soldiers involved followed the Rules of Engagement properly. Soldiers used the Shout, Shove, Show, and then Shoot procedures. They had in fact, fired warning shots and shots to the engine block of the vehicle that was seemingly ignoring signals to halt as they rapidly approached the control point.

Warning shots or shots to the engine block of a speeding car are tricky. Neither are necessarily well-aimed shots. Moving cars and fired bullets often conspire to produce disastrous physics. Ricochets of bullets off metal, pavement, or rocks are unaccountable.

The threat of a vehicle-borne IED was high for the 5th BCT and Task Force 1-21 because we were patrolling Route Irish and Route Senators, around the clock. When units were on roads, static, with a mix of mounted and dismounted troops in a given area, invariably danger lurked. Iraqis drove without regard to traffic signals under normal circumstances. We used Arabic language signs, written and designed by local nationals, standard Iraqi traffic "STOP" signs, and put interpreters on bull-horns and loud speakers to mitigate the confusion that many claimed after incidents occurred. Soldiers, fearful of car bombs, have very short decision cycles to apply Shout, Shove, Show, then Shoot rules to the rapidly unfolding situation. Night time or limited visibility conditions made discerning appropriate action exponentially more difficult in these scenarios.

I concluded the solution to this conundrum had to be resolved in training for the Task Force. Soldiers had to know the rules of engagement and practice the application of the rules instinctively. Any training could not be so regimented that free-flowing variation was not part of the process. No two situations are exactly the same. To train the rules of engagement, we had to develop scenarios and after-action reviews that reinforced the rules of engagement simultaneously focusing soldiers and leaders on the permissive nature of the rules.

Despite all efforts, through the year in Iraq, the Task Force had no less than fifteen incidents where 15-6 investigations were conducted by order of Colonel Lanza. The investigations were conducted ostensibly to insure we had properly applied the CFLCC Rules of Engagement. In all cases the investigations found that the rules of engagement were meticulously and properly applied.

I caution senior leaders attempting to micro-manage combat engagement so meticulously to beware. This micro-management is fraught with great danger. Attention to the following might be beneficial:

- What is your command message when you restrict soldiers beyond the higher command codified Rules of Engagement?

- Can you personally operate under the scrutiny you place your soldiers? Will you accept the punishment you mete out should you fail to meet your own standards?

- Training the Rules of Engagement demands a focus on the permissive aspects, not the restrictive ones.

- Focus less on career protection and more on the soldiers' survival.

- Commanders and unit leaders: you are accountable for soldier's actions in combat. No amount of reliance on the Rules of Engagement or supporting investigations defers or deflects your accountability.

- Train. Train. Train.

The restrictive nature of the rules of engagement coupled with the lack of armored humvees again extolled their fare from Task Force 1-21 on the streets of Al Saidiyah.

Silver Star ". . . on my son's chest!"

Private First Class Christopher N. Fernandez was assigned to A/1-21 FA, known as the "Assassins," as a patrol member in the Renegade patrol. He received the first Silver Star Medal awarded to a First Cavalry Division trooper in the war in Iraq for the heroism he exhibited on May 5, 2004.

Private Fernandez was designated a rocket crewman by Military Occupational Specialty (MOS). Military Occupational Specialty is the Army's administrative method of naming or coding a particular job. The Army matches specified training tasks and skills to specialties. Despite his official designation, Private Fernandez in Iraq performed the duties of a tough, brave infantryman. Private Fernandez, originally from Phoenix, Arizona, was a tall, lanky half-Mexican young man, just 20 years old. He was a quiet unassuming guy who loved to soldier and understood his role on his team. On the day his patrol counted on him most, Private First Class Fernandez performed like a superstar athlete knocking a walk-off homerun in game seven of the World Series. He was magnificent on the battlefield where life and death were at stake.

Renegade patrol was sent into Al Saidiyah to provide security in two mahallas located in the southwest corner of Al Saidiyah. The patrol was specifically to look for particular vehicles we had identified as having been involved in mortar attacks in and around Al Saidiyah. The term we used for Renegade's patrol was "BOLO," an acronym for "Be On the Look Out."

First Lieutenant Ryan Swindell was Renegade's patrol leader. He was an exceptional lieutenant. He was smart, tough, and wanted to excel in everything he undertook. He was eager, but not too eager. He would get excited but he always controlled his emotions well enough to think clearly. When he had to brief, he was always well prepared and could think on his feet. Though he had not been leading the platoon long, he knew all his troops and his technical competence was one of the best among his peers in the battalion.

The Assistant Patrol Leader was Sergeant First Class Landolph James. Sergeant James was as strong as a bull, hardened, and a well-liked non-commissioned officer in the battery. He fretted over his men like a mother hen. He was a good teacher who led from out in front of his troops, always willing to assume the risks necessary to protect his team members. Sergeant James was as brave a soldier as I have ever seen.

Renegade patrol progressed with little or no incident which was typical. In a well-planned, well-rehearsed outfit the soldiers knew what they needed to do, and they did their jobs superbly. The patrol had set in position at two of the four programmed positions. The Patrol Leader directed the patrol to prepare to move to the third location. One of the humvees had been turned off and was sitting in its over-watch position so the soldiers could hear well. Now, getting ready to move, the vehicle would not start. The soldiers tried to get it running but could not get it started.

Lieutenant Swindell radioed his battery Command Post (CP) and informed it of the situation. He then made the decision to forgo the last two positions and return to base. He did not want to be out on patrol with a broken vehicle since this would slow them down. He was aware the enemy looked for this kind of situation to exploit. The patrol leader ordered the soldiers to rig the vehicle for tow.

En route back to Camp Falcon, the patrol moved through Al Saidiyah down the main north-south market street in the town with one vehicle in tow closely behind the tow vehicle. They did not take the same route back that they used heading to their programmed points, a maneuver forbidden in the battalion.

The broken humvee had a 240B, 7.62mm machinegun mounted on a stand in the back cargo hold of the humvee. The back of the vehicle was protected only with "Mad Max" locally fabricated metal armor, since we did not yet have other armor for humvees. Riding in the back were Staff Sergeant Terry Saffron, Private First Class James Marshall, and Private First Class Bradley Kritzer. Private Kritzer was manning the 240B machinegun and the other two soldiers were providing left and right flank security for him.

As the patrol neared the end of a major north-south market road in Al Saidiyah, they approached an intersection. About 300 meters north of the intersection, the enemy sat in an over-watch position. As the towed vehicle passed the trigger point, an IED was detonated.

The IED was a 155mm artillery projectile encased in solid concrete. Encasing the artillery shell in concrete increased the shrapnel sprayed from the blast. The IED detonated on the right side of the towed vehicle. Sergeant Saffron was seriously wounded but conscious.

Private Marshall fought very hard to stay alive, but his wounds were fatal. A large piece of shrapnel went under his right arm and traveled internally across his chest, exiting just below his throat through the chest bone. It left about a five-inch hole. The force of the shrapnel blew his outer tactical vest open. We never found the shell fragment. The fragment tore through his body and exited with such force it flew out somewhere on the road.

Private Kritzer also fought hard to stay alive but his wounds were too extensive. Multiple large, medium, and small shrapnel fragments tore through the right side of his body, piercing his right arm, shoulder, face and head.

Sergeant Saffron, who was furthest from the blast point, tried to lift his weapon and fire at what appeared to be the enemy maneuvering to engage the halted two vehicles of the patrol. But because his arm was shredded by the IED, he could not lift his weapon. Additionally, the right side of his jaw was badly injured and he had multiple perforations from shrapnel fragments.

The back of the disabled humvee was a bloody mess, and the patrol was in bad shape. The tow vehicle sped up within seconds of the blast in an attempt to get out of what they thought was a kill zone. The driver of the tow vehicle, Private First Class Larry Garcia, raced toward the intersection. Ahead on the road was a concrete curb used for channeling traffic in multiple directions in and around the intersection.

The soldiers in the lead vehicle with the patrol leader heard the blast but were more than 300 meters ahead of the blast location clearing the route. They had already crossed the median and were heading east on Route Force toward Check Point 8. They were called back.

As the other vehicles in the patrol attempted to jump the curb of the median, the tow strap on the disabled vehicle snapped and released the vehicle carrying the wounded.

Lieutenant Swindell, the Renegade Patrol Leader, was on the radio talking to the radio operator in the task force Tactical Operations Center. Hearing the desperate nature of the situation, the Operations Sergeant, Master Sergeant Joe Silvas, spoke with Lieutenant Swindell and managed to obtain a relatively accurate report on the current situation from the lieutenant. Lieutenant Swindell reported that he had an incident involving an IED, he thought he had wounded but he didn't know their status or how many. The S3 directed the Battle Captain to inform the Troop Medical Clinic at Camp Falcon to expect wounded and that a detailed nine-line medical evacuation report would follow as soon as it could be put together. I got on the radio to Lieutenant Swindell.

Immediately Lieutenant Swindell reported that he had just returned to the crippled element on Route Force and they were presently taking automatic weapons fire — direct fire — from the buildings across the street. He was very calm and matter of fact, not panicked in the least. I could hear the heavy volume of fire when he spoke.

"Rocket 6, I'll get back to you," he advised me.

The radio went silent. I was concerned. I asked the S3 if we had anything else out and if so could we vector them over to lend assistance. If not, we needed to get the quick-reaction force moving immediately. Major Reinhart, the S3, had already alerted the quick-reaction force, and they were at ready-condition one [REDCON 1] waiting an order to move. But we had another patrol from B/1-21 in a sector that could get to the Renegade patrol quicker. I ordered the S3 to send that patrol and leave the quick-reaction force at ready-condition one; develop the situation. The Operations Sergeant, Master Sergeant Silvas, got on the radio and vectored the B/1-21 patrol to the ambush location.

What Lieutenant Swindell was dealing with was a small-arms far-ambush. The IED was the trigger event for an ambush lying in wait less than a block down from where the blast had occurred. Because the patrol had a good interval and moved quickly with mutual support, the ambush was poorly executed and undisciplined. While the enemy had placed part of the patrol under direct fire, it was not effective against the entire patrol.

Sergeant James had circled back to the disabled vehicle and was laying down a base of fire with his rifle. He was also trying to rally his driver, who had become catatonic from the blast and subsequent series of challenging events. Sergeant James had a good chunk of his right shin sliced off by a piece of shrapnel from the blast. He was not aware of the wound until he turned to clear his radio and collapsed on the ground because his leg gave out when he put weight on it. He crawled to the humvee cab to clear his radio.

Staff Sergeant Timothy Buttz, a squad leader on the patrol from the squad that had not been hit by the IED, dismounted his truck and, with the enemy firing at him, ran to the back of the separated, disabled humvee and began to pull his wounded comrades out. Private Fernandez, following his squad leader, also hopped from his vehicle with his M249 squad automatic weapon. Taking cover behind the hood of the disabled humvee, he directed suppressive fire on the enemy ambush position, allowing Sergeant Buttz to retrieve the wounded soldiers. One-by-one, Sergeant Buttz ran the wounded from the disabled vehicle to his humvee. When Private Fernandez ran out of ammunition for his squad automatic weapon after Staff Sergeant Buttz moved the second wounded soldier, he noticed the M240B machinegun still mounted in the back of the disabled humvee loaded with a belt of ammunition. He ran from behind the protection of the disabled humvee — fully exposed to enemy fire — hopped in the back, grabbed the M240B machinegun, removed it from the bent mount, and fired it from the hip at the enemy ambush position while Sergeant Buttz removed the last casualty in a fireman's carry.

By this time, the others in the patrol had joined in the fight. Lieutenant Swindell saw that three of four wounded were in critical condition. He also assessed that the enemy small-arms fire had subsided. He ordered his patrol to cease firing. By then, the B/1-21 patrol had linked up and was able to assist and take charge of security so the wounded could be evacuated.

Lieutenant Swindell reported the casualties to the Tactical Operations Center and battery Command Post. He informed us the patrol was inbound with four casualties, three critical and one serious. He also updated us on the ambush firefight. The S3 provided a report to the Troop Medical Clinic and the BCT Tactical Operations Center. I briefed Colonel Lanza. I then met up with Command Sergeant Major Hughes, and we went to the medical facility to confirm they were prepared for the casualties.

When I arrived at the emergency room, there was blood everywhere. Private Marshall was on a gurney nearest the main entry doorway. Doctors had fully exposed his chest. Private Kritzer was furthest from the main door, turned on his right side and three medical people were frantically working on him. His head was messed up with a wide, open, gaping wound. Sergeant Saffron's arm, neck, and face were bleeding badly, but he was alert although in excruciating pain. Looking in his eyes, without him uttering a word, I knew he was going to make it.

The doctors had put a chest tube in Private Marshall's side and were doing cardio-pulmonary resuscitation within seconds. First Lieutenant Helms, the Task Force Physician Assistant (PA), was digging in the hole of Private Marshall's chest with his fingers. He looked directly at me as he was doing so and with his expression told me, Private Marshall was dead. Marshall was not moving or really conscious. His eyes were not fully closed, they were fixed straight toward the ceiling but were seeing nothing.

Private Kritzer had a large, grotesque puddle of blood pooling on the floor below his gurney. I walked over toward him and tried to move blood-soaked cloths from the work area of the medics attending him. After a few long minutes I could not watch anymore. The wound to his head was horrific and exposed all. The chaplain had been summoned to the medical clinic. I could see he, too, was struggling emotionally with what he was seeing.

Sergeant James was bleeding profusely from the leg injury but was alert. He was more concerned for the others than for his own injuries. Sergeant James sat on a ledge in the emergency room and I believe he was praying for the lives of his men. He was tough as nails and never once uttered a word for help. When a medic put a dressing on his leg, I don't believe he even noticed.

To see my soldiers in that condition profoundly affected me. This event, though tragic in proportions only soldiers can truly grasp, signaled that we had turned a corner as a unit. These soldiers fought hard and did things right. They fought back and dealt with the horrors of close combat. Tragically, two of them were killed and all of us would have to live with that. But the training and toughness had been indelibly stamped onto the unit.

Sergeant James and Sergeant Saffron would leave Iraq after

a short stay at the hospital in the Green Zone.

These losses and difficult lessons magnified the need for me to toughen up my leadership. It was essential I made sure I remained personally and directly involved with the soldiers and our junior leaders. It was unequivocally necessary that, as the battalion task force commander, I was in the mix every day because at the end of the day I was responsible for all Task Force 1-21 did or failed to do. The lives of every one of these men and women were my responsibility. I understood in the most graphic way just how high the stakes were and understood as I never had before.

12 Patrolling & Training, Leading From the Front

"A piece of spaghetti or a military unit can only be led from the front end." George S. Patton

The sudden loss of soldiers in the Task Force in April and May coupled with the constant pressure the enemy sought to place on us challenged all the leaders in the Task Force in ways none of us had ever experienced before. We had trained hard in the past. Many of us found ourselves in situations earlier in our careers that demanded great personal sacrifice. However, the combat death of soldiers and the constant threat of losing your own life inestimably altered the dynamics of troop leading. Constant presence, looking your soldiers in the eyes to see through to their soul, was absolutely critical to successfully leading in this environment.

One of the key tenets of the "Lanza" Doctrine was constant and direct leader involvement. In his typical lead-by-example manner, Colonel Lanza set the standard for his subordinate task force commanders to follow. Colonel Lanza was out in the BCT sector and beyond every single day. He never took a day off or stayed inside Camp Falcon for a whole day, never. He expected his subordinate commanders to be out in their respective sectors. He wanted them directly engaged in the operations. In the BCT this was absolutely normal. Really, it was matter-of-fact in execution; my peers were out and in their sectors every bit as much as Colonel Lanza or I were out. The nature of fighting in Iraq demanded this practice. Meetings with civic leaders, checking on the progress of civil projects, negotiating problems in the various mahallas, and "refereeing" the factions of people contending among each other required battalion commanders to be intimately engaged.

One of the things I constantly and consistently did was to go out on patrols with the units in the Task Force. This is something many non-military people do not truly understand about military leadership. Officers in too many Hollywood movies or books penned by disgruntled troops are portrayed as aloof, arrogant, sometimes unfeeling careerists. That may be true for some, but most officers are involved closely with their soldiers. They share in the hardships right alongside the troops they are charged to lead. Not only do officers live the hardships and share the pains but they bear the burdens and responsibilities for their units' successes and failures. That's just the way it was in Task Force 1-21. It is how I insisted officers in the Task Force approach their duties. Indeed, officers in the U.S. Army have been right in the melee with their soldiers since the earliest days in 1775 when this Army started.

Commanding in Iraq demanded constant, close interaction with all parts of the organization. Deviating from convention was absolutely called for in this counterinsurgent environment. One of the ways I deviated from standard, conventional senior leader practice was in daily execution of Task Force operations. My peer battalion commanders and all those at or above the battalion level formed Personal Security Teams (PST). These were teams designated and trained to provide personal executive-type protection to commanders. Division staff in fact directed the implementation and training of these Personal Security Teams for commanders, battalion level and above to operate. These teams were generally a twelve-soldier team. The intent of the directive, as I understood it, was for me to maintain appropriate security when operating in sector. A whole patrol, in my mind, met that intent. I chose not to employ a dedicated Personal Security Team beyond the means of my vehicle combat crew for a couple reasons. First, the Personal Security Team, over a short time in sector, was easily identifiable as the Task Force Commander's Personal Security

Team. The same vehicles and the same faces become identifiable to an observant enemy. I did not want to be so easily discernible. Second, I was squeezing every last soldier I
could to meet the troop-to-task demands. A dedicated Personal Security Team was not a luxury I felt the Task Force
could afford. Third, I felt a Personal Security Team would
impede my ability to participate and coach given my personal style of leadership. I wanted to be in the mix, not ancillary to the action.

I went out on patrols. On these patrols, I imbedded myself
with my crew as another asset for the patrol leader to use
in his assigned mission. Always, the Patrol Leader briefed
me and my crew on our mission, task, and immediate action drills in support of the patrol. Doing this gave me critical insights into how the Task Force operated day-to-day. I
knew intuitively and empirically what business practices
functioned and at what level of competence. For example,
after three or four days out on patrol I became keenly aware
that the pre-combat checks patrols conducted before missions were not executed to battalion-prescribed standards.

When I was on the pre-deployment site survey in January
before we deployed to Iraq observing 1-94 Field Artillery, I
noticed, during the patrols, how sloppy the vehicles were
inside, with equipment strewn about haphazardly. Unacceptable, I thought, while riding. I made a note that my
unit would not patrol like this. I surmised that if something as simple as grabbing the medical aid bag were the
difference between life and death, then it mattered where
the bag was stowed and that anyone could get at it quickly.
This was true for all equipment. A standardized designation for equipment located inside patrol vehicles was essential. In all my training in the Army the need to have a
vehicle load plan for combat was always part of the regime.
Good units followed with élan and discipline this kind of
operating standard.

Through my experiences at the Army Maneuver Training Centers, every Observer Controller I ever spoke to or got coached by had a universally consistent comment about units that train there: pre-combat checks were poorly executed by units. They execute better as the training cycle of the unit progresses, but only because lessons were learned the hard way.

My observations of patrols in April and May clearly proved the Task Force did not execute pre-combat checks well. That had to change. And because I was the leader responsible for this organizational shortcoming, I was the one who had to lead the unit to fix it.

My other major observation from personal participation in the patrols at this stage was that patrol leaders did not issue orders well enough to optimally prepare the patrols for action. The patrol leaders were trying to cut corners and skip the orders process because they considered it cumbersome and repetitive, simply restating the obvious, according to them. That was dead wrong. That mentality was a disease of being artillery not infantry. The leaders understood the orders and ingrained directives for artillery procedures but were struggling with transferring those procedures to infantry/cavalry actions. Again, I saw another vulnerability that had to be addressed or people would be killed unwittingly.

Every patrol the Task Force sent out in Iraq had a task and purpose — a mission. Every soldier in the patrol participates and any soldier may need to assume a leadership role within the patrol. My patrol leaders had to learn this, think this way, and then operate accordingly or they would be removed from serving in Task Force 1-21.

Because every soldier had a role and could become a leader it necessarily followed that all soldiers needed to know the mission — the detailed plan — and rehearse. That was the process I communicated to my patrol leaders. This standard I took from Ranger training. I had to coach them to perform to this standard, internalizing it as their own.

By mid-May, I concluded several issues needed to be addressed and where I would direct my leadership to improve the unit and overall performance:

1) Fire and maneuver emphasizing an aggressive warrior ethos that soldiers would have to internalize.

2) Teach patrol leaders how to better conduct patrols as well as direct fire and maneuver, issue detailed patrol orders, and rehearse better.

3) Direct involvement, with input from the Command Sergeant Major in pre-combat checks until demonstrated performance was consistently up to standard.

To deal with the actions necessary to fix these shortcomings, I went to the Battery Commanders. Unfortunately, none had the training, experience, or education in infantry or maneuver tactics to effectively train and educate their lieutenants and sergeants in the art and science of patrolling and patrol leading. None of my subordinate commanders were Ranger qualified and certainly none were infantryman. Five Field Artillery captains and one Chemical Corps captain commanded the subordinate elements of the Task Force.

All these subordinate commanders were highly capable and talented. They could learn and then teach their lieutenants and sergeants, but time was not on our side. Although I ideally wanted to train, teach, coach, and mentor executing a train-the-trainer program, I could not take the time to do this.

At Fort Hood, before deploying, we had already worked together quite a bit. We had focused on platoon tactics but not patrolling and patrol leading. There's a marked difference. Rather than dismissing their positions as commanders, I integrated these roles into the training regimen.

The Battery Commander's Achilles heel was proper inspections and execution of pre-combat checks. The subordinate commanders, their lieutenants, and senior non-commissioned officers neglected their duties in this area and it angered me tremendously. I confronted the subordinate commanders, emphasizing their inability to execute the detailed assessments and enforce the standards. I knew I was ultimately responsible. Obvious to me was that I had not properly taught them what correct pre-combat checks and inspections looked like. I decided I needed to be more forceful and demanding.

One of the clearer lessons for me in addressing the pre-combat checks deficiency is that combat leadership was markedly different from leading in garrison in a peacetime Army. Although many would say there is no difference, those who do so have likely never led in combat. Senior Army leaders are more forgiving in peacetime environments, and that forgiveness generally permeates down through the ranks. It creates a certain weakness and tolerance that does not have a place in a combat Army. I liken it to the difference between practice and game day in sports. Coach is a little more forgiving in practice; he'll yank you out in a game. This is true in combat. I think I was more tolerant and patient with subordinates before we deployed to Iraq. I was very demanding, less patient, and more draconian in Iraq. Though I tried to be measured in my judgments, I never hesitated in Iraq to pull a low-performing leader or confront a situation that needed my attention. You have to be tough in combat or you fail. Weaklings perish in combat or their character inadequacies surface fairly quickly; it's simply too demanding to be otherwise. The stakes are too high.

I had a long discussion with the Command Sergeant Major about the failures in enforcement of rigid and exacting standards with pre-combat checks I had observed. He went out, did some more checks, and concluded, as I had observed, that leaders weren't doing what they were taught and directed to do. I told him I thought he and I should take it on at battalion level, get the standards clearly demonstrated, and drive the point home. Once the units demonstrated they had mastery of pre-combat checks functions then I'd turn that back over to the Battery Commanders. We would then do random spot checks at battalion to ensure the system remained right.

Being in the mix of the patrolling also helped me see what continuing training needed to be done. Though we were in a daily fight, I wanted the organization to stay sharp and trained. Sitting inside the walls of Camp Falcon could be dreary, boring, softening to the troops. I wanted them ready, on edge, and prepared to fight when required to do so. Training is absolutely essential to long-term success in combat. To fight in Iraq for a year and conduct no sustained training was unconscionable to me. I was committed to as robust a program as I could lead and enforce.

The Task Force staff always had to balance between operations — which obviously took precedence — and training. Soldiers could not go 24/7 without respite and survive the year. As I contemplated training in the Task Force, I kept this in mind and balanced the effort.

Training the Task Force while in Contact

In my personal estimation one of the best modern Generals

of our time was General William DePuy. He was the first Commanding General of Training and Doctrine Command (TRADOC) when that Army Major Command was formed in the early 1970s after the Vietnam War. General DePuy was a trainer and educator whose legacy has shaped the Army profoundly and taught all the generations of leaders in the modern Army how to train, educate, and sustain training in the Army these decades since he left command of TRADOC.

In his writings, General DePuy emphasized that training and education are the basis for success in any unit. He saw tough lessons of death and carnage inflicted on units he was associated with as a young officer in World War II. He saw that poor training caused poor performance. Without developing and executing training while deployed in combat, performance could not improve. His ideas and beliefs influenced me long before I got to Iraq. Once there, I understood first-hand what he meant.

I was very much free to do as I saw fit in Iraq insofar as implementation of training programs and their subsequent management. The BCT and higher authorities did very little to promote training. All emphasis was prior to deployment and while in Kuwait. Once soldiers became engaged in the fight in Iraq, there were precious few training requirements. The BCT staff was consumed by the daily operations. The BCT Commander was immersed in the daily grind. Neither gave attention to a robust internal BCT training program. The Division had a training program but I would characterize it as superficial. That neither echelon above the battalion Task Force had a directive training program was fine with me. I wanted the freedom to manage my business my way. Having been in the mix of patrols, I knew what needed to be done, and went after training and training management with vigor and purpose.

In order to make the training relevant and focused I established the priorities and the basis for training. Establishing the priorities was easy. A context for training needed to be shaped. Obvious to me was that patrols were the context in which to shape all training. Everything Task Force 1-21 operated on a day-to-day basis was conducted in a patrol unit of action. Conceptually, shaping all that we trained around this organizational paradigm kept everyone synchronized.

Within the Task Force, I established priorities for training effort and ensured the S3 understood them. I insisted the staff and subordinate commanders pursue training with these priorities in mind: Leader improvement (education of officers and non-commissioned officers); tactics modification/improvement; soldier education; and then Military Occupational Specialty training.

Leader Development

I considered a leader training and education program vital because this was where as a commander I could best influence the whole Task Force. Junior leaders were out dealing with the daily action. They were executing the plans and grand designs of the staff and senior officers of the BCT. Their individual and collective ability to lead, emphasizing the tenets of the "Lanza Doctrine," commanding and controlling combat operations at the patrol level, and realizing the overall task force objectives were entirely dependent on their ability to understand and practically apply the concepts with good procedures and troop-leading skills. There was no substitute for a good leader-development program with personal involvement.

To address this need and focus on the junior leaders, I created the Patrol Leader Program in May 2004. This comprehensive program included certification standards to build a strong, capable patrol leader. Lieutenants and senior non-commissioned officers were required to participate in this program. To be a patrol leader in the Task Force, a soldier had to successfully complete the education and training requirements I established.

The Task Force Patrol Leader Program

The first objective of the Patrol Leader Program was to teach the junior leaders the basics of patrolling and how to lead patrols. I gave classes on the fundamentals of combat and recon patrols, relating the doctrine to the actual experiences they had already acquired. The lieutenants and senior non-commissioned officers related the lessons they learned to each other. This became the basis for the broader program the Task Force fostered and promoted throughout the time I was in Iraq. The Task Force Patrol Leader Program was a cross-fertilization lessons-learned session that the S3 led weekly to extract the good ideas. We always tried to implement ways to be more effective and successful.

At Fort Hood, while training and preparing for deployment, the Task Force staff and command team made a concerted effort to define the training that the platoons needed. We defined it as light infantry tactics training and used Field Manual 7-8, *Infantry Rifle Platoon and Squad* as the basis for training organization and design. Once in Iraq this proved faulty for a few reasons: First, platoons were not our base unit of action. The basic formation and operational unit in Iraq for us was a patrol. A patrol is doctrinally defined as a smaller unit sent out from a larger unit to conduct combat or reconnaissance. Never did full platoons go out on patrol. Always a subset of the whole platoon was employed. We did not have enough vehicles to support whole platoons on every operation. Additionally, with the Division's

Environmental Leave Program, some portion of every platoon's membership was on leave or rotating to or from leave back to the States at any given time. It was impossible to operate as whole platoons day-to-day. We also rotated personnel on and off duty to sustain operations.

Operating through the full spectrum of tactical conflict was possible on any given patrol and this smaller force was more malleable than a whole platoon. All patrols in the BCT and in Task Force 1-21 were mounted or at least started out mounted and then transitioned to dismounted. Thus, the dismounted emphasis of light infantry was of limited value.

The standard weapons mix relied upon in Field Manual 7-8, *Infantry Rifle Platoon and Squad* was not the operating norm for Task Force 1-21. We were not outfitted as a typical infantry unit. We were given an infantry mission and role but not the personnel and equipment of a typical infantry unit. We had to modify our units with assigned personnel and standard equipment for a rocket artillery battalion.

What Field Manual 7-8, *Infantry Rifle Platoon and Squad* provided was a solid basis of understanding from which everyone could further develop. And Field Manual 7-8, *Infantry Rifle Platoon and Squad* had a good section on patrolling. By the summer months, it was time to dig into that part of the book and gain mastery. Personally, I preferred the U.S. Army Ranger Handbook as the doctrinal source of teaching patrolling skills, and it was entirely consistent with Field Manual 7-8, *Infantry Rifle Platoon and Squad* but smaller, compact, and easily carried while on patrol.

The Field Artillery branch is famous for "certifying" all the key positions in the fire support chain to execute indirect cannon and rocket/missile fires. We certify observers, cannon and rocket crewman, and fire direction specialists. At

Ranger School, not everyone earns the Ranger tab, a skills qualification badge worn on the uniform in which a standard has to be met. So, I did not reinvent the wheel, I just went with what was obviously necessary and set up a certification program.

Battery Commanders were required to provide me with the names of the lieutenants and senior non-commissioned officers they considered capable of performing as Patrol Leaders. Each then had to get classroom instruction on:

• Battalion Task Force 1-21 Standing Orders

• Small Unit Leadership Principles

• Troop Leading Procedures (Patrol Military Decision-making Process)

• Ambush Patrols (Mounted and Dismounted)

• Raid Patrol/Cordon and Search

• Recon Patrols

• Patrol Operations Planning

• Rules of Engagement

• Hasty Blocking Positions

• Information Operations Support

The soldiers then had to pass a check ride patrol, which included:

1) An evaluation of the preparation of an actual combat patrol applying the Eight Troop Leading Procedures; the patrol leader had to demonstrate mastery, not simply understanding.

2) A graded assessment of the patrol order. A preset minimum score was required. The patrol orders were observed and evaluated by three captains that I had personally

trained and certified, who were assistant operations officers in the Task Force Operations Section.

3) The patrol order assessment was followed by a ride-a-long from the battery commander.

4) A second patrol reinforcing the demonstrated skills already learned, followed by a ride-a-long observation by me.

5) A formal interview with me, which included an oral quiz about expectations, Task Force policies, and a CFLCC Rules of Engagement review; this provided me a face-to-face opportunity to ensure the patrol leader candidate had internalized the essential fundamentals of patrol leadership expected in Task Force 1-21.

Upon successful completion of this regimen, they were certified. This made a real difference in two fundamental ways. The patrol leaders had confidence in their knowledge and ability to apply it. Second, the Task Force expectations were synchronized at the patrol-leader level. Both of these goals were integral to my leadership.

Many of my peers may wonder where I found the time to implement such a detailed certification process that some might suggest was overkill. The truth is that the training was integrated into the natural flow of operations, so it took no extra time. The performance of these patrol leaders was an issue. They were going out to operate and fight either way. I thought they should be as good as I could make them. As for the criticism of not having it done to standard before deployment, my response is that we met the Division and BCT articulated standard. Once I fully understood the realities of combat in Iraq, I concluded that standard simply was not good enough. Although the articulated standard served as a baseline level of competency, we had an obligation to be better. Lives were at stake. Working better as a team was part of my command responsibility, one I did not take lightly.

By the summer and into the early fall of 2004, I had concluded that in the very near future the Army was going to have to completely rethink its method for training leaders, particularly junior leaders. To maximize effectiveness and minimize loss of life, a very liberal, unconventional, and courageous approach to personnel utilization and training is needed. My situation triggered a reflection deep within me about the Army in which I served.

Although I was operating within the closely-prescribed limits of the military and the command in which I was serving, I knew I was pushing the limits outward to meet the needs of the unit's situation. I was not going to compromise the optimization of my organization. Training and leader development was undeniably necessary to transform my subordinate officers and non-commissioned officers from artillery leaders to infantry-capable patrol leaders and the effort had to be continuous.

I believe that three things most influence the leader development training for the future in the Army. First, with the reduced size of the force, more and more varied tasks have to be performed by fewer people; management of this must become part of the training equation. Second, technological advances have influenced command and control, making information available to leaders who must make decisions in a more refined and quicker manner. Technology has also increased the lethality of weapons. Third, the types of missions the Army is directed to undertake have changed dramatically since the military action in Korea. America fights wars that are undeclared, straddling peace enforcement and actual combat action. Today's wars deal broadly in civil affairs and police-type tasks and demand

that Army and Marine leaders understand public administration from a pragmatic implementation perspective. But
Army leaders today lack the supporting experience and
education. The future requirements demand change.

Future Officer Training

I envision great change necessary within the Army's officer training program. As I observed and worked for twenty years with peers and subordinates, this is what I came
to see.

Because force structure for the Army is moving inexorably toward smaller, leaner, more mobile (deployable) lethal
formations, the demands on leaders to perform more tasks
are ever-increasing. This suggests that the technical com-
petencies of leaders must become broader so leaders can
effectively respond to change and better resolve problems.
I believe instead of having multiple specialized branches
within the Army that compartmentalize task accomplishment, we need more comprehensive conglomerated, ca-
pabilities-based branches, an almost-exact opposite of the
model that worked through WWII.

My idea is for the Army to conglomerate branches and develop broadly-capable and liberally-educated officers who
can learn and apply technical skills easily and quickly. Today the Army has 17 standard branches (excludes specialty
and non-accessions branches). This has come to pass as an
evolutionary process over our Army's history since 1775.
It was appropriate for the preparation of the large, high-
intensity conflict-oriented Army that culminated, in my
opinion, with World War II. It is wholly inappropriate for
the realities of today and tomorrow.

I further believe strongly that all the Services of the Armed

Forces holistically need to adopt the same notion of conglomeration or more refined integration. We no longer need the division of the military Services as we know them now. We need a functional Land Component Force (not the Army and the Marines but one land force deployable by air, land, and sea and sustainable once in theater), Sea Component Force, Air Component Force, Space Component Force, Logistics Support Component Force and Special Operations Component Force. All of these component forces are supported by a political dynamic that must synthesize effort in budgeting, acquisition, doctrine, and force structure. The incredible proliferation of information technology demands this methodology. An organizational design like this optimizes capabilities to solve problems strategically, operationally, and tactically — sometimes simultaneously and sometimes autonomously — but always with maximum flexibility. The whole effort of developing a holistic, true, joint military force seeks this end anyway. The Service traditions and political procedures have effectively stifled this effort since 1986 when major legislation was passed to force the Services to pursue a more robust joint war-fighting capability. The so called Global War on Terrorism and right now, the war in Iraq, expose this national defense shortcoming clearly.

Focusing this argument more narrowly on the Army today, there is need for conglomerations of combat arms; combat support; logistics; civil affairs/psychological operations/information operations; and special warfare.

An Examination of the Combat Arms branches offers further explanatory insight. Until recently, the Army had five major Combat Arms branches and two minor. The majors are: Infantry, Armor, Aviation, Field Artillery and Special Forces; the minors are Air Defense and Engineers. Moving Air Defense, Aviation, and Engineers to combat support and moving Special Forces to its own domain thereby leaving the Infantry, Armor, and Field Artillery in a con-glomerated Fire and Maneuver Arm is more efficient. Officers should lose the specialty designations of Infantry, Armor, and Field Artillery and just be Combat Arms Fire & Maneuver officers. Requirements for officers designated to a Fire & Maneuver Arm would include:

• Technical/Tactical maneuver for infantry: light, motorized, mechanized.

• Technical/Tactical maneuver for armor.

• Technical/Tactical fire support techniques and planning.

• Intermediate proficiency with the weapons systems of the Infantry, Armor, Fire Support, and armed ground support Aviation.

• An intermediate-level understanding and education in Civil Affairs, Psychological Operations, and Information Operations to BCT level.

• Fluency in at least one foreign language.

• Intermediate-level understanding and education in negotiation and contract management.

• Intermediate-level understanding and education in High Intensity Conflict, Low Intensity Conflict, Peacekeeping Operations and Full Spectrum Operations doctrinal application.

The best Combat Arms officers under the current design in the Infantry, Armor, Field Artillery, Special Forces, and Aviation are those leaders who most effectively apply fire and maneuver. Fire support is a technical skill most Armor and Infantry officers simply do not master. Adding fire support ability and training to the tactical and operational level application of fire and maneuver, and then assigning those so-trained officers to units interchangeably would permit refinement of their skills and would achieve the overall effect of producing more capable leaders and combat arms officers.

Courses for Civil Affairs, Psychological Operations, and Information Operations as well as the foreign-language proficiency and negotiation and contract management should be standardized and college-level accredited. By doing this, the acquired skills would be transferable through legitimate accreditation benefiting the officer in the future. Mastery in the technical and tactical aspects of Combat Arms would be acquired by the officer in his unit(s) of assignment through a certification process. Assignment of officers would include positions in any type of Combat Arms unit.

This conglomeration vision would fit right with the present initiatives in the Army to create a force structure based on Units of Action and Units of Employment. A very powerful organization with officers who have a very broad and technically-diverse, combined understanding of warfare and how to apply those instruments to optimal effect would be the result of such an approach. Combat Arms officers would be better postured to fight and operate in a full spectrum, asymmetric, contemporary environment. Additionally, this approach would optimize career-progression opportunities from a human resources management perspective.

Many would say this is not possible: where would the Army get the time and money to educate an officer in this way? There is too much to learn and jumping between maneuver and fire support would be too difficult. I adamantly disagree. First, the academic rigor of Army schools was woefully absent in my personal experience. Army schools are the least intellectually challenging I have ever experienced. Many are simply designed to disseminate the information. Everyone passes with little emphasis on mastery of the subject matter. Second, examine how the Army trains Special Forces officers. This is the paradigm I recommend. The money is available with this perpetually smaller active force. The schools and facilities already exist in the Army. The issue is reorganization and reallocation of resources. The outcome would be profound. The Army would obtain a maximum level of flexibility in officer utilization. At the same time it would provide the Army a heretofore-unimagined capability. Most importantly, officers trained this way would have the capability to bring a synergy and malleability essential for a 30-year career.

This described model and process could be applied throughout the Army. The Army could merge other branches into conglomerated capability. It already has the leaders capable of designing educational paths and standardized instruction, which could create a much more flexible capability. Without this sort of radical regrouping, the Army will continue to struggle with everything from career progression to force capability. The soldiers, non-commissioned officers, officers, and American people in the end suffer the most.

Truly these ideas are not all that new. After World War II, the leaders in the Army who pressed for special operations forces, especially Major General Aaron Bank, saw these needs and advocated addressing of the changing ways of war. "Unconventional Warfare" became the term in vogue. Men who served in the Office of Strategic Services in WWII saw the future in unconventional terms, perhaps too narrowly. They proposed a force or "corps" to deal with the future way of fighting wars rather than a broad based change to the Army. It has taken the Army and national-level political leaders 60 years to appreciate that the conventional Army needs to be a true multi-faceted, responsive, highly-deployable force, more like a special-operations organization than the traditional WWII-styled force. But even that realization has not spawned a quick and efficient transformation; it continues to be slow and confused.

These ideas will likely fail to resound among Army leaders, as they likely will be viewed as "dangerous" or too broad-based. Regardless, this is what is needed. Malleability and flexibility are premium qualities for leadership just as they are for tactical responsiveness. To that end, the Task Force worked laboriously with a training regimen to address tactical modification through soldier education.

Tactics Modification/Soldier Education

The next priority in the training program was to work on adapting tactics and procedures in the Task Force to deal with a rapidly changing environment. As we learned more, experienced more and worked with other units, those lessons had to be inculcated into the organization. We could not just talk about them in the chow hall and then leave these ideas and applications alone. Additionally, educational information for soldiers had to be disseminated and reinforced to sustain a high level of confidence in the team. Good Army training was the only way to get this accomplished.

The enemy learns how we fight through engagement and observation and then adapts his tactics, techniques, and procedures. This is the 'cat-and-mouse' game about which anyone who has fought in a war knows. Learning the lessons and applying them required training.

In Task Force 1-21, we had multiple, formal methods to

exchange ideas and the knowledge gained through experience. One method was "skull sessions" with leaders. Once a week the S3 gathered the available patrol leaders and they batted around experiences and ideas. The S3 served as the facilitator and gleaned the best ideas to incorporate into the unit daily operation.

Another information-gathering and sharing method in which we organizationally engaged was to have one of the officers in the S3 section scour the Cavalry Network [CAVNET] for new ideas, lessons learned, and emerging tactics, techniques and procedures from across the Division in Iraq. The Cavalry Network was a Division-owned, web-based (secured intranet) repository for shared experiences and emerging tactics, techniques, and procedures that all units in the Division could access. The network allowed others to see what units in the Division were doing and recommending for fighting the enemy. This Cavalry Network was a veritable treasure trove of information sharing.

When we found something good on the Cavalry Network we would give it widest dissemination. Often, we adopted as procedure, the best ideas within the Task Force. The adaptation and assimilation then required training.

Another formal process came through the non-commissioned officer-development program the Command Sergeant Major directed within the Task Force. In these classes, ideas and innovations would come to the fore again, from personal experiences.

Regardless of the method or forum, a good idea was a good idea. All good ideas needed an outlet to get to the staff and to me so the idea could be assessed and transformed from concept to executable procedure. We did this very well in the Task force because we all felt strongly this activity was a key to fostering a responsive organization; this is the kind of organization I wanted to lead.

Related to this tactical improvement priority was soldier education. Cultural understanding, rules of engagement implementation, and understanding the "Lanza" Doctrine to effectively fight a counterinsurgency war were essential to long-term success. None of these things were mutually exclusive from tactics fighting against an insurgency. Soldiers today are smarter than ever; formal instruction was key and essential to meet the demands of this war.

Military Occupational Specialty/Sustainment Training

Because Task Force 1-21 was made up of distinctly varied units — two rocket firing batteries, one cannon firing battery, one service and support battery, one chemical company and tangential responsibility for one radar battery — keeping soldiers proficient in their primary Military Occupational Specialty was absolutely necessary. In the Army, all soldiers, non-commissioned officers, and officers have an occupational specialty. This is an alphanumerically-coded position that corresponds to a particular job in a specific field in the grand design of the Army. For example: The majority of soldiers in the Task Force were Multiple Launch Rocket System Crewman with a code of 13M. The alpha-numeric code is an administrative management nomenclature for human resources management purposes. These soldiers are trained to operate the Multiple Launch Rocket System. 13M is their Military Occupational Specialty code.

For the radar unit, training management was very easy because the soldiers were actually executing their unit-designed mission, i.e., operating radars across all of Baghdad. This required them to work daily in their Military

Occupational Specialty field. Also, at least one platoon of the cannon battery was working in their Military Occupational Specialty daily. The remainder, however, worked not in their assigned Military Occupational Specialty but rather as infantry.

The Task Force had three major supplementary missions: 1) fire long-range missiles if requested from Multi-National Forces, Iraq; 2) provide Hazardous Response Teams from the 68th Chemical Company to any requirements the Division directed; and 3) maintain one firing platoon of cannon artillery to engage targets at the discretion of the BCT Commander. This translated into a definite command responsibility of training and sustaining Military Occupational Specialty proficiency in order to execute these missions. Because we could not keep all soldiers up to Army standards in their assigned Military Occupational Specialty, sustainment training priority was placed on meeting the demands of the three supplementary combat missions. Battery commanders had primary training responsibility. The S3 had oversight duties and had to insure standards were met. At no time could the BCT commander request any of the supplementary missions and find Task Force 1-21 unprepared, a reality of which I was acutely aware.

Although Task Force priorities were focused on these things, we did not stop there in our efforts to train and improve. Several other initiatives were emphasized in training and improving the task force while fighting.

Non-Commissioned Officer Development and Sensing Sessions

Command Sergeant Major Hughes led a Non-Commissioned Officer Professional Development program. Each Friday, he assembled the non-commissioned officers who were not out on missions in a meeting hall on Camp Falcon and would instruct them on a specified subject. Most often the subject focused on leadership and tactics executed in current operations. This provided an excellent forum in which to share experiences, techniques, and leader actions.

Another educational program the Command Sergeant Major and I worked together on were broad unit sensing sessions. Every six to eight weeks, we faithfully met with the soldiers of the subordinate commands of the Task Force. The battery was divided into a soldier group and a non-commissioned officer group. Given the intense operations tempo, it was difficult to meet with soldiers, except in small groups and at specific times. Keeping my finger on the pulse of the troops and giving them an opportunity to tell the Command Sergeant Major and me what they were concerned about was important. I felt I needed to have a sense for what they were thinking about, which included everything from their living conditions to the politics of the war. This was vitally important to me as a leader. This forum also allowed the Command Sergeant Major and me an opportunity to educate. We could speak directly to soldiers about the issues we saw and how they should approach them. I could also provide the soldiers with unfiltered guidance and views from my perspective as their commander. This proved to be powerful and very useful to both the Command Sergeant Major and me. To do this kind of thing without allowing it to turn into a destructive complaint session meant Command Sergeant Major Hughes and I had to have thick skin. We had to face critical thinkers and be accountable to them. The soldiers gave me plenty to consider.

In Iraq, stress was high and tension could quickly escalate out of control over seemingly trivial concerns. After witnessing this in other units, I did not want that to happen in ours. Sensing sessions were conducted with frequency in my unit. We found the 6-8 week time frame just right for Task Force soldiers. Soldiers lived in close quarters confined by a 40-foot wall all around Camp Falcon. This kind of confinement wears on soldiers. Sometimes, as I would run around Camp Falcon doing physical training, I considered that this might be how a prisoner felt, although a prisoner did not have to gear up and go out to risk his life every day. A sobering thought. Not one I dwelled on, but that confined feeling certainly crept into my mind on occasion, and something I imagined the soldiers thought about too. One enterprising civilian contractor aptly captured the sentiment in a T-shirt he had made that declared he was an "Inmate of Camp Falcon."

Women serving in units and living at Camp Falcon brought another dimension to combat life in Iraq the year Task Force 1-21 served with the First Cavalry Division. Some women had to endure unique challenges living and fighting in a male-dominated Army. Confined to the forward operating base, young as most soldiers were, and integrated at a level not experienced before in war for the Army, women played a major role in redefining their service in the future of the American Army. Most withstood the rigors of this lifestyle extremely well. This has been a poorly reported story thus far but nonetheless it is a key development for the Army fighting in Iraq.

L to R: Me, my sister Lisa, my mother Luz Maria, my brother Joseph. My father was in Vietnam when this photo was taken in 1967. We lived at Fort Buchanan, Puerto Rico.

Captain Allen Anthony Baumann, my father, in the Republic of Vietnam, 1967.

L to R: Colonel Lanza and me. Just a couple weeks in command by July 2003, I escort Colonel Lanza to my headquarters to brief him on the "State of the Battalion" days after he assumed command of the Division Artillery. Neither of us saw the incredible transformation coming.

L to R: Me, Colonel Lanza. Meeting Robert Ford, political assistant to Ambassador Negroponte, at Camp Falcon Landing Zone before going on patrol to meet with a Sunni Imam. We were both a long way from the tranquil days of July 2003. This was January 2005.

Lieutenant Colonel Bill Salter, Commander 1-7 Cavalry in Baghdad, Iraq.

Lieutenant Colonel Jay Allen, Commander 1-8 Cavalry in Baghdad, Iraq.

Lieutenant Colonel Jim Hevel, Commander 515th Forward Support Battalion, in Baghdad, Iraq

Major Menti was the Task Force S3 when we deployed to Kuwait in March 2004.

L to R (front): Lieutenant Colonel Mark Tillman, 1-77 Field Artillery Commander and me at the rank of major serving as S3 for 1-77 Field Artillery. L to R (back) Captain Steve Caroll, B/1-77 Commander, Captain Glen Fox, HHS/1-77 Commander.

Major Robert "Bob" Marshall, Task Force 1-21 Executive Officer in Al Saidiyah, Baghdad.

Command Sergeant Major Kelvin Hughes and me standing in front of the Task Force 1-21 Headquarters, Camp Falcon.

Crew training in Kuwait days before Task Force 1-21 headed north to Iraq. The "Add-on-Armor" kit was installed to protect the crew cab. In the cargo compartment was mounted an M-249 squad automatic weapon. The siding was wood with sandbags placed between two layers of wood. The floors were lined with either sandbags or kevlar blankets, affording protection against small arms. The IEDs and rocket propelled grenades were another story. Most vehicles did not have this protection. The hummer my team rode in had only sandbags on the floor.

With Captain Kevin Runkle (Assistant S3), Lieutenant Rodney Davis (Executive Officer, A/1-21), and Lieutenant Joe Medina (Executive Officer, B/1-21). We had literally driven onto Forward Operating Base, Camp Falcon when this picture was snapped.

With Major Bill Reinhart (picture left), new Task Force S-3; and Major Bob Marshall (picture far right), Task Force Executive Officer.

Captain Robb Dettmer, TF 1-21 S2 (Intelligence Officer) nicknamed "Dale Earnhardt Jr."

With Naima Faruk, Council Member, Dr. Ali Olbeidi, and Qusay a.k.a. "Las Vegas" one of the 25 interpreters in the Task Force. This photo was taken at the Neighborhood Advisory Council building after a meeting where I introduced Dr. Ali to the council.

With Dr. Ali on a project site July 2004.

L to R: First Sergeant Brian Lindsey, Captain Matt Chambers, and First Lieutenant Ashton Read, the command team of C/2-82 FA.

Major Rob Dixon served as Task Force 1-21, Civil Affairs Team Chief.

Captain Michael Levy, Task Force S5, Civil Affairs Staff Officer.

Staff Sergeant Timothy P. Rogers, PSYOPS Chief for TF 1-21.

Specialist Ellen Terry receives her Purple Heart Medal.

Private Russell Shalk is welding together a unit-fabricated turret.

Major General Peter Chiarelli at Camp Falcon awarding Private First Class Christopher Fernandez the Silver Star Medal for gallantry in combat.

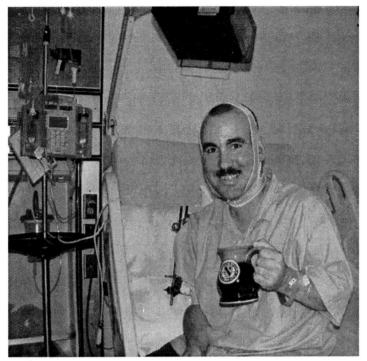

Staff Sergeant Terry Saffron, recovering from surgery in the hospital at Fort Hood, Texas.

Major Kevin Kugel, Commander of 68th Chemical Company.

L to R: Sergeant Sarah R. Vega and Sergeant Rosa M. Olivo, members of "Coyote" patrol attend an operations order briefing in B/1-21, Command Post as they prepare for a raid. Also pictured are front to back: Captain Roberto Mercado (foreground, back of head), Staff Sergeant Jimmy S. Howard, Staff Sergeant Timothy W. Johnson, Sergeant Robert G. Pierce.

Lieutenant Justin H. Richardson, Platoon Leader in A/1-21, with three Facilities Protection Service Guards at the Al Saidiyah Neighborhood Advisory Council administration building. The guard pictured on the far right we called "3 in 1" as we decided he was 3 Iraqis in 1 man. "3 in 1" was killed shortly after Task Force 1-21 left Iraq.

L to R front: Iraqi FPS Captain, Staff Sergeant Curtis Raine, FPS
Commander Major Tahseen, Corporal Jack Slaton, FPS guard, FPS
Captain. Back: "3-in-1" FPS Lieutenant, FPS guard, FPS Lieutenant.

Iraqi Civil Defense Corps soldiers from D/304th Iraqi Infantry in
formation; notice the odd assortment of uniforms.

Captain Chris Van Keuren on the day we readied to convoy north into Iraq.

Command crew L-R: Specialist Anthony L. Jackson, Fadi "Freddie" Fadhil, Specialist Francisco J. Villa

With Freddie (Task Force Commander's "terp") and Specialist Francisco Villa, my humvee driver and body guard.

The Neighborhood Advisory Council before "The Reformation" initiative and probably at its zenith while Task Force 1-21 worked with the council. Captain Tom Pugsley is sitting at the table in his role of chief liaison. I am off the table behind Captain Pugsley with "Freddie" my interpreter. Positioning was very important to the conduct of these meetings. Sending clearly-understood messages and setting favorable conditions.

In the foreground L to R: Staff Sergeant Tobin, Lieutenant Davis, and Sergeant First Class Michael Battles. The other soldiers were mostly men from A/1-21 Field Artillery. This unit, A/1-21, would suffer the most casualties and become the most decorated unit of the Task Force just a year later in Iraq.

Sergeant First Class Michael Battles killed in action October 28, 2004.

Captain Martin Wohlgemuth working with Iraqi National Guard soldiers.

L to R: Major "Jay" Soupene, Task Force S3, me, Task Force Commander, Command Sergeant Major Kelvin Hughes, Task Force Sergeant Major, Major Bill Reinhart, Task Force Executive Officer.

Men and women of Task Force 1-21 Operations and Intelligence Staff Sections.

Iraqis line up in the late morning of January 31, 2005 to vote.

Captain Tom Pugsley, Commander, A/1-21.

13 Women in Combat for the Task Force

"I am not afraid . . . I was born to do this." Joan of Arc

Task Force 1-21 had a sizeable contingent of women in the unit. Twenty-nine enlisted soldiers and six officers were women in the Task Force. A third maneuver element of the BCT, Task Force 1-21 had an unusual personnel amalgamation compared to our sister maneuver task forces; neither 1-7 Cavalry nor 1-8 Cavalry had women assigned (during task reorganization in Iraq, Task Force 1-21 provided a platoon of soldiers from 68th Chemical Company to 1-8 Cavalry, which included three female soldiers). The 515th Forward Support Battalion, a logistics unit, was closer to our composition than were 1-7 Cavalry and 1-8 Cavalry. This particular anomaly worked to our favor operating in Iraq. Women brought unique capabilities and talents to this complex battlefield allowing us to more genuinely and precisely operate through the full spectrum of tactical operations demanded of units fighting in Iraq.

Easily, one of the major stories not well reported in the print or television media covering Iraq was the role of women in the war in Iraq. Women were fighting as infantry/cavalry soldiers throughout the First Cavalry Division. This was executed with the full knowledge, endorsement, and expectation of senior Division leaders; everyone is an infantry/cavalryman first. The Division needed women to serve in this role because we were short-handed. Women fought in Iraq as equals to men in every sense of the notion of equality.

To deal with the challenge of fighting, given the composition of Task Force 1-21, required a direct combat role for women. Our troop-to-task demands were extensive and the Task Force simply did not have enough male soldiers to meet the strain levied from the BCT staff. The largest subordinate unit of the Task Force was 68th Chemical Company which contained all the female soldiers in the Task Force until I moved some to Headquarters Battery and to 1-8 Cavalry. This was not a force multiplier that could sit on the sidelines during the game.

Before deploying, we all knew women would fight as infantry/cavalry in Baghdad. We trained women for direct combat, infantry roles. The fact that women would fight in combat was not an issue of concern for anyone in the BCT; it was just done.

Major Kevin Kugel commanded the 68th Chemical Company in Baghdad. Installed in command as we deployed into Kuwait, he replaced the previous commander who I had no confidence could lead the company in Iraq. By mutual agreement the previous commander abdicated the position and the division chemical staff sent us Major Kugel.

Major Kugel was tough-minded, highly technically competent, and knew precisely how to optimize that unique outfit. He was superb commanding the organization insuring all soldiers, regardless of gender, met the performance standards for fighting in Baghdad.

Amazingly, as late as May 2005, there was debate in Congress about women participating in combat. A House bill sought to codify into law a long-standing Department of Defense policy prohibiting women from serving in echelons below brigade for combat units. According to this Department of Defense policy and the legislation proposed, women were not to be assigned to function in direct combat roles below the brigade echelon.

A news story written by reporter Ann Scott Tyson explains the debate:

Wednesday, May 18, 2005
More Objections to Women-in-Combat Ban
Army Says 22,000 Jobs Would Be Affected;
Service Groups Join Fight Against Bill

By Ann Scott Tyson

A House measure aimed at keeping women out of combat would bar female soldiers from at least 21,925 Army jobs that are now open to them, a senior Army official said yesterday.

The projection of lost jobs comes as opposition to the proposed ban spreads from the Army's senior leadership to include associations representing nearly 145,000 current and former Army and National Guard members.

Lt. Gen. James L. Campbell, director of the Army staff, provided the figure in what Army officials said was a narrow interpretation of the potential impact of the measure passed May 11 by a panel of the House Armed Services Committee, which would ban women from serving in certain support units in an effort to keep them out of "direct ground combat."

"If the amendment . . . to prohibit the assignment of female soldiers to Forward Support Companies (FSC)" applied only to such companies in heavy, infantry, and Stryker brigade combat teams, "a total of 21,925 spaces currently open for assignment to female soldiers would be closed," Campbell wrote in a letter delivered yesterday to Rep. Ike Skelton (Mo.), the committee's ranking Democrat.

In contrast, Republican proponents of the measure said it would affect only a few dozen jobs.

Committee Chairman Duncan Hunter (R-Calif.) seeks to compel the Army to comply with a 1994 Pentagon regulation that bars female soldiers from direct ground combat units below brigade level, said a statement released yesterday by a spokesman for Hunter.

"Presently, the Army is unilaterally assigning servicewomen in land combat units. The committee's intent simply is to codify current Department of Defense regulations," the statement said. Lawmakers and staff indicated that the measure's wording will be different when it is presented for a full committee vote, probably today. The Army says it is complying with the policy.

In a letter yesterday, 27 Democrats on the committee called on Hunter to strike the measure, an amendment to the defense authorization bill, saying it would "tie the hands of military commanders in a time of war" and undercut recruiting and careers of women.

Leading Army groups also rallied to oppose it. Retired Gen. Gordon R. Sullivan, president of the Association of the United States Army and a former Army chief of staff, wrote to the committee this week that the proposed ban would be "confusing" and "detrimental to units."

Opponents also argued that the notion of a clear front line has evaporated in today's insurgent conflicts, casting doubt on the practicality of the effort to restrict women from combat. "Today combat may occur in the desert or on Main Street," wrote retired Air Force Brig. Gen. Stephen M. Koper, president of the National Guard Association of the United States.[15]

My fellow Americans, the debate is over! In the war in Iraq, the Army placed women in organizations that were combat units not in name but in function. This was sanctioned by senior Army leaders, all knew women were sent to units or units were re-tasked in mission and function to operate where direct combat was not only likely, it was expected. Their participation was incontrovertible. Women were trained to participate in direct combat as a direct line of defense, to their credit.

Women in Task Force 1-21 participated in direct combat by design and they wanted to be there. More importantly, they successfully did the job. That politicians still debate this issue is folly and testament to the fact that American political representatives debate issues about which most have no empirical understandings.

Very few Representatives or Senators in Congress have ever served in the military. Of those that have, a small group actually has combat experience. Within the 108th Congress, a mere seven percent of the 435 members have had combat military service experience. None served in the ongoing Iraq war.[16] Apparently, Americans do not consider military service an important criterion for congressional service. This lack of actual military experience has had a detrimental effect on political decision-making about women's roles in combat.

Fighting combat actions, being wounded and exposed to the line of fire in combat during raids, ambushes, recon patrols, cordon and search actions, and executing basic fire and maneuver as infantry is exactly what the women in Task Force 1-21 did for the year I was in Iraq. No one batted an eye or ordered that we not train and deploy women as infantry. Quite to the contrary, training the women in Task Force 1-21 to execute all the standard infantry actions from individual movement techniques to operating as infantry team, squad, patrol members, and patrol leaders was demanded of me from my superior officers. Without hesitation or compunction of any kind, we in Task Force 1-21 did this with élan.

What is clear, regardless of the law and what senior leaders say publicly, is that women serving in Iraq have to fight in direct combat engagements because that is the nature of the war; all personnel, even those in a so called supporting role must be an infantry soldier first. Women in the Army and the Marine Corps have been killed and wounded in Iraq. Consider this report from the front pages of the news in June 2005:

Female Marines Ambushed in Iraq
Four Marines Killed; More Troops Wounded or Missing

By FRANK GRIFFITHS

BAGHDAD, Iraq (June 25) — The lethal ambush of a convoy carrying female U.S. troops in Fallujah underscored the difficulties of keeping women away from the front lines in a war where such boundaries are far from clear-cut.

The suicide car bomb and ensuing small-arms fire killed at least four Marines, and a Marine and a sailor were missing and presumed dead, the military said Saturday. At least one woman was killed, and 11 of the 13 wounded troops were female.

The ambush late Thursday also suggested Iraqi insurgents may have regained a foothold in Fallujah, which has been occupied by U.S. and Iraqi forces since they regained control of the city from insurgents seven months ago.

The women were part of a team of Marines assigned to various checkpoints around Fallujah. The Marines use females at the checkpoints to search Muslim women "in order to be respectful of Iraqi cultural sensitivities," a military statement said.

The group al-Qaida in Iraq claimed it carried out the ambush, one of the single deadliest attacks against the Marines — and against women — in this country.

Lance Cpl. Holly A. Charette, 21, from Cranston, R.I., died in Thursday's attack, the Defense Department said Friday. Three

*male Marines also were killed, the military said. One was iden-
tified by his family as Cpl. Chad Powell, 22, from northern
Louisiana.*

*The high number of female casualties spoke to the lack of real
front lines in Iraq, where U.S. troops are battling a raging insurgency and American women soldiers have participated in
more close-quarters combat than in any previous conflict.*

*"It's hard to stop suicide bombers, and it's hard to stop these
people that in many cases are being smuggled into Iraq from
outside Iraq," President Bush said Friday at a joint White House
news conference with Iraqi Prime Minister Ibrahim al-Jaafari.*

*Current Pentagon policy prohibits women from serving in front
line combat roles, but an increasing number of female troops
have been exposed to hostile fire.*

*Thirty-six female troops have died since the war began, in-
cluding the one that was announced Friday, said Maj. Michael
Shavers, a Pentagon spokesman. Most have died from hostile
fire.*

*More than 11,000 women are serving in Iraq, part of 138,000
U.S. troops in the country, said Staff Sgt. Don Dees, a U.S.
military spokesman.*

*Thursday's attack may have been the single largest involving
female U.S. service members since a Japanese suicide pilot
slammed his plane into the USS Comfort near the Philippines
in 1945, killing six Army nurses, according to figures from the
Women in Military Service for America Memorial Foundation.*

*Fallujah, the city about 40 miles west of Baghdad where Thurs-
day's attack took place, is a former insurgent stronghold invaded
by U.S. forces at great cost in November. It also is the city where
an Iraqi mob hung the mutilated bodies of two U.S. contractors*

from a bridge. On Nov. 2, 2003, two female Army soldiers were in a Chinook helicopter shot down over Fallujah.

The military did not provide the genders of the missing Marine and sailor believed to be in the vehicle that was attacked. They were presumed dead, said a U.S. military official in Washington who spoke on condition of anonymity because the victims have not been identified.

The attack, which raised the death toll among U.S. military members since the beginning of the war to 1,734, according to an Associated Press count, came as Americans have grown increasingly concerned about a conflict that has shown no signs of abating.[17]

Often, in the media, senior Army leaders describe that women are in support units and, in the course of carrying out their duties on the asymmetric battlefield, they are attacked, thus supplying the reason why the women are engaged in combat. "Asymmetric" is a fancy word to say, "The enemy is everywhere." What senior leaders describe is true in word and statement. However, in Task Force 1-21, the truth was a bit more revealing.

From the very beginning of notification for deployment in August 2003, the 68th Chemical Company was assigned to 1-21 Field Artillery. They were, on paper, a separate company of the Division. However, the facts were that for more than four years, the 68th Chemical Company was a subordinate element of 1-21 Field Artillery. The 68th Chemical Company was considered, by my immediate commander and by everyone up through the Commanding General, a maneuver element of the Task Force I commanded in Iraq. Chemical companies in the Army are combat support units by doctrinal definition.

However, the role and expected utilization of this company

was to deploy and fight as infantry/cavalry in Baghdad, Iraq. The mission-essential tasks we were directed to train this company to accomplish as a unit were direct-combat tasks. The appearances simply were not the reality.

When the battalion began training to convert the 68th Chemical Company to infantry and hone the company's skills to operate in Baghdad, Captain Brian Clark was the Company Commander. He worked tirelessly to absorb the tactics, techniques, and procedures outlined in Field Manual 7-8, *Infantry Platoon and Squad*. He led the company through multiple training events that included: close quarters marksmanship, squad and platoon field training exercises focused on urban dismounted and mounted patrolling, platoon offensive operations, cordon and search operations, and raids. These were all infantry/cavalry tasks where the soldiers in the platoons were both men and women, just as they were manned by Army standard for a divisional chemical company. There was no adjustment whatsoever.

Three of the five platoon leaders, First Lieutenant Denise Little, First Lieutenant Dorothy Butala, and First Lieutenant Teri Hennigan, were female officers. The Company Executive Officer, another female officer, was First Lieutenant Chevelle Malone. Each woman had to learn troop leading for a light infantry platoon.

All of them mastered these skills. By the end of 90 days of operating in Iraq the women, not only in 68th Chemical Company, but across the BCT, were trained and expected to operate in patrols as full-fledged members and the officers and senior non-commissioned officers as full-dutied leaders. Several female soldiers were on the Personal Security Team for the BCT commander. Colonel Lanza's .50 caliber machinegun operator was a female soldier, Specialist Medina, who, according to Colonel Lanza, was the best gunner in the Brigade's Headquarters and Head-quarters Company, let alone the Personal Security Team he employed. On these Personal Security Teams the expectation of direct combat was part of the mission the teams served. Assigning any female to this team was an overt admission of an expectation that a direct combat role was expected. The obfuscation occurred because of the brigade echelon that the female soldiers were assigned; this was authorized by regulation. I contend it made sense but subverted the intent of the rule.

Women were also required to participate in every raid the Task Force executed in the BCT sector. In the 5th BCT, U.S. forces always included women on Special Search Teams (SST) to control and interact with Iraqi women and children. Their primary function was to insure that Iraqi women and children were not violated and that their Muslim tradition was preserved and respected. Often, when we raided homes to search for contraband or capture known insurgents, Iraqi women and children were present. Having female soldiers was absolutely essential to mitigating the trauma and negative potential effects of male soldiers handling the Iraqi women and children.

Immediately upon arrival at Camp Falcon in March 2004, I was ordered to provide 1-8 Cavalry with two infantry platoons to augment their undermanned requirements. One platoon I sent to 1-8 Cavalry came from the 68th Chemical Company and included three females, one in each of three squads of the platoon. They fought the balance of the year as a full fledged maneuver unit of the Division without concern or question from any senior leader in the Division. According to Lieutenant Colonel "Jay" Allen, the women attached to his cavalry battalion performed exceptionally well, always meeting his standards in every aspect.

Before Task Force 1-21 ever had to execute these types of

missions and place women into infantry squads and on these Special Search Teams accompanying raid and cordon and search missions, 1-94 Field Artillery from First Armor Division did the same things. We actually took the tactics, techniques, and procedures they had developed, and refined and used them as a basis to establish our Special Search Teams in Task Force 1-21. By no means were we the first in the Army fighting in Iraq to do this kind of training and operating as a norm.

Another significant role women served where direct combat action was threatened daily was in Civil Affairs teams attached to maneuver battalion task forces across the Army and Marine Corps in Iraq. Civil Affairs teams are made up of twelve person teams attached to combat units but often conduct missions separate from the main task force. Many of these teams are led by female officers and include female non-commissioned officers and enlisted soldiers. Female leaders on these teams must be able to plan and conduct missions using the very same processes and procedures as infantry units executing patrol operations. In every instance the civil affairs mission in a combat zone is every bit as dangerous as an infantry mission. Civil Affairs teams often come under fire and must be able to respond effectively. Civil Affairs team members must know and practice the same skill sets and employ the same tactics used by infantry soldiers to operate in this environment.

Some senior Army leaders have stated that women participating in combat was not occurring suggesting that they did not know what they should have and, thus, were unaware; or they are not being forthright. Women were directed, trained, and placed in organizational echelons that absolutely required them to fight direct combat as infantry. Though, technically, in Task Force 1-21 these women were assigned to a combat support unit the 68th Chemical Company, the Task Force had a maneuver, direct combat mission, and these women were fully trained and engaged in the fighting, not as support troops but as infantry/cavalry troops.

In June 2005, a female soldier was awarded the Silver Star Medal for heroism in direct combat against insurgents in Iraq, more evidence that women are already doing that which some Congressional leaders seek to prevent them from doing.

Woman Soldier Receives Silver Star for Valor in Iraq
By Sgt. Sara Wood, USA
American Forces Press Service

WASHINGTON, June 16, 2005 – For the first time since World War II, a woman soldier was awarded the Silver Star Medal today in Iraq.

Sgt. Leigh Ann Hester of the 617th Military Police Company, a National Guard unit out of Richmond, KY, received the Silver Star, along with two other members of her unit, Staff Sgt. Timothy Nein and Spc. Jason Mike, for their actions during an enemy ambush on their convoy. Other members of the unit also received awards.

Hester's squad was shadowing a supply convoy March 20 when anti-Iraqi fighters ambushed the convoy. The squad moved to the side of the road, flanking the insurgents and cutting off their escape route.

Hester led her team through the "kill zone" and into a flanking position, where she assaulted a trench line with grenades and M203 grenade-launcher rounds. She and Nein, her squad leader, then cleared two trenches, at which time she killed three insurgents with her rifle.

When the fight was over, 27 insurgents were dead, six were wounded, and one was captured.

Hester, 23, who was born in Bowling Green, Ky., and later moved to Nashville, Tenn., said she was surprised when she heard she was being considered for the Silver Star.

"I'm honored to even be considered, much less awarded, the medal," she said.

Being the first woman soldier since World War II to receive the medal is significant to Hester. But, she said, she doesn't dwell on the fact.

"It really doesn't have anything to do with being a female," she said. "It's about the duties I performed that day as a soldier."

Hester, who has been in the National Guard since April 2001, said she didn't have time to be scared when the fight started, and she didn't realize the impact of what had happened until much later.

"Your training kicks in and the soldier kicks in," she said. "It's your life or theirs. ... You've got a job to do — protecting yourself and your fellow comrades."

Nein, who is on his second deployment to Iraq, praised Hester and his other soldiers for their actions that day. "It's due to their dedication and their ability to stay there and back me up that we were able to do what we did that day," he said.

Hester and her fellow soldiers were awarded their medals at Camp Liberty, Iraq, by Army Lt. Gen. John R. Vines, Multinational Corps Iraq commanding general. In his speech, Vines commended the soldiers for their bravery and their contribution to the international war on terror.

"My heroes don't play in the (National Basketball Association) and don't play in the U.S. Open (golf tournament) at Pinehurst," Vines said.

"They're standing in front of me today. These are American heroes."

Three soldiers of the 617th were wounded in the ambush. Hester said she and the other squad members are thinking about them, and she is very thankful to have made it through unscathed. The firefight, along with the entire deployment, has had a lasting effect on her, Hester said.

"I think about it every day, and probably will for the rest of my life," she said.[18]

Women Proved Capable

Without question, women are capable of handling the infantry role in Iraq. I expected to report to you that women were unable to carry out the infantry role, they lacked the physical stamina, they could not handle the horrors of close combat, they feared capture and sexual abuse so badly that they couldn't fight and perform their duties. This handle-women-with-kid-gloves attitude is a result of old-school Army, and I truly believed that women would not endure the rigors of infantry close combat. I was wrong, sorely off the mark.

Without exception the women in the Task Force, in every aspect of their job and in every measure of performance, excelled as infantry/cavalry troopers. The old-school Army arguments were simply uninformed. The suggestion that unit cohesion is adversely affected if combat units are comprised of males and females is likewise without merit. Combat requires a great deal of trust between soldiers "in the foxholes," the notion that soldiers are unable to count on females who are not up-to-snuff physically, emotionally, or psychologically and thus detrimental to combat effectiveness and unit cohesion was not borne out by my personal experience. The reality is truly eye-opening.

The Myth of Lack of Physical Stamina

Many believe that women cannot endure demanding, aus-
tere conditions for prolonged periods of time. But I observed no appreciable difference between the women and
the men in the Task Force. They wore all the same gear,
carried the same ammunition and water load, and manned
the SAW, M-240B and .50 Caliber machineguns without
any problems.

Because we moved in patrols in humvees or Fox chemical-detection vehicles this negated the long challenging
walking that is associated with infantry and that was not
required by my soldiers. We lived in barracks on the Forward Operating Base, and almost always soldiers returned
to their barracks daily for rest. Although many patrols
transitioned from mounted to dismounted, the distances
we walked were usually no more than two kilometers and
all the women did this easily even in 120 degree heat. The
nature of operations and the tactics, techniques, and procedures utilized in urban fighting in Baghdad were accommodating to females participating in the role of infantry. Fighting purely-dismounted as light-infantry over extended periods of time likely would physically overwhelm most but
not all women and many men in my basically artillery unit.
Some women can physically handle the rigors of a light-
infantry life, many more than most men believe possible.

Participating in light infantry may be distinguished from
other infantry combat missions. Fighting in Baghdad, with
First Cavalry Division, we most often fought as motorized
infantry. Depending on where units were located, the tactics, techniques, and procedures used were varied and applied differently. Light infantry service demands strenuous
physical capabilities that even many men lack. The lines to
get into light infantry units are not long for a reason; it is
a damn tough living. I do not contend women can serve

in that capacity yet. But there are suitable infantry roles.

Another odd reality affecting women service in direct combat organizations hinges on the Army's method for basic training of soldiers, non-commissioned officers and officers. Light-infantry formations and tactics are the basis for all collective unit and leader assessment training. Simulated direct combat scenarios are generated to create conditions to teach and assess leadership.

Female officer cadets are trained and assessed at Army ROTC Advanced Camp alongside the male officer cadets. Women cadets are expected to perform all the same tasks as their male counterparts every step of the way. The Army uses light-infantry tactics, techniques, and procedures as the standard method and context for unit organization and operation to measure leadership traits in all cadets, both male and female. Many people in America do not appreciate that this is how the Army trains and assesses its officers, a method used to provide a common standard for all officer candidates. If future law or current policy at the Department of Defense prohibits women from direct combat, why would the Army measure its female officers on the same scale as men? That seems illogical and unfair.

While it may be suggested that using light infantry and direct combat scenarios for training and assessment is harmless and merely a training mechanism, I believe that it sends the wrong message and is inconsistent with Department of Defense policy. If an Army trains as it will fight, then this needs to be reviewed and modified.

The truth is that the Army's current methodology is highly effective, and for more than three decades women have proven capable of performing in that environment. And so women ought to be allowed to serve in direct combat units because, on aggregate, they have proven capable.

There are limits in the combat arms. Women can easily serve in tank and artillery units. Some infantry units such as mortar sections and motorized and mechanized infantry units would also be conducive to women's service. There is room for debate with their service in light infantry units. Women can handle mechanized and motorized infantry tasks, and can crew tanks and crew mortar, rocket, and cannon artillery.

If America is going to continue to fight the global war on terror as a limited and undeclared war with an all-volunteer force, the military needs every qualified American willing to serve. Now and into the future, women are essential to the future of our combat force.

Old warriors will think it a sad day when a nation puts its women in combat because not enough men will join the fight. Although they may be right, these are the conditions we face as a result of the decisions of our national political leaders. This nation has collectively chosen this course and women are capable.

It is an incontrovertible fact that in Task Force 1-21, women fought as infantry/cavalry troopers and performed as well as any other unit in First Cavalry Division.

Capture and Sexual Abuse Not Limited to Women in Combat

Another frequent objection to the presence of women in combat is the belief that women are very vulnerable to hideous abuse if captured. In fact, the thought of women being physically and sexually abused is a large part of the resistance to women serving in direct combat units. Admittedly, I am uncomfortable with the thoughts of such treatment. But those sentiments are chauvinistic and unfair to those women who wish to serve. American men are raised to defer to women and to see them as delicate, less physically capable, and more of a sexual object than an equal partner and competitor but this does not diminish their real capabilities and contributions. In short, the problem is with men, not women.

Men captured by Arab insurgents are abused. Is it less horrendous if a man is sexually defiled, his genitals electrocuted, bones broken in beatings, and his head cut off, his execution videotaped in digital format and put on the internet? To be captured by any enemy, whether you are male or female, is a bad deal. I do not think men are more equipped to handle it than women are. The disparate treatment is a result of men's sensibilities more than anything else. All soldiers — male and female — know the risks and realize they can be captured.

Both Jessica Lynch and Shoshana Johnson were captured in Operation Iraqi Freedom I. Although their experiences were horrible, they are no more horrible than what male soldiers have experienced. While the thought of a woman having been captured is deplorable, in this kind of war, women are no less prone to the risk of capture than are men regardless of the restrictions placed on women by Congress.

Adverse Impact on Unit Cohesion Dispelled

The notion that unit cohesion is adversely affected by the presence of women is pure silliness. Land forces units in both the Army and Marine Corps have functioned with females in them for a long time. This has already proven convincingly that cohesion is not an issue.

The sexual tension among young men and women serving in the ranks side-by-side does affect a unit, but it is entirely manageable. I have no particular social attitude about this issue. I know from understanding of human nature that men and women have sex, and when put together they have it more. Although this may shock some, it is natural, and I am not naïve enough to not understand that dynamic. But does that dynamic thwart a unit's ability to function cohesively as an aggregate? I answer no, it does not. Unchecked and uncontrolled, sex among soldiers serving in the same unit certainly can cause a multitude of problems and can tear down cohesion. Commanders have to be attentive and utilize proper disciplinary actions to minimize the impact and insure good order and discipline just as they do for other offenses, which unchecked can also threaten unit cohesion. Examples that come to mind include rampant drug use, alcohol abuse, and thievery. As in any institutional context, equal-opportunity, sexual harassment policies coupled with education can effectively mitigate its impact.

In Task Force 1-21, female and male soldiers served alongside each other as they did throughout the BCT. Sexual liaisons most likely occurred in every unit in the BCT where males and females were put together. However, I witnessed nothing rampant, undisciplined, or out of control where unit cohesion was at risk. When caught, soldiers were disciplined. Most soldiers were not running around having or seeking sexual interaction. Most men and women committed themselves to a year of celibacy and went about their business. Those who use hyperbole to sensationalize sexual misconduct and lost unit cohesion most likely never served a day in the military or in combat and, thus have no factual basis for their opinion.

Women can serve in units below the brigade level in direct combat units and be successful, effective soldiers carrying out their duties and responsibilities with little issue. That was the reality in Iraq in 2004. The debate needs to be about defining the types of direct combat units in which women can serve beyond that which is currently authorized. Consideration to expansion should include:

- Armor tank units

- Mechanized Mortar infantry units

- Cannon artillery units

- Rocket artillery units

- Radar units

Political leaders are not malicious. But the significant lack of military experience resident among political leaders has left a void in their collective understanding. They lack the collective ability to make sound decisions about the roles of women in combat in the 21st Century. This aspect of leadership is significant and should not be discounted by voters in America.

One of the critical dynamics of fighting in Iraq that became difficult to manage was the character of the Iraqi people. The presence of women in combat formations helped immensely, providing us with the capability to materially honor cultural sensitivities and provide insights unique in interacting with Iraqis. These contributions helped us improve our overall effectiveness. Understanding the Iraqi character was a dimension immensely challenging in all we attempted, influencing all political, military, civil, and psychological operations dynamically and at times diabolically.

14 Character and Values in This Kind of War

"All who have meditated on the art of governing mankind have been convinced that the fate of empires depends on the education of youth." Aristotle

A significant part of what defines nations is their unique cultures, beliefs, and behaviors intertwined to form a national character; nations are an amalgamation of its people. The collective character of a people defines a nation. Dealing with the Iraqis, given their unique character, made the complex, exasperating; the difficult, near impossible; the unknown, even more confounding.

As a soldier directly working with a foreign culture as was required in Iraq, I quickly became enamored with the people. I came to feel a strange affection for them. They were so desperately in need of help. On the other hand, many Iraqis have an immature view of Americans. They see us as a people of great power and wealth. The soldiers of America are not distinguished from the average American citizen by Iraqis. They think we Americans can do anything. They look at us as if we were from a Star Wars-like intergalactic force.

Being a person of compassion, a Christian believer, when witnessing the devastation and oppressive life the Iraqis have led all these years under Saddam, I felt an abiding and compelling desire to try to understand them. I wanted desperately to connect with them regardless of their Muslim faith. I connected with them on a human level.

Many soldiers and other officers I served with were easily frustrated by Iraqis and dumbfounded by their behavior. I too was often frustrated to the point of exasperation with some behaviors but I was very careful to control and suppress my frustration. For others, frustration too frequently surfaced and people exercised overt malicious treatment, engaged in sarcastic verbal exchanges, and made backbiting commentary in councils among Americans.

Iraqis are clearly different in manner, response, expression, and beliefs from Americans. We were in their country, uninvited and, to a large extent, unwanted by many. I never allowed myself to forget that regardless of the politics of my country. The reality of having to interact and work with the Iraqis necessitated connecting and understanding who they are so we could work from a position of mutual respect in relationships. I absolutely had to appreciate the character of the people. I had to learn to think as they did so we might communicate best.

One of my first discoveries about Iraqis was that they just were not well-educated by Western standards of measurement. I am not intending to be arrogant or superior with this statement. Depending on the source, the literacy rate among male Iraqis is reported at just over 50 percent. For women it is considerably lower than that.

As an observer with a Western concept of how people should behave and how society and governments should educate the masses of citizens, Iraq's people are woefully deficient. The public education system that Saddam's regime installed did not elevate the masses. Education was not about developing critical thinkers. Indeed, Saddam's objective was the exact opposite.

In Iraqi society, titles were more important than substantive position. That is to say, it was more important to an Iraqi to have the title of "manager" than to be an effective manager. Title carried privilege and stature; possessing the skills and ability to function well in that position was not important. I believe this behavior was rooted in Iraqi culture, but I could not figure out its source. Men exhibited behaviors associated with the need for aggrandizement because of title, which I suspect had to do with Saddam's control and method of rule.

The many expatriated Shia Muslims, who have returned to Iraq after the American invasion and have since ascended to powerful political positions, are well educated. Though their eloquence was often lost in the Arabic-to-English translation, their education was Western primarily through European and American educational institutions, and these men articulated good ideas — by Western standards — for the future of Iraq. These Shia Muslims actually bring ability and broad thinking to the political arena in Iraq. They truly offer the best chance for change, reform, and improvement in Iraq over the next decade. However, they will never bring the Western style democracy we know and understand to Iraq. The greatest hope for Iraq will be keeping enough of them alive and serving long enough to have effect.

From his rise to power in 1979 until 2001, Saddam went about creating an "entitlement society" in Iraq. Almost every Iraqi I ever met believed the government owed them something. The average Iraqi citizen believed he had some inalienable right to a handout from the government. Many Iraqis looked at American Army soldiers as the direct replacement of Saddam's authoritarian government. Iraqis I encountered expected us to provide them handouts.

Because everything under Saddam's regime was a state-owned enterprise, no notion of self-advancement in a capitalistic sense existed. The concept of entrepreneurship does not exist in the mindset of the average Iraqi. With Saddam's regime an Iraqi would not make much of a profit for himself. This would have been dangerous. Everything that was created in society through labor or in arts and sciences literally belonged to Saddam. He was omnipotent in Iraq. If not voluntarily given to him, then he took it forcibly, killing those who would not provide their wealth and business profit to the state or, ipso facto, to Saddam. He made certain that what all Iraqi people needed the government would provide. And Saddam decided what they needed.

Americans cannot fathom the masses viewing Saddam as a deity. But to an impoverished Iraqi, Saddam was God-like. The government existed to perpetuate his omnipotent, God-like status. The combination of wealth, magnificent palaces, spying, torture, information tools, and psychological pressure coupled with the inability for the average Iraqi to think critically combined to create a public that worshiped the dictator Saddam as a God. As twisted as we Americans may perceive it to be, Saddam owned the hearts and minds of most Iraqis. Iraqis believe in persons, not institutions.

Saddam often used garbage collection, sewer management, and electrical-power distribution as a means to control people and segments of society. Public works belonged to the state, and so Saddam made sure the people knew that he could provide or take away at his will. The lasting effect of that type of control and behavior was to create a mindset among the general Iraqi population that the government either provided or withheld, but ultimately that it controlled all. If they wanted or needed anything, the government was the institution to turn for satisfaction.

Assessing behavior from a value-based perspective, the Iraqis simply did not operate at a level which Americans can relate. I do not say Americans have the highest social values in the world. But the mainstream of America basically espouses a Judeo-Christian value ethic as basis for behavior toward others. Iraq's basic Islamic values are not radically dissimilar from Christian or Jewish values, though there certainly are differences. The moral bankruptcy I perceived among the general Iraqi society, I surmised, had more to do with Saddam than Islam. After the fall of Saddam, Iraqis are now trying to redefine themselves along a more Islamic tradition. And America's military — primarily the Army — is in the middle of this rediscovery.

Another complicating and insidious aspect to leading soldiers in Iraq was managing my own frustration with some of the behaviors and poor values exhibited by some American troops and junior officers. Most soldiers exhibited honorable and decent values as they served in extremely difficult circumstances. As well, their volunteerism and committed service manifested in their combat tours was as noble and virtuous an act as any human being can exhibit.

However, the values espoused by too-large a number of soldiers were not the same as those with which I grew up. And it is my personal assessment that values and behaviors among the youngest soldiers and marines serving have eroded in the last 20 years. In general, young people tend to be less considerate, disciplined, and ethical. While there is not wanton degenerate behavior, there is a less mannered and temperate behavior exhibited than that I recall from soldiers serving in 1985, when I entered the Army as an officer. There are many reasons for this. Values among Americans in society are less binding than they were just a decade ago. National political leaders and celebrities, who dominate the world view of young Americans day-to-day in our media-dominated society, set poor examples and are unchecked by society for their clearly unethical behavior. Personal accountability has diminished in an ever expanding social-liberalism in America.

I buttress my perception with that of General Dennis Reimer, former Chief of Staff, of the Army, who saw this same issue among soldiers in the Army years before the foray into Iraq. He sought to do something about it when he brought a program to the Army in 1998-1999, entitled "A Values-Based Army."

I remember one day the small group leader of our class at the Army, Command and General Staff College brought us all a wallet card and a hard plastic dogtag-shaped device. We were instructed to carry these items on our person at all times. On the card and the dogtag were the seven Army Values to which we were all instructed to adhere and internalize. We were reminded that as we went back out into the Army from our school setting, we would be the keepers of the values and set the example for others to follow. The Seven Army Values are:

Loyalty
Bear true faith and allegiance to the U.S. constitution, the Army, and other soldiers.
Be loyal to the nation and its heritage.

Duty
Fulfill your obligations.
Accept responsibility for your own actions and those entrusted to your care.
Find opportunities to improve oneself for the good of the group.

Respect
Rely upon the golden rule.
How we consider others reflects upon each of us, both personally and as a professional organization.

Selfless Service
Put the welfare of the nation, the Army, and your subordinates before your own.
Selfless service leads to organizational teamwork and encompasses discipline, self-control and faith in the system.

Honor
Live up to all the Army values.

Integrity
Do what is right, legally and morally.
Be willing to do what is right even when no one is looking.
It is our "moral compass" an inner voice.

Personal Courage
Our ability to face fear, danger, or adversity, both physical and moral courage. [19]

The howling began almost immediately. We were all newly-minted majors and absolutely taken aback that our Chief of Staff would have the audacity to question our values. "Good God, has he gone mad?" many of us thought.

The fact was that General Reimer was not too concerned with us. We were transitioning to becoming senior officers now. We had become the infamous "they" as organizational leaders in the institution. We were to steward his institutional "Values Based Army" initiative.

He was concerned with what he saw as an erosion of values among young soldiers, non-commissioned officers, and new officers which manifested in their poor behavior. The Army would have to teach values not learned at home or in the public school system or other institutions in America so that it could function at its desired level.

The encroachment of eroded values among young people recruited into the Army was significant. It was clearly a factor in the grand scheme of leading soldiers in combat in Iraq. And this will continue to be an important issue in the future. As long as our political leaders choose to commit Americans to wars like this one in Iraq, the measure of success and ultimate victory lies, in part, in the values our nation's soldiers display in war dealing so closely with other cultures and peoples.

Fighting counterinsurgent wars is markedly different from fighting conventional wars, because the insurgents are among the people. Insurgents do not wear a uniform, do not always occupy a position of tactical or strategic value, and do not try to hold any particular piece of ground. Rather they attempt to kill Americans or cause catastrophe to affect behavior or influence political situations. To get at this enemy, American troops must be among the people. Soldiers must discern the good-guys from the bad-guys, eyeball to eyeball. Invariably, cultures will clash as surely as diametrically-opposed purposes clash.

For Iraqis, their first consideration was always about themselves. They constantly seek what they could freely get for themselves. I never came across an Iraqi, not one, who spoke about or genuinely expressed a community-first attitude about an issue. If penetrated, the self-centered-behavior proclivity gave way to their familial and tribal interests immediately. Nepotism and favoritism were expected and absolutely normal behavior.

In Al Saidiyah, the major enclave in Task Force 1-21's sector, tribe preceded local community, which fell lower on the hierarchical priority than other interests. The residents, city leaders, shopkeepers, and security forces all grouped into familial and tribal associations. Loyalties formed around these entities, closing off the greater needs of the community at large. This worked against our hope of establishing a local government that considered all people in an inclusive manner. Iraqis are not community-minded in the same sense that Americans understand that notion. Changing this behavior, I believe, was a key to winning.

An indictment of the general moral character of Iraqis was

the overt disrespect they had for each other. Iraqis fought and killed each other over gasoline. I recall one occasion where I had to step between two arguing Iraqi security forces men who were ready to shoot each other over gasoline. At one of the gas stations in Al Saidiyah, the Ministry of Oil employed a 20-man guard force to enforce the Interim Iraqi Government rationing rules for gasoline. A group of men from a nearby Iraqi police station came to the Al Saidiyah gas station, cut to the front of the line, and brought plastic cans into the gas station to fill them up. The Ministry of Oil guards told the Iraqi police that filling cans was not allowed in the rationing rules and to leave, of which the Iraqi policemen already were well aware. One of the Iraqi policeman argued that his position and title allowed him the right to take the gas in plastic cans. I arrived as the arguing became heated. I walked over to the men and, with my interpreter, intervened. As I approached, a Ministry of Oil guard pointed his AK-47 rifle at the Iraqi policeman in charge of the group who, in turn, raised his AK-47. Other soldiers with me from A/1-21 grabbed the Ministry of Oil guard and Iraqi police officer and disarmed them. It happened very quickly. There was no doubt in my mind, had we not intervened, that one or both of those men would be dead.

On other occasions, when we were not present, Iraqis were killed or Iraqi security force units wounded or killed other Iraqi security force members in an effort to steal the gas they felt they needed. Many times, attacks — one-on-one shooting confrontations — occurred at gas stations for similar reasons among civilians waiting in gas lines.

To kill each other over perceived slights and insults is symptomatic of a social system out of balance. Muslim faith teachings do not endorse this. But few Iraqis are true Muslims devotedly following their faith. They are a mystery. On the one hand, their education and daily family and tribal interactions are governed by Muslim faith teachings.

On the other, they almost wantonly dismiss those tenets for personal convenience. From my perspective this was a society of people who use faith to achieve gratuitous desires much more hedonistic than religiously-based Muslim ideas and faithfulness. Clearly this practice was not followed by all Iraqis. However, it was the standard among many of those that I observed and dealt with in Iraq.

I witnessed Iraqis dismiss their faith for the convenience of the situation. An example of this is "Pleasure Marriages," a practice my Iraqi interpreter explained to me. This Shia-Muslim sanctioned practice allows a sexual relationship between a Muslim man and woman in circumvention of the technical sin of adultery. What occurs is a Muslim man, who has a sexual interest in a Muslim woman, can have an imam marry the couple for a specified time period agreed upon in advance among the parties. During this time, the couple has sexual "pleasure" with each other; afterwards the sex must stop.

Sunni do not believe in such duplicitous practice and do not condone pleasure marriages. A Sunni would candidly cheat on the marriage vow but not with the convenient relationship the Shia endorses.

I believe that much of what ails the Iraqi society is rooted in poor public education. The masses of Iraqi society have not had access to an effective, valued public education system. While in Iraq, I compared the situation to my experience in America and concluded we are a nation challenged to value what we have accomplished in public education. American pundits cynically criticize our public education system. Granted, there is much room for improvement in the American public education process. But there is much more right and exceptional about the system than wrong. Only one day serving as a soldier in Iraq brought this home to me in a very personal way.

The public school system in Iraq was pathetic by my Western standard of measure. The schools were filthy, decrepit, and almost unsuitable for use. No self-respecting community anywhere in America would stand for the conditions of sanitation nor allow the filth that exists in the public schools of Baghdad.

While commanding Task Force 1-21, we focused many projects on schools in various communities of our sector. Because I believe so strongly in education as a means to build a society, I never passed on an opportunity to do my part to improve this sector of Iraqi society. The classrooms in most public schools in Baghdad were as simple as the single room schoolhouses of 19th century America. Iraqi children are not in school long enough to learn much. They engaged in instruction for four hours a day. The instruction was well rounded but not refined. Few critical thinkers exist in Iraq due to the distrust and oppression. Iraqis believe 100 percent of what they see on television, not questioning it or realizing that the media have agendas and opinions they promote. The blind belief in the media was evident from the conversations I had with many Iraqis.

Although a lot of Iraqi adults claimed to be educated and to hold advanced degrees, conversing with them leads to a contrary conclusion. Because Iraqis do not see themselves as free and empowered, I believe many suffer from a low self-image. As a result they seem lost, unguided, and accommodating rather than aspiring or driven people.

I realize that I am imposing a Western assessment of Iraqi behavior and it may be that their culture demands such an outward appearance in behavior. But, I think Iraqis behaved this way because of conditioning, oppression, and a poor public education system, all of which can be remedied. Any remedies must be consistent with Iraqi culture and religion, and that takes time.

To further depict the Iraqi character and behavior of which I speak, examination of a few prominent words in their language is insightful. To me two words in Arabic, more than any others, help explain the Iraqi mindset. The first is "Inshallah." This means "God willing." So what's in a word or phrase? No matter how trite or how serious a conversation was going with an Iraqi, at some point when a "yes" response or a commitment response would be appropriate, an Iraqi would shrug and say, "Inshallah," God willing. This was the supreme cop-out or deflection of personal responsibility. In the Army, serving as an officer, personal responsibility is hugely valued. This "Inshallah" response became anathema to me. Generally, in Western societies there is some expectation of accepting personal responsibility for actions, albeit not as pronounced as in the military. To an Iraqi, personal responsibility and accountability are not concepts they ascribe. Things may go badly because they are beyond one's control and God's will was not in their favor. As well, the reverse is true and things may go well which is good. Either way, God's will determines the outcome, not the individual's. Later in my tour I would hear "Inshallah" and I would follow that up with, "OK, what are you going to do to help God achieve his will?" I would get some very curious looks.

The other phrase that Iraqis use — less openly among Westerners but nevertheless strongly believed in — is "Kaffeck", which means, "As you like." This phrase says a great deal about Iraqis too. It is about accommodation. If you are willing to allow another to define the terms of accommodation then what do you really stand for? Again, Americans generally are not so willing to acquiesce to another's will or desires. At some point Americans believe that one must have a position or be accountable for something they believe in. By deferring psychologically, a person is held accountable for nothing at all. What does that espouse? It is abomination to an American but completely normal to an Iraqi.

Combined, "Inshallah" and "Kaffeck" are an insight to the Iraqi people. It is as if they place themselves in the position of victims in most situations. Unaccountable for a belief or certain position, one is readily a victim of everything.

That the Iraqi people harbored some less-than-desirable character traits necessarily adversely impacted all that the Task Force did in our sector. Managing and directing negotiations, Iraqi security force training, civil affairs operations, information campaigns, and daily interactions between soldiers and citizens in the towns and villages of our sector were affected by Iraqi character traits, and we had to master an understanding of the differences if we hoped to accomplish anything meaningful. The clash between American and Iraqi character and behaviors was constant and a dimension to fighting in Iraq of which leaders had to be aware. Salient to success for the Task Force was managing this dynamic.

With these early assessments, the Task Force began to shape events, fight the enemy, and negotiate with Iraqi clerics and community representatives residing in our assigned sector. The key to success was building relationships to secure and stabilize our sector. Every day was a day to learn and improve.

The effort to fight and win in Iraq will continue to be hugely difficult for young Army and Marine Corps leaders who must deal with this character clash every day. Unit training and soldier education were absolutely essential to succeeding in this environment. Task Force 1-21 committed strongly to training and educating soldiers and leaders about the differences. We worked techniques and strategies to mitigate the differences and manage the problems presented by these character issues. Some units did this very well and others were woefully inept. First Cavalry Division and 5th BCT made a concerted effort to incorporate this training and education into all units under the First Cavalry Division flag.

As commander of Task Force 1-21, I knew understanding the Iraqi character and our ability to work through the problems presented by the cultural differences was essential to success. The efforts to work with the people in our sector and to train the Iraqi security forces required a heightened level of understanding and competency in cultural relations.

We were continually tested. The Facilities Protection Service, Iraqi police, and Iraqi Civil Defense Corps — all Iraqi security force elements — were integral to our daily operations. Unfortunately, their level of competency, training, and equipment were in question when we arrived in March 2004. 1-94 Field Artillery did a good job of forming the organizational basis of these Iraqi security forces elements. It was up to us to take the forces to the next level and make them effective.

15 Iraqi Security Forces—Keystone Cops in Action!

*"It is easier to find men who will volunteer to
die, than to find those who are willing to endure
pain with patience." Julius Caesar*

The strategic and political decision in Coalition Provisional
Authority General Order Number 2 disbanding the Iraqi
military resulted in all BCTs in Iraq having to absorb the
training mission of building a new Iraqi military. In his
book *My Year in Iraq*, Coalition Provisional Authority Director and Presidential Envoy, L. Paul Bremmer III, explained
his decision describing that the political advice he received
concluded, because of the American invasion, there was no
Iraqi Army to reconstitute. Those Iraqis serving in the military that were not killed or captured simply quit and went
home to their families. Military bases, equipment, weapons, and ammunition were looted thereby further disallowing any reconstitution. According to Bremmer and the
Coalition Provisional Authority, there was absolutely nothing left to reconstitute.[20]

I strongly disagree. Iraqis would have reformed for a pit-
tance of payment. The military could have lived in tent
cities. A reconstituted Army did not necessarily require
bases with all the facilities of hard-stand buildings. Over
time they would need these, but to reconstitute the Iraqi
Army this was not necessary. That weapons and ammunition disappeared and were looted should have given pause
to decision-makers about the overall desperateness of the
situation. How could the further disenfranchisement of so
many produce a favorable situation? It was inaccurate to
conclude a method of reconstitution was impossible. The
decision not to reconstitute the Iraqi Army did not consider how a new Iraqi Army would be brought to life or

who would take charge. That is to say, there was no detailed, comprehensive plan in place to support a decision to rebuild the Iraqi Army anew. The better solution for the Coalition Provisional Authority at the time would have been combining efforts of reconstitution with rebuilding. To outright disenfranchise the officer corps of the military most profoundly set the condition for an insurgency to take root. Bremmer improperly factored the vital implementation aspect of the decision to rebuild the Iraqi Army anew. And, based on his own account, no senior military leaders were politically adept enough to provide that guidance and steer the sagacious diplomat to a better decision. Bremmer had no personal understanding of what his decision levied on the U.S. Army in Iraq, and he received no good military advice in making the decision. Having never served in the military, Bremmer knew relatively little about the parameters of the undertaking, and as a career diplomat this could not be expected. Military leaders had a duty to provide him with better advice.

The time needed to execute a total rebuilding effort and the subsequent effects on security, general law and order, as well as the political effect of disenfranchisement of a tribal, Sunni-dominated, officer-heavy military served the cause of the burgeoning insurgency in Iraq. I spoke with many senior Iraqi military officers living quietly in Al Saidiyah who repeatedly told me their former colleagues were involved in the insurgent effort. "You gave them no choice," they would tell me.

This Coalition Provisional Authority decision directly linked a strategic decision to a tactical implementation consequence that was nearly untenable. In spring 2004, the battalion task forces of the many BCTs throughout Iraq were charged with the mission of training, equipping, and fielding a new Iraqi Army. As a commander of one of those battalion task forces, I can testify we were provided no additional personnel, equipment, funding (at our executor level), or practical advisory-assistance type training to execute the significant task of building a new Iraqi Army. We had to figure it out for ourselves and with whatever resources we could muster.

Complicating matters, the Iraqi security forces that Task Force 1-21 dealt with upon our arrival were disparate organizations. Three key organizations required our direct involvement as a Task Force: Iraqi Civil Defense Corps (precursor to the New Iraqi Army), Facilities Protection Service, and the Iraqi police. All Iraqi security forces operating in Al Rashid in March 2004 were poorly trained, led, and resourced. Because Task Force 1-21 lacked the numbers of troops needed to accomplish the many varied missions assigned, we relied on the Iraqi security forces to make up the difference. In the first three months none of these organizations materially benefited the mission for the Task Force.

That the Iraqi security forces were in pitiable shape in April 2004 only magnified the most glaring need for Al Saidiyah, which was local security. Nearly none existed. Without a capable local police force the need to provide security around the clock in the Task Force sector proved to be a significant daily challenge.

While officially there were Iraqi policeman and a so-called police force, it was not comparable to an effective police force as Americans understand. Task Force 1-21 had no direct control over any Iraqi police organization at any echelon. Iraqi police could operate — or not operate — in Al Saidiyah. No master plan or effective leadership functioned to insure services were provided in a comprehensive manner. No local government directed the Iraqi police; rather, the Ministry of the Interior, a national-level organization, controlled the Iraqi Police Service. This nationalized police system infringed on the ability of the local Iraqi police to focus on local police work. So Iraqi police did whatever they independently chose to do. No independent local funding, recruiting, or daily operating was part of the design. In the configuration and administrative organization that existed the year Task Force 1-21 operated in Baghdad, the Iraqi police were completely incapable of providing local policing capability. During Saddam's era a national Iraqi police force existed to enforce the law of Saddam. Not materially changing this force from a national organization to a locally-administered and directed one, with a focus on protecting and serving the citizenry of the neighborhoods of Baghdad, allowed an ineffective dynamic to perpetuate.

The fact that there was no local governing or policing capability meant the American military had to fill the void. In my sector, the American military was looked upon to serve as the local government and police, a role for which we were never resourced or effectively empowered to carry out. This lack of local policing evidenced in 2004 and early 2005 remains true today: local governance has no efficacy in Iraq, which is the critical failing of the strategy in Iraq.

Security, whether it is military or civil law enforcement, must have a localized component to be successful on the larger national scale. The whole is the sum of its parts. For law enforcement, the insurgents fully understand that if the Iraqi police get strong and established in the local enclaves of Baghdad — that is, through the adoption of an effective "protect and serve" doctrine — they will lose. The Iraqi police were high-value targets for the insurgents the year Task Force 1-21 served. Iraqi police stations were prime and relatively-easy, soft targets.

One of the most gruesome attacks I was privy to occurred in the summer of 2004. A police station in the BCT sector was brutally attacked. An Associated Press (AP) report described it:

Jordanian terrorist Abu Musab al-Zarqawi's militant group claimed responsibility for the attack, as it had done for a highly coordinated assault on a police station west of Baghdad the day before in which insurgents killed 16 police, looted the station's armory and freed dozens of prisoners. The claim, like the previous one, appeared on an Islamic Web site known for such statements and could not immediately be verified.

This was the type of barbarism we dealt with daily. Although American soldiers could not round up suspected insurgents and execute them; that is exactly what the insurgents did. Soldiers saw this. As a leader I had to understand and deal with the emotional and psychological aspect this had on soldiers. The rules that insurgents live and operate under are vastly different from those that American soldiers have to honor and respect, and while most Iraqi citizens wanted law and order, none know how to obtain it.

Our predecessors, 1-94 Field Artillery, used an organization called the Facilities Protection Service to fill the local security void in Al Saidiyah and throughout their sector. This Facilities Protection Service existed under Saddam's regime. They were a left-over organization after the U.S. invasion and the toppling of the existing regime. 1-94 Field Artillery preserved and employed a contingent of these men. They were paid by the Army to serve in an augmenting role essentially providing local policing as an interim solution to the burgeoning, yet dysfunctional, Iraqi police force. We inherited this group. From the outset, it was clear to me they were a disjointed, poorly-trained, poorly-resourced, and almost-dangerous organization. To me, they were the Keystone Cops, Iraqi style.

Under the Saddam regime, the Facilities Protection Service was established to protect key government facilities throughout Iraq, much like Pinkerton guards in America.

Armed with an AK-47 rifle and wearing a uniform with a light blue shirt and sleeve brassard embossed in bold white letters with the letters "FPS" for Facilities Protection Service, along with a badge identifying them as Facilities Protection Service security, these men were expected to deter attacks and stop the planting of IEDs in key sections of Area of Operations Rocket. They operated around the clock in eight-hour shifts. Curiously, Iraqis were enamored with badges. To an Iraqi, a badge was some symbol of prestige. Ostensibly, the more badges an Iraqi had, the more important a person he was. Under Saddam's rule, a position with a uniform and, I suspect, a badge denoted prestige and this belief continued.

When we arrived in Iraq and assumed control of the Facilities Protection Service, the men were paid:

 TF 1-21

TF 1-21 FPS PAY

RANK	NUMBER	AMOUNT	TOTAL
MAJ	2	300,000 dinars (approx $230)	600,000 (approx $460)
CPT	5	221,000 dinars (approx $170)	1,105,000 (approx $850)
SOG	56	198,000 dinars (approx $152)	11,088,000 (approx $8,512)
GUARD	257	179,000 dinars (approx $138)	46,003,000 (approx $35,466)
TOTAL	320		58,796,000 (approx $45,228)

FPS Pay Chart

Figure 15.1 — Pay scale for Facilities Protection Service guards.

Generally Facilities Protection Service guards were uneducated, unable to even read or write, and paid a mere $138 a month stipend for the task of risking their lives against a determined insurgency. That their performance was for the most part substandard was foreseeable. Many would work only one month, collect their pay, and disappear. There was little loyalty to their fellow Facilities Protection Service comrades or to Iraq. Some were wounded or killed doing their job. When shot or killed, some were perpetrating crimes or were wantonly engaged in corrupt activity. But there was a group that tried hard to serve to their full capability most of the time.

We also assessed that a number of the guards were actually hardened insurgents who had infiltrated the Facilities Protection Service. They joined to either set others up to be killed in attacks or just to collect a $150 that month to help their families survive by doing nearly nothing.

My typical observation of these Facilities Protection Service guards was a small group congregating at a checkpoint and openly presenting themselves to the fast moving traffic along the highway on Route Irish or Route Senators. Rarely would guards venture too far from a fixed checkpoint location to deter an insurgent from planting an IED.

On the occasions they were attacked, the Facilities Protection Service guards often sprayed fire in the direction of the attack, indiscriminately wounding or killing Iraqi nationals, or hitting nothing at all. After the dust cleared, there would be dead Facilities Protection Service guards and a story about an attack having occurred but not much else.

For example, one day two guards ventured above an overpass and walked, one in front of the other, a few feet apart along the edge of roadway. A car drove by, shot both guards dead, and continued down the road at a high rate of speed. When we received the report about the incident approximately 15 minutes later, none of the Facilities Protection Service guards could tell us what had happened. And until we rounded up Iraqi civilians in the vicinity who told us what they saw, we were unable to piece together sufficient information to reconstruct the incident.

Iraqis did not seem to care when a Facilities Protection Service guard was killed. In fact, many felt the Facilities Protection Service guards got what they deserved for collaborating with the American soldiers.

Obviously, our assessment of the Facilities Protection Service and its effectiveness was cynical. We knew many things had to be done quickly if we were going to improve the situation and make the organization a viable force able to truly assist us in our efforts in sector. And because LOO 2 directed us to "Employ Iraqi Security Forces," as part of the campaign plan to secure the Al Rashid district, we had to find a way to make this force more viable.

It was apparent that the Facilities Protection Service guards needed better equipment and pay to upgrade the quality of men volunteering to serve as a guard. Next, the guards needed training on how to patrol and work to defend the neighborhood or facility that needed guarding. Guards also needed an appreciation of how to protect themselves from attacks and, when attacked, how to fight as a team.

Training of the Facilities Protection Service also required that guards learn how to report information to allow us to follow up and act on the information. Lastly, and perhaps most salient, the organization needed better mid-level leaders.

We had inherited a structure that had two branches or contingents to the Facilities Protection Service. One branch was assigned to protect the two highways in our sector, which was referred to as the "Highway Branch." Ali Saleem Ali was the major in charge of the Highway Branch.

The other branch was the "Al Saidiyah Branch." In the Al Saidiyah Branch, the guards were positioned at key locations in static checkpoints. Each mahalla had a contingent of guards. Generally, the guards were from the neighborhoods they patrolled which facilitated local security. The Facilities Protection Service guards had great familiarity with the area and the people; and, therefore, many had a vested interest in protecting the people in the neighborhood. Unfortunately, this also set conditions for potential corruption. Tahseen Ali Hussein was in charge of the Al Saidiyah Branch.

1-94 Field Artillery did a superb job of working with the Facilities Protection Service and developed strong relationships. The Facilities Protection Service contingent they handed over to us was 320 guards strong. Immediately upon our arrival, we were directed by the BCT staff to transfer 50 guards and two Facilities Protection Service Captains to 1-8 Cavalry to support their needs, as they were dreadfully short.

Though the Facilities Protection Service guards were very poorly equipped, not well led at the mid-level, and their training was deficient, they showed signs they might ultimately provide value to the Task Force as scouts. With improvement, this was a force that could really augment our efforts. With proper direction and training the men serving in the Facility Protection Service could perhaps one day effectively integrate into the Iraqi police force or serve in the New Iraqi Army.

To improve the standards of performance, I assigned a Facilities Protection Service Leader Team to work with the two Facilities Protection Service Branch Majors. The team, Lieutenant Jayson Luckey, Staff Sergeant Curtis Raine and Corporal Jack Slaton, took charge of the Facilities Protection Service. Their tasks were to reorganize the Facilities

Protection Service, develop a detailed training program, and to work with the Task Force Executive Officer, Major Marshall, and the Task Force S-4 to better equip the force rapidly. In general, they had the responsibility of developing a comprehensive program to bring the guards from a poorly-disciplined and ineffective organization to one that could genuinely provide support to the Task Force. The idea was to make the Facilities Protection Service a viable, contributing security force.

Lieutenant Luckey led the team. He was a tall, athletic, young officer, with a smile that could light up the room. Lieutenant Luckey quite literally was my most improved lieutenant in the Task Force. His taking on the management of the rascally Facility Protection Services characters and the interpreters was a growing experience for the Lieutenant.

Lieutenant Luckey was assisted by Sergeant Curtis Raine. Sergeant Raine would quickly become the "go to" person in that group. Sergeant Raine was a seasoned non-commissioned officer, who stood about five feet, nine inches, with a round, happy face that either smiled or snarled depending on what people around him were doing. Well-loved by everyone, Sergeant Raine was loud, direct, and gregarious, and he had an amazing sense of humor. Sergeant Raine had served in the Marine Corps when he was younger. This non-commissioned officer was superb. No one possessed a more dedicated spirit than he did. I never gave him a task or mission that he failed to accomplish, exceeding the standard routinely. More importantly though, he was smart, energetic and committed; all qualities I leveraged for the benefit of the Task Force. He was ideally suited to work with Iraqis. No one who served was more resourceful, innovative, or hard-nosed than Sergeant Raine.

Helping Sergeant Raine on the team directing the Facilities

Protection Service was Corporal Jack Slaton. Corporal Slaton was the perfect, trusty apprentice to Sergeant Raine. He was a lanky, 5' 10" young man who always exercised good, common sense, and possessed good problem-solving ability. I called him "Baseball 6" which was a take-off of a radio call-sign because he had been in the Texas Rangers AAA baseball system in his earlier days. He was a talented athlete. Corporal Slaton loved motorcycles, baseball, and Texas. He also had some earlier life experience with law enforcement making him ideally suited to train the Facilities Protection Service volunteers. Additionally, he had a great personality ideal for working with the Iraqis and helping them work together. The Facilities Protection Service leaders and many of the guards respected and genuinely liked Corporal Slaton; they listened to him when he gave them direction.

The problems resident in the Facilities Protection Service were the same as those experienced in the Iraqi Civil Defense Corps, the legitimate ground military component of the Interim Iraqi Government. The Iraqi Civil Defense Corps battalion that served in support of the 5th BCT in March 2005 was, by my best description, a "Rag-Tag Army."

Iraqi Civil Defense Corps – A "Rag-Tag" Army

The Iraqi Army was completely dismantled in Operation Iraqi Freedom I by the Third Infantry Division and the Marine Corps contingent in Iraq. Those Iraqi soldiers who were not killed or captured, scattered. Many went home and others became the soldiers and leaders who presently serve in the ranks of the insurgency.

The Coalition Provisional Authority policy rejecting any effort to reassemble the Iraqi military that served Saddam meant that whatever Army Iraq would have would be one built anew, with precious few former Iraqi Army officers and leaders in charge. Much like the Facilities Protection Service guards, the soldiers that volunteered to serve in the Iraqi Civil Defense Corps were characters of questionable ability and quality. Easily too, most were Shia since the Sunni were not committed to the rebuilding of an Iraqi military. The Sunni soldiers already had a cause and new insurgent army to serve. The expulsion of infidels now was added to the reasons to serve in the ranks of the insurgency.

The company of the Iraqi Civil Defense Corps that Task Force 1-21 inherited was D/304th Infantry. While on the pre-deployment site survey, I met the Company Commander of D/304th and its First Sergeant. The First Sergeant was a very charismatic man. He loved Americans and tried to act, dress, and behave like an American non-commissioned officer though he barely spoke a word of English. He was a jovial, barrel-chested, tough guy. He was a confident and natural leader. He could physically beat-up any soldier in the company. He was the perfect First Sergeant to lead this loosely-banded group of men who wanted to be soldiers. He had one serious flaw, though: he was illiterate. Despite this shortcoming, I chose to keep him in the First Sergeant position because his other abilities offset this shortcoming. I knew, though, that down the road, he would have to either learn to read and write or leave the Army.

The Company Commander was a reserved, bright officer who I surmised could handle the unit. He was willing to learn and, clearly, he had a lot to learn. Typical of officers in the Iraqi Civil Defense Corps, he had a penchant for demanding privileges because of his position. This behavior was supremely tough to manage and frequently got in the way of accomplishing tasks and solving problems. The Company Commander had a fondness for seeking the easy road and avoiding tough training and personal risks. He was not leading from out front but rather pushing from behind.

When I returned to Iraq after the pre-deployment site survey with Task Force 1-21, I found the First Sergeant was still in place but Captain Dilawer, a new Company Commander, was now in charge. The previous commander was elevated to the battalion staff and was now the battalion's S2, Intelligence Officer.

The new Commanding Officer was cut from the same cloth as his predecessor and had the same inclination for privilege.

The Iraqi Civil Defense Corps company that Captain Dilawer commanded was ill-disciplined, untrained, and poorly equipped when we inherited them. The First Armor Division leadership had given 1-94 Field Artillery little assistance and support. 1-94 Field Artillery literally had their hands tied rendering this situation miserable. Little equipment was provided to the Iraqi Civil Defense Corps and the company had no vehicles. Worse, the Iraqi Civil Defense Corps company had very limited logistical support from any entity other than 1-94 Field Artillery. 1-94 Field Artillery justifiably did not trust the Iraqi Civil Defense Corps. It was difficult to discern which soldiers were committed friends and which might be insurgents. The Iraqi Civil Defense Corps was infiltrated.

1-94 Field Artillery had tight, positive control of the Iraqi Civil Defense Corps company and integrated patrolling with their own patrols but that was the extent of their involvement. 1-94 Field Artillery taught us enough to understand the organization, where it had been, and made good recommendations on how we could improve the company.

Amazingly, the First Cavalry Division and the BCT handed the battalion task forces responsibility to train and ready this Iraqi Civil Defense Corps company to fight but absolutely no resources were provided to accomplish the objectives.

Initiatives generated within the Task Force to spend our allocated funds or creatively outfit the soldiers by providing our equipment to the Iraqi Civil Defense Corps company ran into one obstacle after another. It was absolutely maddening. Each battalion commander requested necessary resources to Colonel Lanza and he supported us in every way he could. He simply had nothing coming from above to distribute. That did not change the order that we train the newly-minted Iraqi Civil Defense Corps and we did the best we could. In reality, it was not very much at this early juncture.

Many Iraqi Civil Defense Corps soldiers wore dress shoes, sandals, or other personally owned shoes because they had no boots. Some soldiers wore Mission Oriented Protective Posture suits or over-garments. These are the hot, nuclear, biological, and chemical protective suits made famous by the media during Desert Storm. The suits are designed for soldiers to function in tactical field environments, but they are bulky and uncomfortable. In hot weather, these suits are miserable and impractical for daily wear. The Iraqi soldiers wore them in the stifling heat because they were the only uniforms they had. Others wore old Saddam-era Army uniforms, which caused problems among the ranks and offended some Iraqi Civil Defense Corps soldiers. Almost none of the soldiers had helmets or any other military headgear. They looked like a band of militia more than an Army.

No Iraqi Civil Defense Corps soldiers had body armor of any kind. None had load-bearing equipment to help them carry their ammunition and water, essentials for any infantry. To organize the Iraqi Civil Defense Corps company was going to take more than just fleeting effort. These soldiers had to become an integral part of my Task Force formation. Amazingly, our Army displayed absolute ignorance about how to train and build a foreign Army such as the one in Iraq.

In the 1960s, our Army had done this very thing in Vietnam.

The Military Advisory Assistance Command was created to build the Army of the Republic of Vietnam and help the South Vietnamese fight the communist North Vietnamese. Where did all that knowledge and after action information go? Why were we so inept thirty years later? Why did senior Army leaders act as if they were doing something new and cutting-edge? I found the Army severely lacking in this whole arena and it frankly upset me. The Army was absolutely incompetent in this effort when we arrived a year into the war.

Later in my tour, Lieutenant General Petraeus, who early in the war commanded the 101st Airborne (Air Assault) Division operating in Northern Iraq, returned while I was fighting with the First Cavalry Division, and he took charge of building Iraq's burgeoning security forces. No doubt, he went back to the old-school lessons of Vietnam to shape a competent organization to undertake the huge task of re-forming these Iraqi forces.

In 2007 General Petraeus was named Commander for Multi-National Force – Iraq, and he has significantly up-graded the overall effort to train the Iraqi Army. This is significant but perhaps too little too late. The lesson the Army must learn is to retain the capability honed through this experience and institutionalize the process for the future because this, America, is the future.

As I looked at the reality of our situation training the Iraqi Civil Defense Corps, it occurred to me that if we could build a new Iraqi Army on equal par with the organization, logistical support, and tactical capability of the Army of the Republic of Vietnam, this would be another significant nail in the insurgents' proverbial coffin. The U.S. Army in Vietnam built the Army of the Republic of Vietnam extremely well. That the Army of the Republic of Vietnam did not fight well in the final accounting had more to do with their lack of will to win and low commitment to the Republic of Vietnam cause rather than the structure and design of their national Army.

Unlike the Army of the Republic of Vietnam, the Iraqis have the will to win and reclaim their country from the al-Qaeda, Iranian and Syrian Sunni opportunistic intrusions. They have the capacity and capability to settle the internal discord between religious sects, but only with time, growth, coaching and mentoring from the U.S. military. With the force structure, education, and logistical support similar to the Army of the Republic of Vietnam, I strongly believed that this fledgling Iraqi Civil Defense Corps could tip this war to the effective control of the Iraqi government. With that, the U.S. and the Iraqi government could focus on the civil rebuilding efforts of restoring the infrastructure and the economy of Iraq.

Feeling as strongly as I did about what effort we needed to put forth to get the Iraqi Civil Defense Corps into better fighting shape, I put my Headquarters and Support Battery Commander, Captain Christian Van Keuren, in charge of training this company. The other task force commanders chose to use young captains, not yet in command of American troops, to lead these Iraqi units. Most of these captains performed well. But I chose a currently-serving battery commander to take on this role for Task Force 1-21 because I saw the challenges as monumental in scope and complexity and believed this required a senior, seasoned officer with command experience to work the details and press the Iraqi Civil Defense Corps to higher standards.

Captain Van Keuren, who we all called "VK," was the perfect officer to do this. VK was a very deliberate thinker. He loved soldiers and soldiering and had a great conceptual mind. He could devise exceptional training plans and had proven this to me before we ever deployed. Back at Fort Hood, his training plans were never bland or rudimentary. He was innovative, creative, and technically competent with his designs. He was the best battery commander in the battalion at this kind of thing.

Together we dusted off an old Army program General William Westmoreland used in Vietnam called RECONDO, short for Reconnaissance-Commando, and modified the program methodology to fit our needs and situation. Captain Van Keuren had read a great deal about RECONDO and, though it was not an old Military Advisory Assistance Command program per se, he felt it was one that fit our existing situation. From that foundation, I sent him off to design a comprehensive training program.

Making the Iraqi Civil Defense Corps a viable and capable force that could operate independently in a variety of tasks, including reconnaissance, raids, ambushes, and combat patrols, was our goal. Planning operations and handling their weapons safely was another. To get to a capable level of competency would take great effort and required significantly-improved logistical support. The sad state of logistics was a constant impediment in our initial effort. We had to figure out how to overcome the equipment problems. Developing leaders and changing the character of the Iraqi Civil Defense Corps soldiers was another clear effort we would have to pursue vigorously.

Captain Van Keuren understood the many problems very well. He was allotted a week to put together a 90-day program to improve the Iraqi Civil Defense Corps. The 90-day program was broken into tasks, which were required to be performed in 30 day increments. As the soldiering improved — or deteriorated — we planned to make adjustments.

The work we had to do with the Iraqi security forces was very challenging. Despite the monumental task that lay ahead, we believed with effort and a plan we could help improve these forces. With élan and vigor we dove into the tasks.

Throughout the training process, the Advisory Support Team led by Captain Van Keuren was frustrated with the limited resources and constant pressure from the BCT and Division to get the ICDC into combat operations. Despite the frustration, Captain Van Keuren and his team worked tirelessly to meet the training demands of Iraqi Civil Defense Corps soldiers. Over time, the company would improve as the Advisory Support Team did their best to train the Iraqi soldiers. This part of the mission, however, only represented a fraction of the overall effort. Another very critical aspect to operating full spectrum in this complex environment was the management of civil operations and civil projects to rebuild our little part of Baghdad. Civil operations were the focus of Task Force 1-21.

16 Civil Military Operations

"I don't think our troops ought to be used for what's called nation building." George W. Bush (October 11, 2000)

Standing on the streets of any city block in Baghdad in the late spring, early summer of 2004 it was obvious that the city needed to be rebuilt. Iraq, after the Gulf War in 1991, was devastated by the horrible government that ruled Iraq and the United Nations sanctions that limited outside access to Iraq. The U.S.-led invasion to topple the regime of Saddam Hussein further destroyed the once-exotic Arab city. Infrastructure in the capital city had deteriorated so badly that people were overwhelmed with the decrepit nature of Baghdad. Iraqis had no idea and little means to fix their neighborhoods. The BCT and Task Force 1-21 did not take long to begin focusing effort on civil affairs. Project development focused on restoring infrastructure entailed most of what the Task Force did from the summer of 2004 until we left in March 2005.

During my few weeks on the pre-deployment site survey in January 2004, and in the early weeks of our effort in Al Saidiyah, I was astounded by the pathetic state of the environment. I expected the year-old American presence to have produced a much better living condition for Iraqis. After the invasion, which had concluded almost a year earlier, appallingly little noticeable improvement to the infrastructure, cleanliness, or civil operations of Baghdad was visible. The electrical power was on for a few hours a day; trash was piled up in the streets; street lights and traffic signals were inoperable; bombed-out buildings were still in rubble and not cleaned up; broken down cars, abandoned machinery, and building material were strewn along the roads. Most of Baghdad looked more like a scene from the Hollywood movie "Terminator" than a city where millions lived.

I could not fathom what strides the previous American forces or the Coalition Provisional Authority had made. My eyes told me that very little had been realized. I have no idea what mess existed after May 2003 when the initial offensive operation of Iraqi Freedom I seemed to wane. I concluded it was unfair for me to judge the previous efforts as ineffective. But, constantly in my mind was the thought that had I been the leader responsible for post-invasion Iraq and managing the cleanup effort if, after a year this was all I had to show for my efforts, I would be ashamed. Intuitively, I felt something was amiss. I vowed to make sure that when the Task Forces' year was up, we had to have something to show for our efforts. We could do much better.

No units in First Cavalry Division were professionally or comprehensively trained to conduct civil military operations on the scale required in Baghdad. Nor were any units particularly adept at project development for rebuilding decrepit or non-existent infrastructure. Regardless, that was where the focus of our efforts in Baghdad had to be.

While a presidential candidate in 2000, George W. Bush argued that the military should not be used for nation-building. When Bush won the election, his directives to the Secretary of Defense steered the military away from civil operations. President Bush discounted President Clinton's efforts in Kosovo and Bosnia as frivolous and not a proper application of military power. Therefore, upon his assumption of office, the Army (in fact the U.S. Armed Forces) was not pressed along a path to develop a robust civil operations capability. The Army in which I served was not well trained to nation-build Iraq or any other for that matter.

The Division efforts to focus on civil military operations began in earnest at Fort Hood, about 100 days before we deployed. But that effort merely scratched the surface, and we certainly did not gain the requisite expertise needed to broadly impact the situation once we arrived. Most of our lessons were learned on the fly in Iraq through trial and error.

Colonel Lanza understood immediately that the learning curve was steep. The organization we replaced did not have a well-developed, refined, effective method for managing civil affairs projects which represented the cornerstone of practical activity with civil affairs in any sector of Baghdad; this is precisely why Al Rashid had not progressed much in the year before we arrived. The First Armor Division did all it could to develop a program but it amounted to trifling little considering the scope of the work that needed to be done. In fairness to First Armor Division, the financing and support resources were nearly non-existent during their time in Iraq during Operation Iraqi Freedom I. Colonel Lanza quickly sought to bring order and process to the project development effort. Project execution was the centerpiece of civil military operations.

The first six weeks in the country, we toiled mightily to figure out how to develop, process, and execute good civil projects. We matured rapidly as a team. The process to manage and administer projects became well-refined by the third month the BCT was in Iraq. Colonel Lanza developed a comprehensive, BCT non-lethal targeting process that included this component for developing civil projects in Al Rashid. We had no "book" to follow, so he and the BCT staff literally wrote the book.

At the BCT level determining the right projects to pursue and ultimately execute was considered a "targeting process" and was described like this by Colonel Lanza:

Rather than achieving the traditional kinetic lethal effects on an enemy military force, the brigade had to achieve more subtle effects on the civilian population while maintaining the ability to execute lethal effects on the insurgents.

*The priority was always force protection while the brigade con-
tributed in Al Rashid to the overall movement of Iraq toward
security.*

*Achieving effects, such as gaining the trust of the local nation-
als, ultimately led to HUMINT [human intelligence] for the
brigade's soldiers who then contributed to the precision targeting process. The 5th BCT also sought to build Iraqi responsibility for political and business affairs, critical infrastructure and
security, developing local institutional responsibility to help
achieve security and then stability in Al Rashid.* [21]

At the Task Force, we had to apply more pragmatic efforts
in determining the effects we would pursue with each project. Anything we hoped to achieve had to be in conformity
with the BCT concept. Deciding what targets or projects to
undertake had a functional component and pragmatism to
the process that was difficult to manage. Our Task Force
project selection goals were to pursue projects that, from
a practical standpoint, the Task Force had a reasonable expectation of getting funded and achieving successful results within our assigned sector. Politically, my task was
not simple. I could not pursue a project that may have been
good for the political situation in Al Saidiyah, but for which
I had no chance of receiving BCT support. Until I knew a
project would be funded by the BCT, I could not discuss
the possibility with Iraqi local nationals. By prematurely
discussing a project, I ran the risk of creating expectations
that could not be realized to imams, sheiks, or residents.
And that situation was worse than doing nothing at all. I
had seen others spend weeks recovering from the breakdown of trust created by unfulfilled "promises;" therefore,
the Task Force staff, my subordinate commanders, and I
were careful not to engage in this sort of communication.

To further explain, for the 5th BCT of First Cavalry Division, the BCT Commander decided what was done and

what was not. As commander, it is correct that he insure the integrity and right purpose for the administration of projects across the Al Rashid district. That is his responsibility. However, the method chosen and executed relegated the Task Force to lobbying for a project. Every Task Force project had to be "sold" to receive funding, and because funds were limited, priorities had to be set. Colonel Lanza controlled all the money. Whatever we task force commanders were doing, he used this process to ultimately control all we did in sector. This necessarily meant the fight was BCT-dominated. From my view this was a significant mistake. Tight BCT control was problematic because it did not allow for the right balance of flexibility in targeting and control. This methodology also suggested Colonel Lanza knew better what was right in the task force sectors than did the commanders operating in the area. This centralized process necessarily meant local flexibility was limited. Though the BCT leader and staff rhetoric was "decentralized BCT operations," the truth in execution was exactly the opposite.

Under the centralized control methodology, task force commanders were unable to make deals and negotiate situations as we saw fit. In the fluid and politically charged environment in which we operated, time and action were of the essence. Missed opportunities could rarely be recovered. Because in the end we had to "ask Dad for money," we always had to negotiate the maze of the BCT staff procedures to get a project approved. Time, momentum, and initiative were always at risk under this approach. Convincing Colonel Lanza that some particular project was important all too often ran contrary to his ideas. Worse yet, the bureaucracy created in the approval process created an inordinate amount of time spent building "gee whiz" slides and preparing laborious arguments for a project that bordered on ridiculous at times. For Task Force 1-21, competing with the other two maneuver task forces who had larger sectors to cover, almost always relegated us to third priority on allocation of funds for projects. This positioning exacerbated my personal frustration.

These inherent shortcomings did not paralyze us. It changed the dynamics to less flexible and timely project action time cycles. Delusional, the BCT staff believed they were very timely and action-focused. The reality was we were unable to achieve the optimum effect because the process was tedious, slow, and cumbersome. More importantly, this further illuminates the tedium of our efforts to affect the rebuilding effort in Baghdad. Extrapolate that across the military in Iraq and the situation quickly becomes patently obvious that we might not find timely success.

This is critical to understanding the military failures in Iraq. Civil affairs and projects to improve the infrastructure of the townships of the various districts of Baghdad relied on this haphazard process. BCTs across Iraq conducted their efforts to execute projects differently everywhere. This disparity and disjointed process only confused matters for military personnel and Iraqis alike. Senior commanders who held the purse strings tightly choosing not to distribute resources to lower level commanders out of distrust created a condition that inhibited success.

The approach which would have better served the situation would have been to decentralize and allow a budget for battalion task force commanders. Battalion task force commanders understood and lived the nuances of their assigned sectors; rightfully, they should have been empowered to direct the civil affairs action in total. Command guidelines and standards from Multi-National Forces, Iraq through divisions and BCTs down to battalion task forces should have been provided, monitored, and institutionalized in the military operating across all of Iraq. Emphasis on lowest-level application should have been the focus to maximize malleability for the determination and execution of these civil project efforts. Unfortunately, this just did not happen. Instead, control was kept at the BCT echelon in our case, causing a process that was easily politicized within the military organization above and beyond the American–Iraqi interaction day-to-day in the townships. Failure was assured.

I would have gladly accepted a smaller budget than my sister task forces because I was supremely confident I could manage mine better. The BCT could oversee the task force commander's management budgets to insure discipline in the program. All task force commanders asked more than once for a budget, but to no avail. While I appreciated that Colonel Lanza had his reasons for controlling the money in this manner, I felt it communicated distrust.

The other aspect to "Detect" in Task Force 1-21 that was extremely challenging was working with the Neighborhood Advisory Council and other "leaders" in Al Saidiyah (imams, sheiks and tribal leaders). These were the people that we had been sanctioned to work with in selecting which projects to pursue. Because the Neighborhood Advisory Council was never a politically viable or a legitimate governing entity in Al Saidiyah, it complicated our efforts to work it. The imams, sheiks, and tribal leaders were referred to as "powerbrokers" by the BCT. I was unsuccessful in implementing a genuine effort in cooperation with the so-called powerbrokers because I never found an openly visible and operating powerbroker in Al Saidiyah. Many Iraqis claimed to be sheiks, imams of import, and tribal leaders, but they were really front men.

I had a simple metric for assessing whether I was dealing with a powerbroker. When a particular Iraqi's influence demonstrated observable, significant behavioral or political shifts in people, then, I knew we had touched on a power source. But I never saw this on a meaningful scale in Al Rashid. Thus the results of negotiations never achieved long-term, viable political change in Al Rashid. Through the direction of various projects targeted at or in concert with the Al Rashid District Advisory Council members, some actions were carried out, but few were truly significant achievements. The BCT used self-aggrandizing metrics and, unfortunately believed them. The idea of seeking these people out and leveraging their influence was a dead-on accurate method. But the follow through to find them and accurately measure their influence never truly materialized.

Because the Coalition Provisional Authority ordained the advisory councils as a quasi-legitimate organization, albeit with no power but "advisory" in the neighborhoods of Baghdad, we worked with them as best as we could. The advice I sought from the Neighborhood Advisory Council was how, where, and for what purpose we could execute community projects to benefit the people who lived in Al Saidiyah. Unfortunately, I found the men who sat on the council were not very learned or altruistic. Community spirit was not something these men exuded. In some cases, the council members were literally out for themselves seeking projects for personal benefit. Corruption among these men was pervasive in contradiction to the tenet of their Islamic faith. Because they were so obvious about their personal greed we saw through the charade and we were very careful to avoid supporting any project to the personal benefit of a council member. Captain Levy, the Task Force Civil Affairs Officer, and Captain Pugsley, the Battery Commander tasked with direct liaison to the Neighborhood Advisory Council, were constantly solicited by council members for "support" on amazingly farfetched ideas and schemes for projects. The council members saw the money and little else. Because much of the time the council was intransigent and immature, devoid of character and shameless, we made our own observations about the community. We then conducted a detailed analysis and developed ideas for projects based on observed needs.

The process was intricate to convince the Neighborhood Advisory Council of the importance of the projects we believed needed to be implemented. Knowing the members were flawed in character, power, and ability did not diminish the overt need to work with them. The "dance" we had to choreograph was to insure that ultimately, no matter what we as American military did, the Iraqi residents of Al Saidiyah could not hang on to the belief that the American military governed them. This was, I considered, a fatal flaw in the American effort across Baghdad. All American military leaders knew that Iraqis taking charge and having responsibility for self-governance at the local level was salient to success, but few practiced a procedure to truly empower the Iraqis.

The initial process we employed to handle civil projects had no chance of success. The Task Force staff would determine what we believed was needed and then find a contractor to build whatever was required. 1-94 Field Artillery had started several projects, including a soccer stadium, construction of a Neighborhood Advisory Council administration building, a street cleaning project, and school building restoration projects. All were worthwhile projects. None were initiated or overtly supported by Iraqis. Upon our arrival, we blindly continued working on the projects but soon met with failure. Iraqis wanted to distance themselves from the perception of collusion with Americans. This was the primary nemesis of all project efforts. Among the many things that adversely impacted our efforts to conduct civil military projects were:

• Because insurgents threatened and killed them, almost no Iraqis wanted to have open association with Americans.

• The character of Iraqi so-called powerbrokers was suspect at best. Guarding against graft was difficult. "Playing the ends against the middle" was a common practice.

• Contractors were also of dubious character. Many were well versed at overstating a contract in order to steal money.

• The payment system for contractors was exclusively cash, which had pitfalls for both Americans and Iraqis.

Most Iraqis were easily intimidated. Those who came forward to work or assume responsibility for projects did so mostly for personal gain or money. Culturally, responsibility or accountability are not the common way an Iraqi relates to his fellow Iraqi or to anyone else for that matter. Externally ascribing to a so-called powerbroker the responsibility of accountability was fallacy and ensured failure. Iraqis do not function in accordance with American standards. Demanding that they do so did not change the reality. Other than pursuing money for personal gain, there was no other compelling reason for an Iraqi to risk his life. The politics at the local level were never favorable for open cooperation with American forces. Therefore, in our implementation of most projects, the best we ever achieved in the Task Force was a highly localized effect. Entire community involvement never took root under our initial methods.

I found that unless there was a political backing at the local level for a particular project, there was little chance the work executed would survive very long. The many soccer fields, parks, and community playgrounds that all the task forces of the 5th BCT had built fell into disrepair or were not used much because of the association with the American Army. There was no political efficacy at the local level. The projects that were not the Iraqis were always considered "American" in the eyes of the community residents. Though the Iraqis won the contracts and hired the labor, the work was constantly monitored by a U.S. Army Civil Affairs team or by unit commanders who were responsible for the ground in which the project was being built. While inspection and monitoring made perfect sense to Westerners, it only put an American face on the project and essentially undermined any consideration by the Iraqis of the projects as their own.

After a few obvious failures, the Task Force changed our operating method. We employed a more comprehensive scheme attempting to account for the shortcomings of a flawed system. By the summer of 2004 we began presenting civil project ideas at a council meeting. Once the project was placed before the council, the members would debate the need for the project and attempt to devise a system to implement it. We provided ancillary technical support but never dictated their choices. I also insisted that when we suggested an idea or concept, a council member had to sponsor the project. Sponsorship meant that a council member became an advocate, coordinator, and pseudo-inspector of the project. The sponsor went to the project site and checked on the progress, talked to the contractor and, through my interpreter answered any questions or issues I had. Iraqis rarely spoke to me directly unless it was in a council meeting. This council member/project sponsor was also required to obtain a non-council member imam or sheik to sponsor the project in the neighborhood. This almost completely placed an Iraqi face on the project, at least as far as the capabilities we had allowed. Money still came from the Task Force; the Neighborhood Advisory Council had no revenue.

For Al Saidiyah, there was no shortage of civil project needs. The process of determining a project to pursue was not clear-cut. A great deal of subjectivity and intuition was built into it. Additionally, it demanded significant effort at negotiation and interpersonal communication. Politics, culture, and local relationships were all tied into the dynamic process. Once projects were fixed and funded at the task force level, we had to track their progress. We also had to assess whether the project had the intended effect. We quickly discovered that every project had unintended consequences. Sometimes projects spawned horrible unintended consequences like the deaths of workers or contractors. This assessment was vital to the successful implementation of the project.

In my judgment, many Army units are notorious for massaging the statistics to correlate with the commander's intended desires. Although this did not occur wantonly in the 5th BCT, the assumption was that the right metrics had been utilized, and I never felt that was true. While task force commanders were consulted on what defined the Measures of Effectiveness or the Measures of Performance, the advice was largely ignored by the BCT staff and commander when it came to execution. I personally made several attempts to explain to BCT staff members that the Measures of Effectiveness had to be more closely based on what Iraqis thought and perceived. But that appeared to fall on deaf ears. The response was allowing Iraqis to define anything the American military did was a losing proposition for performance assessment and outcome — and that would be too risky.

The BCT consensus was to produce results from a familiar position of control and comfort, and this was the course chosen to follow. The echelons of the staff and the command system, thus, were permitted to digest their own "numbers" and define the performance. Later they would pat themselves on the back for a "job well done." To do the politically shrewd and unpopular but bold act of understating the performance and defining it in Iraqi terms was too precarious. The easier choice was to stick with the familiar safe methodology and define the metrics ourselves.

No matter what projects we tried to implement, the Iraqi character always pre-empted our credible, altruistic projects. My experience was that local interest in projects was often very limited. Association with Americans was politically very risky for most Iraqis. The way Iraqis behaved and reacted to the American military was more political than cultural or religious based. The social behaviors that we found challenging occurred because we did not attempt to change the political climate at the local level. Instead, we attributed the behaviors to cultural and religious nuances. But changing the local political situation was where we needed to focus effort to change behaviors in Iraqi populace at large.

The Pink Hindenburg

One of the more famous projects Task Force 1-21 was involved with was a place called the "Sewing Factory." Before the war this factory operated as a state-owned enterprise. A woman, Ms. Shafa, headed up this factory. Colonel Lanza learned Ms. Shafa wanted to re-establish the business. A female Captain "Emissary" from the BCT happened upon this woman at a District Advisory Council meeting. Colonel Lanza decided Ms. Shafa had some promise and began an effort to help her revive the sewing business. The factory was located in Task Force 1-21's sector. Therefore, I inherited oversight of this project. Because it was Colonel Lanza's brainchild, I didn't have to run the usual "selling" gauntlet.

I thought success of the project required that I become more familiar with Ms. Shafa. She told us she could employ over 1000 workers and produce uniforms for the new Iraqi Army and other items that would be useful. The facility had, since the invasion, fallen into complete disrepair. The industrial sewing machines and everything in the building had been looted and gutted. It was clear that refurbishing the sewing factory would be a huge enterprise.

Colonel Lanza saw this as a boon. By application of LOO 5, "Economic Pluralism and Business," this factory represented a great opportunity. Returning the factory to operations and supporting the economy in the process, this project had the potential to make a statement and pick up momentum for the whole BCT campaign. Potentially, this project meant:

• Significant employment opportunities: a thousand people with steady jobs, mostly women.

• Producing viable products, affecting the area for the long term.

• Could steer this part of Baghdad down a road to free market or entrepreneurial development. Because Al Saidiyah had enough affluent and educated people the probability of success was better than 50/50.

I was in full support of Colonel Lanza's vision in this refurbishment project. The Task Force staff and I worked very hard to make our efforts successful. This was a true opportunity for the BCT to significantly and positively influence the community. It could also permit the BCT to seize the psychological initiative in this sector of Al Rashid. Word would get out that this was a real success story and potentially have a positive ripple effect.

Unfortunately, we went at it all wrong. In the end, I failed the team because of my complete ignorance of the reality with which we were dealing. The project was completed and it became a showcase stop for VIP visits on the Al Rashid "Tour de Force" as I called it. But within two months of completion the whole project proved to be nothing more than a "sham." The sewing factory had to be garrisoned with the Task Force's contingent of Facilities Protection Service forces to keep insurgents from leveling it.

We followed all the rules. We hired a contractor, local labor, monitored the construction progress, negotiated the purchase of sewing machines, and visited frequently with Ms. Shafa to make sure her needs and her wants were met. We indeed restored a premier facility and had a big grand opening ceremony bringing in Arab media and key members of the Al Saidiyah Neighborhood Council and Al Rashid District Council. When the project was done, the best we could claim was moderate success. A project was completed and local effects were achieved but no lasting improvement occurred in Al Rashid. From the beginning, the subterfuge was at work.

Ms. Shafa had no idea how to run a business. She lied about the workers. She told me repeatedly that she would fill the building with over 1000 workers a day. As we neared completion of the facility, she told my interpreter that most of the workers would work at home, not in the building. When I challenged her on this, she told me that was the way Iraqis did the work before. She was not going to make all of them come in to the building. This, she considered was too dangerous because Americans built the factory. I was completely taken aback.

Having no choice but to accept this situation, the next "bomb" was that Ms. Shafa expected me to get sewing contracts for her. The BCT gave her a huge contract to produce children's school backpacks for the upcoming school year. The factory did a great job with this. The BCT staff then went to the Iraqi Interim Government to obtain a contract for the production of uniforms with some moderate success. Unfortunately though, this was the entirety of Ms. Shafa's business. Once those contracts expired, there was no work to sustain the factory. She lacked the entrepreneurial skills and business savvy to generate more contracts and develop a clientele. That the factory then sat there, decaying and crumbling, as far as Ms. Shafa was concerned, was not her responsibility. She could not comprehend that as the factory leader and chief executive officer, that the job to maintain the business and develop it into something viable was hers. Essentially, Ms. Shafa was handed a gold mine courtesy of the U.S. Army but had no idea what to do with it.

These were the facts:

• Ms. Shafa had no business acumen.

• The facility was not cared for as in cleaned, maintained or improved in any way.

• Ms. Shafa wanted Americans to stay away. She felt the insurgents would attack because of American presence and association. But she wanted our help to generate business.

• The Neighborhood Advisory Council and District Advisory Council public support did not translate to viable political support. Most of the council members hid and none had the power to influence substantial business support for the project.

• The community did not care about supporting the business even though it employed Iraqis citizens and improved their communal condition.

My failure was an inability to see all this in advance. I was incapable of steering the internal BCT politics in a direction that would have screened Ms. Shafa as a businessperson. We needed a means to select another, more capable candidate. I should have been able to tell Colonel Lanza that Ms. Shafa was not the right person to run the sewing factory and brought him another.

I desperately wanted to ignore the facts of the failures associated with the Sewing Factory project and other smaller ones like it. I easily could have continued the charade of appearances but that would never lead to an improved condition. I learned my lessons. The Sewing Factory project was indicative of all the projects we were doing in our sector and this tendency toward failure despite enormous commitment repeated itself in other task force sectors throughout the BCT sector. Publicly, we all talked up our projects, but the painful reality was that most ultimately collapsed. I am certain that once the Task Force left Iraq, those projects that appeared to have had some measure of localized positive effect most likely fell into shambles.

Through the experience borne of repeated failure, I figured out a way to succeed with projects. We could execute projects that would last and be supported by Iraqis. But it would require shrewd political work to tip the balance in our favor. Imams and low-profile behaviors on our part were the keys. Those were coupled with legitimate local ownership. In the last four months of time the Task Force was in Iraq, my criteria for pursuing a project had evolved to this:

• Does the project have imam consensus from the Al Saidiyah Imam Council?

• What local person, businessman, or entrepreneur is backing the project and what are his demands?

• Are they reasonable and feasible?

• Is he stepping up to be the Iraqi owner face on the project?

• What is the marketing strategy for the Iraqi owner or group that wants to take control of the project?

• Does he have a viable business plan?

Only if the assessment of these questions were favorable would we press for funding for the project from the BCT.

Another factor that significantly contributed to the failure of projects was the BCT staff and commander's penchant to actively advertise the projects initiated. The BCT staff and commander believed this would help gain local support for the actions and demonstrate to the masses that the Americans were here to help make their lives better; that the motives of America were honorable, noble, and peaceful. Logically, that approach all made good sense. But, again, this was a very Western way of thinking. Iraqis wanted our help without an overt association. This signaled to me that the entitlement mentality and thievery machinations dominated the Iraqi mindset. The Iraqi association with Americans began and ended with the money.

Because the Iraqis felt fear from exposure of cooperation with Americans this approach of advertising served only to antagonize the situation. Additionally, if the insurgents were having difficulty deciding what target to next select, they could simply look at the local paper where the BCT advertised to tell them where the next big American project would occur. There was literally no way the 5th BCT or Task Force 1-21 could guard all the facilities and projects under execution. We did not have enough soldiers, American or Iraqi. That is why the premium on Iraqi control was so high in my mind.

Executing projects to create statistical records that claimed the organization had been successful, while impressive, was ineffective and dishonest, accomplishing little at the expense of a lot of money. This was the odd dichotomy, I felt. Collectively it appears that we were doing much when in fact we were not. Iraqis were staying for life and we were leaving after a year. Without the sustaining mechanisms in place to buttress our efforts, we accomplished very little. Had the 5th BCT remained in Al Rashid another year with much the same leadership, the outcome might have been much more beneficial.

After the invasion in March 2003, the effort to rebuild the nation found Iraq in civil conflict among its factious people. This reality, clearly evident in daily operations, was mitigated by the American military presence. In Baghdad, most Iraqis are caught in the crossfire of a Sunni-directed insurgency that seeks to throw Americans out of Iraq and Shia who seek a legitimate means to the political power they have been denied for many years. Only after the removal of the American presence can Sunnis more narrowly focus the fight on the Shia to reclaim their lost political dominance and national power.

The entire time in Iraq, I knew we were standing between the tinderbox and the flame that this civil discord represented. American military leaders have to prevent the Sunnis from regaining power, simultaneously rebuilding the country and setting conditions for democracy to flourish with all sects participating willingly. This requires Americans to indirectly teach Iraqis how to participate in a free market economy and democratic government process.

These facts complicate so profoundly the demands on Army and Marine commanders who have the precarious task of trying to work through the civil affairs actions that they must direct. No military commander can walk into Iraq and expect to have success without understanding these dynamics and realities. Constantly rotating forces requires that these and other significant lessons be re-learned, setting efforts back continually. Even more challenging is that these constant rediscoveries confuse the sensibilities of Iraqis. The civil project administration component of this was a difficult aspect of the operation and will continue to be.

Part Three

17 A Wind of Change

"Everything is very simple in war, but the simplest thing is difficult. These difficulties accumulate and produce a friction which no man can imagine exactly who has not seen war." Karl von Clausewitz

By fall of 2004, the 5th BCT had learned many lessons and significantly improved its ability to conduct civil affairs operations. The BCT made huge strides gaining the initiative throughout Al Rashid. Change across the sector was detectable. Relationships were solidifying across the sector between BCT Army leaders and Iraqis in the communities of our respective sectors. Task Force 1-21 began to make inroads among imams and Neighborhood Advisory Council members connecting with some local sheiks in the area who had the ability to influence large numbers of residents in Al Saidiyah. Civil Military Operations led by soldiers of the Task Force included infrastructure repairs (roads, sewers, buildings, schools), employment opportunity, civic beautification efforts, medical care projects, and agricultural assistance. These infrastructure repairs coupled with our aggressive tactical operations (area searches for cached weapons, home searches, security patrols, and quick responses to criminal activity supporting the Iraqi police) were beginning to show signs of positive effects throughout the zone.

A clear change in the general attitude and behavior of the local nationals in sector was evident. Mortar and rocket attacks all but stopped in Area of Operations Rocket. The people were friendlier and engaged with us. Iraqis who had previously avoided venturing too far from their homes were jamming the market streets well into the night. Iraqi security forces support grew — ever so slightly — among the Iraqi citizens across the BCT zone. The Iraqi police recruiting rapidly increased as did the recruitment for the Iraqi Army. Training and logistical support for all Iraqi security forces was now on the mend. All these positive signs indicated progress and improvement.

Telling in our efforts as a BCT, and especially prominent in Task Force 1-21, was our sensitivity and attention to culture. We had now gained a deeper understanding of the nuances of the Iraqi culture to affect behavior. The key in the Task Force to understanding the culture as a means to affect behavior were our interpreters.

"Terps" Make Us a Better Task Force

The Iraqi interpreters group working in the Task Force was a tremendous asset. Throughout our time in Iraq, the Task Force had worked very hard to nurture and develop the interpreter pool we inherited from 1-94 Field Artillery. By fall 2004, we had developed very good relations with the Iraqi interpreters.

1-94 Field Artillery handed over thirty interpreters, referred to as "terps" by American soldiers, to Task Force 1-21 in April 2004. This "terp" reference actually was a term of endearment and not derogatory. In the Army, the soldiers of every war develop their own language that only those who served of that time know and understand. For Iraq veterans, "terp" is one of those words.

While we were there, the interpreter system in Iraq was not too elaborate. Iraqis who wanted to help U.S. forces with their mission signed on with Titan Corporation, a contracted company. Interpreters were paid about $400 a month. This was great money for an Iraqi. Titan Corporation screened the candidates, giving them a translation skills test and conducting a superficial background check.

A more detailed screening was undertaken by the Army units at the forward operating base where the interpreters were sent to work. The language skills test could not have been too difficult because we had a handful of interpreters who did not speak English well.

Upon our arrival, I readily realized that these Iraqi men and women were a huge asset. They spoke English and had learned from soldiers in 1-94 Field Artillery a great deal about Americans. They understood how Americans acted, thought, and operated. And obviously, they knew a lot about their people, rendering their insights invaluable.

Insofar as those interpreters we inherited, the best we could discern was that very little further screening had been undertaken by the BCT from First Armor Division once they arrived at the operating base, Camp Falcon. On base, interpreters were required by Army rules to wear a badge, but most ignored the rule and did not wear their credentials. The First Armor Division BCT we replaced did not enforce the standards and Iraqi interpreters had run of the place once inside the base walls. Many interpreters also had personal cell phones. Upon our arrival, we felt their freedom of movement and unmitigated use of cell phones had to be stopped. Although we wanted to trust them, this was not reasonable because we could not know which interpreter was a friend and which might be an insurgent or sympathizer.

Once Task Force 1-21 took over for 1-94 Field Artillery, some interpreters quit out of loyalty to 1-94 Field Artillery and distrust of us because we were the new guys. Also I had immediately implemented changes in the daily operation of interpreters that some did not like. All were required to wear their badges. Cell phones were not authorized for use on base except when supervised by Task Force soldiers and a second interpreter whom we trusted was present. An assessment of the English skills of all the interpreters was required and those whose skills were not deemed effective were dismissed from the Task Force and sent back to Titan for re-training or reassignment that was up to Titan, their employer. This caused others to quit because they thought the new standards were harsh and unfair. In all, about ten interpreters voluntarily resigned during the hand-over period.

1-94 Field Artillery had implemented a program where the interpreters were set on schedules with each of their subordinate batteries. The majority of the interpreters worked day shifts; very few worked at night. This was in keeping with 1-94 Field Artillery's approach of avoiding night patrolling. Interpreters were fearful of operating at night, but this was not going to work for our operations, because we were determined to be out at night, protecting and interdicting insurgent operations. I realized we needed to keep the interpreters on the team but they would have to overcome their fear and work at night when needed.

One of the first major hurdles we had to address was the interpreters' need for personal protection armor, specifically kevlar helmets and tactical-armored vests, which I believe they should have already had when we took over. When on the pre-deployment site survey, I had noticed the interpreters' lack of protective gear and inquired as to why. I was advised that the First Armor Division was trying to resolve this problem, but clearly had not yet succeeded by April 2004. Inquiries to Titan Corporation about outfitting interpreters with helmets and body armor revealed that Titan officials believed that supplying this type of equipment was our responsibility. But Army units were not resourced with personal protection gear for interpreters through the Army supply system.

Protecting the interpreters was critical to success and providing them with protective gear was imperative. I wanted as many interpreters working as possible. They served as the cultural bridge between my troops and the local nationals we would encounter.

The administrative issues for us relative to management of interpreters were scheduling, pay, retention, and addressing the innumerable personal problems which arose daily. We wanted them happy so they would not quit. On many occasions, my non-commissioned officers working with the interpreters became frustrated with me because they wanted some fired for behaving like teenagers. But I was very insistent that we work with the interpreters and teach them about personal accountability and professional behavior. This was admittedly tough. Like most of their fellow Iraqis, they didn't think or work like the American Army. I encouraged soldiers to be tolerant and teach. As a matter of policy, I adopted the three-strikes-you're-out formula.

This approach paid off because later, when the going got tough across the BCT and the other two task forces were down to paltry five or six interpreters, Task Force 1-21 had 25, and they were extremely loyal and highly competent. Keeping interpreters feeling like true members of the team was an essential ingredient of our success. This effort set conditions for our preparations for the critical election in January.

Iraqis are a familial and tribal people. I consciously used this cultural behavior to create for the interpreters a sense of belonging to the 1-21 tribe or family. Unlike many of my peers, I typically did not preach the family metaphor for the Army units I led, choosing instead to address them as members of a team. But with interpreters the family metaphor was expedient.

The method we devised for employing the interpreters was simple. We had two shifts for them to work: day and night. All interpreters were divided up and assigned habitual associations with the batteries. We did this for two reasons. First, we wanted to build relationships and understanding between units, leaders, and interpreters. This further resonated with the tribal and familial associations that Iraqis culturally gravitate toward. Second, we wanted the interpreters to learn the operations areas of the units and start building relationships with designated local leaders and people in the various communities. Developing these relationships and establishing consistency would help in our future tactical, civil military and psychological operations.

Every patrol in the Task Force was required to go on patrol with an interpreter. This was vital to Task Force operations. I indirectly learned that many of the patrols of my sister task forces went out with no interpreters. How they managed, I could not understand. Frequently, situations arose that demanded good, effective communication, and I considered it very dangerous to patrol without an interpreter. To maintain a proper stance and execute capable patrols able to respond and relate to local nationals while on patrol demanded an interpreter's contributions. This was a fundamental to internalizing the "Lanza" Doctrine and effectively executing the Five LOO, Oasis campaign plan.

Shortly after assuming non-commissioned officer leadership and management of the Facility Protective Service/ Interpreter Liaison Staff, Sergeant Raine worked out a solution to supply each interpreter with body armor and a kevlar helmet when he/she went out on patrol. Through the Command Sergeant Major and subordinate unit First Sergeants, Sergeant Raine gathered ten outer tactical vests that were extras in the batteries and companies. They were placed in the administrative office where the Facilities Protection Service/Interpreter Liaison Staff Section issued them to an interpreter as he accompanied a patrol on a mission. Major Marshall, the executive officer, obtained ten kevlar helmets from Camp Taji and they were also consolidated with the body armor in the liaison office for central issue to interpreters. Whenever an interpreter went out with a patrol, he/she went to the Facilities Protection Service/Interpreter Liaison Staff Section administrative office where a helmet and tactical vest were issued. This immediately made a difference in how the interpreters perceived their importance in the Task Force and how we felt about their presence in the unit. In a short time, the relationships the soldiers and officers in the battalion formed with our terps was quite strong.

The insurgents made a concerted effort to kill as many interpreters and Facilities Protection Service guards as they could uncover in a concentrated assassination campaign. These insurgent groups were hidden among the locals in the mahallas. No one wore a sign saying, "I'm an insurgent," so it was difficult for interpreters to identify who would "rat them out." Some interpreters took up the habit of covering their faces with masks to hide their identity. But most wanted to wear the desert camouflage uniforms exactly like the ones the soldiers wore to better blend with the soldiers in patrols.

I allowed my interpreters to cover their faces as a protection measure. Almost every interpreter in Task Force 1-21 was threatened, attacked, or — in four cases — killed. Several were shot but not fatally. We nevertheless lost their services because they quit working as interpreters.

Major Marshall also procured desert camouflage uniforms from the Army Central Issue Facility at Camp Taji, and we assigned, on a temporary basis, these uniforms to interpreters. I was admonished by BCT Command Sergeant Major Gerry Shindler for doing this, who told me that interpreters were not allowed to wear U.S. uniforms. I ignored that profound pronouncement from the Command Sergeant Major in favor of protecting my interpreters from a more sinister threat than a pissed-off Command Sergeant Major, like the killers outside Camp Falcon making good on their sinister threats. The uniforms interpreters wore had no U.S. insignia, they were sanitized uniforms.

I believed the interpreters' contributions and their culture mattered and tried to be sensitive to my appreciation of their way of thinking, working, and acting mostly deferring to their ways when differences arose.

The lives that interpreters led in their efforts to help the U.S. military build their nation is painstakingly explained in May 2005:

For Interpreters, Working in Iraq Is a Deadly Proposition
Terrorists 'Trying to Hurt Us by Hurting Them,' U.S. Army Captain Says

By JIM KRANE

(May 22) — It's one of the most dangerous civilian jobs in one of the world's most dangerous countries: translating Arabic for the U.S. military in Iraq.

One by one, little noticed in the daily mayhem, dozens of interpreters have been killed — mostly Iraqis but 12 Americans, too. They account for 40 percent of the 300-plus death claims filed by private contractors with the U.S. Labor Department.

Riding in bomb-blasted humvees, tagging along on foot patrols in Fallujah or dashing into buildings behind Marines, translators are dying on the job, but also facing danger at home: hunted by insurgents who call them pro-American collaborators.

"If the insurgents catch us, they will cut off our heads because the imams say we are spies," said Mustafa Fahmi, 24, an Iraqi interpreter with Titan Corp., the biggest employer of linguists in

Iraq. "I've been threatened like fifteen times, but I won't quit. A neighbor saw me driving and said, 'I am going to kill you.'"

That fate befell Luqman Mohammed Kurdi Hussein, a Titan linguist and Iraqi Kurd captured by insurgents in October. A video of the 41-year-old's beheading was posted on the Internet.

Another Titan employee, Sudanese interpreter Noureddin Zakaria, was luckier. He appeared as a hostage on an Oct. 30 broadcast by Al-Arabiya television, saying he had been captured in Ramadi. His kidnappers later released him.

In a more recent attack in Baghdad in late March, two carloads of insurgents gunned down five Iraqi women traveling home in a car from their jobs on a U.S. base. All were killed, the Iraqi police reported, and at least one of them was a translator.

The efficiency with which insurgents hunted down Titan contractors worries the U.S. military. As militants killed them in growing numbers, usually in ambushes off base, the Army and others began housing Titan workers on military bases or in Baghdad's fortified Green Zone.

"There was a period when it seemed translators were being targeted on a daily basis," said First Sgt. Stephen Valley, a U.S. Army reservist who worked with Arab journalists in Baghdad. "There was virtually no way to protect these people."

Most Titan linguists now live on U.S. bases.

More than 4,000 translators work for San Diego, Calif.-based Titan, which supplies the U.S. military with Arabic- and Kurdish-speaking linguists. In April, Titan reported a 23 percent increase in revenues, or $559 million, a company record. Titan said its contract with the U.S. Army is its biggest revenue source, worth up to $657 million by the time it expires.

The human cost has been high. The U.S. Labor Department reports 126 death benefit claims for Titan workers in Iraq out of a total 305 for contractors as of mid-May. The Titan death toll includes 12 Americans, and possibly some non-translators, the company said, with another 149 wounded.

"This is a war zone. Our people are embedded with literally every military unit in Iraq, facing the same life-threatening dangers as our U.S. combat forces," Titan spokesman Wil Williams said. "We have lost more personnel than any other American contractor covered by (U.S. government) insurance because of our unique, critical and dangerous mission, and because of the intensity of the insurgents who seek to discourage Iraqis from serving their country."

Titan's toll — which includes both violent deaths and accidents — is far higher than any of the hundreds of civilian contracting firms in Iraq, including those with many more workers.

For example, Halliburton, the Houston-based contractor with 50,000 employees spread between Iraq and Kuwait, has had more than 60 employees and subcontractors killed in the war zone, more than 250 wounded and one worker unaccounted for, spokeswoman Jennifer Dellinger said.

Many deaths don't show up in the Labor Department statistics under the name Halliburton because often claims are filed under subcontractor names. The 305 death claims with the Labor Department represent only part of the toll for American and other civilian contractors in Iraq. The true figure is difficult to estimate because many firms don't publicize workers' slayings. The U.S. troop death toll is over 1,620.

In Iraq, translators are seen as a critical link between U.S. troops and Iraqis.

"They were important to our mission, and terrorists were trying

to hurt us by hurting them," said Army Capt. Joseph Ludvigson, who was based last year in northern Iraq.

On Baghdad's hostile western outskirts, the Army has conducted memorial ceremonies for slain Titan interpreters, said 1st Cavalry Division Maj. Derik Von Recum.

The first, an Iraqi woman, was killed in July, "shot execution-style at her home in front of her family," Von Recum said. The second, an Iraqi man, stopped coming to work in November. It took a few days to figure out insurgents had kidnapped and killed him, Von Recum said.

"The two we lost were like family to us," he said. "I wish we could have provided them with better protection."

But some Iraqis working for Titan said they spent months on the job before being issued helmets, body armor, and ear- and eye-protection given to U.S. troops and foreign contractors.

Titan's Williams said Iraqi workers now get the same Kevlar helmets and vests issued to U.S. troops. "Following some initial equipment shortages, our Iraqi personnel now have the equipment they need where and when they need it," he told The Associated Press.

One Titan interpreter said he completed more than 100 missions without body armor and a helmet. The man spoke on condition his name wasn't used because he didn't want to lose his job.

This reporter, who spent more than a year in Iraq, accompanied Iraqi interpreters who wore no body armor or helmets on many U.S. military missions.

"You look around and see the soldiers and the international press with you, and they're all wearing the proper protection. What about me? I'm one of the team," said the Titan interpreter, *who emerged uninjured from two convoys blasted by roadside bombs.*

The interpreter said he asked his U.S. Army commander why the troops and the American civilians — some also in Titan's employ — had body armor and helmets, but not the Iraqis.

"After a while they decided it was wrong. They gave it to us," he said.

A Titan translator with no military background said U.S. troops allow him to carry an AK-47, after having taught him to shoot it. The 31-year-old Iraqi said he opened fire on insurgents when his convoy came under attack near Baghdad in March 2004. He was slightly wounded.

"I saw an American soldier killed right in front of me," said the translator, who didn't want his name used because he feared for his life.

"The insurgents were shooting at us from the rooftops. I was trying to shoot them too. The soldiers yelled at me: 'Hey, don't try to be a hero. Get down!'"

He said he has survived three ambushes, but a co-worker with Titan was killed by a mortar round on a U.S. base in Baghdad.

The dangers commuting to work are as bad as the on-the-job hazards.

The Titan translator who had to ask for body armor said he alters his route, schedule and the cars he takes to the U.S. base where he works. He never stays more than a few nights in one house. And he wears a black ski mask to hide his identity while on patrol.

"I stay with neighbors, sometimes with my family, with my wife's family, my uncle, my parents," he said. "If anyone recognizes

you, and says, 'Hey, I saw you with the soldiers,' that's when you're done."

Another Titan contractor, who didn't want his name published for fear of retribution, keeps a pistol in his lap when he drives.

"I don't talk about my job," he said. "If you keep your mouth shut, no one is going to know who you are or what your job is."

Money is the chief reward. The interpreters say monthly salaries start at $600 and range as high as more than $1,000 for those who take the most dangerous missions. That pay is big by Iraqi standards, where many survive on less than $100 a month.

Under those salaries, U.S. government death benefits for families of slain Iraqi translators would range from $300 to $700 a month, according to a formula in the Defense Base Act, which sets a maximum payout of less than $4,190 a month.

Valley said he was amazed Iraqis would show up to replace a translator who'd been killed.

"They were putting their lives on the line for what seemed to me a ridiculously small amount of money, but to them it was the highest salary they had ever earned," Valley said.

Valley said his office helped negotiate a new salary scale that made their translators "some of the best paid Iraqi civilian workers in the country."

"If we couldn't protect them from the insurgents, we could get them a higher monthly salary," he said. [24]

The Task Force had several exceptional interpreters, who were well skilled in both English and Arabic. Some of them were more than mere translators; they could go beyond just translating and delved into the subtler skill of negotiating, deftly bridging the cultural divides.

I spent the majority of my time dealing with issues in Al Saidiyah, where the greatest concentration of people and problems occurred for the Task Force. Early in my tour of duty, when I went into that area, I engaged many of the same people but each time with a different interpreter. Some interpreters were more adept at conveying my message than others, while others were noticeably scared in the presence of some imams, which simply was unacceptable. I became exasperated when, in the middle of a discussion with a tribal leader or a Neighborhood Advisory Council member, I had to stop and inform the interpreter of developments he did not know. I decided I needed one dedicated interpreter who could manage the constant and intricate negotiations I was dealing with daily in order to maintain continuity and progress.

Curiously, the BCT staff told me that using a single interpreter was detrimental to operations. Their logic: A soldier's rapport can be hurt while using a single interpreter because civilians become too accustomed to one interpreter. This phenomenon had been seen in the Balkans multiple times: civilians see the interpreter as the 'voice' of authority. When the soldier is not present, either the civilians will ask the interpreter to do things or the interpreter will make statements that the civilians believe are messages from the military personnel. This can be quickly abused and results in the military personnel losing authority with the civilians. Throughout the deployment, civilians have constantly requested to speak only with a specified interpreter. It does not matter who the interpreter is, the soldier is the person the local national should be talking to.

The staff officer's recommendation was that interpreters should be rotated regularly so local national civilians would not get too used to them. By rotating interpreters on a regular basis, local nationals quickly realize that the military person is the one with whom they should speak, not the interpreter. This is especially true for the Battalion Commander.

Such reasoning suggested Battalion Commanders have no discipline and insinuates that Battalion Commanders don't have the sense or command and control experience to manage their interpreter(s). In reality, interaction and relationship-building was occurring so quickly that rotating interpreters was a losing proposition. Those who did not have a single, consistent interpreter that they trusted, respected, and with whom they worked well, were significantly less effective than those who did. While I respected the BCT staff warning because it was foreseeable that interpreters who were left unchecked and given free reign could be mistaken as the voice of authority, continuously rotating interpreters would have led to certain failure. Despite this warning I received from the BCT staff, I was very aware that Colonel Lanza employed one dedicated interpreter to assist him. I chose to follow his example.

Finding Freddie

Dismissing the advice of the BCT staff, I turned to my staff for a recommendation of a dedicated interpreter. I had personally interacted with many interpreters by May 2004 and thought that Akeel was the best I had encountered. Sergeant Raine suggested an interpreter who went by the Americanized name, Freddie. All the interpreters had Arabic given names but many had assumed American aliases, a practice that started before First Cavalry Division arrived in Iraq and stuck. Freddie was assigned to support the Task Force Civil Affairs team. He had been working with them for several months by May 2004. Since I did not know Freddie, I rejected that recommendation out of hand.

Sergeant Raine insisted that I interview Freddie before rejecting him. He told me Freddie was the best interpreter he had encountered in Iraq and the best candidate to serve my needs. Reluctantly, I agreed to an interview.

Fadi "Freddie" Fadhil was a young 25-year-old who stood about 6′ 2″ and was thin, well kept, and in good physical shape. On initial impression I could tell he was obviously very smart. He spoke English better than any interpreter I had met before. He even understood American-GI slang. He was poised, respectful, and polite. I was amazed with his demeanor and instantly liked him. He expressed reluctance to work exclusively for me but I explained the urgency of my need and that I needed someone who appreciated the nuances of the negotiations I was carrying out and who could absorb the details sufficiently well so as to pick up where we left off despite breaks in the process. He agreed to a temporary commitment.

In a very short period of time Freddie, was able to directly assist Task Force 1-21. We quickly made strong inroads into the Al Saidiyah community. He was magnificent. His intellect, mastery of the American and Iraqi cultures, and his knowledge of the area were phenomenal. Under Freddie's interpretive and negotiation skills, the relationships we built and nurtured were substantial and resulted in the unit's success. Those in Al Saidiyah quickly learned who Freddie was and that he was the direct line to me. Freddie was very loyal and he never operated independently, this was quite impossible given that he lived on the Forward Operating Base and he truly appreciated that this was not allowed. His loyalty to me and the Task Force was beyond reproach.

Freddie and I quickly developed a strong, binding friendship. He rapidly assimilated my methods, was a quick understudy of my approach to problem-solving, and understood my goals in various initiatives and projects. Freddie accompanied me on every patrol and became part of my combat crew that included Specialist Francisco J. Villa (driver and body guard) and Specialist Anthony L. Jackson (.50 Cal. Gunner). Freddie was soon my right hand man in my day-to-day dealings with Iraqis and I trusted him implicitly.

The bond I formed with this young man was profound. Because we spent so much time together and he risked so much providing incredible support at tremendous personal risk, Freddie became one of my soldiers in a very real sense. That other Iraqis saw our relationship as such a strong friendship, I think, also helped them see me as not an arrogant American but a person who cared about them. Because I had a dark complexion with a white Anglo and Puerto Rican mixed heredity, I could look Arabic easily; this could not be discounted in personal interaction. My driver, Specialist Villa was half Mexican and half Honduran. He wore a moustache, he had a dark brown complexion, and he looked very much like an Iraqi. Many kids teased and asked how I got an Iraqi driver. We used to tease Specialist Villa, warning that if we ever got attacked and he was the sole survivor he could strip out of his uniform and run off naked into the crowd; no one would mistake him for an American, they'd think he was Iraqi. Freddie perpetuated our team dynamic, taught us Arabic and Iraqi customs while on patrols, and helped us make quick connections and expert translations for me and the crew.

What Freddie did to assist me was significant, requiring him to assume incredible personal risk. Freddie actually began working as an interpreter for U.S forces in Iraq in March 2003. He worked for the 101st Airborne Division, Air Assault, the 82nd Airborne Division, the First Armor Division and then us in the First Cavalry Division. Any officer would love that line-up on their professional resume. Freddie is fluent in both English and Arabic, possessing the ability to read, write, and translate in both languages. I relied on him to work through business contracts with local city and religious leaders. He was fully committed to the ideals of liberty and democracy and fully supported a free and prosperous Iraq.

What Freddie provided the Task Force directly and the U.S. Army through his loyal, continual service was strong linkage between us and Iraqis in sector who could help us accomplish our mission. He was a one-man command and control center. Carrying two radios and a cell phone, always trailing me everywhere I went; these tools were necessary to execute command and control. He interfaced with the Iraqi police, the leaders in the Iraqi Army Company attached to the Task Force (D/304th Infantry), and with the Facilities Protective Service leaders at various sites in Area of Operations Rocket. He also provided me detailed descriptions of cultural nuances, coaching me on proper customs and courtesies in a variety of situations. He even taught me enough Arabic to help attract Arabs to me in very meaningful interpersonal ways. From this, I was able to connect with people, civic leaders, and, in a few cases, aggressors to the Coalition cause for negotiation and conciliation.

In June 2004 I began an earnest effort to begin a large scale development project in Al Saidiyah. Freddie and I consulted on the nuances of how to approach our negotiations with Sheik Ali, the powerful Sunni imam, who operated from the Shakir Al Abood mosque in east Al Saidiyah to establish the conditions to get a project started building a police station. This was the same cleric that months earlier would only meet me on the street in front of his mosque. This entailed coordination and then several private meetings in the quarters behind the cleric's mosque. This was unheard-of access and hospitality for a Muslim cleric to allow a military officer this close to the mosque in the view of his people. This was accomplished partly because Freddie knew precisely how to set up the meetings to preserve face and respect cultural sensitivities. The end result was that the imam endorsed the effort and aided in the broader negotiation with the Neighborhood Advisory Council to broker the deal and get the project started.

The Task Force had established close ties to Iraqi security forces, primarily the Iraqi police, Iraqi Army, and Facilities Protection Services. To accomplish our daily mission in my sector I had to interact with these forces and coordinate actions of my patrols with these other Iraqi agencies. Freddie was my way into the leaders of these security forces. He communicated via radio and cell phone, fielding calls and directing actions keeping me informed of significant actions to battle-track various situations. He was in every sense the equal of any of the six subordinate company commanders working for me. His command of situations and understanding of what must be done were almost clairvoyant.

Freddie also directly assisted the efforts to secure and stabilize the Task Force sector by developing highly competent and reliable human intelligence sources. In Al Saidiyah to know what is occurring in the neighborhoods with regards to terrorist and criminal activity with the vast culture divide, we needed informants helping in our efforts to assess and target insurgents. Freddie helped by developing sources. On multiple separate occasions we were able to secure what we called "targetable" information resulting in combat raids to capture insurgents operating in Al Saidiyah. No other interpreter was more valuable in this assistance than Freddie.

One of the most difficult challenges we faced was trying to discern the character of people we had to deal with to accomplish our mission. Freddie had the uncanny ability to assess his own countrymen's character and motives. Because he understood the cultural norms and many of the behaviors of people under the regime of Saddam Hussein, he could very quickly decipher the code of characters that sought contracts with the U.S. government for reconstruction efforts. He would translate for me in negotiations and be able to advise me after our discussions concluded on the character of the contractor. Because part of my responsibility as a battalion task force commander was to be a good steward of taxpayer dollars, this was very important to understand and not make mistakes. Additionally, if we let contracts to a disreputable contractor the people in the community would judge us negatively. Worse, projects could and would go awry, which truly risked too much in effort and possibly lives. I observed many other commanders struggle with this problem. Freddie kept me on track and we never steered off course and I dismissed upwards of fifteen contractors over the months Freddie was with me in Baghdad.

During patrol operations Freddie would help with traffic management and warnings to the public when confusing situations arose. Captain David Norris, the Assistant S-3 on staff, had served as an enlisted man in the Army Military Police Corps before going to Officer Candidate School and becoming a Field Artillery officer. He had made a suggestion to me that we purchase and install siren and loud speaker systems to place on our humvees to use for traffic control and communication with local nationals. Across the Task Force, on our humvees we installed loud-speaker systems much like those that police patrol cars have. Freddie would get on the loud-speaker and direct people, crowds or moving traffic to provide for and support the secure movement of the patrol. By having him do this, the local nationals appreciated our deference to speak to them in Arabic providing directions and we were able to minimize danger to our soldiers by moving people away from potentially dangerous situations. Freddie was very good at this as were all the Task Force interpreters.

When I had to position Iraqi security forces I often consulted with Freddie because he would make very sound recommendations for placement based on how Arabs live and travel within a community. While that may sound trivial, it is not. Where people congregate, modes of transportation used, and high traffic areas are cultural and custom-based. Freddie understood this dynamically and advised me well on how to use Iraqi forces to complement our tactics. To do this I had to trust and share tactical plans with him. I trusted him. What I found amazing was his ability to learn our tactics so quickly and then depict the complementary implementation of Iraqi forces.

Freddie was an unmatched connector. He, on my behalf, established very effective rapport with a variety of significant actors in my sector. He directly connected me to every imam in my sector, the police chief of the neighboring township and two outlying communities, the commander of the Iraqi Army forces in our district, and several Ministry Directors in the Iraqi Interim Government. He was able to do this through his considerable interpersonal skills and initiative. Doing this allowed me to solve many difficult and delicate problems often with just a phone call, whereby I would communicate my intent and Freddie would directly communicate this to whomever I was seeking assistance from. He was absolutely superb at this. The number of security issues resolved without fighting but rather through negotiation was incalculable but undoubtedly attributable to this tactic that I could not have employed to this effect with another interpreter.

Consequence management is a significant part of the responsibilities I had as a battalion task force commander. Consequences from urban combat can range from damaged buildings to Iraqi civilians who are killed or wounded in the street fighting. When these incidents occur we had to go into the streets and assess damages. We had to help the people understand what happened and why it happened. We also had to understand the local Iraqi's point of view and make sure we genuinely internalized their concerns and mitigated the effects on their lives. Again, Freddie's sharp and insightful interpersonal skill and connection coupled with his ability to advise me on custom and behavior always made the outcome positive.

Freddie was a key player on my staff. His daily contribution was necessary and integral to our success. I have no doubt these relationships formed all over Iraq with soldiers, leaders and their interpreters. Sergeant Raine's recommendation to use Freddie could not have been more right!

The most profound contribution the interpreters made for the Task Force was to integrate our military mission with the local effort to win over the common Iraqi. We had to be connected. Fighting an insurgency demands connection, development of trust, and collusion on resolving quality of life issues for people. Winning against an insurgency is completely localized in scope. Interpreters were the connectors and bridge builders for us. We could not have enough of these heroic people.

Focus on the Local Fight to Win the National Victory

Militarily, we in the First Cavalry Division and particularly in the 5th BCT focused on a counterinsurgent effort in the Al Rashid district of Baghdad. For Task Force 1-21, local governance was vitally important to winning in Iraq. Though the decided course to pursue national, democratic governance prevailed at the highest echelons, the real fight I knew was at the local level. Establishing capable local governance, in my mind, was strategic and the key to winning against the insurgency.

Examining insurgencies, it is no secret that their fundamental basis for sustaining operational capability is garnered through local support. Interdicting that support was the key to defeating the insurgent effort in Al Saidiyah. Without local support, no insurgency can survive. Don't believe me — believe Mao Tse Tung: that's his proven contention. The place to attack an insurgency is at the local level. Counter the insurgent argument with deeds that demonstrate the sanctity of your political argument, and thereby defeat the premise of the insurgent's political arguments, and you win. That, I concluded, was the essence of counterinsurgency, plain and simple.

For our efforts in Iraq, many senior military leaders and American diplomats contended that winning the people held the key to victory. But, no one could ever pragmatically define what winning the people meant. By what means do you win the people? How do you win a foreign culture that despises you for who you are? Many use conciliatory practices mixed with retribution as the means. "Carrot and stick"— Iraqis must do this and behave thusly to earn rewards. When they don't cooperate, they are punished. I disagreed with this method.

The means had to be positive development of local self-governance and building strong public education. In the 1960s we did not do this in Vietnam, although countless efforts were pursued. The Coalition Provisional Authority, carrying out the will of the national strategic effort in Iraq, made the same mistakes we committed over 33 years earlier in Vietnam and missed that in the effort too.

The Coalition Provisional Authority disestablished the Iraqi military, disenfranchised the Sunni, and exacerbated the conditions of strife internal to Iraq through a series of questionable decisions. The continuing national strategy struggles because for America to win in Iraq, the Iraqis must nurture legitimate local governance. It is a wonderful thing to move the national government of Iraq toward assuming full, legitimate control of the nation. But the national government has done precious little to thwart the insurgency. That is not easily achieved. L. Paul Bremmer III's Herculean national level effort and top-down political approach to rebuilding Iraq needed a robust and dedicated local, bottom-up effort directed by Army and Marine Corps task force commanders acting simultaneously to win in Iraq. The latter piece was missing. For the American military, the only chance of success is through mastery of the cultural nuances of the people aimed at modifying and directing behaviors to garner legitimate local political dominance.

The culture of Arabs is rooted in tribalism. Arab culture is male-dominated, sheik-led, religiously-based, and rests on strong familial organization. It is all very locally-minded and focused. American policy in Iraq has not exploited this fundamental truth about Iraqis. But the insurgents have!

This phenomenon is not new to America's counterinsurgent history. In Vietnam the American military ran into the same problem. The Vietnamese were mostly agrarian, village-dwelling, very familial, and local-thinking people. In Saigon were many well-educated and capable Vietnamese, but they did not completely represent the Vietnamese national population. It's much harder to focus information operations, civil affairs efforts, and psychological operations at a distributed population. Even more, it's damn tough to penetrate historic, generations-long familial ties.

In the Vietnam War there were multiple efforts to overcome this problem with robust civil affairs projects, but they generally failed. They failed because most projects never had local leader control from legitimate "powerbrokers." These same phenomena exists all over again in Iraq. Legitimate local leaders must be nurtured, protected, and allowed to possess and control resources to their own perceived utilization. Benefits must be realized and based on the cultural traditions and mores of the Iraqi people to expect a chance of success in countering this insurgency.

Coalition efforts also have to focus on teaching and nurturing an effective democratic process. The governance in the neighborhoods, in local governing bodies must retain the Muslim tradition of the people. It must also allow for the Iraqis to decide their own direction. Coalition military and civilian leaders must only coach, teach, and mentor. Let the Iraqis decide the issues and resolutions. Americans must defer and mostly just support the Iraqi leader's decisions. Again I do not divulge this as an original political ideology. I merely echo the discovery and wisdom of T.E. Lawrence. These are the things I concluded would win in Al Saidiyah.

18 Local Political Action and Reform

"Some people wanted champagne and caviar when they should have had beer and hot dogs." Dwight D. Eisenhower

I translated the esoteric concept of "gaining the support of the Iraqi people" to the pragmatic action of developing a democratic, self-governance capability in Al Saidiyah. Having a means to accomplishing self-governance and defining, practically, the idea of "gaining the support of the Iraqi people," meant applying it to my little corner of Baghdad. Local governance through an entity that represented the people, tended to the critical business of the community, and did so in a culturally relevant and supported means defined the way of winning for me.

All my personal studies on the operational art as it applied to counterinsurgency and my experience through the summer months and fall of 2004 showed me that in every U.S. Army effort to defeat an insurgency in the past, the standard paradigm failed. The standard paradigm focused on carrot-and-stick approaches to directing and controlling local and national leaders. Information dissemination efforts were intended to directly appeal to the masses.

The masses of any nation are too disparate and distributed to permit a single approach. The people have never been won quickly and decisively by any foreign power. Unless a foreign power is willing to commit a generation of time to the fight, their odds for success are not good. It does not appear the U.S. is willing to commit to the time and sacrifice necessary to ultimately establish a strong democratic people in Iraq. The insurgents are of course more patient because the political situation always favors patience. By changing the political dynamic, the initiative can be wrested from the patient insurgent enemy.

The counterattack with the best chance for success given the American, democratic, national political will has to focus on changing behavior and building local governance throughout Iraq. I believe this to be the most profound means to affect the overall political situation to favor the U.S. effort.

Insurgents' propaganda exploits the idea that the "occupier" cannot help, and is in fact stealing the people's freedom. The rationale is that foreigners cannot bring local nationals their identity, wealth, and freedom. Insurgents maintain the hero and liberator role. They demonstrate the capacity to attack when and where they choose and further demonstrate that the "occupier" cannot stop them. They operate with impunity and take on an air of invincibility. Insurgents count on the people to support them with sustenance, cover, and fighters.

These messages generally resonate and succeed because what the "occupier" does not effectively do is attack this insurgent message with deeds. That is to say, "occupiers" fail to profoundly change the condition of the average citizen favorably — through their own self-determined leadership — uncorrupted, and community minded, and then defend the salient systems built to improve lives. Information campaigns attempt to convince the people that the "occupiers" are friendly and want to help. However, this actually supports the insurgent message because the "occupiers" do the real work, provide the money, and furnish the technical know-how, and then insist that projects follow their prescribed processes. Those people who attempt to support the "occupier's" efforts are then turned into collaborators and stooges. History has shown this to be true and the way this can be countered is with a directed political shift.

The necessary shift, I believe, has to be a broad U.S. policy shift away from a national, top-down implementation of "democracy" to a policy that directs resources and effort developing capable local governance entities throughout the many mahallas of Baghdad. This bottom-up political strategy would more directly influence the political situation to U.S. favor and attack at the heart of the insurgents' policies against American efforts: Focusing bottom-up has critical benefits:

• Allows democracy to grow locally developing a solid foundation for national level democratic and political processes to flourish

• Focuses effort on community residents' basic needs that are not being met by an inept national government

• Directly impugns the insurgent program at the community level where the insurgents focus their efforts

By the end of the summer of 2004, I understood this and so did my staff. Supported by good intelligence, which elaborated in specific terms this concept of the Iraqi insurgency, allowed us to further develop strategy and execute a tactical program to counter the insurgency in Al Saidiyah.

The Election that Wasn't

The only entity I had authority to work with to establish some semblance of local governance was the Neighborhood Advisory Council. A/1-21 Commander and chief liaison to the council, Captain Pugsley, the S5 (Civil Affairs Officer), Captain Levy, the Civil Affairs Detachment Team Commander, Major Rob Dixon the S3, Operations Officer, Major Bill Reinhart and I concluded that the Neighborhood Advisory Council had to be changed through new membership. We came up with the obvious solution of setting up a local election. Because the sitting members clearly were not representative of the neighborhoods that made up the enclave of Al Saidiyah, we had determined that the sitting council was inept; a change was the first step in achieving the goal of self-governance, which was consistent with impacting the politics of Al Saidiyah to favor the Coalition objectives.

The ineptness of the council manifested in many behaviors and design problems. Council members were mostly Shia. Al Saidiyah was mostly Sunni. No council member had been elected. I never learned how these individuals were selected to sit on the council. The most plausible story I heard is that they volunteered to the 1-94 Field Artillery, A Battery Commander, who was liaison to the council, and that was all that was required.

There were risks inherent with sitting on the council as we soon found out. The few Sunni on the council argued incessantly with the Shia over trivial matters. Mohammed Zamil was the only well-educated man. He was a trained Iraqi attorney, who was nearly impossible to work with because he objected to everything and constantly choked the discussions with threats of legal action. His behavior was comical and frustrating. Not a single member of the council was community minded. The primary concern of each member appeared to be obtaining from us money, gun permits, pistols, cell phones, and a stipend payment for their service on the council. No parliamentary procedure existed. No one wanted to pursue any ordered process, not even an Arabic traditional tribal meeting format. The council could not conceive, articulate or direct project selection, development, and execution processes for even the simplest of projects. The council had no budget and failed to develop resources to provide for a budget for the people, which nearly ensured the failure of this entity. The Neighborhood Advisory Council could do nothing important. Without a budget, the council effectively had no power. And because the Americans brought the money, the condition for failure was set because the Iraqis understood who held the purse and, thus, where the real power resided. At best the Neighborhood Advisory Council could only be viewed as a puppet organization. This was, of course, powerful psychological ammunition for the insurgents' cause. Steering the council to formulate a few projects in hopes of generating money through rental fees and taxation of profits at a very low rate was an idea we tried to seed. But we could never get the council to pursue this. The council simply did not understand the concept. No matter what service-minded project we proposed or attempted to coach the council toward, the process invariably broke down and turned into a corrupt, money-grubbing effort on the part of most council members. Two women sat on the council. Neither ever showed up for the meetings.

Frequently, if a serious incident occurred in or near Al Saidiyah, the council attempted to avoid meeting for a few weeks out of fear. And constantly we prodded them back to the table.

Our point in holding an election was the desire to directly and decisively change the current ineffective situation. We sought to affect the political circumstances in Al Saidiyah in accordance with a master plan designed to attack the insurgents at their heart. Executing the election meant that the people would choose who represented them in the neighborhood, giving efficacy to the council. It would generate some political fervor at the local level allowing the issues that concerned the Iraqi's out on the street. Because the majority of people living in Al Saidiyah were professors, lawyers, doctors and senior military leaders in Saddam's regime, we hoped to see better-educated and more administratively experienced people selected as council members and believed community minded goals would follow. We hoped at the grass roots level the Iraqi people would have a front-seat education in democratic processes and become enthusiastic about the future. An election would set conditions from which great momentum could be built.

The staff dove into developing an election plan. The biggest challenge would be to obtain the support of an election to the sitting council. Explaining why we needed to have an election and doing so without insulting the present members was a delicate dance indeed.

I committed to a four-week process to promote the idea to the council members. Captain Levy suggested the notion would be more palatable if we did not replace all the members but rather picked a number of seats to replace. The sitting council could then decide of that number which seats specifically would be open for election. Someone came up with the term "refreshing" — i.e., the election would be to "refresh" the council — which stuck.

Captain Pugsley introduced the idea to the Neighborhood Advisory Council, without giving the members a reason why the election would occur. The focus was instead on the mechanics. Several meetings later, I explained why an election was needed. First, I pointed out, many had sat on the council for a long time and it was appropriate to seek new people to serve their community. Second, some members habitually did not attend meetings and perhaps had lost interest, which was not proper, according to Muslim teachings. Thus sitting members had to act to correct this impropriety. Third, I showed them the demographics of the population by mahallas demonstrating that this council did not truly represent Al Saidiyah.

Amazingly, this worked and the Council agreed to an election. The individuals then wanted to work the administration of executing the election process. I walked out of that meeting feeling like we had finally made some progress. The whole staff felt fantastic about this apparent success. Unfortunately, our feelings would be dampened quickly by policies that denied our initiative.

The political fight with the BCT and the higher echelons of the military in Iraq was an abject failure for me. When I pitched that I was working through setting the conditions for a local election I was shut down immediately. Colonel Lanza wanted to support me and, in fact, considered a local election for the District Advisory Council but quickly found out this was not allowed by the Multi-National Forces, Iraq.

It was explained to me that the United Nations representative, through the U.S. State Department, had ordered no local elections occur for fear they would interfere with the national elections. We were further directed that we were in no way to instruct or attempt to educate the Iraqi people about election processes or democracy. The logic was that local elections might cause confusion and adversely affect the national election process. Further, local governments did not exist and the Iraqi national government would be the entity that would determine and formulate how local governance would be implemented, not the U.S. military. For military entities to interfere with the national election process would be detrimental to the national strategy.

With regard to education, the military — and the United States in particular — could not be perceived as tainting or slanting the elections process by direct involvement. And while this actually made some sense to me, I believed there were other ways of educating the Iraqi people besides the military. But I did not see any United Nations or other entity engaged in a large-scale effort to do so.

Many Iraqis thought the existing semi-chaos they were living in since the invasion was democracy. Many still think status-quo is the best that democracy can provide. I believe a major failure on the part of the U.S. national strategy is the deliberate effort to avoid teaching the academics and processes of democracy to Iraqis.

As I worked daily with the Iraqis I found it absurd that at the national political level we appear to believe we can invade a country that has been ruled despotically for over 30 years and then, through some declaration and United Nations directed effort, change it into a functioning democracy. Without any democratic tradition the people have little understanding of how to run a democratic government.

While it may seem unfathomable to Americans, the information age of internet and satellite TV had not reached the masses of Iraq until after the invasion. The news and information we Americans had readily had since the late 1980s and into the 1990s simply were not available to the average Iraqi. Seeing a democratic world through television and internet has never been resident in Iraq. Iraqis, on average and in aggregate, have no intellectually-developed idea about what democracy is or how to exercise that in their political lives. They need academic lessons and a practical, local-level exercise of the democratic way of governing.

The poor security in place adversely affects the ability to educate the Iraqi populace on democratic principles. Poor security is tied to the security forces — American or Iraqi — able to be deployed throughout the mahallas of Baghdad. It is the decisions of American national political leaders which are accountable for the too few boots-on-the-ground that creates these second and third orders, negatively impacting the grand scheme and subverting the path to victory in Iraq.

A unit of the United Nations, or perhaps some non-governmental organization, strategically placed in locations throughout Iraq could teach and train about democracy, setting conditions to changing the will and behaviors of the Iraqi masses. The Iraqis need some instruction and basic understanding beyond "this is a ballot and here's how to vote."

I wanted desperately to teach and train the people of Al Saidiyah about democracy and the ideals of democracy. As John Locke's ideas had been used and tied democracy in America with Christianity, so too could we do the same with Muslim teachings. For those who take the time and look at Muslim teachings, democracy definitely correlates. I believe this is the best way to teach democracy in the Middle East.

At this juncture, unable to hold local elections or train or teach democratic principles, I had to either abandon my idea or redesign it to work within the previously undefined parameters that had now been made clear. I opted for the latter.

Since there could not be any elections, the next best thing was to hand-pick replacements. Of course, if the Task Force did the picking there would be no material change in conditions. Therefore, no one from the U.S. Army could choose the replacements. This was a big problem. Another option was to have the sitting council members choose new members, which was better but not much. With nepotism and tribalism, this approach would only result in the placement of relatives and close friends working in the same vicious cycle of failure.

The only thing that I believed would work and possibly preserve some efficacy required imam involvement. Imams are generally respected, and Iraqis listen to them and follow their advice. Almost every mahalla in Baghdad has a mosque. Linking democratic processes directly to imams was salient to success. I knew this was a sensitive approach. Americans and the U.S. government might not endorse this manner of replacing council members out of fear that a theocracy like that in Iran might emerge. The American democratic tradition separated church and state. But, I believe that this fear is unfounded. A poorly-educated and oppressed society like that of Iraq derives great benefit from and clings to religion. If there is any hope for success, it is impossible to extract religion from government in Iraq right now. To positively affect the political situation at the local level, I believe, we need to embrace the religious aspects of the people of Iraq and marry these to the local democratic processes. Time, experience, and education would allow the Iraqis to evolve into their own democratic state as the people choose to define it, not in a way Americans or any other Westerners might. If the goal for the U.S. is to truly establish a democracy, the main effort has to be local, and tied to the Muslim tradition.

The imams of the Sunni and Shia mosques had to become players in the political process and endorse the Neighborhood Advisory Council. Instead of having an Imam Council and Neighborhood Advisory Council, I foresaw one powerful council, capable and more representative of Al Saidiyah. Merging the two seemed to be the best answer to achieve my goals without an election.

An informal Imam Council had come to life in May 2004. Over the summer months, the Task Force had several contentious engagements with imams from Al Saidiyah. Colonel Lanza had pressed all the subordinate task force commanders to pursue developing relationships with imams. I had pursued this with great vigor but with little positive result until the fall of 2004.

The Imam Council of Al Saidiyah

As early as June 2004, the Task Force embarked on a reso-
lute effort to form a viable imam council. The purpose of
pursuing this effort was to bring another entity of people
with a strong reputation and some modicum of stature in
the community into the political process. Working with the
imams and developing an understanding of the real situation through interaction and relationships, it became obvious that a more formal council with true political power was possible through this group. The people followed
their imams.

After fits and starts in the earlier months with little substantive progress, by early September 2004, the Task Force
had formed and operated productive meetings with a bona
fide Imam Council. The idea and effort to form a council to
negotiate and discuss community issues took form and we
stood up an Imam Council. I was chief liaison to this council and Khalid-Al Husseini, whom we called Dr. Khalid
because he had a Ph.D. from the University of Baghdad in
Economics, was the front man for the imams. He worked a
relationship and position whereby he served as a connector and council director. Dr. Khalid was about 5' 9" and
spoke English quite well. He was very polite, professional,
and open to working with me on a variety of issues. He
was a Sunni and attended the Al Aksa mosque in central
Al Saidiyah.

Dr. Khalid coordinated directly with the imams. He served
as the go-between for me and the Al Saidiyah Imam Council. He maintained rosters of the members, phone numbers, and handled all administrative tasks. We met twice
a month and conferred on an agenda before the meetings.
This relationship and operating method were vital to my
plan in Al Saidiyah. To be successful, Dr. Khalid had to
be viewed as trustworthy and legitimate by the imams of

the council. He had to be able to deal with the Task Force yet not be perceived as a collaborator. This was obviously an extreme challenge for him and for me as well because I could not allow the situation to break down. The slightest mistake by either of us could result in his death.

Now, I know through personal experience and a very deep understanding of the political dynamic, insurgents were in our midst. Fooling the imams while still talking to them in these forums was tough. No doubt, the imams sitting at the table in these meetings were insurgents or sympathizers reporting to someone about my plans. All the better, I felt, because they were close and I could control the message. Privately I worried that they might believe that eliminating me would alleviate some of their problems. But after some reflection I concluded that I'd be ready if they tried; after all, the show must go on. Dr. Khalid and I met in the conference room of the Neighborhood Advisory Council building every other week.

Dr. Khalid worked with great effort to keep the imams coming to the meetings and talking directly to me. I represented the U.S. Army to the imams. I was careful to address only issues of Al Saidiyah although the imams frequently attempted to expand our topics to include issues affecting all of Baghdad. Because that was not my scope, I avoided any expanded conversations, much to the frustration of some of the imams. Almost every meeting I conducted with these men I made sure that Chaplain Boyer was present. We commenced the meetings talking about religious issues and the imams read prayers from the Koran. Because I am no Muslim, I was careful not to read or quote the Koran. But I was comfortable with quoting the New Testament and encouraged Chaplain Boyer to discuss theological issues with the imams. The imams loved this. We never proselytized. Everything was kept in the context of working together and cooperating as men of God and human beings who sought to make a better world for all people. While that sounds idealistic, it worked well to gain their attention, trust, and respect, which I felt was necessary to have meaningful negotiations.

Chaplain Boyer and I had an ongoing agreement that we would defer to the imams on issues of religion. Our objective was to generate confidence, trust, and some familiarity. I hoped the imams would speak comfortably so we could conduct effective business and religious discussions were a natural topic for these men.

Dr. Khalid ran the meetings while I sat at the head of the table. This was not my choice; it was the imam's. I thought I should sit among the group and be a participating member but not the decision-maker. The imams insisted I sit at the head of the table, and I did so to appease them. I disarmed and stripped myself of body armor before meeting with the imam council to show respect and trust.

When confronted with problems and asked what I would do, I kicked the problem back into the middle of the table for further debate, following T. E. Lawrence's guidance to let them solve the problem. Although I might not agree with the solution from a practical standpoint, because it was theirs I endorsed it as best as I could. This mesmerized them. What mesmerized them more is that I would always resource their solutions by helping devise a method to implement the solution or provide financing to realize their solution or marshal manpower to achieve their solution, always in good faith. In time, the imams began to trust me and believe I was there to help them.

One of the major issues the Al Saidiyah Imam Council determined I could help them with was repairing mosques in Al Saidiyah. According to the members of the Al Saidiyah Imam Council, the previous battalion had made promises to provide repairs but had never delivered. Although I had my doubts about that claim, because 1-94 Field Artillery was very good about keeping promises and careful about what was promised, because the council members felt so strongly and voted for a universal repair program, I decided to help them. With Dr. Khalid's help, the council was forced to define what repairs would be undertaken. I then allotted a budget to them from which to work. I sought equity and balance in the allocation of the resources. The council had to work through all of the details and then present a proposal. Because Colonel Lanza controlled the money, I had to go to him to fund the project. It was not an easy sell, but he supported the Task Force. Dr. Khalid put the details into action and, within three weeks of the initial discussion, action and repairs were being conducted. This repair project sparked the fire needed to build momentum with the Al Saidiyah Imam Council, which led it to do more things for the community.

Within the Imam Council there were two distinct political alliances, divided along Sunni and Shia lines. Sheik Ali Al-Jabouri, a Sunni imam, was the most powerful figure. He did not come to these local-level council meetings. Sheik Naal was the most powerful Shia imam. He made occasional appearances at the council meetings to talk to me. Both sent surrogates to watch me and listen to me, and then report what went on among the imams. Sheik Ali Al-Jabouri thought I was naïve to this game, but I knew exactly who he sent and when he reported back to the imam because we watched the quarters behind his mosque regularly. One of my interpreters had a contact in Al Saidiyah who routinely reported to him. That informant regularly advised me on the activities of Sheik Ali Al-Jabouri.

Never did we get all the imams of Al Saidiyah mosques to the negotiating table at the same time, but the majority of imams were present. The Al Saidiyah Imam Council despised the Neighborhood Advisory Council. The imams felt the Neighborhood Advisory Council was illegitimate and incapable, often telling me that the Neighborhood Advisory Council did not speak for Al Saidiyah, which I took to mean, did not represent the people of Al Saidiyah.

Having the two councils pulling against each other was a losing proposition functionally and politically. Merging the two provided some hope of creating an organization that would meet the goal of creating a representative body committed to community development and substantially alter the political dynamics of Al Saidiyah to more favorable conditions.

Imams were extremely reluctant to openly engage with the Coalition and were wary of open political collusion with imams of opposing sects. The hardest thing for me to appreciate was that these men of God, who follow essentially the same Muslim teachings, could not get along and work together for the greater good of the people and their country in these dire circumstances.

But the Catholics and Protestants of Ireland have not done that for centuries, either, so it isn't an anomaly. I just found it frustrating. This was truly more tribal than religious, more political than pragmatic, and more selfish than altruistic. But that is the real world of Iraq. The imams, too, wanted more for themselves than for the Iraqi people, just like their counterparts on the Neighborhood Advisory Council. Time and effort might have overcome these shortcomings, but at the time I had to work with what I had.

The New Design of the Neighborhood Advisory Council

Changing the council members was critical to the future success of local governance in Al Saidiyah. Reforming the council by legitimately destroying the old political regime and creating a new one in an evolutionary manner was no easy maneuver. The staff devised the "Refreshment Program," which merged the Al Saidiyah Imam Council and the Neighborhood Advisory Council. Imams like Sheik Ali Al-Jabouri and others whose support would be perceived as collaborating with the enemy were encouraged to stay away but asked to provide a representative from their mosque. The representative had to be a respected and well-known individual who attended the mosque and had a college education. There were no other stipulations. Because Sheik Ali Al-Jabouri and Sheik Naal had agreed to help me seat this kind of Neighborhood Advisory Council, I had the means to check each representative. If anyone tried to pass off a representative who didn't meet our stipulations, the two imams would tell me. Only one of the 16 mosques attempted to do so and Sheik Ali Al-Jabouri fixed the problem quickly.

Several dynamics were in operation with the newly configured council. Mahallas and mosques were tied to one another, which is how the Iraqis function day to day. Representation correlated directly with the imams and the people at the same time. Better-educated people were sitting on the council, which we believed would improve productivity, and discussions among council members would be more constructive, and democratic. As the people of Al Saidiyah learned who was sitting on the new council, efficacy was quickly achieved.

By late October the combination of the Imam and Neighborhood Advisory Council program was just starting to come to life. I was confident that, once in place, the work to get a budget and realize better authority in the township was achievable. And my confidence grew. Though all of our initiatives, projects, and operations were not successful, most were effective. The soldiers and junior leaders in the Task Force were extremely confident in all we were do-ing. I sensed they understood how their daily actions af-fected the larger Task Force effort. The people in Al Saidi-yah were clearly expressing a greater trust and confidence in our support. By no means was it ideal, but Area of Op-erations Rocket was the most stable in Al Rashid. We were achieving our goal of implementing a local governmental body to spearhead community development and building momentum to take the effort to the next level.

The Iraqi security forces that worked with us turned a cor-ner ever so slightly too. The long term Task Force effort to make the various organizations of the Iraqi Security Forc-es viable was gaining credibility and capability. Not yet where we wanted the Iraqi soldiers, Facility Protection Ser-vice guards, and our interaction with Iraqi police forces, much progress had occurred parallel to the political gains we were realizing. The situation looked promising.

19 Iraqi Security Forces Show Promise

"Remember upon the conduct of each depends the fate of all." Alexander the Great

The Iraqi Civil Defense Corps had improved considerably since the summer of 2004. Logistical support was the one critical area where greatest improvement occurred. Training had matured and the Task Force's Advisory Support Team made huge strides teaching and mentoring the company. For some reason, completely unknown to me, the Iraqi Civil Defense Corps name was dropped and the Iraqi National Guard name was given to this organization and the Iraqi 304th Infantry Battalion.

Many achievements were realized by the fall of 2004. Captain Van Keuren and his team were able to get uniforms and institute standards for wear which made a significant difference in the appearance of these forces. Public confidence in the Iraqi National Guard improved. This was not achieved just because an Army was fielded. Appearance, action, treatment of citizens, and professionalism were part of the process of building a competent military in Iraq. Captain Van Keuren and his Advisory Support Team were doing an effective job of turning D Company, 304th Iraqi Infantry into a capable fighting unit.

Along with uniforms the companies of the Iraqi 304th Infantry Battalion began to receive other pieces of equipment like helmets, small radios, and better vehicles. In order to keep track of this equipment, supply management and control procedures were set in place. The Advisory Support Team taught the Iraqi National Guard non-commissioned officers and junior officers how to manage this. Captain Van Keuren taught his counterpart, Iraqi Captain Dilawer, how to take charge and account for the assigned equipment. Captain Van Keuren then showed Captain Dilawer how to maximize the life of the equipment through maintenance and inspection standards.

The Iraqi National Guard Company trained hard in Basic Rifle Marksmanship, Primary Marksmanship Instruction, and Close Quarters Marksmanship techniques. This training was vitally important to ensuring that Iraqi National Guard soldiers could handle their weapons effectively and hit the enemy insurgents when using their rifles. The Iraqi National Guard soldiers were notoriously poor shots. Luckily, so were most insurgents.

Training squads and platoons had progressed well enough that twice-daily autonomous and integrated Iraqi National Guard patrols were able to be placed on Route Irish to augment our patrolling of that challenging route. The Iraqi patrols did an outstanding job. Advisory Support Team members accompanied the patrols and helped them manage confrontational situations which occasionally occurred with local citizens.

Despite the improvements, many challenges still confronted us. One of the biggest problems we encountered was supplying the Iraqi National Guard with armor vehicles. Iraqi vehicles had no armor, and we had no way of securing any with armor for them. I was told by the BCT staff that the likelihood of Iraqis securing any armored vehicles for our Iraqi National Guard company while we were still in country was slim. We helped them by putting on "Mad Max" armor, but I knew this was not a very viable permanent solution.

Absenteeism of soldiers in the Iraqi National Guard was a continual problem. On occasion, the commander would contact Captain Van Keuren and report he could not field a patrol because he did not have enough soldiers. This was particularly so around Shia holiday times or significant religious events. Other times, the Iraqi National Guard Company would not be able to perform because soldiers were scared and refused to go on patrol. Generally, this happened after the Iraqi company or a sister unit had encountered a major engagement with the enemy where casualties had been taken. When casualties were involved, word spread fast and the Iraqi soldiers were not mentally committed enough to risk combat in close proximity to a devastating action. As Americans, we found this behavior unconscionable. To the Iraqis, this was quite normal and actually expected behavior. It was as if the soldiers were paying homage to and expressing solemn grief for fallen comrades. Although heartsick and grief-stricken when fellow soldiers are killed or seriously wounded, American soldiers do not quit simply because the enemy got the best of you one day. Certainly, an Army cannot flourish, fight, and win if it shuts down after every lost life. Although these shut-downs were not frequent occurrences in the Iraqi National Guard Company, they happened enough to adversely affect the Task Force patrol operation.

One of the major efforts the BCT placed into Iraqi security forces improvement action was to recruit more heavily and oversee a rigorous selection process compared to that which we had inherited. First Armor Division did an excellent job of establishing the Iraqi Civil Defense Corps and started the processes of association and training, but the overall effort was in the infant stages. At the juncture we arrived, the effort had to take the processes to the next level.

Recruiting required a great deal of advertising through the local areas of Al Rashid, which had to be followed by strict security since insurgents targeted many Iraqi police and Iraqi National Guard recruiting sites for attack. The two most common attack methods were car bombs and walking suicide bombers.

Colonel Lanza set stringent conditions for recruiting drives. Generally, these personnel recruiting goals were determined after consulting with the Iraqi National Guard or Iraqi police officers. Colonel Lanza then assigned oversight responsibility to a whole task force of the BCT. He physically inspected and checked the security measures at the recruiting site to insure there was no chance for insurgent success against our efforts. The BCT never suffered an attack at a recruiting site that caused U.S. or Iraqi casualties. In fact, we were attacked only once. Thus, our overall efforts to recruit were very successful in the Al Rashid District of Baghdad.

Another challenging problem we faced from the beginning of our dealings with the Iraqi National Guard was command and control. Obviously, we did not speak the same language, our cultures were markedly different, and the level of professional military education and training were very different. Initially, Captain Van Keuren bridged the gap with a constant presence and a good interpreter rotation to support the training effort in the Iraqi National Guard Company.

By the fall, as autonomous operations were being conducted, we worked two methods of command and control to insure competent and effective patrolling by the Iraqi National Guard. First, members of the Advisory Support Team always accompanied the Iraqi National Guard on patrols. The Advisory Support Team had an armored humvee and communicated with our Tactical Operations Center during all operations with the Iraqi company. Second, my interpreter, Freddie, carried a walkie-talkie with a five kilometer range on his person and monitored the Iraqi National Guard command net. He was adept at deciphering what he heard on the radio and reported. This allowed him to quickly pass along critical incident information to me as it was occurring. These measures were highly effective, allowing for better support and partnering with our Iraqi National Guard company. The Iraqi National Guard also approved of these measures because they felt truly cared for and were directly included in the process.

To more acutely solidify the feeling of partnership and true integration, the Iraqi National Guard Company Commander became an integral part of the Task Force daily battle-update briefing sessions, twenty-minute staff and commander updates given to me. Iraqi Captain Dilawer sat in and briefed on his unit actions for the day, speaking in Arabic with a translator who would then brief back in English. This arrangement was ideal for both units.

One problematic area of concern with the Iraqi National Guard involved "battle tracking," one of the major functions of any Tactical Operations Center. Essentially, battle tracking is the process of recreating the movement and integration of information through reports from all units onto a map or digital display. The map or digital display is typically maintained in a Command Post where decision-makers assess, analyze, and make decisions about the operation.

When Iraqi National Guard were part of the Task Force operation, reporting relevant information to higher headquarters in the Tactical Operations Center in order to "paint a full picture" was challenging. Only Category II, security-cleared interpreters were permitted in the Tactical Operations Center of the Task Force. In Task Force 1-21, we only had one Category II-qualified interpreter. To overcome our problem, we posted the Category II interpreter in the Tactical Operations Center during operations. When this was not feasible, we relayed information from a Command Post established in the Interpreter/Facilities Protection Service office down the hallway from the Tactical Operations Center. This worked well but added a layer of complexity and placed more people between the message and the report, which meant time and accuracy were potentially reduced. That procedure was the best we could do to maintain effective battle-tracking activities with the Iraqi National Guard.

The Iraqi National Guard's growth and development were part of the overall BCT campaign plan to employ the various elements of the Iraqi security forces so as to make them more capable throughout the Al Rashid sector. Many soldiers across the BCT were serving as members of advisory support teams in their respective task forces. They were hard at work trying to rapidly improve the Iraqi National Guard capability, professionalism, and effectiveness. Clearly, we all understood and believed the Iraqis could form a capable government to direct these forces autonomously sometime in the future. None of us believed this would occur in our year in Iraq, but we all worked as though it were imminent.

Besides the Iraqi National Guard, the other major element of the Iraqi security force was the Facilities Protection Service. By the fall of 2004, much had changed with this organization, too. The Facilities Protection Service grew within our Task Force and we began to use them extensively. Unfortunately, financial support for the Facilities Protection Service was drying up. By September, I had to actively lobby Colonel Lanza to keep the Facilities Protection Service operating. I was the only commander seriously doing so. Ultimately, the support to retain the Facilities Protection Service Protection Force was lost, and Colonel Lanza shut the organization down.

The Death of FPS—Long Live the Temporary Iraqi Infrastructure Security Force

The decision to inactivate the Facilities Protection Service came as a heavy blow. In Colonel Lanza's eyes, the Facilities

Protection Service had not provided an exceptionally-competent function for the BCT, and I had failed to make the case that it had done well for Task Force 1-21, so far. Colonel Lanza made the determination to shut down the Facilities Protection Service. I was extremely frustrated because we had worked and invested much time and effort to improve the capability of this force. More importantly, to operate optimally, we needed the rudimentary capabilities provided by this organization to supplement the efforts of my soldiers.

I pointed out to Colonel Lanza that the Facilities Protection Service provided good surveillance and a deterrent presence. The Task Force did not have the forces to cover the area sufficiently without this support. Employment that the Facilities Protection Service provided in Al Rashid was vital to the long-term goals of security and stability. In time, with training, and the proper resources, the Facilities Protection Service would improve and provide more robust capability. We just needed to keep working the program.

But the fatal problem I had in convincing Colonel Lanza to maintain the Facilities Protection Service was it was not exceptionally competent at fighting the insurgents. Before it was dismantled, we had worked incessantly to improve the Facilities Protection Service ability to fight. Because the volunteers were so poorly educated, and many were almost destitute, it was quite a task to teach and develop the guards. It took much more time than normal training. I believed that patience and good treatment, coupled with improved leadership among the members of the organization, would pay off in the long run. But my attempts to persuade fell on deaf ears. No one seemed to be willing to commit the time.

A lack of peer support truly doomed my efforts to lobby Colonel Lanza to maintain the organization. Lieutenant Colonel Salter and Lieutenant Colonel Allen were exasperated

with their Facilities Protection Service contingents and justifiably so. When they were polled, both essentially said,
"Get rid of them."

As the decision came down, part of me knew this would
prove costly. Intuitively I felt that the Facilities Protection
Service would manifest its value once the service was no
longer available. And that was exactly what followed.

Once the Facilities Protection Service was defunct, I directed the Task Force staff to find other employment for the
250-plus Facilities Protection Service guards we had in our
contingent. Many guards of our Facilities Protection Service were frantic about losing their jobs, creating a delicate
balance. We wanted and needed to keep the trust of the
Iraqis we had employed in the Facilities Protection Service
to preserve a good relationship. I worried the displaced
guards might take this as a slight and decide to become
insurgents as pay back. The only way to mitigate this was
to help them with other employment.

Colonel Lanza was clearly concerned about the unemployed
Facilities Protection Service guards. He worked hard with
his staff to address this condition. One serendipitous cir-
cumstance was that a major Iraqi police recruiting effort
had begun in Baghdad in mid-September. We worked with
the BCT staff and Iraqi contacts in Al Saidiyah to transport
as many Facilities Protection Service guards to Iraqi police recruiting locations as we could. We hoped they would
serve in Iraqi police jobs, and many took us up on this offer. This clearly reduced the tension and stress of the dis-
placement of Facilities Protection Service guards.

Sometime around the first week of October, I learned that
Colonel Lanza never truly wanted to dismantle the Facilities Protection Service. The lack of money allocated to support the Facilities Protection Service was the real issue.

Division provided BCTs with a stipend to pay for the Facilities Protection Service to operate in their respective districts. Colonel Lanza was advised that at the end of the fiscal year (30 September) the money would no longer be available; thus, his decision to dismantle the Facilities Protection Service.

The loss of funding was because the U.S. military authorities of Multi-National Forces, Iraq wanted to honor the Interim Iraqi Government's political decision placing all Facilities Protection Service under the direct control of a specified government ministry and requiring that ministry to fund it. While that made great sense, the Facilities Protection Service we had in Al Rashid would be dismantled by the owning ministry without analysis or assessment of the guards and would effectively place over 500 people in the unemployed ranks of Al Rashid.

Behind the scenes, Colonel Lanza reviewed the options with his operations and legal staffs. They were trying to figure out a politically viable way to preserve the Facility Protection Service without violating the Interim Iraqi Government's request to Multi-National Forces, Iraq. The BCT also had an obligation to meet the orders issued by the Commander of Multi-National Forces, Iraq, General Casey. The resulting solution became the formation of another organization, the Temporary Iraqi Infrastructure Security Force.

This solution appeased the political situation. Creating the Temporary Iraqi Infrastructure Security Force provided a significant functional need for the BCT and yet met the requirements of the political situation.

For Task Force 1-21, the Temporary Iraqi Infrastructure Security Force solution and its implementation was a double-edged sword. We had successfully found jobs for most of the Facilities Protection Service guards which depleted our ranks. But we gathered the staff, civil affairs experts, and Iraqi local leaders who supported our efforts in Al Saidiyah, and started anew. And in reality, we created a better solution than the one we had essentially inherited before.

In a three-hour meeting with the Battery Commanders and key staff members, we worked out a new concept for recruiting, equipping, training, and posting of Temporary Iraqi Infrastructure Security Force in our sector. Shortly after deciding to adjust the Temporary Iraqi Infrastructure Security Force, I had to select a leader to direct the Temporary Iraqi Infrastructure Security Force and chose an Iraqi gentleman we called Major Imad.

Before the Facilities Protection Service was dismantled, Iraqi Majors Tahseen and Ali were running the branches of the Facilities Protection Service. As we began to adjust to the realization that the Facilities Protection Service would no longer be funded, Major Tahseen found a new job working in the Green Zone as a security guard. Major Ali was offered and accepted a position as a logistics purchaser for our Task Force. Thus, we were without a viable leader for the new force.

I was introduced to Major Imad through some former Iraqi Army intelligence officers who lived in Al Saidiyah. In August 2004, a young man named Isam arranged a meeting with these officers. They wanted to consult with me about employment opportunities for them in the Temporary Iraqi Infrastructure Security Force. I explained what we were trying to do with the Temporary Iraqi Infrastructure Security Force and we needed men to serve in the ranks. We were looking for 200 Iraqi men.

These former Iraqi intelligence men committed great effort to secure guards for the Temporary Iraqi Infrastructure

Security Force. They also recommended Major Imad to serve as the commander. Although I was initially concerned that these men might be working to infiltrate the Task Force security effort, after discussions with the staff, we concluded that their open association with us would keep them in check. If they were enemy infiltrators, keeping them close would allow us to control them. If they were not, then we were forming a relationship from which to build a more viable security force with former military men leading the organization. This would help us to form a better Iraqi protection force. Such was the ambiguity of operating in Baghdad.

Major Imad Proved Incompetent

Once I had decided to hire Major Imad, I introduced him to the Neighborhood Advisory Council. He explained all the goals he hoped to accomplish. He described how he was going to lead the organization and announced a recruiting drive. Major Imad asked the Neighborhood Advisory Council to allow him use of the administration building. He also obtained the council's help in communicating that he was recruiting. He further laid out a plan to provide full-time guards at the Neighborhood Advisory Council building to protect the council members when they were present. Captain Pugsley explained to the Neighborhood Advisory Council the Facilities Protection Service was being dissolved, but the Temporary Iraqi Infrastructure Security Force was available to replace its functions.

The council was thrilled with the plan and immediately threw their support behind Major Imad. Though not all members were supportive of the change, all agreed the potential for improvement was great and each member wanted to improve the situation.

The implementation of Major Imad's plan followed fairly quickly. Sergeant Raine worked with Major Imad and set-up a recruiting and sign-up operation at the Neighborhood Advisory Council administrative building. While on patrol, I went to the Neighborhood Advisory Council building and checked the progress of the recruiting operation. The line of potential recruits for the new Temporary Iraqi Infrastructure Security Force exceeded 300 people, stretching outside the building.

Sergeant Raine and Corporal Slaton meticulously screened, documented, and credentialed all the new guards. Additionally, they issued uniforms, vests, and hand-held radios to the guards. Major Imad supervised the overall operation, and we felt confident that the new Temporary Iraqi Infrastructure Security Force would be a huge success.

Sergeant Raine and Corporal Slaton also worked directly with Major Imad, providing him with special new equipment we had purchased. They worked out a training program and interfaced with Temporary Iraqi Infrastructure Security Force guards selected by Major Imad. The two-man American advisory team assigned to the Temporary Iraqi Infrastructure Security Force developed a "train the trainer" program, whereby Corporal Slaton trained selected leaders and then those leaders, under his direct supervision, trained the rest of the guards. The idea was to get culturally-appropriate training and instructional design into the process. Corporal Slaton was the ideal non-commissioned officer to conduct the training because of his extensive civilian police background. Sergeant Raine handled the overall logistical support operation and assisted with training. This dynamic duo performed minor miracles daily with the Temporary Iraqi Infrastructure Security Force.

After the initial phase of training was completed, Sergeant Raine came to me raising a red flag. He warned that although Major Imad appeared to be capable, he was, in truth, a fraud. Sergeant Raine explained that Major Imad was doing nothing more than taking care of his cronies and Major Imad's leadership was elitist and perfunctory. He feared Major Imad would lie, cheat, and steal under the guise of a caring and capable leader.

I absolutely trusted Sergeant Raine's assessments. He worked so closely with Iraqis daily, he clearly knew more than anyone in my command about how Iraqis thought and behaved. Sergeant Raine had an impeccably and brutally honest streak in him. When he spoke, I listened.

Just a week after Sergeant Raine came to me with his concerns, the situation with Major Imad deteriorated rapidly. Within days of his assuming command of Temporary Iraqi Infrastructure Security Force several insurgents openly threatened Major Imad in Al Saidiyah. Apparently, insurgents had seen him checking his guard posts in town and, through various sources, figured out that he was in charge of the Temporary Iraqi Infrastructure Security Force. In the first week of October, insurgents attempted to kill him when he was driving on Route Irish. They failed to hit him in their assassination attempt, but he was sufficiently rattled. The next day, he called Freddie and told Freddie to inform me that he had quit.

The sudden resignation of Major Imad left the Temporary Iraqi Infrastructure Security Force in slight disarray. Sergeant Raine went to the senior Temporary Iraqi Infrastructure Security Force Captain and offered him the job of interim commander. We then scrambled to find a new Commander.

Major Tahseen, in the meantime, had monitored the situation through informants in Al Saidiyah and learned that a commander was needed. He had taken the Green Zone security guard position only because the Facilities Protection Service had been dismantled. He was skeptical about the likelihood the Temporary Iraqi Infrastructure Security Force actually would be established. But once he heard that the new organization was in full operation and better resourced than the Facilities Protection Service, he wanted to come back. His family resided in Al Saidiyah and that is where he wanted to be. He contacted Freddie and requested a meeting with me to ask to come back and take charge of the new organization. We hired back Major Tahseen immediately.

Major Tahseen brought order to the Temporary Iraqi Infrastructure Security Force, and he knew precisely what needed to get done with the guards. He brought along with him his best subordinates from the former Facilities Protection Service and placed them in key leadership positions. He and I sat down with Sergeant Raine and went through the details of the changes between the two organizations. Major Tahseen saw the new equipment, listened to our training demands, and was briefed on our new-fangled deployment plan. He offered suggestions for refinement which were valuable and exactly the sort of support I had hoped he would provide. He had a renewed commitment to Task Force 1-21 and our efforts in Al Saidiyah.

After the meeting I spoke with Major Tahseen without the rest of the staff. I told him that while it was great that he had come back to serve with Task Force 1-21 I was a little skeptical about his motives. He shrugged off my concerns and stated he hated the Green Zone. He never wanted to leave the Task Force but he needed to feed his family, which was a motivation I understood and respected. Now, more than ever, he was convinced the way the Task Force operated was much better than what he had experienced elsewhere. In his own words he "wanted to work with a winner."

I told Major Tahseen I was pleased to have him back and we agreed to talk and to maintain daily contact. We shook hands. "Shukran [Thank you]," I told him. Then I said, "Tahseen, we have an election coming in January; we need to be ready. You will have a big role in that. It's up to you and me to make that work."

He smiled, placed his open hand with his palm over his heart, which is the custom in Iraq, and simply said, "Inshallah [God willing]."

I replied, "Moshee [OK]," and left the conference room where we were meeting.

20 Death and Respite

*"Go Sir, gallop and don't forget that the world was
made in six days. You can ask me for anything
but not time." Napoleon Bonaparte*

By mid-October 2004, the Muslim holy time of Ramadan
was fast approaching. U.S. forces throughout Iraq became
very sensitive and nervous around this time of year. During Ramadan, the gates to heaven are open to Muslim
martyrs and the gates of Hell are closed. Acts of kindness
and sacrifice for one's religion are magnified thousands
of times during this period. Men who make the "ultimate
sacrifice" in the name of Allah during Ramadan are promised entrance into paradise where seventy-two virgins
await them. For the passionately destitute Muslim fanatic,
this was a particularly enticing promise. For American soldiers, Ramadan was a time of heightened danger.

In Task Force 1-21, we had already started a training series on Ramadan to ensure soldiers throughout the Task
Force were aware of the threats that lay ahead and were
prepared intellectually to deal with those threats.

Insurgents renewed their indirect fires campaign at the end
of September and into October. We began to take mortar
and rocket fire daily in Camp Falcon. The Ramadan season
not only contributed to a surge in indirect attacks on the
base, it also increased attacks on patrols and Iraqi Security
Forces in the Al Rashid district. In fact, throughout Baghdad the number of attacks rose but they were manageable.

During Ramadan, Colonel Lanza wanted focused efforts
with all Iraqi security forces. Combined U.S.–Iraqi security
force operations and autonomous large-scale (battalion-
sized) Iraqi security force operations were put together by

the Iraqi National Guard. A spike in attacks in the vicinity of Check Point 8 and against patrols transiting just north of Check Point 8 on Route Irish were originating from the mahallas northeast of Check Point 8 in 1-8 Cavalry's sector. I talked with Lieutenant Colonel Allen, the 1-8 Cavalry Commander, about undertaking a combined operation to cordon and search that area and press the enemy to either fight us or push them away from Route Irish.

We struggled with the BCT staff to find relief in the existing, heavy-patrolling schedule to execute this combined operation. The operation had been conceived in early September, but unfortunately the limited available manpower and other more pressing priorities defeated our efforts to get the operation launched.

Finally, in late October, Colonel Lanza worked out the tactical situation which allowed a battalion of Iraqi National Guard and elements of 1-8 Cavalry and 1-7 Cavalry to go into the mahallas northeast of Check Point 8 in an attempt to neutralize the insurgent activity in this area.

Task Force 1-21 had been securing Check Point 8 with a 24-hour presence. We had a patrol at the checkpoint in a defensive posture, and Facilities Protection Service guards were on foot, patrolling the immediate area in and around Check Point 8 for at least a month starting the end of September 2004.

The combined Iraqi National Guard and 1-8 Cavalry operation was set to launch in the early morning hours of October 28, 2004. I had been in my Tactical Operations Center until about 3 a.m. on October 28th. I retired to my quarters across the hallway from the Tactical Operations Center of the Task Force headquarters at 3:15 a.m., hoping to get some sleep before my 7 a.m. wake-up call.

Sergeant First Class Michael Battles, Rest in Peace

Before my wake up call, I heard a huge BOOM! The explosion sounded like it was immediately outside Camp Falcon. The boom was so loud that it woke me from a dead sleep. I sat straight up in my bed and had one thought, "Please God, don't let that be my guys!"

For a reason that to this day I cannot explain, instead of running to the Tactical Operations Center, I got out of my bunk and started to put on my uniform. While doing that, a runner came in from the Tactical Operations Center and told me an IED exploded at Check Point 8 and soldiers had been wounded. Partially dressed, I went into the Tactical Operations Center and tried to discern what was happening.

Initial reports said a patrol from B/1-21 had been wounded under the overpass at Check Point 8. No other information was available. I told Master Sergeant Joe Silvas, the Task Force Operations Sergeant, to develop the situation, get accurate reports, alert the Troop Medical Clinic that we may have casualties coming in, and to keep everyone calm, to figure it out. I also instructed the S3, Major Reinhart, to assemble the Quick Reaction Force patrol and advise my crew to be ready to roll as we were going to Check Point 8 immediately.

I left the Tactical Operations Center and finished gearing up to head out. Command Sergeant Major Hughes was already dressed for action and wanted to come along. After I finished gearing up, I returned to the Tactical Operations Center to get my M4 rifle, where Sergeant Silvas reported that we had three wounded. Quietly, Sergeant Silvas confided just to me that the situation he suspected only two soldiers were wounded and that the one had actually been killed. I tried not to think about the loss of a life.

I left the Tactical Operations Center and went out to the front of my headquarters building to meet with my crew and vehicle. On my way, Major Reinhart ran out and verified Sergeant Morris B. Harrison, Jr. and Private First Class Keith R. Schulteis were wounded but that Sergeant First Class Michael Battles was killed. I was despondent. I thought about it, absorbing what I just heard and then went to tell Command Sergeant Major Hughes the bad news. He was visibly upset but supremely composed.

Sergeant Battles was a man I had known very well. I met him early in my tenure of command. He was the Chief of Firing Battery (Smoke) for the First Cavalry Division Salute Battery. Shortly after I took command of 1-21 Field Artillery, I attended the 4th of July weekend festivities that the First Cavalry Division put on at Hood Stadium. Part of the program required the Salute Battery to fire a salute to each of the 50 states. Lieutenant Rodney Davis and Sergeant Battles were in charge. Before the event I spoke with each of them. Later, they performed perfectly, firing precisely every three seconds without error. Sergeant Battles had the team so finely tuned they executed all 50 shots, without a misfire.

Sergeant Battles was also an extremely gregarious, fun-loving non-commissioned officer, who was a strong disciplinarian, mentor, and coach. To the younger soldiers, he was somewhat of a father figure. Every one of us in the Task Force had a personal association with Sergeant Battles, and the battalion took his death very hard because of that.

I believe Sergeant Battles was one of the very best non-commissioned officers in the battalion. I had many conversations with him, out on the artillery firing ranges at Fort Hood when we were conducting field training, and out on a launcher, working through a technical problem. Sergeant Battles was constantly teaching me. We had a very good professional and personal relationship.

In Iraq, I had frequent contact with Sergeant Battles because of his involvement with the Patrol Leader Training
Program. He always had great experiences to share, and
he helped me teach others. The day Sergeant Battles died a
part of me died, too.

Based on our investigation, insurgents set two IEDs along
Route Irish in advance of the cordon-search operation.
We believe one IED was placed about 700 meters north
of Check Point 8 and a second, larger IED, was placed at
Check Point 8. Through observation of previous incidents,
the enemy knew our cordon distance for an IED was about
500 meters. Therefore, they placed an exposed IED along
the northbound lane of Route Irish at a distance that ensured U.S. and Iraqi security forces would be closer to the
second, more-powerful and well-hidden IED. Their plan
worked to perfection.

Sergeant Battles moved his patrol south from the initial IED
position, which was closer to the underpass of Check Point
8. While repositioning elements, the southern half of the
cordon developed a gap. As was typical of Sergeant Battles,
instead of wasting time directing others to cover the gap,
he dismounted his armored humvee and ground-guided
his vehicle to fill the gap. As the driver maneuvered the
humvee into a covering position on the north side of the
overpass, the concealed IED which had been placed at the
check point was remotely detonated.

Private Schulteis was in the gunner station on top of the armored humvee. He was protected by the gunner's shields
we installed. Private Schulteis was knocked unconscious
from the blast concussion and he slumped inside the truck.
Sergeant Harris was driving, and although the door was
open to the right side where Sergeant Battles was standing talking on the radio, Sergeant Harris was not killed by
the blast. Unfortunately, the heat and explosion concussion

knocked him from the vehicle onto the ground on the left side of the humvee.

The extreme heat from the blast turned all the metal of the vehicle searing hot almost instantly. Both Sergeant Harris and Private Schulteis were burned. Sergeant Battles had his left lower leg blown off and he was peppered all over his torso with shrapnel that cut through him. Miraculously, he was not killed instantly, but he was in bad shape.

Captain Martin Wohlgemuth, a Fire Support Officer assigned to 1-7 Cavalry now serving as the chief of their Advisory Support Team working with Iraqi National Guard troops, arrived at the scene and directed the evacuation of the wounded. Captain Wohlgemuth was a superb young officer. He had a penchant to be free-wheeling, the kind of independent-minded leader who thrived in an advisory role with the Iraqis. Captain Wohlgemuth had been wounded earlier in our tour. He described the incident in which he was wounded on the evening of 29 August 2004:

The Fire Support Platoon was spending a week at the Iraqi National Guard compound, and I was manning a rooftop observation post with a few Iraqi National Guardsmen (we'd had sporadic drive-by shootings west of the compound near the elementary school and took turns manning observation posts). At 2130 [9:30 PM] we had a single car involved in a drive-by shooting, but it drove away. An hour later, a single black sedan stopped in the school parking lot and two individuals dismounted and began walking toward the Iraqi National Guard compound. About 100 meters away, they both pulled AK-47s from behind their backs and opened fire on the guard tower in the northwest corner of the compound. Two Iraqi National Guardsmen returned fire from inside the tower and I returned fire from the rooftop in a sandbagged position. When the Anti-Iraqi Forces saw the secondary position (next to the tower) one fired at my position. I ducked into the position as it was hit with a few rounds. The position was only one sandbag deep, and one of the rounds passed through the sandbag and I caught the rico-chet in my cheek. I returned fire, killing one.

Captain Wohlgemuth directly supervised the effort im-mediately following the IED explosion and got the three wounded soldiers first aid. Specialist Peter A. Owen was the medic on site who directed and rendered first-aid ef-forts. Captain Wohlgemuth made sure the chaos was re-stored to order and all action was taken to continue se-curing the area, treat the wounded, and prepare them for medical evacuation. He made the decision to take the wounded directly to the Combat Army Surgical Hospital in the Green Zone located about 15 minutes away rather than to the Troop Medical Clinic about 10 minutes away. Captain Wohlgemuth realized that Sergeant Battles' best chance for survival was treatment at the Level III care hos-pital. Although it was the better judgment call, in the end his wounds were too extensive and Sergeant Battles died in the emergency room at the Combat Army Surgical Hospi-tal in the Green Zone.

As I raced to Check Point 8, I received confirmation over the radio that Sergeant Battles was killed. I re-routed to the hospital in the Green Zone while the S3 proceeded to Check Point 8 and implemented the necessary tactical ad-justments.

I felt literally sickened, sorry, and responsible. Keeping myself together and setting an example for my soldiers I could show compassion and concern but I could not break down, despite the fact that every fiber in me wanted to. That would come later and privately.

The death of Sergeant Battles and the memorial service I had to lead the Task Force through were my last acts before departing for a scheduled tour of leave in the U.S. I was worn out by the time I reached the first week of November. This leave could not come at a more opportune time for me. But tactically, politically, and pragmatically in terms of directing civil operations I knew we would lose time.

Leave was a big issue for senior leaders across the Division. In 5th BCT it was a hypersensitive issue among the command group. None of us wanted to leave our formations as we were fighting. Major General Chiarelli, much to his credit, ordered all battalion commanders and BCT commanders to schedule and take leave. We had no vote. He knew we needed it and that our effectiveness was at issue.

I was personally concerned that the system set up for soldiers to take leave did not guarantee all soldiers would have a scheduled leave during their one-year tour of duty. I felt I could not take leave if even one soldier in my Task Force was denied the opportunity. The soldiers came first as far as I was concerned.

I had Command Sergeant Major Hughes and my adjutant, Captain Eric Willis, put together a very detailed analysis of the Task Force Environmental Leave Program which specified a schedule that ensured every soldier had a guaranteed tour of leave. Once we fashioned a fail-safe schedule, and all the command team had gone and returned, I scheduled my leave dates. I chose early November to return to the U.S. because I had to comply with the Commanding General's orders that battalion level and higher commanders leave not be taken during Thanksgiving and Christmas. Additionally, by late November, preparations for the Iraqi national elections would be too high a priority to permit tours of leave for senior leaders. By November more than 80 percent of the soldiers in the Task Force had gone on leave and returned.

I truly believed I could have pressed on without taking

leave, but the break proved revitalizing for me in many ways. Being in a place where I did not have to worry about incoming mortar rounds, snipers, or ambushes and IEDs was a tremendous relief.

Leave, Going Home and Getting a Respite

The odyssey of traveling from Iraq to the U.S. was an adventure. The process to get home on leave started with finding a way to Baghdad International Airport either by helicopter from Camp Falcon, a convoy set up by 515th Forward Support Battalion, or hitching a ride with a patrol that had business scheduled at Baghdad International Airport. Since I knew I was leaving November 5th, I hitched a ride with one of the Task Force's patrols that was already scheduled to go to Baghdad International Airport that day.

At Baghdad International Airport, all the soldiers departing on leave mustered in a formation at the makeshift terminal and were assigned a flight on a U.S. Air Force C-130 departing for Kuwait. In Kuwait, we were assigned flights to one of three airports that served as major hubs for returning service members. Dallas was one of those hubs. But the plane I was assigned broke down on the flight line at Baghdad International Airport and so the 10 a.m. departure was delayed to 3 p.m. and then again until the next day.

Because I was on a tight timeline, I worried I would not get out of Iraq in time to be back before Thanksgiving Day. Under normal conditions, a leave cycle takes about 21 days from start to finish. Concerned about complying with the Commanding General's orders, I went to the flight operations officer in charge of the military flights and finagled a ride on another working aircraft.

I was able to depart for Kuwait only 24 hours behind schedule and was back in the U.S. the following day. By email my wife was able to advise me that Sergeant Battles' funeral would be in San Antonio on the same day my flight landed in Dallas. Although I desperately wanted to make it to the funeral, the time and distance made it impossible. I simply could not make it from Dallas to San Antonio in time. I was particularly upset because I could have made it had I departed as originally scheduled. To this day, missing Sergeant Battles' funeral haunts me.

My wife and son met me at the Dallas-Fort Worth Airport when I arrived. Easily, this was one of the most surreal moments in my life: going from the world that was Iraq with its stress, filth, noise, threats, heat, stench, dust, and sleeplessness; and then, almost too suddenly, finding myself in the quiet, civil, tranquil, happy, clean, cool environ of a November day in Texas. It was wonderful and strange all at once. I realized on the ride home just how tired I was.

At the airport in Dallas, there were throngs of people who lined the walkway from the gate exit to the terminal where my family was waiting. They cheered all of us arriving and thanked us. The well-wishers waved American flags, held out signs, and the entire place was draped in bunting and balloons. It was nice.

I did not want to be cynical but I noticed that these were veteran military men and women, not average Americans off the street. Although I personally appreciated the show of support, in the back of my mind I realized the gesture belied a different reality. I had seen my father come home on leave from Vietnam in 1971 and there was just my mom, my brother, my sister and I. No one else cared a bit. At least someone seemed to care for us. I pushed that concern from my mind because it just didn't matter at that moment. I was excited as I embraced my wife and hugged my son.

The ride from Dallas to Fort Hood, where we lived, was about three hours long. As we approached every underpass along the route, I found myself unconsciously scanning left and right, trying to see what vehicles or people were moving over the top. Overpasses are particular points of danger in Iraq. I had been on patrol almost every single day I had been in Iraq. Several underpasses had to be traversed on the routes through the Task Force sector. The enemy often placed IEDs on the sides or into the overhead road with a blast pattern aimed downward to kill anything passing below. Our tactic for negotiating an underpass was to speed up in our approach and begin evasive maneuvering going in one spot and coming out from another, unpredictable spot underneath. Every soldier in the vehicle had a scan sector to watch during movement.

The other thing about underpasses that had gripped my mind was the association they had with death. Sergeant Battles was killed at an underpass. A simple highway underpass habitually—almost instinctively—reminded me of fighting in Iraq. While home on leave, I began to realize that this combat experience in Iraq had indelibly impacted my life.

Because I could not make it to Sergeant Battles' funeral, I appeased my heart by promising myself that I would personally visit Sergeant Battles' widow and his little boy. They lived at Fort Hood on the post as did I. My third day home, with my Rear Detachment Commander, Captain Wayne Wallace alongside, I went to Sergeant Battles' home.

Sergeant Battles' wife was Panamanian and a wonderful Army wife who had invested much in her husband Michael and in Army life. Michael Jr., their son, was a beautiful little boy who looked so much like his father that I could not hold back my emotions when I met them. I hugged Mrs. Battles and we cried together for several long minutes. I apologized through tears and anguish.

She wanted to know what happened and I told her all I knew about the incident. I explained to her all the things Sergeant Battles had done in the battalion and we talked about what kind of man he was. She seemed comforted. Michael Jr. had asked her if his dad's left leg was hurt because he had woken in the middle of the night on the day Sergeant Battles was killed complaining of pain in his lower left leg. Mrs. Battles wanted to know if anything happened to her husband's left leg. This question shot through me with a flood of emotion. I lost my composure again as I told her that her husband's left leg was severed below the knee from the blast.

Mrs. Battles asked me if she could meet with Private Schulteis and Sergeant Harris. Both soldiers were at Brooke Army Medical Center in San Antonio and my wife and I had already planned a trip to visit them. I invited her to join us on the trip.

Two days later, we went to Brooke Army Medical Center and met with the two soldiers. Mrs. Battles wanted more details from them. She spoke with them privately. Neither recalled much after the blast since both had been knocked out. Although Sergeant Harris had only been unconscious for a few seconds, after he became lucid he was so disoriented from the explosion and the chaotic aftermath, he simply could not provide her the detailed information she sought. And Private Schulteis had no recollection other than the BOOM!

Private Schulteis seemed to recover mentally and physically fairly fast. Because he had little recollection of the events he was able to process the trauma well. But Sergeant Harris' recovery was much slower. He had trouble sleeping with the lights off and, although his wounds were not life-threatening, he had hand burns and internal throat burn injuries from having inhaled scalding air from the blast.

Several days after returning from Brooke Army Medical Center, I received an email from my second in command, the Task Force executive officer, Major Marshall, back in Iraq. Some more disturbing things were happening in my absence. When I left Iraq, Major Marshall had assumed command of the Task Force. Before I departed we had made an agreement that we would not communicate unless soldiers in the Task Force were wounded or killed. Whatever else happened, Major Marshall would handle it and I would live with his decisions. I did not want to command the battalion through email or over the phone while I was in Texas. I trusted Major Marshall and knew I had a great team that would do the right things without me.

The message from the executive officer advised that Sergeant Robert N. Myers, assigned to 68th Chemical Company, was wounded by shrapnel from a rocket propelled grenade. He was hit under his armored vest with a hot piece of metal. He was stable but had been medically evacuated to the surgical hospital in the Green Zone. I was told he would be evacuated to Germany within 24 hours and was expected to live.

Other than this bit of bad news, my time home was wonderful. I slept a lot and spent as much time as I could with my son. He was in school during the day. But when he got home, we spent time together. The first week at home passed nicely. I tried not to think about Iraq too much. I did not watch the news. I listened to the quiet. Listening to the quiet was relaxing and I tried to do that as much as I could.

During the second week I became filled with dread and was anxious. Each day that passed drew me nearer to Iraq. The last two nights, I barely slept. I received another message from Major Marshall. He informed me that the Neighborhood Advisory Council building had been blown up by insurgents. Additionally, the insurgents had targeted and blown up the building we had been restoring for establishing an Iraqi police station.

Immediately across the street from the Neighborhood Advisory Council building, my vision was to establish an Iraqi police station along with the council in the center of Al Saidiyah. Apparently the vision was too close to realization for the insurgents, and they directly attacked the effort while I was away, obviously indicating they were very close to us.

When I heard this news, I was distressed. I was angry. I was confused. We had worked so hard and made a great deal of progress only to have the centerpiece of our efforts literally blown up in a day. I decided in my last days at home that I needed to change my strategy and tactics once I returned to Iraq.

The enemy had stepped across a line and had committed to stopping the Task Force efforts. Initially, I struggled to understand why the insurgents had chosen these targets. We had them guarded with Iraqi police and Temporary Iraqi Infrastructure Security Force guards. But this apparently did not deter the insurgents at all. They had actually driven to the buildings and told the guards that if they did not leave immediately, they would be killed and their families would be killed. The guards offered no resistance, abandoned their posts, and left. Clearly, the guards lacked commitment — at least not enough upon which to stake their lives. I worried about Colonel Lanza's reaction. I could already hear him asking, "Why didn't you protect these buildings better? The enemy control Al Saidiyah, not you." I pushed those thoughts from my mind.

I had a few days left at home. There was nothing I could do from Fort Hood. Major Marshall sent me a follow-up email outlining all the actions he had taken. I had agreed with his approach, which focused on three things:

1) Searching for the insurgent cell that executed the attack.

2) Taking steps to clean up the mess and rebuild.

3) Shifting more Temporary Iraqi Infrastructure Security Force guards and more Iraqi police support, along with more Iraqi National Guard, to the area in an attempt to demonstrate we would not be deterred and that construction workers would be substantially protected.

More would have to be done, but until I returned, I was not entirely sure what more I wanted to do. I knew the staff would be developing information, gathering intelligence, and preparing recommendations for me to consider immediately upon my return.

A day or so before my scheduled departure from Fort Hood, I received another email from Major Marshall. He was ordered to leave the battalion to work at Division Headquarters having recently been selected for promotion to Lieutenant Colonel. Apparently Division needed him more than the Task Force. I was amazed that the BCT staff could not delay his reassignment for a week until I returned. Major Bill Reinhart, the S3, was required to assume duties as the executive officer and the Task Force commander in addition to his regular responsibilities until I returned.

I didn't sleep the last night before going back to Dallas to catch the return flight to Kuwait. My wife and I stayed up most of the night and discussed what was ahead for us in the Army. I told her this was likely the end of the road for me. I explained to her the Army was not going to allow Field Artillery officers to command BCTs. I did not want to serve ten more years as a staff officer. I felt I could do better in civilian life. We also talked about the last time I was deployed to the Middle East and the expectation that I would likely be headed right back sooner than later. We discussed my son and how this impacted him. I was close to the magical twenty-year mark and if I could get out of Iraq with my life maybe there was something better for us. We made no definitive decision but the conversation was started.

I was again dreading leaving her and filled with anxiety about my son. I wanted to get back to the soldiers and the Task Force. I loved with a passion that words cannot adequately describe commanding soldiers in the Army. But I knew that this command was going to end at some point. Never having the chance to command again made service in the Army unattractive for me.

My wife drove me the three hours back to Dallas. I tried to stay serene and worked my mind toward Iraq. We said a tearful goodbye and I calmed myself by knowing November was almost over and we would be back together in March, just four months more. I told my wife and son that would happen with conviction as I kissed them goodbye and headed down the terminal ramp to the gate.

Returning to Iraq was more of an adventure than leaving had been, as it took four days of travel to get back to Camp Falcon. Upon my return, I received more bad news. Hamza, the Neighborhood Advisory Council Chairman, had been assassinated in his home two days earlier. He had gone to a Sunni mosque — although he was Shia — and confessed before the congregation that he had "collaborated" with the Americans. He was afraid for his life, and wanted to renounce his association with Americans, and live a peaceful, Muslim life. He had only sought to help all Iraqis by serving on the council.

After his confession Hamza wept and had ostensibly been granted forgiveness by the gathering. But that night insurgents, most likely from the Shakir Al Abood mosque, came to his door, knocked, asked to speak to Hamza, and shot him multiple times with AK-47s until he was dead.

What was so perplexing about this development with Hamza was that he had earlier expressed a staunch commitment to pursuing noble, community-minded goals even in the face of threats. Several times he had come to me and said that the council wanted to take a break because they were threatened. I had told him that unless he and the others on the council persevered in the face of these threats, no progress could be made. Quitting the work because of threats played into the hands of the enemy, I had explained. He always agreed, saw the wisdom of that, and declared he was a patriot who "wanted to die serving a new Iraq."

I was grief-stricken about Hamza's death. I had mentored and encouraged him, and felt personally responsible. The investment of time, energy, and emotion coupled with the personal relationship we had formed was imprinted on my soul. I felt his death was directly tied to my leave. He made the bold move to give his confession while I was gone and, therefore, I was not there to counsel him against this. I knew once he divested himself he would never be able to remove the stigma of his association with Americans. Had I returned sooner, perhaps his desire to purge himself of his association would have been avoided. Again, I had to hold personal pain and grief I felt so deeply inside because others were looking to me to lead the way. In the military, you cannot lead if your emotions are out of control. And so my grief remained private and inward. Although I felt a desire to avenge his death, I knew that, as an Army leader, I had to be careful to separate my personal feelings from the military business I was charged with carrying out.

The assassination of Hamza solidified in my mind what the next phase of the Task Force campaign would be. It was time to become more aggressive with the insurgents in Al Saidiyah. We needed to challenge them as directly as they had challenged the Task Force.

21 Wolf and Bear

*"Tactical agility is the ability of a friendly force to
react faster than the enemy. It is essential to seizing,
retaining, and exploiting the initiative."* [25]

Major Marshall had departed Camp Falcon and the Task
Force before I returned from leave. In his absence, Major
Reinhart assumed the duties of executive officer and de
facto commander of Task Force 1-21; and Assistant S3, Captain David Norris, served as S3, as he had previously done
when Major Reinhart had been on leave in September. Colonel Lanza knew I needed an S3 immediately.

I asked for Major John "Jay" Soupene to serve as Major Reinhart's replacement. I met Major Soupene in August 2003,
a few months after I took command of 1-21 Field Artillery.
I had seen him in action a few times when he served on
the Division Artillery staff in the Division Fire Support Element. We had also worked together at Fort Hood when he
led an investigation related to the suicide of an incarcerated soldier. I really liked what I saw in his staff work. I had
privately communicated my interest in having him serve
as an S3 or executive officer in 1-21 Field Artillery when
an opportunity arose. I mentioned my interest in having
Major Soupene serve as S3 to Colonel Lanza. When we deployed to Iraq, Major Soupene was working on the Division staff. Shortly before Major Marshall's departure, Major Soupene was released from the purgatory assignment
at Division and was reassigned as the Information Operations officer at the 5th BCT. Colonel Lanza was reluctant to
give him up but knew I needed a major to serve as the S3.
The S3 position in a task force is a premier job for any major. Serving in that position with a unit during combat was
an even more significant career opportunity.

Major Soupene and I very quickly formed what I jokingly called "a Vulcan-mind meld," a reference to the Star Trek television series. Indeed, the two of us thinking in synchronicity on key operations issues was serendipitous. For me, the significance of our quick compatibility shored up my confidence upon my return from leave. I believed that time had become more critical. The margin for error for the Task Force's course in the coming weeks was minimal. The fact that Major Soupene and I arrived at similar conclusions about the need for change independently of each other was helpful and refreshing. Major Soupene brought a new perspective and a lot of knowledge, know-how, and institutional understanding to the Task Force. He was energetic, eager, very bright, and he intuitively understood what needed to be done. That Major Soupene had previously served at BCT and Division, which are both echelons above the battalion, made an impact organizationally and with me.

Major Reinhart had done a tremendous job as the Task Force S3 through November. With the untimely reassignment of Major Marshall, he ascended to Task Force Executive Officer. Major Reinhart was ideally suited to move up to the executive officer job. Losing Major Marshall was hard for me personally because he was the check and balance to my personality. He was also a great officer who served the Task Force very well. Although not a combat loss the impact of his departure felt similar.

The new command team which had literally been reorganized while I was away came together quickly. Although we had lost a key player in Major Marshall, I was very grateful that the unit did not miss a beat. In a few short weeks, we actually ascended to the next level of competency and effort.

After thinking for days about the situation in Al Saidiyah, I decided the Task Force needed to be more aggressive and direct with the people in sector. For the past several weeks, the BCT staff directed events, which amounted to a deluge of supporting requirements for the BCT. We also had to respond to the BCT staff's obsession with Route Irish security, which seriously impeded the Task Force's ability to operate in sector the way we wanted and needed.

By this juncture, I believed that tactically, the Task Force had to become completely unpredictable to the enemy. We needed to fashion a bold strategy and assume risk with Route Irish requirements reducing patrols there to get more heavily back in sector, thus focusing effort with the residents in Al Saidiyah to set favorable conditions for the elections that were coming in January.

I met with the new command team and shared my ideas without putting much "meat on the bones." In fashioning a strategy, I wanted their opinions and perspectives; in particular I was interested in knowing how they envisioned the unfolding of our future course. Everyone knew I was frustrated with the destruction of the Neighborhood Advisory Council building and future Iraqi police station building. I was very upset that Hamza had turned and made some sort of odd confession to the Sunni Shakir Al Abood mosque members and then was assassinated. And I was filled with contempt over the death of Sergeant Battles. But, despite my personal frustration, I was amazingly focused on my vision for the Task Force.

The staff had prepared a detailed briefing to bring me up to speed on the myriad of things that had gone on while I was away on leave. The brief included a gamut of issues ranging from tactical to administrative matters including the most trivial of events that had happened while I was away.

After my formal briefing and informal get-reacquainted time with the new command team, I met privately with the new S3, Major Soupene. I asked him his opinion of the substance of the briefing, explaining to him that I wanted to come up with a way to deter the insurgents by conducting more robust operations designed to knock them off their game plan. I was concerned that we might have been getting too predictable. We had clearly been on the right track with our efforts, because when the insurgents went to the heart of our program, they exposed themselves. Now, it was time to use that vulnerability to defeat their future efforts.

Before I returned and immediately following the bombing of the Neighborhood Advisory Council building, Major Marshall and Major Reinhart responded by setting the Task Force on a more aggressive pursuit of insurgent activity. Major Marshall led the task force through two large cordon-and-search missions in Al Saidiyah.

Major Soupene requested a couple of days to delve a little deeper into the recent operations and assess some ideas he had after listening to Major Rinehart and his operations and intelligence staff. He and Major Rinehart conferred directly in their hand-off of duties. I could tell a plan was forming in Major Soupene's mind, but he was cautious about approaching me with it. I appreciated his deliberateness and issued him some planning guidance. We needed to increase the number of raids and conduct more robust cordon-and-search operations. Our intelligence-collecting efforts needed to focus support for the precise application of raid and cordon-and-search operations. We had to find the insurgents in their sanctuaries, ferret out the weapons and ammunition caches, and make certain the insurgent cells in and around the Al Saidiyah area felt watched and uneasy every day leading up to the election. Our strikes had to be perceived as random with more patrols.

With these parameters, Major Soupene and his staff worked

out a conceptual plan of action. Major Soupene's supporting staff really consisted of the Operations and Intelligence (O&I) sections of the Task Force, which was a rather large group.

S3 officers manage the integration, analysis, and synthesis of operations and intelligence. Operations depend on intelligence in an insurgency war. That is to say, to have success in this kind of war depends on the ability of units to assess, analyze, and then focus unrefined intelligence to a high level of precision. This vastly improves the likelihood that a raid or cordon-and-search mission will yield the capture or defeat of an enemy insurgent cell. The accurate processing and handling of intelligence is the essence of fighting an insurgency at the battalion task-force level.

Colonel Lanza had preached the importance of developing precise intelligence and synthesizing our operations and intelligence into one homogenous entity. We worked especially hard at doing just that. And so by this point in late November 2004, it was time to press the Task Force into operating at the next higher level. We had developed sources inside Al Saidiyah and worked them persistently. Major Soupene and Captain Dettmer, the S2 Intelligence Officer, wanted to go faster, further, and work more intensely to set conditions for the elections.

Right after Thanksgiving Day 2004, Major Soupene brought me into his office and, with select members of his staff, laid out a very comprehensive plan for what he called the "Wolf and Bear" concept for operations. Essentially, his idea was to increase the patrols in Al Saidiyah, place more Iraqi National Guard patrols into Al Saidiyah, and re-align the Temporary Infrastructure Security Force in the town. This, he believed, would result in better protection and response to anticipated threats to the election effort. Major Soupene centered the Wolf and Bear plan around the idea of agility, meeting my intent of developing an operational scheme that was long-term, agile, and aggressive keeping insurgent cells off balance all in one.

The "Wolf" portion of the Wolf and Bear plan involved the use of multiple patrols. The patrols were designed to roam Al Saidiyah in patterns that appeared random to the enemy but that were actually specifically designated patrols. No patrol schedules on any given day were the same. We already had a standard practice of varying routes but the enemy had discerned how many patrols we used on a daily basis. Wolf increased and modulated the numbers, times, and frequencies of daily patrols.

The "Bear" part of the plan called for four major Task Force cordon-and-search operations between the end of November and Election Day on January 31, 2005. Utilizing the staff systems and, based on detailed intelligence reports, specific areas of Al Saidiyah became the targeted sites of Bear. Where we had a high degree of suspicion insurgents were quartered, where their supporters hid them, or where weapons were stashed we went in with a Bear-operation to cordon-and-search large areas and trap insurgents inside the net or capture their weapons before they could be moved.

In order to carry out the Wolf-and-Bear plan, we had to reduce civil projects. Manpower was limited, and committing to Wolf-and-Bear meant something had to give. This was a tough decision because we had made huge strides improving conditions for the people in our sector. But given that our work on civil projects did not prevent the attacks we had recently suffered, I decided to undertake the Wolf-and-Bear plan. That the national elections were imminent meant that priorities had to shift, and so I was willing to reduce civil action for more combat operations so as to set the right conditions for the secure execution of the national elections.

The operations tempo would be high for the Task Force and sustaining them for the ten weeks leading up to the election would be very demanding on soldiers. But to do otherwise would be a greater risk to the mission.

Built into the Wolf-and-Bear plan was the flexibility to adjust patrols and increase, decrease, or move projected cordon-and-search operations as intelligence information dictated. Most importantly, the entire sector residents, Iraqi police, insurgents, and unaligned militias would have to adjust to our changes. As long as we remained unpredictable, swift, and tough in our efforts to neutralize insurgent operations, we would, at a minimum, disrupt their anti-election efforts. In a best-case scenario, we would defeat the insurgents before the elections were held. Implementation of the Wolf-and-Bear plan meant we would seize and hold the initiative through the elections. This, above all, was essential to guaranteeing success in the elections, which was truly the seminal event of our tour of duty in Iraq. I loved the plan and committed to it one-hundred percent.

Providing the Task Force with an exceptional, dynamic plan to regain the initiative in our sector was a great achievement by itself, but Major Soupene also brought the Task Force a renewed focus on the Task Force training and leader development programs. I had privately suggested that I thought we had become stale in our training and we needed to lift the organization through more vigorous leader and soldier training events. Major Soupene reacted by enhancing many of the existing programs and adding a few relevant new systems to give us the edge we seemed to be have lost.

Wolf operations immediately began to work well. Increased patrols around the clock made a noticeable difference in Al Saidiyah. Fewer incidents of crime occurred and the locals were openly grateful for our more frequent patrols. On the other hand, the BCT staff complained incessantly that we did not have enough presence on Route Irish. We did not have enough soldiers to do both right. I massaged the BCT staff S3 and did all we could to not allow the focus to shift from the critical mission. It worked.

The first Bear-type Task Force cordon-and-search mission was Operation Wake-Up Call. We quickly followed that up with Operation Kickoff and then Operation Interception. Each of these operations yielded some multiple detainees and a huge amount of contraband.

Throughout the weeks from the end of November through the end of December, leading to the election when the BCT would again dictate much of what we would do, the Task Force relentlessly worked Wolf-and-Bear. There were significant gains and great success in changing conditions in Al Saidiyah.

Our field intelligence sources and Temporary Infrastructure Security Force guards confirmed that suspected insurgents in Al Saidiyah were confused. Incidents of attacks were down and in the mosques people who were caught in the middle were talking about feeling more secure. The Shia imams were openly declaring they and their followers in Al Saidiyah would vote. In a predominantly Sunni enclave of Baghdad, this was significant. The conditions for elections from psychological and political perspectives were set to our favor by late December.

22 First Iraqi National Elections

"A better world shall emerge based on faith and understanding." General Douglas MacArthur

Since early in our deployment, Task Force 1-21 and all units in First Cavalry Division had known that the pivotal event of our tour in Iraq would be the Iraqi National Elections. The elections were scheduled for January 31, 2005. Setting conditions for the successful execution of the elections in Baghdad was the responsibility of Major General Chiarelli, First Cavalry Division Commander. For the Iraqis, a people in turmoil since Saddam's ousting just over a year earlier, the election was a key step toward building a viable future with a representative government. The political lines were drawn along traditional boundaries of conflict between Sunni, Shia, and Kurds. Saddam's regime, since the 1990's, insured that the differences among the people were sharp, emotional, and prone to resolution through violence.

In Task Force 1-21 there was no more critical event and no more meaningful activity we could focus upon in our small slice of Baghdad. Our job was clearly defined. We had to set the conditions in Area of Operations Rocket to insure Iraqi citizens could get to the polling places and vote, risk-free.

The series of large-scale cordon-and-search operations the battalion conducted, coupled with our vigorous effort to patrol in Al Saidiyah, went a long way toward improving security and achieving the stability we sought in Al Saidiyah. Although the setting of conditions tactically was vital, political condition-setting was even more important. To give the residents of Al Saidiyah a legitimate chance at participating in the election and to achieve real security and stability the two had to be balanced and complementary.

By mid-December 2004, the Neighborhood Advisory Council of Al Saidiyah was fully recovered from the assassination of Hamza. Though the Neighborhood Advisory Council building was destroyed, the council continued to meet at another venue and conducted the business necessary to keep moving forward with reforms and improvements in Al Saidiyah. Naima Faruk was chosen to be the Neighborhood Advisory Council chairman. He was fearless toward the insurgents and their frequent threats.

The Task Force had also initiated an Information Operations Campaign to make sure the insurgents knew we were rebuilding the Neighborhood Advisory Council Building, Iraqi police station, and starting many community projects. We embedded these messages in the literature and talking points for patrols as we engaged the people daily on the streets about the coming elections.

Critical to the success of the elections in Al Saidiyah was to counter the message of the insurgents and Al-Qaeda terrorist cells. Their message was threatening. They were selling an apocalyptic description of Election Day. Insurgent cells warned that mass destruction, suicide bombers, rocket and mortar attacks would erupt across all of Baghdad. Those who voted were called traitors to Iraq and to Muslim followers throughout the world. Their message was relentless: "All sheep would be slaughtered who participated with the Americans to sell Iraq."

Our message was less sinister but no less stern. We used a layered approach. First, the "Wolf and Bear" tactics created a greater presence resulting in the searches of hundreds of homes, and allowed us to place tanks and other armor on the streets almost weekly from mid-December until election week. This was significant because Task Force 1-21 previously had no armor to put on the streets. Accomplishing this required the support and participation of my sister battalions. The presence of tanks had an enormous psychological affect on Iraqis in Al Saidiyah.

Second, we detained over 30 suspects and confiscated hundreds of weapons and thousands of rounds of ammunition. In all these raids and searches, what was found and hauled away was made clearly visible to the people. We made a minor production of it. We did this because in Arab culture, word travels quickest by storytelling and rumors. I wanted big stories and outrageous rumors on the street in the neighborhood. If stories and rumors exaggerated our success and effort, then so much the better.

Third, we interacted directly with young men and as many former military officers as we could find in Al Saidiyah. My lieutenants and senior non-commissioned officers led patrols specifically to engage this population and tell them we will control the air and land in and around Al Saidiyah. Any who challenged us would be killed with the full force of the American Army. I believed this approach would level the playing field, and perhaps convince anyone who was considering disruptive actions to reconsider.

I knew, too, that the other major component to setting the necessary conditions in Al Saidiyah required imam cooperation. Pragmatically I realized actions of the imams would probably have the most profound impact on the entire situation. Given that Al Saidiyah was primarily a Sunni enclave, voter turnout would be highly dependent on imam leadership.

Because Imam Ali Al-Jabouri of the Shakir Al Abood mosque was the chief cleric of the Sunni in Al Saidiyah, I concentrated our efforts on him. I knew the others would do as he directed.

With Ali Al-Jabouri, matters were very complicated. Since

May 2004, I had nurtured a relationship with the imam. In the beginning, I had no idea of the depth of his influence within the Baghdad Sunni community. Learning later that he held a position of leadership for all Sunnis of Baghdad west of the Tigris River, and appreciating the scope of his influence over so many Sunnis, I realized that most likely he was involved with the insurgent resistance of the Coalition. How deeply involved he was, I could not discern.

The intelligence apparatus in First Cavalry Division apparently thought the depth of Ali Al-Jabouri's involvement with insurgent activity ran deeply. The BCT's chief Intelligence Officer, Captain Alvarez, advised me that Special Operations wanted to detain him. The timing could not have been worse. I asked to see the evidence and target folder implicating him. I also went to Colonel Lanza and discussed the matter with him. Although I had no doubt Al-Jabouri was capable, the folder revealed nothing of substance against the imam.

Colonel Lanza was caught in the tension between the Division staff's desire to detain the imam, and my concern about the adverse impact to the stability and execution of elections in Al Saidiyah detaining the imam would have. I proposed that we keep surveillance on him to ensure he did not disappear but delay a raid operation by Special Operations until the day after the elections. With some trepidation, Colonel Lanza agreed and was able to convince the First Cavalry Division intelligence staff that this approach was best.

I was assigned the diplomatic task of keeping Sheik Ali Al-Jabouri in Al Saidiyah and leveraging his position to support the elections. It was crystal clear that the Sunnis were against the elections. The Sunni mantra appeared to be that voting in these elections was tantamount to betraying the "cause." Hard core supporters vowed never to vote.

Anything the Coalition said or did would not change that. But I knew if their clerical leader told them to vote, it would be as if Allah decreed that voting was "moshee" (Iraqi for "OK").

I knew I had to meet with the imam and begin the process of garnering his support. But his support could not just be some tacit, feel-good commitment. Rhetoric and polite appeasement would not be satisfying. The imam had to be willing to do something, especially on Election Day.

My interpreter, Freddie, arranged a meeting at the imam's quarters behind his mosque where we had always met in the past. Although I planned to meet with him multiple times before January 31st, I would take it one meeting at a time, practicing immense patience. My objective in our first sit-down was to talk about the election, i.e., what it meant to the Task Force and his point of view. I envisioned that we would debate the world much like two neighbors grousing over politics back home. From there, I would work my way to what I wanted from him.

From December through mid-January, I met with Imam Ali Al-Jabouri three times. The first meeting we pledged to keep talking and politely disagreed about the future of Iraq. He wanted to talk about U.S. policy and I wanted to talk about Al Saidiyah. Every reference he made to U.S. policy I tried to reduce to its application in Al Saidiyah.

The second meeting allowed for some headway toward my objective. He understood that I wanted to avoid bloody confrontation on the streets of Al Saidiyah these few more days before the election. He pledged to me, man to man, he would not let the situation deteriorate to violence. Though he only committed his support and influence to the sphere of his followers at his mosque, I knew the breadth of his influence and accepted his pledge to keep his little piece of

Al Saidiyah peaceful. Unspoken, we both understood the impact of his commitment.

In our third meeting, I sought to press him to publicly support the elections by telling the people in Al Saidiyah the streets would be safe. I wanted him to get on the loudspeaker in his mosque and in his address, tell the people their safety is guaranteed. This he would not agree to do. He told me that if he were to do that, he would become a target of the insurgents. He then confided to me that he was aware that he was a target of U.S. forces, which to me was a confirmation of his deep involvement with the insurgency. I already knew he was a High Value Target for Special Operations and the First Cavalry Division. That Ali Al-Jabouri knew he was a U.S. target meant he had intelligence sources high and well-placed in the Iraqi Interim Government and Iraqi Army. Of course, I played dumb. I did the best acting job I could muster, dismissing his comments as his nervousness and imagination run amok. Unable to secure his public endorsement of the elections, I contented myself in knowing he at least would work to keep the status quo in Al Saidiyah. And this was enough because I was prepared to psychologically and intellectually maneuver on Election Day. If he were contained at home in his quarters behind the mosque and neutralized from demonstrating overt resistance on Election Day, that would more than suffice. And I had another trick up my sleeve for Election Day, if things weren't going well, in the form of Major Tahseen, my Temporary Iraqi Infrastructure Security Force Commander.

Integral to the Task Force security plan for the election were the various services of the Iraqi security forces. In the Task Force sector we had the Temporary Iraqi Infrastructure Security Force, Iraqi police, and the Iraqi National Guard. Captain Dilawer, who commanded D/304th Infantry, the Iraqi National Guard Company supporting Task Force 1-21, by this time in January had been sent to the Iraqi National Guard Battalion to serve as the S2 Intelligence Officer when his predecessor quit due to threats to his family by insurgents. Captain Dilawer's executive officer was simultaneously elevated to Company Commander, which was fortuitous for us because he was a better leader and officer than Captain Dilawer. The Iraqi National Guard deployed to each of our polling sites and literally garrisoned those sites. The polling sites covered almost all areas of Al Saidiyah.

During the three days leading up to the elections, the entire staff and all leaders in the Task Force were heavily engaged in patrolling and preparing for Election Day activities. Constant checks and logistical support patrols were sent out from Camp Falcon to ensure the Iraqi National Guard troops, Iraqi police units, and Temporary Iraqi Infrastructure Security Force remained in place to carry out their duty of protecting the voters.

After initially deploying the Iraqi National Guard and Temporary Iraqi Infrastructure Security Force, we quickly realized the allocated forces were insufficient. Because Multi-National Forces, Iraq command had directed that no Coalition forces would occupy any polling site, I could not deploy soldiers from Task Force 1-21 to polling sites. We were authorized only to support and advise the Iraqis at the polling sites, so as to avoid any perception that the U.S. was directly influencing the voting. This election process was Iraqi-directed from security implementation to actual election polling administration and everything in between. We were there to assist indirectly and no more.

In my mind this was exactly the right call. Intuitively, I knew that executing this any other way threatened the perception of the legitimacy of these elections. However, I also knew that administering and logistically supporting the election was likely beyond the capabilities of the Iraqis.

Iraqis lacked the organizational skills and experience to administer this election without some small measure of support. Logistically, Iraqis did not have the systems, transportation, and organization to support the distributed Iraqi security forces units deployed. We suspected this from the outset of our efforts to develop the defense plan. Captain Aaron Bright, the Task Force S4, Supply Officer, briefed the executive officer, Major Reinhart, that the Iraqi security forces did not have an effective service and support plan. The difficulty of supporting multiple sites, multiple agencies, and the complex restrictions on movement presented a management problem that exceeded their current logistical abilities. Anticipating this problem early and taking compensating actions was critical to ensuring a legitimate election. The Task Force staff did a great job of developing a support plan. Early on, Captain Bright informed the Iraqi security forces leadership in Al Saidiyah of the help we could provide to shore up their existing service and support plan to establish the defense and inner cordon. Doing this allowed the Iraqi security force units to focus on their defense preparation tasks thus avoiding serious distractions from the mission. This also fostered the sense of teamwork and cooperation that proved invaluable on Election Day.

I walked the fine line between assisting them and avoiding direct involvement to keep the election activities at each polling site on track. Even without insurgent attacks, conducting the election was a challenging undertaking. With the real threat of terrorist attacks constantly looming, the endeavor was monumental.

Two weeks before the elections, the BCT was still scrambling to make sure that the polling sites were properly identified. Information from the Independent Electoral Commission of Iraq (IECI) was sparse and mostly inaccurate by the time it filtered down to BCT level. As hard as the First Cavalry Division staff tried to make sense of the information, it always failed to match up with the reality of the situation on the ground in the sectors. The First Cavalry Division gave all the BCTs the best information available. The actual clarity came from a bottom up refinement process that worked well in the BCT. This part of the preparation was critical to the successful support of the Iraqis. To progress orderly in the election process, units had to know some key things:

• Where the polling sites were physically located on the ground?

• Are the sites up and running?

• Who's manning them?

• When are the ballots arriving?

• How are ballots being transported?

• Who was administering the voting process at each site?

• When were the poll workers arriving?

• How are they being logistically supported?

Limited security resources had to be allocated to support the defense plan overlaying the election administration effort. Essentially, the BCT sought to garrison the polling sites with static, reinforced Iraqi security force units in an inner cordon. These units had to be visible and demonstrate to the people that all the polling sites were well secured.

BCT forces supported the static defense with mobile patrols. These patrols could maneuver against any threat from an outer cordon position. By sustaining an outer cordon, any terrorists seeking to get close to a given polling site had to get through significant barriers and U.S. patrols first. Terrorists also could not be mobile because movement restrictions were in place and reasonably well enforced.

The Interim Iraqi Government declared that all traffic, except military, police, and emergency medical vehicles, was forbidden from movement on the roads from 9 p.m. the night prior to the elections through 9 a.m. the day following the elections. Vehicles authorized for movement had to be marked with distinctive stickers applied the night prior to the vehicle curfew. Everyone was concerned that insurgents would get these markings and use them to penetrate the outer and inner cordons to detonate a huge explosive-laden ambulance or military truck. The markings were critical to the rules of engagement for this operation. All government officials, Iraqi police, Iraqi Army and Iraqi Special Operations units were informed of this marking system.

Emergency Vehicle
Window Stickers

FLUORESCENT STICKERS, 6" X 4" AND STICKY-BACKED, COME IN 3
COLORS AND SHOULD BE ATTACHED TO THE APPROPRIATE VEHICLE:
GREEN – WITH THE INITIALS: 'IA'
ORANGE – WITH THE INITIALS: 'IPS'
WHITE – WITH THE SYMBOLS THE RED CROSS AND A RED CRESCENT

Figure 22.1 — Markings for Iraqi vehicles on Election Day 31 January 2005.

In addition to the coordinated and mutually supporting inner and outer cordon configuration, we employed air support. First Cavalry Division provided a robust helicopter scout and attack air support defense package to each of the five BCTs in the Division. For our Task Force, air assets belonged to the BCT. We had a very flexible and responsive command and control system that allowed air support to move where it was needed in the BCT sector. On Election Day, the plan was to employ these assets wherever needed under BCT control.

One significant factor helping us prepare for a successful Election Day was finding and working closely with the administrators of the IECI in Al Saidiyah. Literally, all the BCT task force commanders were in the streets of their respective sectors looking for and trying to make face-to-face coordination with the local designated IECI representatives.

In several meetings two weeks before the actual elections, with the BCT Commander and his staff, we were asked about the Al Saidiyah IECI representatives. I had been unable to identify or arrange a meeting with anyone. Luckily for the Task Force, our relationships and efforts with the Imam Council paid off. Imam Naal, who was a member of the Al Saidiyah Imam Council, contacted Freddie, my interpreter, a week before the election and told us who the IECI representative for Al Saidiyah was and where we could meet with him. A few days before the election, Sheik Naal opened his mosque to the IECI director in Al Saidiyah and his people where he fed them and protected them from insurgent attacks.

We arranged a meeting to pick up the Al Saidiyah IECI director on the street not far from Imam Naal's mosque. We took him to a polling site on the south side of Al Saidiyah where we conducted a meeting to determine what help he needed.

I was not completely surprised that Imam Naal helped us in this way. Imam Naal was a Shia and the most respected imam on the council. He was very clever and played his cards well. He knew these elections were vitally important to Shia Muslims in Iraq and did what was necessary to facilitate their success in Al Saidiyah. A very patient man, Imam Naal was all about small, progressive steps.

In the meeting with the local Al Saidiyah IECI director, we were able to help him coordinate placement of his workers in the right polling sites and ensure they had food and water. We supplied the Iraqi National Guard soldiers and the IECI workers with all the things they needed. By doing so, we eliminated 90 percent of their problems, which allowed them to focus on their mission. Because they weren't running around looking for food and water, Iraqi soldiers could patrol, man their defensive positions, and focus their attention toward security matters. The IECI workers were able to set up polling sites and make preparations for expeditious handling of voters.

The Task Force worked doggedly to provide the logistics for the Iraqis. We also built the defensive positions for the polling sites. This included emplacing wire and barrier obstacles to restrict and canalize movement in and around the streets of Al Saidiyah. We sought maximum control of all movement in Al Saidiyah. Obviously, our goal was to wrest the initiative away from any group that wanted to attack. Our plan was to take away any insurgent movement and maneuver while maximizing ours. Simultaneously, we intended to bring direct, overwhelming fire onto any insurgents who dared to try anything.

Election Day—Apocalypse Now?

By the early morning of January 31st, Task Force 1-21 was braced for a serious fight. I was extremely confident that if the battalion had to fight, we would easily defeat the enemy. However, to me, a fight before or during the polling was ominous and meant we had failed in all our other efforts. "Supreme excellence consists of breaking the enemy's resistance without fighting," was advice from Sun Tzu I remembered as we prepared for the elections.

The Wolf-and-Bear tactical programs coupled with the political maneuvering of the factions of Shia and Sunni leaders, former Iraqi military officers, and the work with imams were all aimed at breaking the enemy's resistance without fighting. In my preparations for Election Day in Al Saidiyah, victory without a fight was the consistent goal.

Several days before the election, Major Soupene had reconnoitered a great location to place the Task Force Forward Command Post. This Command Post would serve as a Tactical Operations Center deployed into the battle space of the Task Force to manage the units in the inner and outer cordon protecting polling sites in Al Saidiyah. He selected a school building situated a block away from the Shakir Al Abood mosque. This location placed us within a kilometer of Route Irish to our east, which represented a high speed avenue of ingress and egress. It also served as the boundary between Task Force 1-21 and 1-8 Cavalry, one of our sister units in the BCT. If they needed support from us, or vice-versa, we could get there quickly. We had designed routes presuming the enemy would seek to cover the obvious lines of movement to interdict any reaction forces moving laterally across sectors.

By 7 a.m. on January 31st, the worst incident we had dealt with was rocket fire. Two salvos landed north of Al Saidiyah, a few meters out of sector. The explosions obviously scared the residents. By 8 a.m., small groups of people started coming out of their homes and walking to the polling stations.

For the next 90 minutes, the numbers of Iraqis who ventured out to vote were small. Major Soupene went through a systematic check of all polling sites to assess how voter turnout was shaping up. All the polls were open, but the numbers of people were small. We had expected this, but I was concerned that the fear factor was dominating the psyche of the residents.

Major Tahseen came to the Task Force Command Post to discuss his assessment of the small voter turnout. He told me that the Iraqis would start coming in larger numbers as the few who came out to vote passed the word that it was safe to vote. He suggested contacting the mosques to have the imams announce over their speakers that the residents should go to the polls and vote, an idea I fully supported.

By noon, we were inundated with voters throughout the sector. The polling stations literally had long lines of men and women, young and old, waiting to vote. This presented a significant security concern because we knew the crowds would be targets.

The media pundits in Iraq, throughout the Arab world, and in the United States had proclaimed that the elections would fail. The threats of the insurgents were well broadcast by all media across the international community. But a funny thing happened on the way to the polls. Few of the media talked to the Iraqis who had an affirming voice rather choosing to speak only to those with a dissenting voice consistent with the media's political agenda, and even fewer had faith in the U.S. Army and U.S. Marine Corps.

Election Day Outcome in Al Saidiyah

The election process in Al Saidiyah went well. But it was not incident-free. The insurgents who had promised to attack all the polling sites and wreak havoc in some apocalyptic, chaotic rain and hail of bullets and fire across Baghdad managed no more than the launching of haphazard indirect mortar and rocket attacks. None of these attacks were effective in the Task Force sector or the BCT sector at large.

Two significant incidents occurred in the Task Force. The first was about as difficult an event as any commander is required to handle. Iraqi soldiers operating with A/1-21 on the west side of Al Saidiyah shot and seriously wounded the Iraqi Interim Government's Minister of Electricity. He was driving in a BMW automobile in the early morning on Election Day with two other Iraqi men. He was in violation of all security rules imposed by the government in which he served as the head of a ministry. He had no markings on his vehicle as was required. Worse, when attempts were made to stop him with hand and arm signals and other non-lethal means, he tried to evade and escape. He moved his vehicle at a high rate of speed toward several checkpoints. Soldiers from A/1-21 fired warning shots from an observation point atop a nearby apartment building. The Iraqi National Guard soldiers at the ground level checkpoint mistook the warning shots for a signal to fire on the vehicle and they placed a high volume of lethal fire on the BMW, severely wounding the ministry official. The vehicle careened off the road, hit a curb, and stopped. The American Army medic nearest the location immediately began to work on the three wounded occupants, one of which was the Iraqi Minister of Electricity. Meanwhile, the Task Force Physician Assistant was dispatched to the scene with the Task Force ambulance. Lieutenant Scott Helm was on the scene within five minutes. He went to work with the medic and ultimately saved the man's life.

At the Task Force Command Post, we received a report that a car with three Iraqi males was taken under fire and there were wounded. No U.S. or Iraqi Army soldiers were hit, just the men in the car. Immediately, Major Soupene, the S3, went about ascertaining the casualties' identities and the incident details to prepare a report to send to the BCT battle staff. A few minutes later, we were told the identification badges indicated the three Iraqi men in the BMW were from the Iraqi Interim Government's Ministry of Electricity. This identification quickly spawned a million questions. Did we have a friendly-fire incident where soldiers failed to follow procedures? How could we be so cavalier? I got on the radio and sent the commander from A/1-21, Captain Tom Pugsley, to investigate and gather the details and report commander-to-commander. Although I was tempted to head over myself, I decided to go only if the battery commander's report warranted my presence. I still had an entire sector to direct; one incident could not consume all my attention.

Major Soupene, meanwhile, worked on getting assessments about the incident. Our initial read was that soldiers from A/1-21 fired on the vehicle because it was unmarked and was not supposed to be on the road in accordance with all directives published and announced across Iraq prior to Election Day. Even so, I was upset that soldiers would take that as license to engage with lethal force. We had always practiced "show, shout, shove, and shoot." As I contemplated it for a few minutes in solitude, I decided I would not over-react. I decided I was confident the soldiers did what we worked hard training them to do. The facts from the initial command inquiry would come out soon enough; I would deal with those results. So, I went back to focusing on managing the big picture, letting the S3 and the battery commander work through the situation, gather facts, and then assess what had occurred.

Lieutenant Helm patched up the three men and evacuated them to our level II medical facility. Colonel Lanza showed up at the Task Force Command Post about an hour later. I briefed him on what we knew, updating our initial reports to his staff. Although he indicated he was satisfied with our handling of the situation, he wanted to know the results of the investigation. Clearly, this incident would elevate to high levels since a high ranking official in the Interim Iraqi Government had nearly been killed.

After the local commander's inquiry investigation was complete a more formal 15-6 investigation was conducted on this incident and we eventually had to forward this to Division. I believe the report was reviewed at even higher levels. The investigation found that the ministry official violated almost all the designated safety procedures and, though awful, the soldiers acted within the strict limits of the Rules of Engagement and had carried out their duty properly.

The second serious incident that occurred on Election Day went much differently. On the north side of Al Saidiyah, a platoon of A/1-21 was attacked by a small, dismounted, insurgent infantry squad armed with grenades and AK-47 rifles. After the polls closed, this insurgent squad attempted to attack one of the polling sites where we intended to consolidate the ballots from our sector. Whoever was informing the insurgents had given them the right information about which polling site to attack.

Lieutenant Adam Jacobs' platoon was assigned to the outer cordon security for one of the sixteen polling sites in the Task Force sector. After the voting was over, they were attacked with a ground assault originating from a palm grove across a four-lane highway on the northern boundary of Al Saidiyah. Lieutenant Jacobs had positioned his observation posts perfectly to respond with enfilading fire from the rooftops with squad automatic weapons and M-16 rifles. The platoon fought the enemy squad element to a standstill keeping them in the palm grove and not allowing them to cross the highway. To gain the initiative and protect his soldiers, Lieutenant Jacobs requested attack helicopter support from his battery commander, Captain Tom Pugsley. Captain Pugsley pushed the air support request to the Task Force Command Post where I was at, about three kilometers away. The S-3 called to the BCT and requested the air scout and attack aviation assets. The BCT passed the air assets to the Task Force and Major Soupene vectored the air support in from the southern part of the BCT sector and then notified me the air attack team was inbound. I decided to pass the attack aviation element directly to Lieutenant Jacobs who was in contact with the enemy fighting the close engagement. Lieutenant Jacobs talked the aircraft onto the target and then lazed the center point of the enemy formation for the pilots. The pilots ripped 14 rockets at the enemy position, ending the fight decisively. All the practice and training we had done the past months paid off, however fleeting a moment it was.

The rest of that evening and into the early morning hours of February 1, 2005 we provided security and logistical support to the Iraqis so they could move the thousands of ballots cast to central collection points. This election was the first of more to come. It was a proud moment for the Task Force as we accomplished our mission and created the conditions for profound change in Iraq. It was definitely something that could be built upon for the future.

What I believe many Americans did not understand about the Iraqi National Elections in January 2005, and that the American mass media buried in the aftermath, is that Iraq, on January 31st, 2005, made a bold and historic attempt to step into the light of freedom and democracy. Iraq moved inexorably away from yesterday and embraced tomorrow. In the grand scheme of the so-called global war on terror, this step by Iraq into the light may well signal the beginning of a new day in the Middle East. Although time and events ultimately decide, at this point of the conflict, Iraqis tried to make an honorable move toward free self-determination.

23 Taking Stock, Finding No Solace

*"This was my chance to help these people to have a life
like ours. The price was worth it, in my heart" SFC
David J. Salie, KIA — February 14, 2005, Iraq[25]*

The resounding success of the Iraqi National Elections was
the crowning event for the Task Force in our one year tour
of duty. Al Saidiyah was as secure a place as one could
hope for in Baghdad on January 31, 2005. The soldiers and
young Task Force leaders had performed magnificently.
Our ability to work with and support the various elements
of the Iraqi security forces allocated to Task Force 1-21 was
first class. The one concerted insurgent attack we faced was
convincingly defeated in a very short amount of time and
had no impact on the election outcome. All the systems put
in place to secure Al Saidiyah worked superbly. I was very
proud of the soldiers of the Task Force.

Though many senior American politicians, diplomats, and
military leaders touted the success of the elections as the
death knell of the insurgency, I knew better. The qualification of success lay in the potential for a democracy to grow
and build in Iraq. Because the Sunnis were the basis of the
insurgency, I understood the insurgency would continue
since generally the Sunnis did not endorse the elections.
The only way to defeat the insurgent efforts was by countering its political arguments and that requires a broad,
unified effort, with a local dimension to the process which
was not commonly pursued during the time Task Force 1-
21 operated in Baghdad. The election turnout and outcome
merely provided a glimmer of hope.

By the first week in February 2005, I was able to take stock
of all that the Task Force had done. Overall, Task Force 1-21
had realized tremendous organizational development and

growth; we had made monumental strides. Contrasting that, though, were our efforts to improve the situation in our piece of Baghdad, which had progressed only a little. I had hoped for and worked tirelessly to match my vision with reality, but I knew we had fallen short. There was truly unfinished business. We needed another year.

As a military organization, Task Force 1-21 had truly gone through a complete metamorphosis, successfully transforming from a conventional rocket artillery battalion to a counterinsurgent infantry/cavalry task force that had a high degree of capability. We were able to execute, quite effectively, our part of the Five LOO Oasis Campaign directed from the BCT. All soldiers of the Task Force mastered the everyday jobs of operating as infantry/cavalry. They had grown and were quite adaptable and capable of handling a variety of situations professionally and with great discipline. Regardless of the assigned Military Occupational Specialty of soldiers in the organization, all had become quite skillful in all the basic infantry soldier tasks that were required of them. They were also proficient in conducting expert reconnaissance, civil affairs support and psychological operations support. Most importantly, all of the soldiers were able to fight the enemy effectively in close combat.

Junior leaders had developed a sharp edge, a self-confident swagger, and a permanent warrior ethos that they had not arrived in Iraq with. Clearly, they were more-seasoned masters of the Army-sanctioned troop leading procedures as well as skilled in the art and science of applying small-unit tactics to engage and defeat an enemy force. Across the myriad of operating systems that an Army maneuver battalion must function, the Task Force was operating optimally in combat for many months. Their growth was nothing short of phenomenal.

With respect to improving the condition of the average Iraqi residing in the mahallas of Al Saidiyah, we had brought about improvement. We took security and stability to a level higher than we received. Although not readily discerned, the measure the Task Force applied was an assessment of the criminal and insurgent activity, which was compared with that across Al Rashid. And Al Saidiyah was in fact, significantly less volatile than other enclaves of Al Rashid.

The Iraqi security forces moved ever so slightly and incrementally to a higher level of competency. But here, too, we had not overcome the shortcomings plaguing these forces. Much work lay ahead.

The Iraqi Army elements that worked with the Task Force were still not completely capable of planning and executing autonomous operations. The Iraqi Army supply system had improved but still did not attain the level of effectiveness needed to support the growing numbers of soldiers so that they could fight with confidence and without direct American help. Leaders were getting better and the soldiers that filled the ranks were becoming more competent, but they were not able to perform without significant coaching and mentoring. In short, they were not able to go it alone yet.

This assessment left me feeling somewhat melancholy. I was very self-critical and refused to indulge in the back-slapping self-aggrandizement that was sprouting around me. I had no illusions about what very little progress we had made. I had hoped to have progressed further than we had. I knew there had been no lack of effort and we had done our very best with every resource we had available; however, had we been given more latitude and better resources, I believe we could have done more. And the Iraqis needed much more.

The Slaying of Dr. Khalid

My personal feelings of glum were exacerbated by another difficult event. In the first week of February 2005, one of the cruelest realities of my year in Iraq would occur. My friend who had served as the Imam Council Coordinator, the gentleman we called Dr. Khalid, disappeared.

At the last Neighborhood Advisory Council meeting I attended before departing Iraq, Dr. Khalid behaved oddly. He had been at the meeting for about ten minutes and then told me he had to leave. As Dr. Khalid rose from his chair to leave, I walked to the door with him and asked what was going on.

"Colonel Booman, I have been threatened many times these past few days. I must make some distance for awhile. It is ok, not a problem. I must go." His face was flush. His eyes told me he had a deep-seated fear.

"How can I help you? Do you need protection? I can have you live at Camp Falcon for a few days," I told him.

He refused and simply said, "Colonel, I must go."

I never saw him again, not alive or dead. Dr. Khalid was gone.

On February 4th, my interpreter, Freddie, received a phone call from Omar, Dr. Khalid's son. Omar reported that some masked men had abducted his father from their house in Al Saidiyah. According to Omar, some armed men, most in civilian clothes, blocked with their cars the two ends of the street where Dr. Khalid lived. They broke into Dr. Khalid's house and took him along with his car, cell phone, paperwork of his anti-terrorism organization, and letters of recommendation from Americans.

Omar further described, "The ones who came to our house were six men with radios and weapons. All of them were wearing face masks. Four of them were wearing civilian clothes, while the other two were wearing a uniform that looked like an Iraqi police uniform with lieutenant rank. Their cars were a black Mark and a brown Toyota Corolla, both muddy, with right-side steering wheels and no license plates. I could see one of their badges and it was red with black writing and a horizontal layout."

Dr. Khalid's son also mentioned that on their way out of the house, he heard one of the abductors whispering to someone on the radio saying, "Yes sir, we are the Iraqi police commandos."

Omar kept trying to call Dr. Khalid's cell phone but it remained switched off. The next day, February 5th, someone answered the phone and identified himself as Lieutenant Alaa, and let Omar talk to his father. Dr. Khalid told his son that he was at a police station but not the Al Bayaa police station, the station closest to where Dr. Khalid lived. Dr. Khalid told his son that the people were very friendly and understanding, and said that somebody in Al Saidiyah had given a false report about him to the Iraqi police.

Then someone took the phone from Dr. Khalid and said, "Everything is ok, your father will be fine. We are located at Zayoona, Jammaya area, in front of the building of the new Ministry of Culture and Media. Just have someone from the American Forward Operating Base call us and verify that Dr. Khalid is good and clean."

After receiving Omar's report, Freddie repeatedly called Dr. Khalid's cell phone but it was switched off except for one time when somebody answered, saying that it was not Dr. Khalid's cell phone and he doesn't know any Dr. Khalid. After that, the phone remained switched off.

Five hours later we learned Dr. Khalid's fate. An Iraqi police patrol found Dr. Khalid's car in Al Saidiyah with his dead body in the trunk. My friend had been shot two times in the head and two times in his chest. The car was taken to the Al Bayaa police station and Dr. Khalid's body was taken to Yarmook hospital.

Freddie came and told me the bad news. I wanted to go see Omar but Freddie told me that going to see Omar would endanger him. Freddie was right; I felt responsible and there was nothing I could do.

We tried to figure out what happened. Who were the men that abducted Dr. Khalid and then killed him like this? What message were they trying to send? Dr. Khalid seemed to know he was going to get killed. Why wouldn't he let me help him? Despite all our intelligence efforts, we never definitively learned the answer.

I turned to Freddie and Omar who as Iraqis might provide the best guesses as to how Dr. Khalid may have been murdered. Their assessment was that the men who abducted and killed Dr. Khalid were not insurgents but rather a militia force operating inside the Iraqi police organization. The red badges and the description matched Army commandos, Iraqi police commandos, or Iraqi police intelligence special quick-reaction forces.

In their opinion, these incidents were tied to an earlier assassination of one of the Shia Neighborhood Advisory Council members, Hanoon. After Hanoon was killed, his tribe threatened many Sunnis in Al Saidiyah and held them responsible. Hanoon's tribesmen called for blood revenge. On several occasions Dr. Khalid had been accused by Hanoon's tribesmen of having been involved in Hanoon's assassination because he was a prominent Sunni in Al Saidiyah. There was a very good chance that the men who murdered Dr. Khalid were avenging Hanoon's earlier assassination. Such is the nature of Iraqi behavior and a significant aspect of the war that is happening in Iraq.

Of all the possibilities, this seemed the most plausible. Though I did not want to believe this, the explanation made sense. The diabolical and sinister hatred that manifests itself in violence and blood vengeance among Iraqis is not easily assuaged even by the mighty American Army. Pursuing practical work is exponentially more complex in this environment. Dr. Khalid's death was illustrative of the many miles of distance yet to be traveled in Iraq.

Thankfully, for Task Force 1-21 the end was nearing. In a few weeks the advance parties of the Third Infantry Division would arrive. We would press on to handing off our sector to a unit of the Third Infantry Division and Iraq would begin to fade into memory. The hand-off would prove to be even more telling about the ineffectiveness of the American military leadership in Iraq. For the entire BCT, though, the arrival of Third Infantry Division was very exciting.

The Third Infantry Division—Handing Off the War

Prior to the arrival of their advance parties, the Third Infantry Division made the decision not to establish a BCT headquarters at Camp Falcon. Apparently, their plan was to have a battalion task force about one-quarter the size of 5th BCT take control of the Al Rashid district of Baghdad. Upon hearing this and seeing the hand-off plan, I was flabbergasted. What we were undermanned to execute, they were going to attempt with a significantly smaller force. All the gains the BCT and Task Force 1-21 had made in the past year would evaporate within the first month 3rd Battalion, 7th Infantry Regiment (3-7 Infantry) was on the ground. There was simply no way to sustain the gains with such a small force.

Since the BCT sector would be reduced to leadership by a mere battalion task force meant Task Force 1-21's sector would necessarily be replaced with a company. A captain would command and manage the affairs of Al Saidiyah. We had barely made headway with a 683-soldier force and now D/3-7 Infantry would have less than 150 soldiers to attempt to sustain the inroads we had made. Few Army captains have the depth of experience needed to handle an area this large and complex. I hoped the commander of D/3-7 Infantry was so blessed. But after our first meeting, it was patently obvious to me that he was not. He certainly was not incompetent, but he did not have the experience and seasoning to assimilate all the subtleties and nuances of this counterinsurgent fight.

Regardless of my misgivings about the program the new division would employ, the reality was that all the standards the Iraqis in Al Rashid had become accustomed to were about to dramatically change. This did not bode well for progression to occur in the overall American effort. I hoped that this situation was an anomaly in the bigger scheme of things across Baghdad.

The overall Army force replacing First Cavalry Division in Baghdad was smaller in size and radically different in scheme. The direct overlay we had meticulously executed with First Armor Division set conditions for success. In one changeover, I felt, all our work was going to disintegrate. I was heartsick about that, but again, I had no power to influence this. Senior leaders in the Army had to manage this process and, from my vantage point, I could plainly see these leaders were not tending to this issue.

While the handover was going on, the Task Force was simultaneously preparing to depart Camp Falcon and road-march in convoys out of Iraq to Kuwait, reversing the process by which we had deployed, and head back to Fort Hood.

I had one last serious piece of business to attend to before I could end my war in Iraq. I had been working for months to save my interpreter from a certain fate of assassination after the Task Force departed from Iraq. The hand-off process was pathetically lacking between American military units, the Iraqi terps were in a very precarious situation. The murder of Dr. Khalid proved to me that once we were gone, Freddie would be next. The previous attempts on his life already merely brought this point home more directly. I was willing to give all my professional and personal efforts into saving Freddie from that fate. Time was running out.

Saving Freddie

Saving Freddie, to me, meant getting him out of Iraq and to the United States. Although it was not imperative that Freddie ultimately get to the United States, it was the only way I could conceive to directly help him after leaving Iraq with the Task Force. I did not believe Freddie would be safe anywhere in the Middle East because I feared insurgents or terrorists might find him and exact their revenge. The vengeance factor runs deep among Arabs, much deeper than most Americans realize.

With the assistance of several people and going through a very rigorous process with the United States Customs and Immigration Service, Fadi was able to get an "O" category visa to assist in the post production effort of a New York filmmaker who had made a film entitled "Interpreting Iraq". The film chronicled Task Force 1-21 preparing for and executing our part of the Iraqi National Elections.

Freddie would travel to Amman, Jordan on February 5, 2005 and await the official papers for his authorization to go to the United States. It was a bittersweet day for me. I was still concerned that he was in danger but happy the process had begun to get him out of Iraq before the situation changed so radically he would not likely survive.

Freddie's departure was symbolic of how I related to this war and my role in it. I had come with idealistic, maybe even romantic notions about war, certain we were going to win. I left feeling disillusioned and feeling unsuccessful; not something I was used to in my Army career. I spent a year giving my heart and soul to helping the Iraqis, but few tangible rewards were realized. Nothing was clear-cut and I had felt awfully lonely most of the time. Despite the many failings, somehow we left the situation better than we found it. But I knew that all we had done was not enough. I am left with a longing to do more.

24 Home Sweet Home and The Mahalla Plan for Victory

"It is fatal to enter any war without the will to win it." General Douglas MacArthur

For me, the war is over. Once we returned to Fort Hood, all the soldiers of the Task Force went through the business of acclimating to a new world back in America. After a year of fighting, toiling, sweating, bleeding, crying, and dying in Iraq, our new task was to dismantle the Task Force and reassemble 1-21 Field Artillery. And then we could rest.

I would soon be surrendering my beloved command to another officer who would carry the colors of 1-21 Field Artillery on the next leg of the unending command marathon. I dreaded June 30, 2005, with as much anguish as I had felt the weeks before March 15, 2004, when we departed for Iraq.

In March 2005, while we were in Kuwait re-deploying, I made my final decision to retire at my twentieth year of service. I knew that I would not only be giving up the battalion command, I would be giving up the Army. The Army was reorganizing to fashion a BCT-centric organizational design across the force. All division artillery organizations were programmed for dismantling. Field Artillery Colonels had commanded these organizations; now they would no longer exist. Moreover, Field Artillery officers would no longer be considered by Army competitive command selection boards to command any of the new-fangled BCTs. The new Army no longer had any room for Field Artillery officers to command these formations. I loved to command and I knew this Army decision severely limited my professional options. I could see no way to achieve my personal and professional ambitions in this new system.

Dreams die hard and admittedly I was very depressed about letting that dream go. I was cutting myself from the team because the senior leaders of the Army had decided because of my specialty branch in the Army — I and all my peers — also designated Field Artillery, were not fit to command a BCT. I didn't want to serve in an organization that could be that shortsighted in its decision-making. I had served for twenty years and had given the Army every ounce of myself every day of those twenty years. I was proud of my contribution. I felt I could compete based on my record and that, if selected, I could do as well as or better than any in that peer group. The Army is a vast organization and decisions like this are made for the good of the organization. And though I was never made privy to the policy behind the decision, I had to make a decision and fortunately I had the freedom to leave. It was a bittersweet decision, but it was the right one for me.

In August 2005, I left Fort Hood and the Army and drove north on Interstate 35, returning to the only other place I could call home, the Twin Cities of Minnesota. Though I grew up an Army brat, I had attended high school in Bloomington, a Minneapolis suburb, and I had graduated from college at the University of Minnesota. My wife was originally from the south side of Minneapolis and her family resides in the Twin Cities metropolitan area. And, my mother and her husband lived in Shoreview, Minnesota. I felt returning to Minnesota was the right thing for us.

In tow with my wife, son, and me was Freddie. He had become more than a brother in Iraq and I wanted to help him become an American as I sensed the fate of Iraq in the final accounting will be abandonment by America. To help Freddie become an American, I felt he needed to come with me. We all went to my mother-in-law's home in Apple Valley, Minnesota. I was worried that having Freddie would be awkward and unnatural to my in-laws, Donald and Nancy Crews, and to my mother. But surprisingly, all welcomed and supported Freddie with open arms.

Freddie lived with us at my in-laws until October 2005, when he moved into an apartment. We continued to work on his immigration status and pursued permanent residency in the U.S.

From August 2005 until March 2006, we negotiated our way through the labyrinth of the immigration system first seeking to secure an H-1B visa and then political asylum. In November 2005, Freddie completed his application for political asylum. While we were waiting for a ruling from the Immigration and Naturalization Service (INS), we were informed that a recently-passed law in January 2006 might conclusively resolve Freddie's case. A provision in the National Defense Authorization Act of 2006 would grant permanent residency and a green card to fifty Iraqi or Afghani interpreters who had served for 12 months or more as translators for U.S. military units that passed a military background check. A general officer had to testify to the applicant's qualifications in a written letter to the United States Customs and Immigration Service (USCIS). The applicant was also required to pass a medical examination.

We secured a letter from Lieutenant General Peter Chiarelli. Freddie easily qualified and is one of the first applicants for this permanent residency opportunity under the new law.

On March 15, 2006, Freddie received official notification granting him political asylum in the U.S. for an indefinite period. Persistence, patience, hard work, conviction, and faith secured this opportunity for Freddie. Perhaps this formula can prevail for America's efforts in Iraq.

Through all my experiences in Iraq the most compelling truth I discovered is that winning decisively for the American effort is tied to one thing: local democratic governance. It is the missing piece to the very complex puzzle. All the military effort in the world will not realize decisive victory unless it is focused and capable of setting the conditions to establish local democratic governance across Iraq. My vision for victory is different from the one being pursued today.

My Vision for Victory: "The Mahalla Plan"

The mahalla is the smallest area of a district neighborhood in Baghdad (or any major Iraqi city). The mahalla is where the insurgents plan operations and where they hide among the families and tribe members; in short, it is where they dominate. The mahalla also represents the locale where seeding democracy has the very best chance of providing a reliable foundation to undergird the national democratic effort. Simultaneously, it is in the mahalla where Americans and legitimate Iraqi government can directly assail the insurgents politically. Just as in the U.S. "all politics is local", so too in Iraq. Baghdad is the capital city, and as Baghdad goes, so goes Iraq. Therefore, America must shift its political focus to the mahalla level of day-to-day life in Baghdad.

I firmly believe a modification of strategy and change in methods by senior political and military leaders to bring harmony to the politics of Iraq through a bottom-up governance approach is the best road to victory. Not only that, but the experience of our unit in Iraq shows that the U.S. military has the means and capability in 2007 to put this plan into practice and can expect it to succeed.

My proposal for "the mahalla plan to victory" is as follows:

The capital city is divided into districts and neighborhoods made up of mahallas within those districts. The Coalition

Provisional Authority established neighborhood advisory councils, District Advisory Councils, and a City Advisory Council, a system that continues to function to this day. This political structure can be used to accomplish the goal. In my vision, these entities would be re-named "Neighborhood Council", "District Council", and "City Council", dropping the "advisory" tag. Each council would be assigned a governing functional role with a budget provided by the existing national legislature to use in their areas until some other revenue mechanism can be installed to sustain each entity. To establish representative councils, the sitting City Advisory Council would draw residential boundaries, defining very specifically which blocks constitute each district and each neighborhood. Each level council would have a specified number of members and each would have an administrative support staff. The ethnic, religious, and social representation would occur through the natural election process. All councils would have a member elected among the council to be the council leader. All council members would serve two-year terms with chairmembers serving for one year.

An Imam Council for each echelon must also be formed. This council would be determined by the imams of each mosque in a given neighborhood locale as designated by the boundaries assigned by the Baghdad City Council. The District-level and Baghdad city-level Imam Council would vote members from each of the mahallas. Imam councils above the neighborhood level would have six imams. These imams would elect a fellow imam to lead the Imam Council at the District and City level. This Imam council would be required to hold an advisory role for the respective governing council. Because the Muslim faith directly affects all that occurs in the mahalla, the political efficacy of any governing entity in the neighborhoods of Baghdad requires this close interaction. Americans will not understand this, as it is not something the American public is familiar with. Imams and the powerful influence of the Muslim faith among the masses cannot be discounted. Discounting this aspect of Iraqi life and politics has stifled what the American military has been trying to do for years in Baghdad.

For the governing councils, local elections to seat these councils, placing money in the hands of residents in neighborhoods to govern the spending, and mentoring the councils to govern the parts that make up the whole would directly attack the insurgency. This approach stands a better chance of stabilizing the situation more directly and faster than attempting a top-down, national, democratic installation of government. But shifting the political governance mechanism and paradigm alone is not enough. The security program must also support this design.

So, parallel with the political line of local governing organization, Iraqi police precincts need to be established along traditional lines and directly associated with neighborhoods or mahallas, and leadership within the Iraqi police must answer to the local councils. This would shift the present day national police force into a localized one that serves the needs of the neighborhoods, districts, and ultimately the city.

Each neighborhood should have an Iraqi police station house built in a mahalla of the neighborhood boundaries. Each district needs a precinct station headquarters and the Iraqi police could have a police captain running the station houses and a police lieutenant colonel running the precinct headquarters. If the neighborhood councils had influence with the security of their neighborhoods through interaction with a responsive Iraqi police force stationed amid the council's jurisdictional boundaries, local security would be more readily managed and effectively directed. Again, all is predicated on a representative council and its power to dispense money through a budget based on council-established priorities.

Local policing is but one component of security. There remains a military component to winning this war. The military component must also be factored into the equation if the insurgency is to be defeated.

The most important military entity to success in Iraq is the Iraqi Army. A Military District of Baghdad could be established if it does not already exist. Units of the Iraqi Army should be assigned specific neighborhoods and districts matching the established political boundaries. The unit size for a neighborhood must be at least that of a battalion. The unit size for a district must be at least that of a brigade. The commanders of the units assigned at the neighborhood level and the district level would work with same-level Iraqi police commanders and report to the councils on security matters. Iraqi brigades should establish bases with headquarters in each district of Baghdad from which operations should be directed and long-term presence established. This model and organizational design should set the necessary conditions for a synergistic association among the political, military, and police leaders. The effect of their collaborative efforts would be to secure the local areas of Baghdad and politically marginalize and militarily isolate the insurgent entities. Insurgents operate in the mahallas, politically, logistically, and militarily. Therefore, that is where they must be assailed.

Obviously, the other key component in the major military organization is the United States armed forces. Applying this model, a significant reduction in American Army and Marine combat forces would follow. Instead, robust advisory teams would be established to serve three key advisory functions: local democratic political mentorship, military advisory assistance for the Iraqi Army units, and police advice to local Iraqi police leaders. The design of these teams would have to be unconventional in that the Army and Marines might not be the sole entities to provide these mentor-coaches. I see Army Special Forces officers and teams taking the lead role for the military component of this design. I envision a U.S. State Department person, an Army officer (Special Forces), and a seasoned police officer from a police force of a large U.S. city forming a triumvirate leadership team. Each would have a supporting staff organized into flexible governance advisory teams. Initially, the Army officer would serve as the team leader. But as the situation developed and the insurgency waned, a natural shift to state department or police mentor-coach personnel assuming primary leadership of these governance advisory teams would follow.

To facilitate the mentor-coach process and overlay all the governance advisory team actions would be a highly competent Iraqi Interpreter Corps. The formation, special training, and careful distribution of a specially-skilled and well-trained pool of directly-assigned interpreters could make a profound difference in the direction of this war for Americans. Communication between Americans and Iraqis is vital to success. Having competent, highly-skilled, and well-integrated interpreters would qualitatively elevate the effectiveness of operations and assist the Iraqi citizenship in realizing self-determination. In Iraq today, this capability is haphazard at best and misses the mark of the full potential of effective communication among Americans and Iraqis. In this kind of war, interpreters and cultural interface in a highly-competent manner is essential to mission accomplishment and is widely overlooked as a salient part of the operations process.

What I propose could easily be established with the existing resources and designs with which Iraqis and American military leaders are already familiar. This local paradigm would not require much modification within the existing systems.

I do not advocate the abandonment of the national democratic-political effort. But perhaps a less aggressive effort is warranted. Iraq does not succeed or fail on the formation and immediate success of a national democratic government. That proposition is already failing. There is too much dissension, inequity, and too many old scores to settle for national democratic government to take root without a viable local effort to ignite the process. A combined bottom-up and top-down approach that first emphasizes the bottom-up and then later transitions to a more robust top-down approach will work in Iraq.

The current program has proven indecisive and a politically abject failure for the Iraqis and Americans alike. The only viable entity in this whole war effort has been the U.S. Army and Marine Corps. But neither can win the war of insurgency because it is not militarily assailable. It is the triumvirate of political, military, and civil action orchestrated and synthesized with a mindfulness of cultural context in which it is applied that must occur if the United States and her allies have any hope of a decisive victory in the many struggles that lie ahead.

Exit Strategy

America can win decisively in Iraq but to win, the senior political and military leadership must adjust fire far more radically than they appear to be willing to indulge right now. Time is of the essence. Additionally, this war in Iraq must have an end in sight and a means by which to let go of Iraq's dependence without abandoning that which America has created. In short, America needs a viable exit strategy.

The United States holds a unique position now after four years in Iraq. That position is one whereby the senior political leaders can transition the war to one of less American military presence without full and unconditional abdication of its goals in Iraq and the region.

The Iraqis have moved inexorably toward a national representative democratic government. The Iraqi military capability has improved and will continue to gain strength through refined capability. When local democratic governance develops into something capable and effective, the ability of this society to democratically pursue and ultimately realize self-determination becomes more likely.

The forthcoming American military role that should be pursued in the very near future is one of reduced presence and full transition to a military and civil affairs advisory assistance role.

Politically, the United States is hard-pressed to continue on a path of escalation and open-ended commitment to Iraq. There is in fact a war on terror and the global nature of that war cannot be monopolized by one country at the existing pace of funding. Our military also cannot sustain this commitment without exceptional cost to the all-volunteer system and the future national defense needs of this nation.

In 1958, when the U.S. began to get involved in Vietnam, the war became a gradual and continuous escalation of involvement. The early American military efforts in Vietnam saw the implementation of the Military Advisory Assistance Command, Vietnam (MAACV). This organization provided American military advisors to help build and develop a capable South Vietnamese Army known as the Army of the Republic of Vietnam (ARVN). While the politics and situation are radically different in Iraq than they were in Vietnam, the organizational functional capability of an organization like MAACV, in my view, is exactly what can help in this contemporary operational environment. The application of this process must be the reverse and functionally serve as the mechanism for de-escalation in Iraq. To extricate from Iraq, the military needs to implement a Military-Civil Advisory Assistance Command, Iraq.

Doing this will allow for significant reduced combat troop presence in Iraq, leave a capable and viable coach-teach-mentor operation functioning in Iraq, and likely reduce the political stress in the American electorate simultaneously providing a viable capability to assist the Iraqis while not abandoning their needs as we have created them with our incursion into their national affairs to protect against the threats to America since 2003.

The critical conditions that must be met are:

- Local governing councils must be democratically seated and fully funded to support a local governance capability that does not function right now in Iraq

- Iraqi police must be completely localized and responsible to the local councils

- Iraqi Army must have fielded the requisite divisions as determined by General Petraeus and declared ready by General Petraeus

- A Military and Civil Affairs Advisory Assistance Command must be established, prepared, and ready to assume full operational control of support actions in Iraq

- State Department must get in the act by deploying and fielding Mentor Support Teams to assist as advisors to the Iraqi Government

This method and the critical operational details of the execution can be worked out by the professionals serving in the military and State Department.

The process of de-escalation needs to begin in 2008. By doing this, America begins to hand full governance responsibility and self-determination to the Iraqi people. After all, that has to be the principled outcome of any American effort in Iraq consistent with our national values and the purpose for which America goes to war: to free the oppressed and defend freedom.

Endnotes

[1] Coppola, Francis F., *Apocalypse Now*, quote of character "Captain Willard" played by actor Martin Sheen, 1979.

[2] Ranger Training Brigade, *Ranger Course Pamphlet*, Retrieved from: http://www.benning.army.mil/rtb/RANGER/pam/rgrcourse.htm

[3] Graphic built using Earth Google satellite imagery

[4] Lanza, Stephen, Colonel, U.S. Army, *Field Artillery Conference "Lines of Operation Brief"*, May 2005.

[5] Sun Tzu, *The Art of War*, A U.S. Army Monograph, translated by Lionel Giles, edited by Brigadier General Thomas R. Phillips (USA), 1963, p. 96.

[6] U.S. Army Field Manual 3-0, *Operations*, Headquarters Department of the Army, June 2001, p. 1-16.

[7] Chiarelli, Peter, Major General and Commanding General-First Cavalry Division, *Oasis – First Cavalry Division Campaign Briefing (public media version)*, January 2004, chart #3.

[8] G3 Section, *Oasis Campaign Brief*, First Cavalry Division "Oasis" Campaign briefing chart, April 2004.

[9] Kipling, Rudyard, *If*, Retrieved from: http://www.swarthmore.edu/~apreset1/docs/if.html

[10] Hal Erickson, *All Movie Guide*, Retrieved from: http://movies.channel.aol.com/movie/main.adp?tab=synop&mid=6864&uid=5532

11 Coalition Provisional Authority, *Baghdad Citizen Advisory Council Handbook,* Third Edition, November 2003, Chapter 5.

12 The Supreme Council for the Islamic Revolution in Iraq (SCIRI), Ayatollah Mohamad Baqir Al Hakim, Retrieved from: http://www.sciri.btinternet.co.uk/English/About_Us/Badr/badr.html

13 Lieutenant General McKiernan, Commanding General-Combined Forces Land Component Command, *CFLCC Briefing-Rules of Engagement,* Headquartered in Doha, Kuwait 2004.

14 Daniel Williams, *Italian Calls U.S. Gunfire Unjustified--Account of Reporter Wounded In Iraq Differs From Military's,* Washington Post Foreign Service Sunday, March 6, 2005; Page A18 Retrieved from: http://www.washingtonpost.com/wp-dyn/articles/A10647-2005Mar5.html

15 Ann Scott Tyson, *More Objections to Women-in-Combat Ban,* Washington Post Staff Writer, Wednesday, May 18, 2005, Retrieved from America Online May 2005.

16 Amer, Mildred L., *Membership of the 108th Congress: A Profile,* CRS Report for Congress, 25 October 2004, p. 6, Annex pages 1-3.

17 Griffith, Frank, AP, *Female Marines Ambushed in Iraq,* June 25, 2005, Retrieved from America Online June 2005.

18 Wood, Sara, U.S. Army Sergeant, *Woman Soldier Receives Silver Star for Valor in Iraq,* American Forces Press Service, Washington, June 16, 2005, Retrieved from AFPS June 2005.

19 U.S. Army, *Seven Army Values,* Retrieved from: http://www.army.mil/cmh-pg/LC/The%20Mission/the_seven_army_values.htm

[20] L. Paul Bremmer III with Malcom McConnell, *My Year in Iraq*, Simon & Schuster, New York 2006, p. 54-60.

[21] Stephen R. Lanza, Field Artillery Journal, *Red Team Goes Maneuver: First Cavalry Division Artillery as a Maneuver BCT in Operation Iraqi Freedom II*, Volume X No. 3, May-June 2005, p. 12.

[22] Stephen R. Lanza, Field Artillery Journal, *Red Team Goes Maneuver: First Cavalry Division Artillery as a Maneuver BCT in Operation Iraqi Freedom II*, Volume X No. 3,May-June 2005, p. 12.

[23] Stephen R. Lanza, Field Artillery Journal, *Red Team Goes Maneuver: First Cavalry Division Artillery as a Maneuver BCT in Operation Iraqi Freedom II*, Volume X No. 3,May-June 2005, p. 12.

[24] Associated Press writer Jim Krane; story filed from Dubai, United Arab Emirates.

[25] U.S. Army Field Manual 3-0, Operations, Headquarters Department of the Army, June 2001.

[25] From a videotape left behind by Sergeant First Class David J. Salie who recorded the video to be played in the event of his death which, unfortunately, came to pass. David Salie's brother, Captain Brian Salie, served with TF 1-21 our last few months in Iraq, and replaced Major Rob Dixon as the Task Force's Civil Affairs Team Chief.

Glossary — Acronyms and Army Terms

Active Duty – Full-time duty in the active military service of the United States. This includes members of the Reserve Components serving on active duty or full-time training duty, but does not include full-time National Guard duty. Also called AD.

AIF – Anti-Iraqi Forces — This is the euphemistic term military planners used to describe insurgents. At the battalion task force level we generally just called them "enemy" or "insurgents." Almost all the insurgents we encountered were Iraqis.

AO – Area of Operations — An AO is an operational area defined by higher headquarters. AOs allow commanders to employ their organic, assigned, and supporting systems to the limits of their capabilities. Commanders typically subdivide some or all of their AO by assigning AOs to subordinate units. Subordinate unit AOs may be contiguous or noncontiguous. When AOs are contiguous, a boundary separates them. When AOs are non-contiguous, they do not share a boundary; the concept of operations links the elements of the force. The higher headquarters is responsible for the area between noncontiguous AOs. AO Rocket was a contiguous AO within the 5th BCT of First Cavalry Division and shared boundaries with 1-7 Cavalry and 1-8 Cavalry, sister maneuver units of the 5th BCT.

Army Brat – A term for someone who grew up while their parent or parents serve or served in the Army. While the term "brat" is commonly utilized in a derogatory manner; in military communities, brat is neither a subjective or judgmental term. One either is a military brat or one is not, its usage is unrelated to that of "spoiled brat".

Army Doctrine – Fundamental principles by which the

Army or elements thereof guide their actions in support of national objectives. It is authoritative but requires judgment in application.

Army Ranger – A soldier specially trained in airborne, air assault, light infantry and direct action operations, raids, infiltration and exfiltration by air, land or sea, airfield seizure, recovery of personnel and special equipment, and support of general purpose forces (GPF), among other skills. An Army Ranger is expert in the implementation of patrolling techniques to accomplish specified missions.

Army Transformation – Describes the future-concept of the U.S. Army's plan of modernization. Transformation is a generalized term for the integration of new concepts, organizations, and technology within the Army of the United States. This future concept was in the process of implementation when Task Force 1-21 of 5th BCT of First Cavalry Division was ordered to Baghdad, Iraq. First Cavalry Division was deployed prior to that division's direction by Department of the Army to undergo transformation and redesign to the BCT centric force.

Battalion – In military terminology, a battalion consists of two to six companies typically commanded by a lieutenant colonel. Battalions vary in size based on the Army branch in which they are organized; generally, 300-1000 soldiers are organized into companies and subordinated under a battalion headquarters. A battalion task force is one that is formed for duration to accomplish a specified task. 1-21 Field Artillery became a battalion task force when C/2-82 and 68th Chemical Company were organized under the battalion headquarters to conduct operations in Baghdad.

BCT – Brigade Combat Team — The Army has recently transformed the whole institution to a force structure predicated on the Brigade Combat Team as the base formation. Before Army Transformation, the Army was constructed around a Division force structure. The U.S. Army shift to the organizational foundation of its ground forces from large heavy armored and infantry divisions to "Brigade Combat Teams" was necessitated by a need to have a more expeditionary force. BCTs are easier to airlift and considered to be more adaptable under a doctrine for U.S. Army forces to fight full spectrum. These BCTs have about 3,700 soldiers and are commanded by an Army Colonel of Infantry, Armor and, effective in 2006, Field Artillery. In 2004-2005, First Cavalry Division was not organized in the new-fangled BCT structure of the Army, although this terminology, BCT, was used to describe ground maneuver brigade formations in the division. First Cavalry Division started their execution of the Army Transformation Plan about 90 days after redeployment from Baghdad, Iraq in the summer of 2005.

BIAP – Baghdad International Airport

BOLO – Be On the Look Out

Bradleys – This is what we called the Army's main armored Infantry Fighting Vehicle. It was called the "Bradley Fighting Vehicle" by the Army, in honor of General Omar Bradley of World War II fame.

Combat Arms (CA) – In the U.S. Army, the units that actually engage the enemy in combat; e.g., the infantry, armor, or field artillery are combat arms. Before Army Transformation the Army had seven combat arms branches: Air Defense Artillery, Armor, Aviation, Engineer, Field Artillery, Infantry, and Special Forces. Since Army Transformation, combat arms branches are obsolete. They are now classified under Maneuver, Fires & Effects (MFE) with more branches than just the former combat arms added in this category.

Combined Arms – Combined arms is the synchronized or simultaneous application of several arms such as infantry, armor, field artillery, engineers, air defense, and aviation to achieve an effect on the enemy that is greater than if each arm was used against the enemy separately or in sequence.

Command Post (CP) — Similar to a Tactical Operations Center, this is a term used generally for command and control and functions at the company echelon or below. It is literally the command and control node for a company/battery/troop-sized unit or below. These can also be mobile or field command and control centers for higher echelon organizations.

Commander's Critical Information Report (CCIR) – In Army units commanders establish information reports they consider high priority or sensitive in nature that demand their attention in a timely manner. Nested in the operational or administrative priorities at each echelon, these reports are vital to organizational communication and action. In combat, these reports are vital to operations and frequently reviewed.

Counterinsurgency (COIN) – Political and military strategy or action intended to oppose and forcefully suppress insurgency.

Decide, Detect, Deliver and Assess (D3A) – The methodology used to drive the targeting process is Decide, Detect, Deliver and Assess (D3A). In Iraq the 5th BCT used this methodology and applied it to non-lethal targeting objectives for civil affairs project development. We viewed projects as targeting efforts in our counterinsurgent effort.

Division (Army) – A division is a large military unit or formation usually consisting of around ten to fifteen thousand soldiers. In most armies a division is composed of several regiments or brigades, and in turn several divisions make up a corps. In most modern militaries, a division tends to be the largest combined arms unit capable of independent operations; due to its self-sustaining role as a unit with a range of combat troops and suitable combat support forces, which can be divided into various organic combinations.

Field Artillery (FA) – This is a branch of the Army. The Army has multiple branches. Field Artillery is the branch that operates indirect weapons systems and fire support systems throughout the Army. Fire support coordination is the fundamental function of the branch.

Field Grade Officer – A field-grade officer holds the rank of Major, Lieutenant Colonel or Colonel. In a typical Army battalion there are three or four such officers out of 35-45 officers assigned. These are the upper level ranks of the regular officer corps. Above field-grade officers are General-officer ranks. Until recently, in the Army, an officer typically attained field-grade rank after 12 years of commissioned service. These are the institutional level leaders.

Fire Support – Fire Support is a military term referring to long-range firepower provided to a front-line unit. Typically, fire support is provided by artillery or aircraft, and is used to soften or weaken the enemy before or during an assault. In this book, references to fire support officers are to those Army leaders trained in the art and science of planning, coordinating, observing, adjusting and reporting effects of indirect fires. Because the mission was so radically different in Iraq, these skilled leaders were used to plan non-lethal targeting seeking effects through civil projects and psychological operations. Also, many were placed in roles to manage information operations for commanders.

FLIR – Forward Looking Infra-Red

Forward Operating Base (FOB) — Task Force 1-21 was located at FOB Falcon also known as Camp Falcon. For a short time the FOB was called Camp Ferrin-Huggins after the first two soldiers from the 82nd Airborne killed in action from that FOB. The 82nd had a unit assigned to this

FOB before First Armored Division units and First Cavalry occupied the base. The 5th BCT of First Cavalry Division was the third occupant of this FOB.

Force Protection (FP) — Conserving "the force's fighting potential so that it can be applied at the decisive time and place. This activity includes counteractions taken against enemy forces making friendly forces' systems and operational facilities (including operational formations and personnel) difficult to locate, strike and destroy. This task includes protecting joint and multinational air, space, land, sea and special operations forces, bases, and lines of communication from enemy operational maneuver and concentrated enemy air, ground and sea attack, natural occurrences, and terrorist attack. This task also pertains to protection of operational-level forces, systems and civil infrastructure of friendly nations and groups in military operations other than war." Tasks associated with protecting the force such as rules of engagement, preventive medicine and dispersion can be found under other operational activities. What becomes clear is that FP is more than security, and the process to accomplish the task successfully requires proactive, deliberate action. It is a process that entails the planning for and application of military assets to minimize the effects of hazards and hostile activities that can impair friendly force effectiveness.

FPS – Facilities Protection Service — This organization existed during Saddam's regime. It was an organization that provided local security to facilities of special interest to the regime and/or Ba'ath Party. When the 5th BCT arrived, the brigade headquarters we replaced from First Armor Division had employed almost 300 of these men to provide security at key points in sector ostensibly to deter anti-Iraqi forces from planting IEDs.

Full Spectrum Operations – The spectrum of military operations the U.S. Army must have a capability to operate within range from domestic disaster relief to strategic nuclear war and everything in-between. For our purposes, Task Force 1-21 had to operate in a counterinsurgent methodology maximizing unit adaptability to functionally execute civil affairs tasks, reconnaissance tasks, through to actual combat tasks and, on occasions, all of these within the same patrol mission.

Humvee – (HMMWV) High Mobility Multipurpose Wheeled Vehicle — The humvee is the Army's ¾ ton prime mover and main command and control and utility vehicle. The body of the humvee is made of composite fiberglass. In Iraq the need for armored humvees quickly surfaced due to the need to have a wheeled vehicle that could maneuver well in urban terrain and provide protection to troops from IEDs the low-tech enemy used as an "equalizer." Armored track vehicles, while able to provide solid troop protection from IEDs and decent firepower often were imposing, not easily maneuvered in urban terrain, and also tore up the infrastructure of villages and towns, counter-productive to a mission to reconstruct decrepit areas in Iraq.

IA – Iraqi Army

IED – Improvised Explosive Device — The media has dubbed these "roadside bombs." IEDs certainly can and often are roadside bombs but they are not limited to this operational deployment. In Vietnam these IEDs were most often called "booby traps." They are a low-tech yet highly effective weapon employed against U.S. forces in Iraq. Urban terrain affords easy and widespread use of this weapon. By far the IED accounts for the majority of casualties in the war. The enemy was and continues to be able to use this very effectively against American forces because Army and Marine units constantly patrol mounted and drive the roads in predictable patterns. There are too many places these devices can be placed and not enough security forces to cover the ground to prevent their emplacement.

ICDC – Iraqi Civil Defense Corps — After the Coalition invasion of Iraq the first efforts to field an Army of Iraqis was named the Iraqi Civil Defense Corps with the intention these units would augment and support Iraqi Police to provide for civil order and localized security. This organization eventually became the Iraqi National Guard (ING) and then the New Iraqi Army (NIA) and now just the Iraqi Army (IA).

Imam – Name for Muslim cleric.

Insurgent – A member of an irregular armed force that fights a stronger force by sabotage and harassment.

IP – Iraqi Police — Also known as the IPS or Iraqi Police Service or Iraqi national police force. While Task Force 1-21 operated in west Baghdad, this force was dominated by Shia and infiltrated by multiple hostile Shia militias. It was also highly corrupt, poorly led and badly administered. There was almost no local focus by these policemen and no political connection of these forces to the many mahallas that make up Baghdad.

ING – Iraqi National Guard

KIA – Killed in Action

LOO – Line(s) of Operation — The Five LOO Plan was also known as the First Cavalry Division Campaign Plan, "Oasis." A line of operation is a distinct commodity area from which operational activity is vested to accomplish a mission. Army units operate along multiple lines of operations simultaneously and continuously.

MOS – Military Occupational Specialty

MTOE – Modified Table of Organization and Equipment Every Army organization has a documented organization and equipment table. This is an official document by which units work to resource a given organization.

Maneuver Units – Typically in the Army, infantry and armor organizations are considered maneuver. They are so named because they maneuver their weapons and troops to close with and kill the enemy. They have vehicles and weapons designed for this purpose. Additionally, their soldiers, non-commissioned officers and officers train extensively to refine and master the art and science of fire and maneuver. This is the essence of the U.S. Army.

National Guard (Army) – United States Army reserves recruited by the states and equipped by the federal government; subject to call by either.

NIA – New Iraqi Army

O&I – Operations and Intelligence

Organic Assets – Assigned to and forming an essential part of a military organization. Organic parts of a unit are those listed in its table of organization for the Army.

Outer Tactical Vest (OTV) – A camouflage vest worn as an outer protection garment. Armored protective plates are mounted inside sleeves of the vest in the front and the back. On the outside are nylon webbed straps where soldiers can affix their combat gear: ammo pouches, first aid kit, canteen carriers, grenades, earplug cases and the like. When fully outfitted this vest adds about 60 pounds of extra weight to a soldier or marine.

Patrol – A smaller unit sent out from a larger unit to conduct combat or reconnaissance operations. Task Force 1-21 was organized into platoon elements as the base organization. We quickly discovered that operations conducted were not executed with whole platoon elements but rather as patrol elements. Because the operational tempo was high and rotations were necessary for rest and recovery, patrols became our unit of action. Our entire organizational training, command and control, and tactical operations were constructed around a patrol system.

Platoon – A unit composed of two or more squads. It is the basic tactical unit, usually commanded by a Lieutenant. In the Army, Lieutenants in command of a platoon element are designated Platoon Leaders because they have no institutional command authority and do not exercise UCMJ authority. In the Marine Corps, Lieutenants who command platoons are designated Platoon Commanders.

PST – Personal Security Team — These were teams designated and trained to provide personal executive-type protection to commanders. Units had to take personnel from within their units to form and operate in this manner. The size of these teams varied, but generally 9-12 soldiers were on these teams.

Reserve Component (Army)— A reserve component of the United States military is an organization of service members who generally perform a minimum of 39 days of military duty per year and who augment the active duty (or full time) military when necessary. The reserve components are also referred to collectively as the Guard and Reserves.

ROE – Rules of Engagement

ROTC – Reserve Officer Training Corps

SAPI (Small Arms Protective Insert) – SAPI is a plate used in the Interceptor body armor, a new-generation bullet-resistant vest. The kevlar Interceptor vest itself is designed to stop projectiles up to and including 9mm submachine rounds, in addition to fragmentation. To protect against rifle fire in critical areas, supplemental plates are needed. A SAPI is made of boron carbide ceramic. It is able to stop up to three rifle bullets of caliber smaller or equal to 7.62 mm and muzzle velocity smaller or equal to 2,750 feet per second (838 m/s). The ceramic plate is backed with Spectra shield, a material up to 40 percent stronger than Kevlar.

The individual plate weighs about 4 pounds, and costs about USD $350 to produce. There is one for the front of the body, one for the back. The mechanism of effect lies in absorbing and dissipating the projectile's kinetic energy in local shattering of the ceramic plate and blunting the bullet material on the hard ceramic. The Spectra backing then spreads the energy of the impact to larger area and stops the fragments, preventing an injury of the wearer.

Stand-off – This is a military tactical term that refers to the time and space separation sought to employ weapons against an adversary. To employ direct fire weapons, a weaker force often tries to create distance whereby they can employ their available weapons to effect but also have time to disengage and get away from a pursuing adversary; a very commonly used tactic by Iraqi insurgents.

SST – Special Search Team — This was the name that we gave to female teams used to support operations to search Muslim women and children. We inherited this name from 1-94 Field Artillery as they taught us the tactic, technique, and procedure. The BCT adopted the name and the practice.

Task Force – A semi-permanent unit created to carry out a continuing task.

Table of Organization and Equipment (TO&E) – A table of organization and equipment (TOE) is a document published by the U.S. Department of Defense which prescribes the organization, manning, and equippage of units from divisional size and down, but also including the headquarters of Corps and Armies. We in 5th BCT and Task Force 1-21 operated from what is known as a Modified Table of Organization and Equipment. This is a document that modifies the TOE in regard to a specific unit.

"Terps" – Interpreters — This was a slang name commonly used by the troops to describe Iraqi interpreters working in the units. Task Force 1-21 had and sustained 25 "terps" our year in Iraq. We were the only Task Force in the BCT capable of operating every patrol with a "terp" embedded.

TOC – Tactical Operations Center — Battalion echelon and higher headquarters operating in a tactical environment manage operations and coordinate actions through a Tactical Operations Center. The TOC is the nerve center for tactical command and control of a battalion.

Transfer of Authority (TOA) – When one U.S. Army command replaced another in Iraq this was known as a Transfer of Authority.

Uniform Code of Military Justice (UCMJ) — The Uniform Code of Military Justice is the primary means by which the U.S. Military enforces discipline. It includes both high crimes punishable by death, and matters which would, in civilian life, be considered serious employment infractions. It also contains what amounts to catch all common law crime provisions, "Conduct Unbecoming" (Article 133) and the "General Article" (Article 134). Procedurally, the Uniform Code is the most protective of the rights of the accused that it has ever been, although conviction rates under the Code remain very high.

Unit of Action — The term used by Task Force 1-21 to refer to the standard, primary unit size and type employed for operations within the battalion task force.

WIA – Wounded in Action

The Soldier's Headstone

Across the way
His body lay
I sat alone
Looking at that strange headstone
There was a helmet, some boots, and a gun

In the distance a setting sun
My desire was to run
Where to, what for, my God my son
There was a helmet, some boots, and a gun

This was my dream
My silent scream
This was their notion of esteem
There was a helmet, some boots, and a gun

All I remember
Every year in September is…
A helmet, some boots, and a gun
A man I loved and his questioning son

By Michael A. Baumann (8/20/1986)